REVOL

WRITTEN AND ILLUSTRATED BY

REVOLVER

VERTIGO
DC COMICS

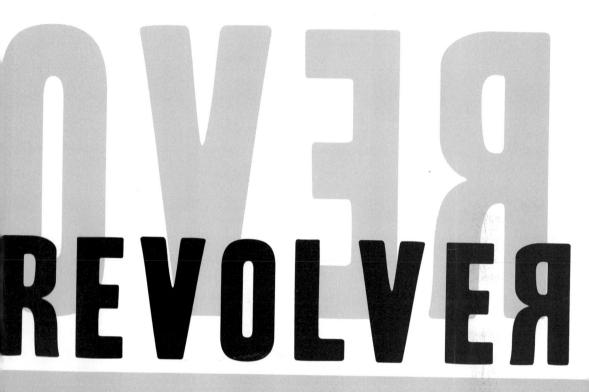

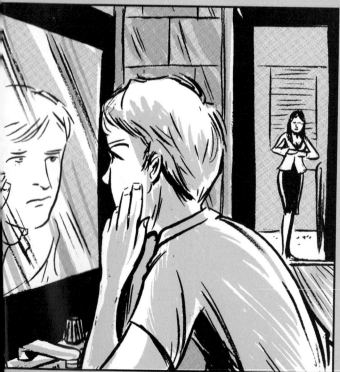

MATT KINDT

LETTERED BY
STEVE WANDS

For Sharlene. 11:11!

Karen Berger SVP-Executive Editor
Joan Hilty & Bob Schreck Editors
Sarah Litt & Brandon Montclare Assistant Editors
Robbin Brosterman Design Director-Books
Curtis King Jr. Senior Art Director

DC COMICS
Diane Nelson President
Dan DiDio and Jim Lee Co-Publishers
Geoff Johns Chief Creative Officer
Patrick Caldon EVP-Finance and Administration
John Rood EVP-Sales, Marketing and Business Development
Amy Genkins SVP-Business and Legal Affairs
Steve Rotterdam SVP-Sales and Marketing
John Cunningham VP-Marketing
Terri Cunningham VP-Managing Editor
Alison Gill VP-Manufacturing
David Hyde VP-Publicity
Sue Pohja VP-Book Trade Sales
Alysse Soll VP-Advertising and Custom Publishing
Bob Wayne VP-Sales
Mark Chiarello Art Director

REVOLVER
Published by DC Comics, 1700 Broadway, New York, NY 10019.
Copyright © 2010 by Matt Kindt. All rights reserved. VERTIGO, all
characters featured in this publication, the distinctive likenesses
thereof and related elements are trademarks of DC Comics. The
stories, characters and incidents featured in this publication are
entirely fictional. DC Comics does not read or accept unsolicited
submissions of ideas, stories or artwork.

Printed in the USA. First Printing.
DC Comics, a Warner Bros.
Entertainment Company.
HC ISBN: 978-1-4012-2241-3.

SUSTAINABLE
FORESTRY
INITIATIVE

Certified Fiber Sourcing
www.sfiprogram.org

Fiber used in this product line meets the
sourcing requirements of the SFI program.
www.sfiprogram.org NFS-SPIC0C-C0001801

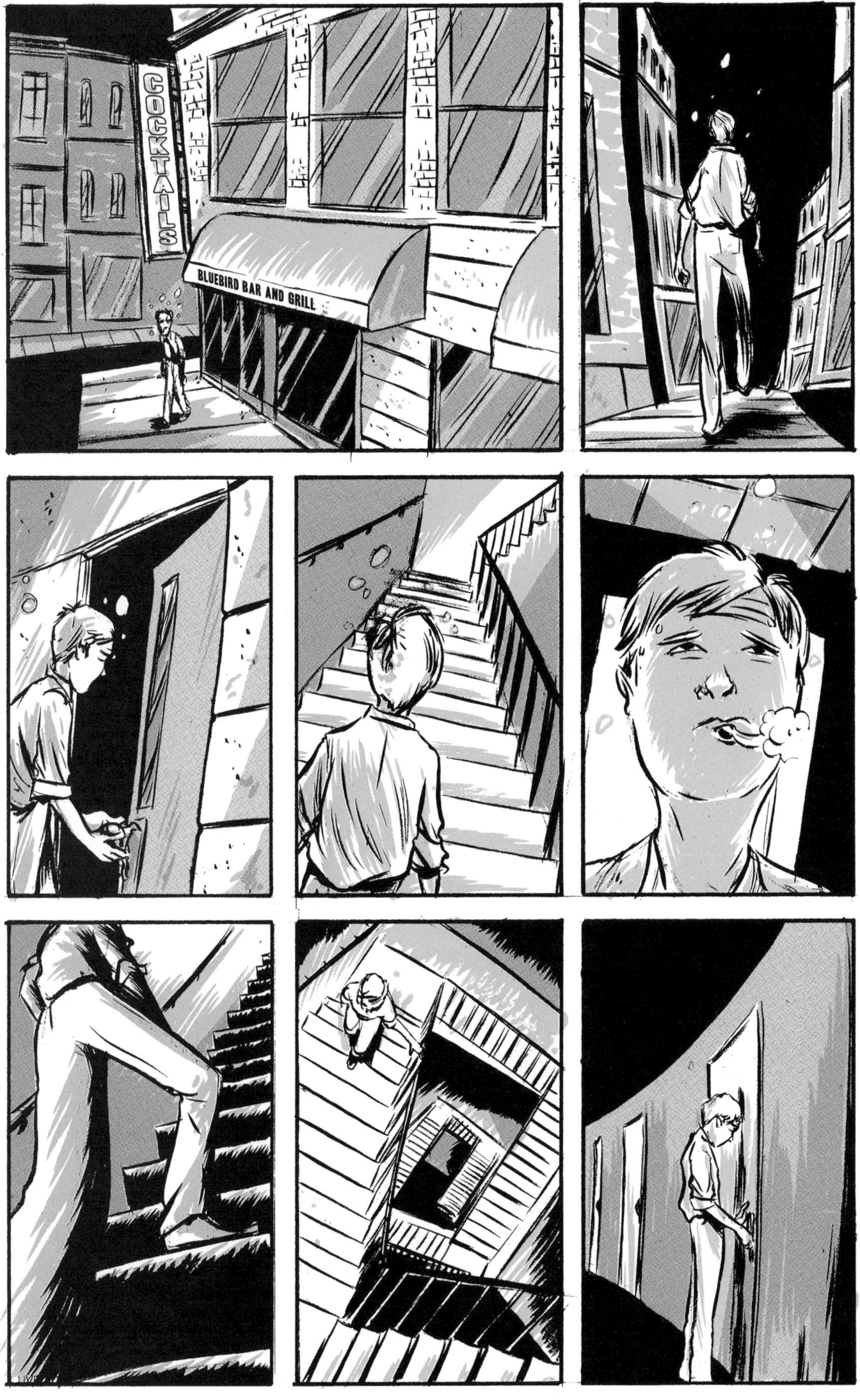
COCKTAILS
BLUEBIRD BAR AND GRILL

ADE ROUTE IS CLOSING MANY STREETS IN DOWNTOWN. ROUTE **ONE** WILL GO THROUGH THE MAGNIFICENT MILE AND END NEAR

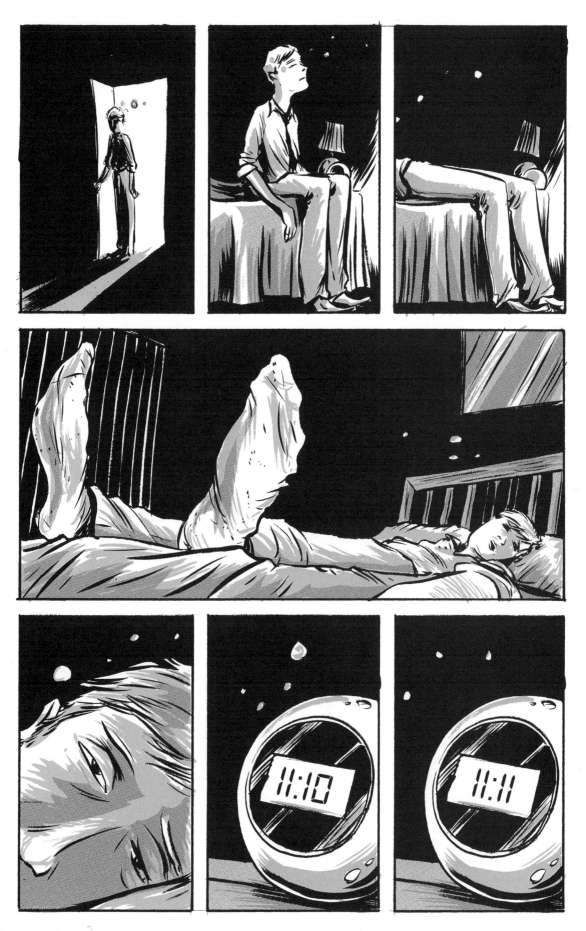

ARE SCATTERED OVER THE ATLANTA METROPOLITAN AREA. **TWO** SKYSCRAPERS DOWNTOWN ARE CLEARLY BURNING. THE CAU

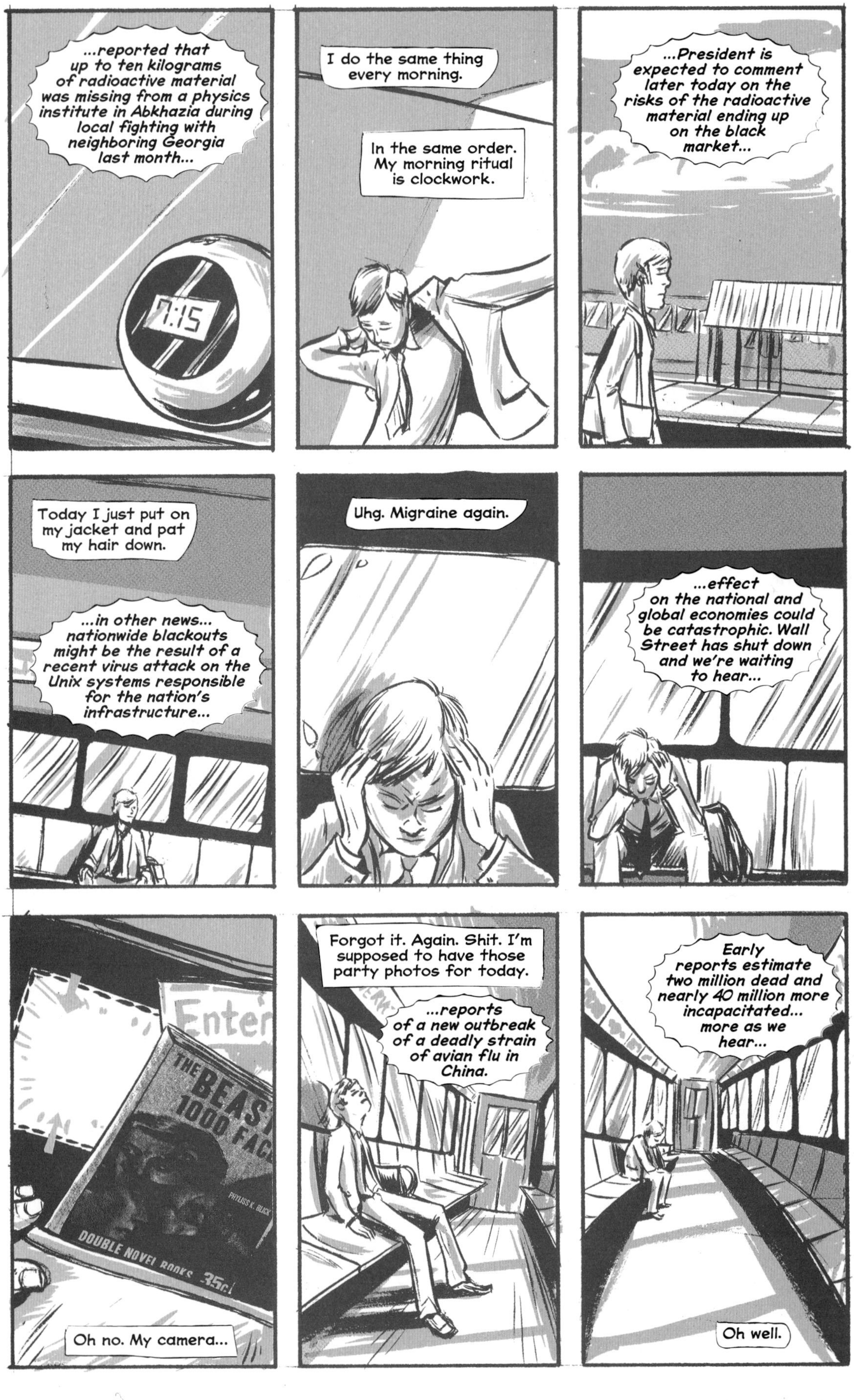
...reported that up to ten kilograms of radioactive material was missing from a physics institute in Abkhazia during local fighting with neighboring Georgia last month...
7:15
I do the same thing every morning.
In the same order. My morning ritual is clockwork.
...President is expected to comment later today on the risks of the radioactive material ending up on the black market...
Today I just put on my jacket and pat my hair down.
...in other news... nationwide blackouts might be the result of a recent virus attack on the Unix systems responsible for the nation's infrastructure...
Uhg. Migraine again.
...effect on the national and global economies could be catastrophic. Wall Street has shut down and we're waiting to hear...
DOUBLE NOVEL BOOKS
35c
Oh no. My camera...
Forgot it. Again. Shit. I'm supposed to have those party photos for today.
...reports of a new outbreak of a deadly strain of avian flu in China.
Early reports estimate two million dead and nearly 40 million more incapacitated... more as we hear...
Oh well.

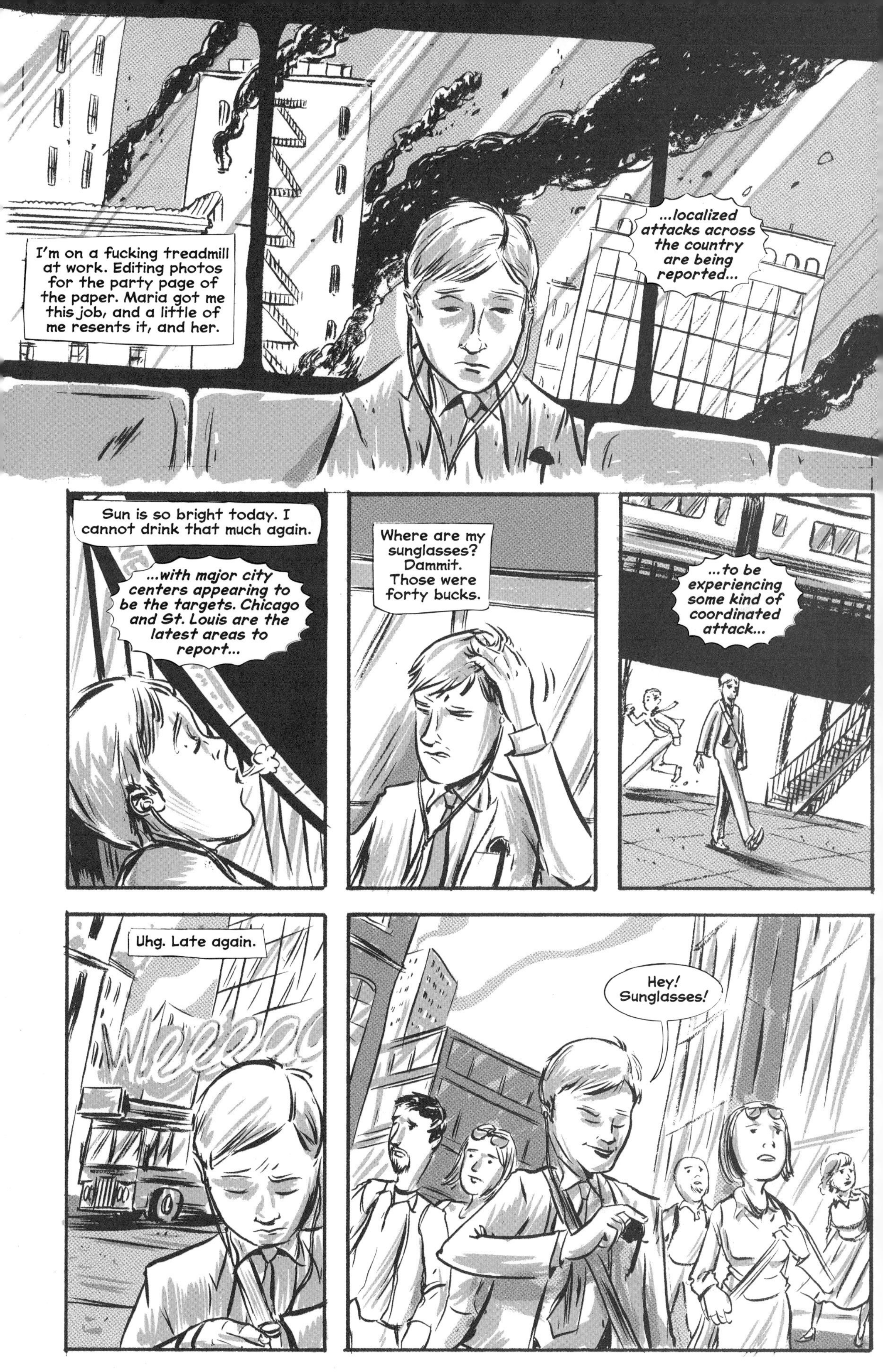
I'm on a fucking treadmill at work. Editing photos for the party page of the paper. Maria got me this job, and a little of me resents it, and her.
...localized attacks across the country are being reported...
Sun is so bright today. I cannot drink that much again.
...with major city centers appearing to be the targets. Chicago and St. Louis are the latest areas to report...
Where are my sunglasses? Dammit. Those were forty bucks.
...to be experiencing some kind of coordinated attack...
Uhg. Late again.
Hey! Sunglasses!

E MIDWEST, REPORTS ARE COMING IN OF A TRAIN COLLISION IN KANSAS CITY. **FOUR** CARS WERE CARRYING RADIOACTIVE MATER

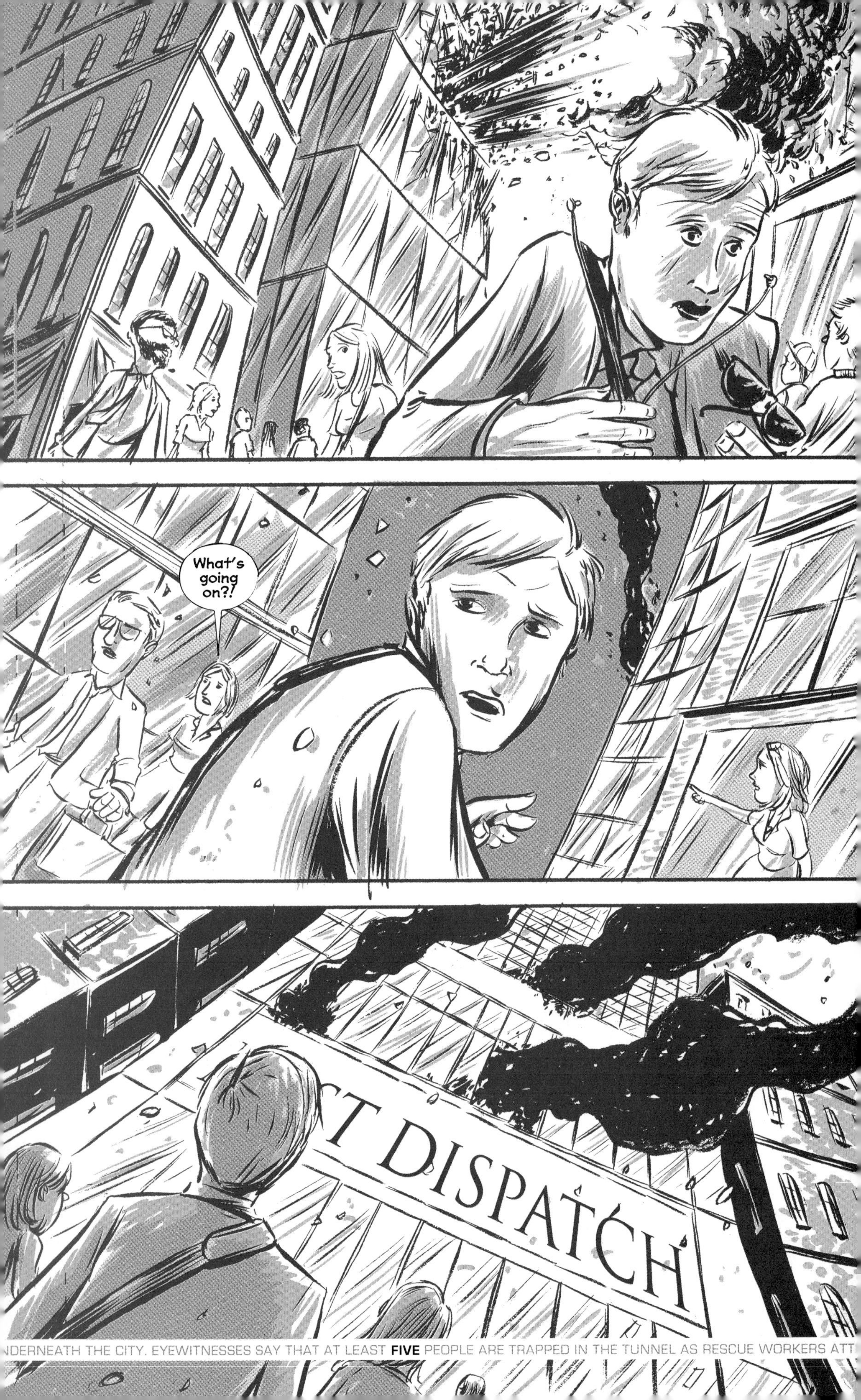
What's going on?!
DISPATCH
NDERNEATH THE CITY. EYEWITNESSES SAY THAT AT LEAST **FIVE** PEOPLE ARE TRAPPED IN THE TUNNEL AS RESCUE WORKERS ATT

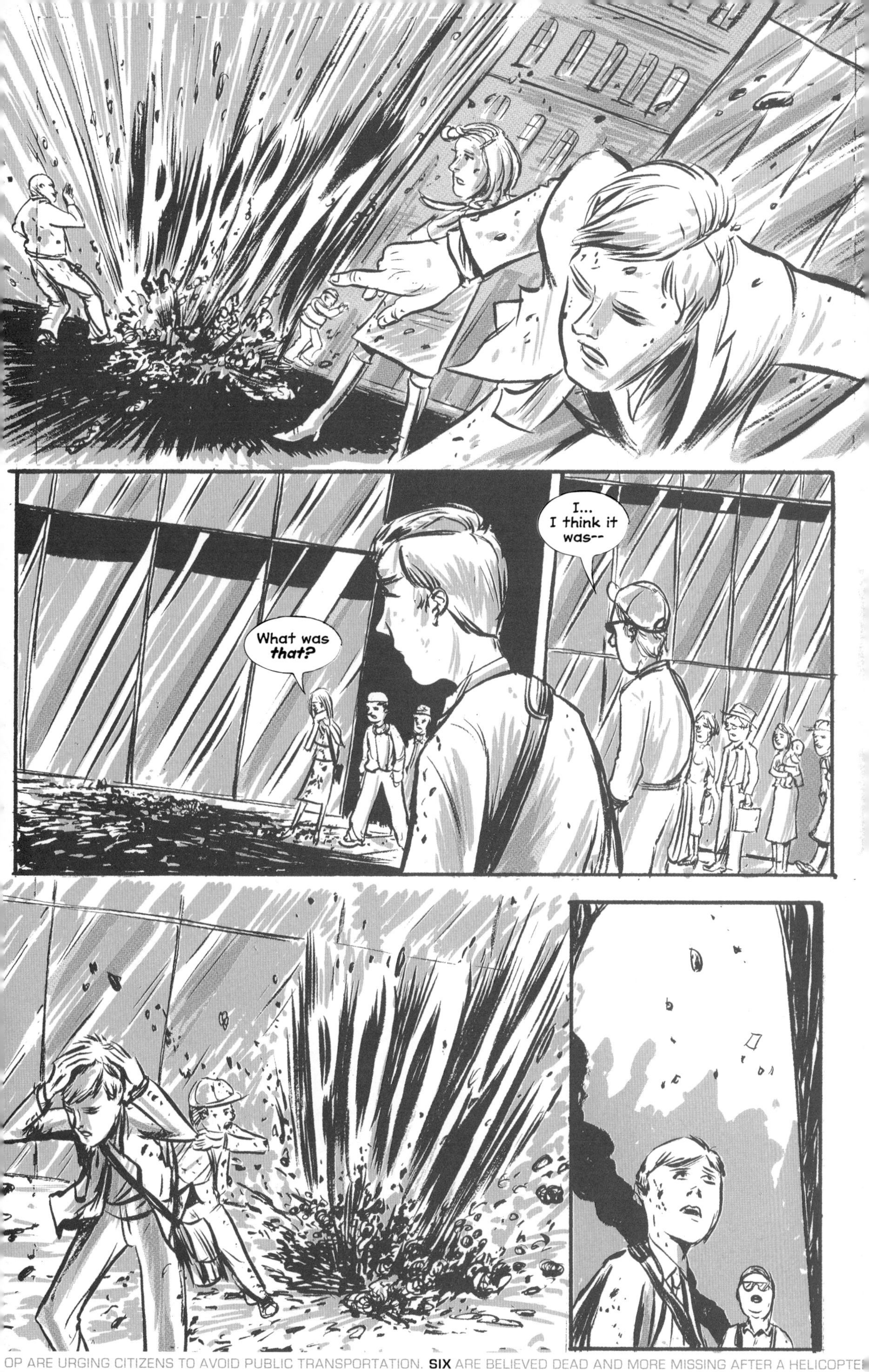
What was *that?*
I... I think it was--

OP ARE URGING CITIZENS TO AVOID PUBLIC TRANSPORTATION. **SIX** ARE BELIEVED DEAD AND MORE MISSING AFTER A HELICOPTE

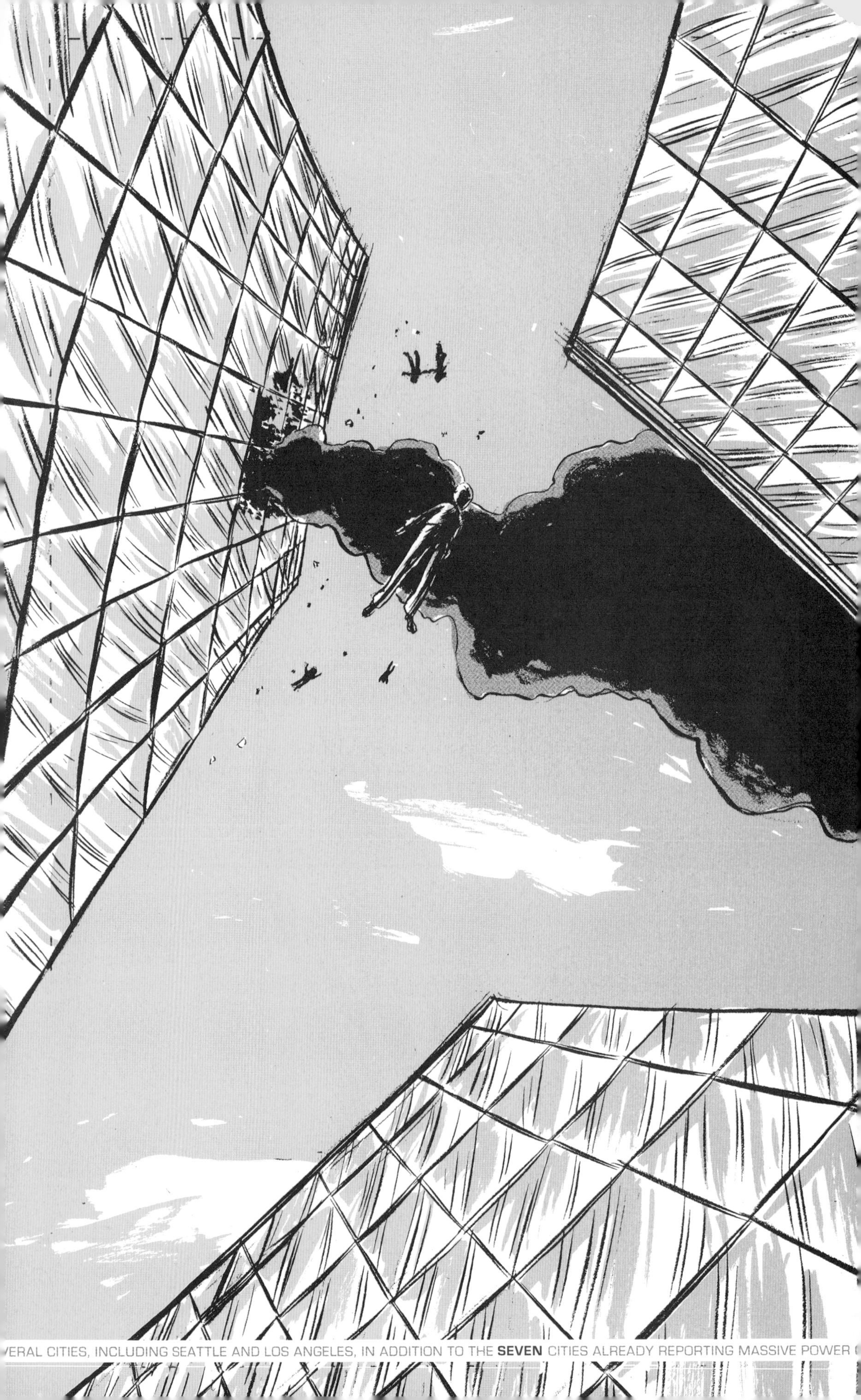
ERAL CITIES, INCLUDING SEATTLE AND LOS ANGELES, IN ADDITION TO THE SEVEN CITIES ALREADY REPORTING MASSIVE POWER

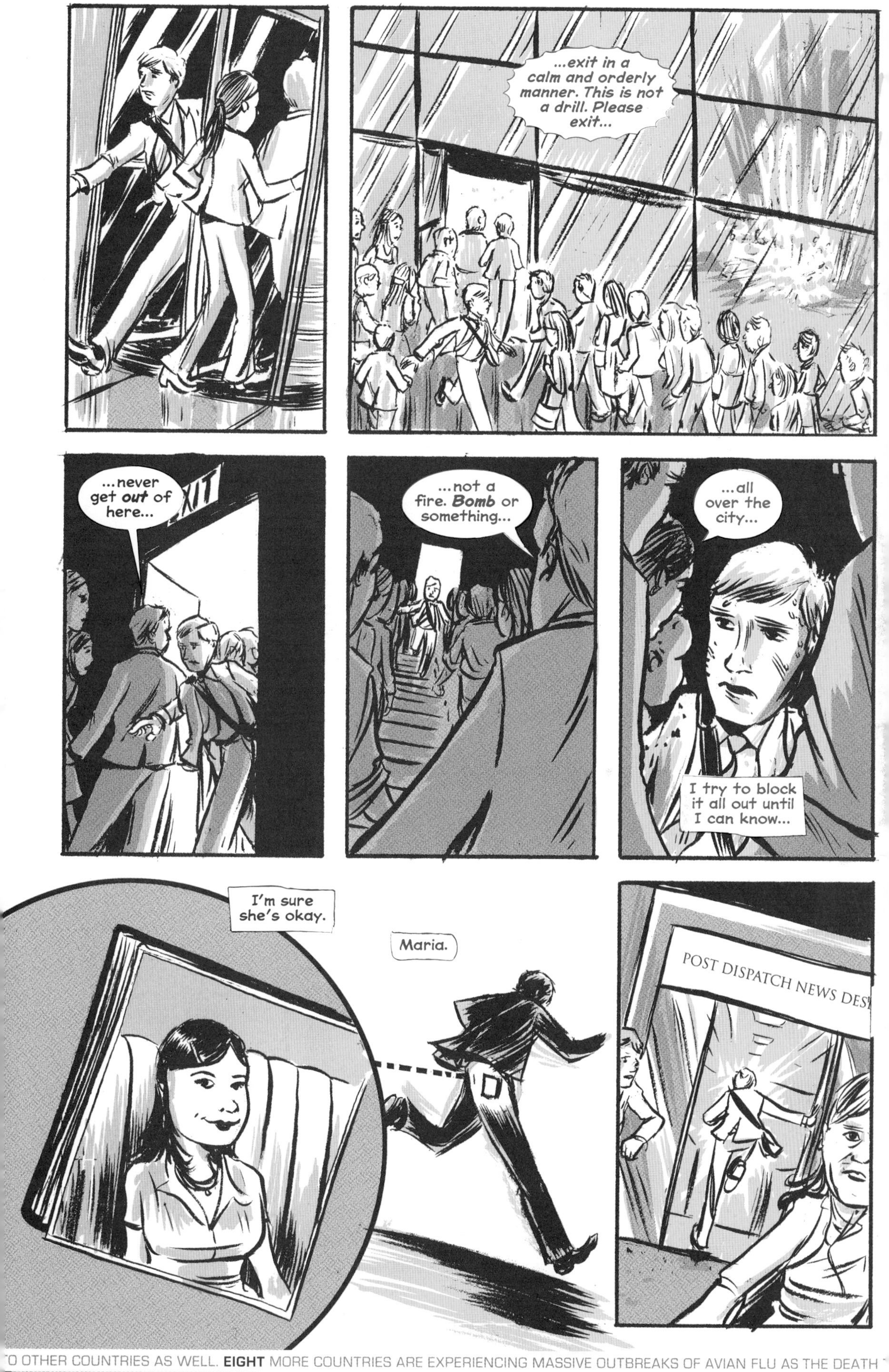
...exit in a calm and orderly manner. This is not a drill. Please exit...
...never get *out* of here...
EXIT
...not a fire. *Bomb* or something...
...all over the city...
I try to block it all out until I can know...
I'm sure she's okay.
Maria.
POST DISPATCH NEWS DES

O OTHER COUNTRIES AS WELL. **EIGHT** MORE COUNTRIES ARE EXPERIENCING MASSIVE OUTBREAKS OF AVIAN FLU AS THE DEATH

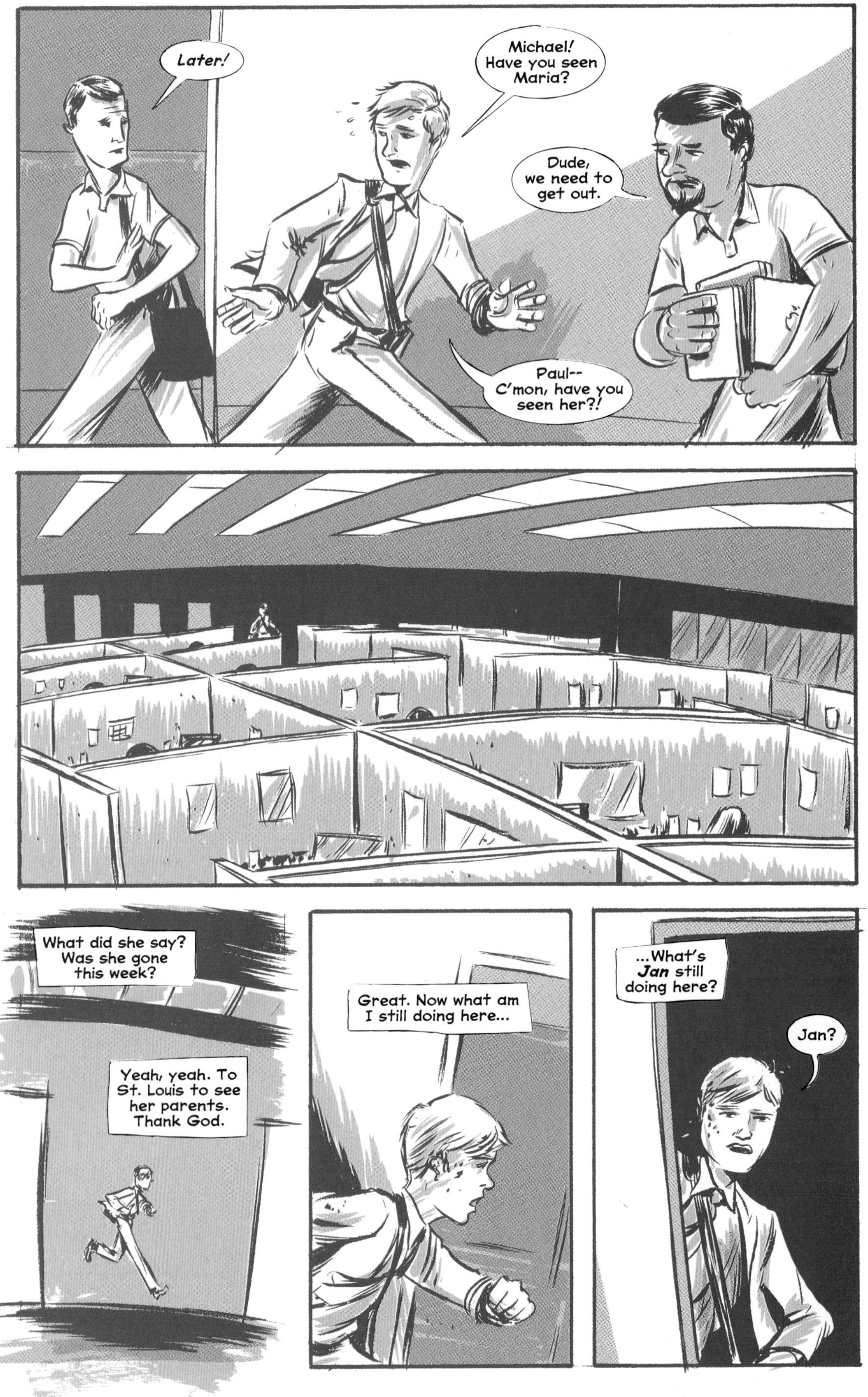
Later!
Michael! Have you seen Maria?
Dude, we need to get out.
Paul-- C'mon, have you seen her?!
What did she say? Was she gone this week?
Yeah, yeah. To St. Louis to see her parents. Thank God.
Great. Now what am I still doing here...
...What's *Jan* still doing here?
Jan?

VERAL RANCHES IN TEXAS THERE ARE REPORTS THAT **NINE** HOMES HAVE BEEN ROPED OFF BY POLICE AFTER MASS SUICIDES SPR

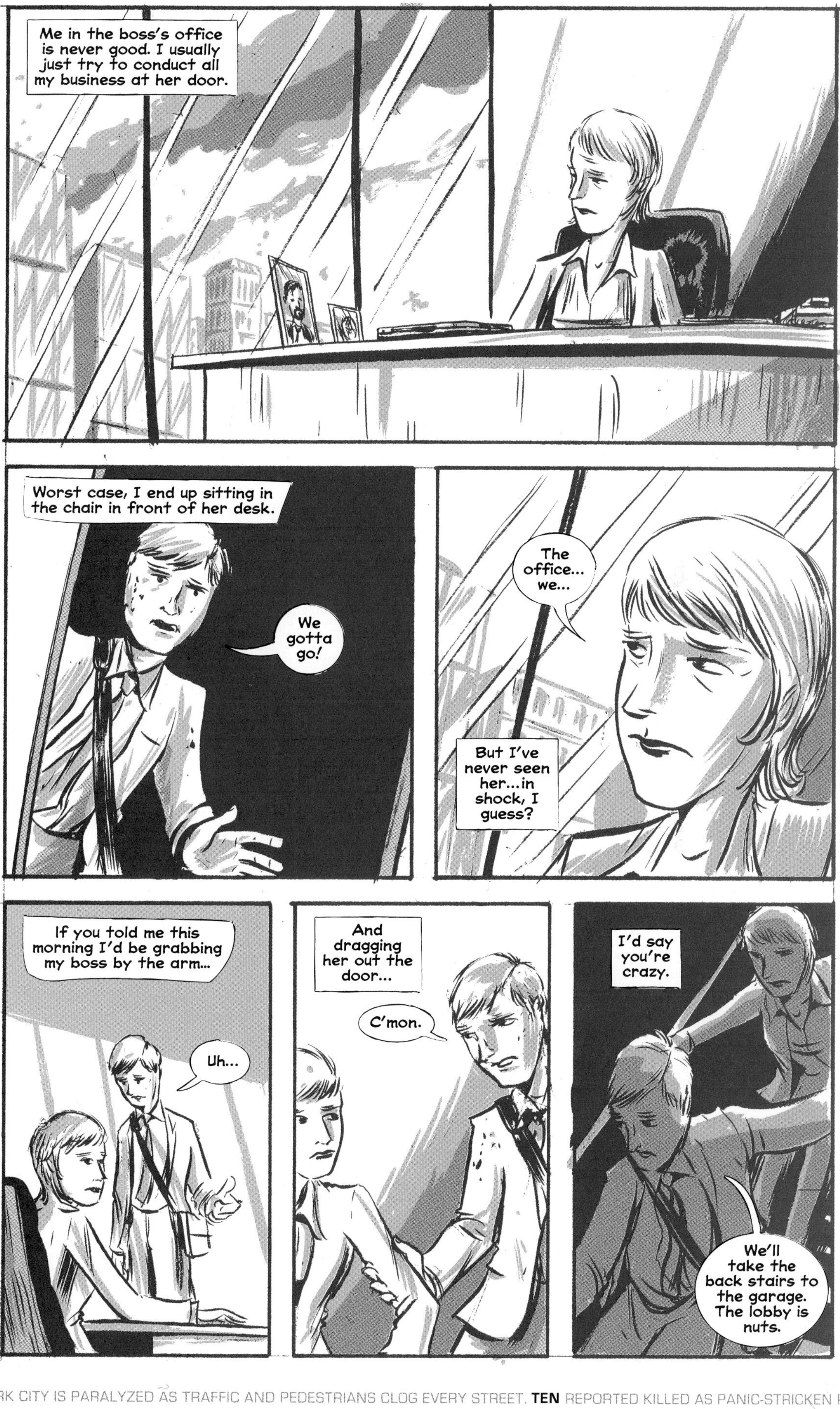
Me in the boss's office is never good. I usually just try to conduct all my business at her door.
Worst case, I end up sitting in the chair in front of her desk.
We gotta go!
The office... we...
But I've never seen her...in shock, I guess?
If you told me this morning I'd be grabbing my boss by the arm...
Uh...
And dragging her out the door...
C'mon.
I'd say you're crazy.
We'll take the back stairs to the garage. The lobby is nuts.

'ORK CITY IS PARALYZED AS TRAFFIC AND PEDESTRIANS CLOG EVERY STREET. **TEN** REPORTED KILLED AS PANIC-STRICKEN PEDES'

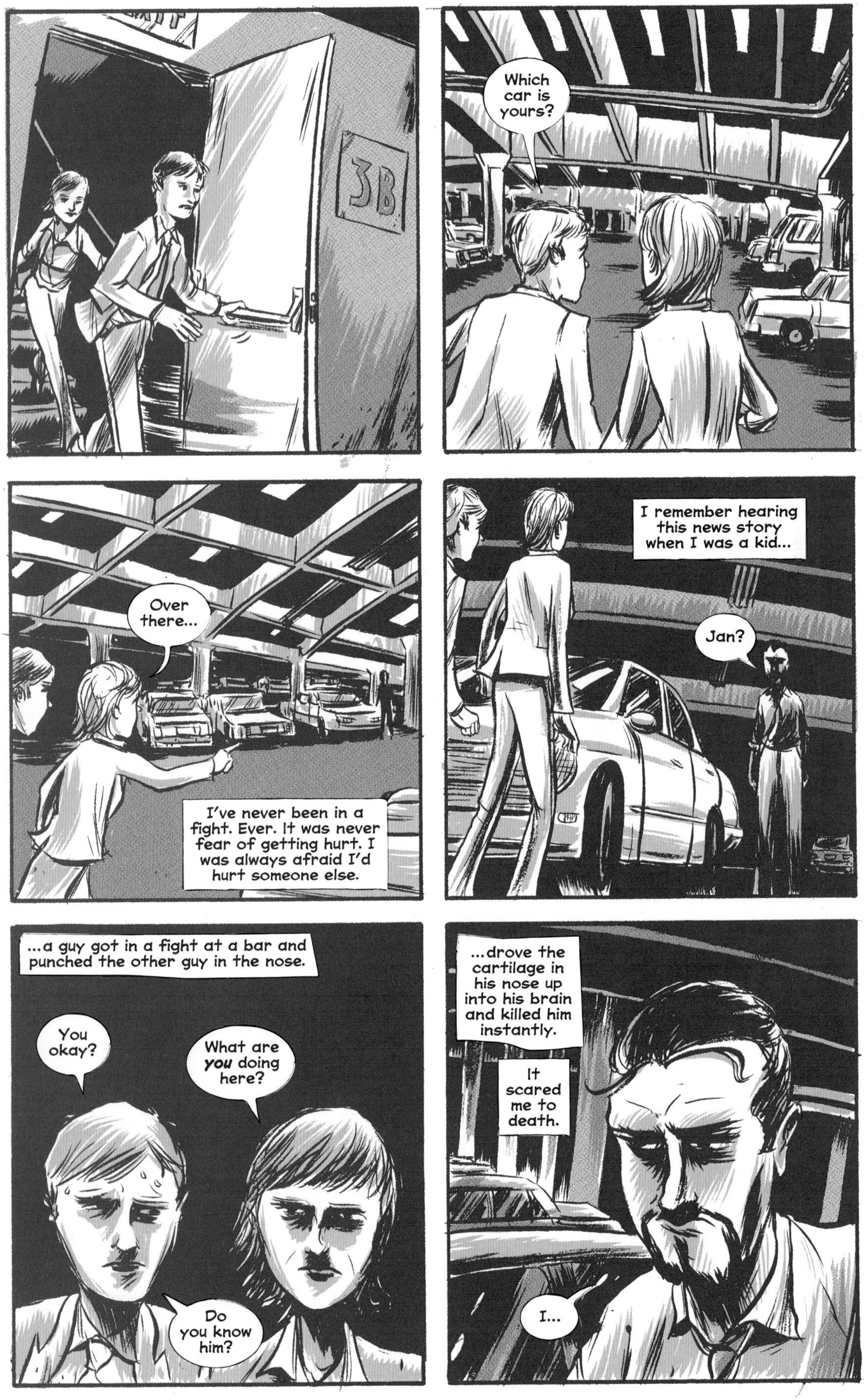
3B
Which car is yours?
Over there...
I've never been in a fight. Ever. It was never fear of getting hurt. I was always afraid I'd hurt someone else.
I remember hearing this news story when I was a kid...
Jan?
...a guy got in a fight at a bar and punched the other guy in the nose.
You okay?
What are *you* doing here?
Do you know him?
...drove the cartilage in his nose up into his brain and killed him instantly.
It scared me to death.
I...

REPORTS FROM PHILADELPHIA CONFIRM **ELEVEN** ARE KILLED IN FIGHTS AND RIOTING AS THOUSANDS ATTEMPT TO ESCAPE THE

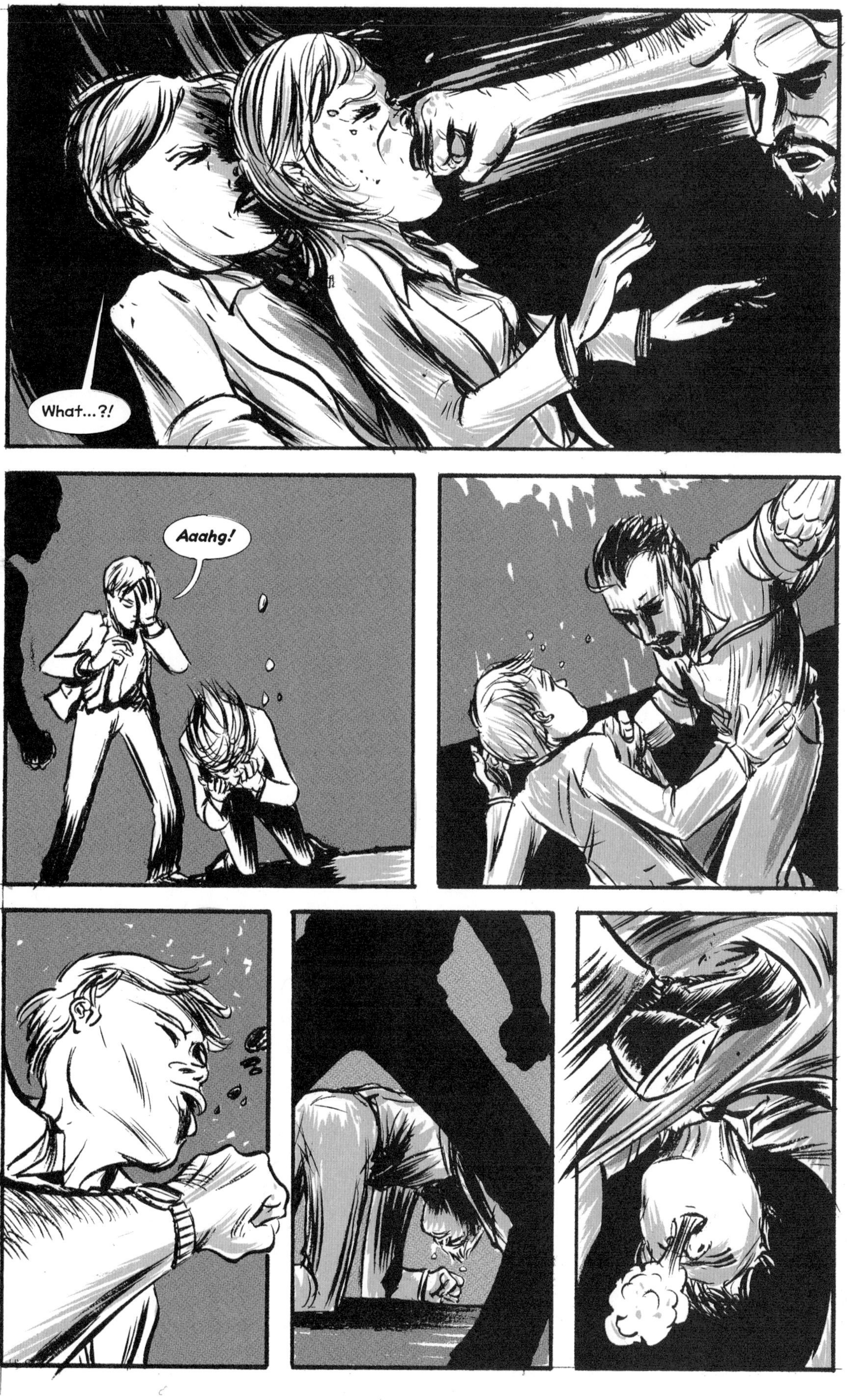
What...?!
Aaahg!

ON AS TO WHAT TO DO WITH THE PRISON IN JOLIET. **TWELVE** GUARDS KILLED IN THE PRISON RIOT SO FAR AND MORE INJURED I

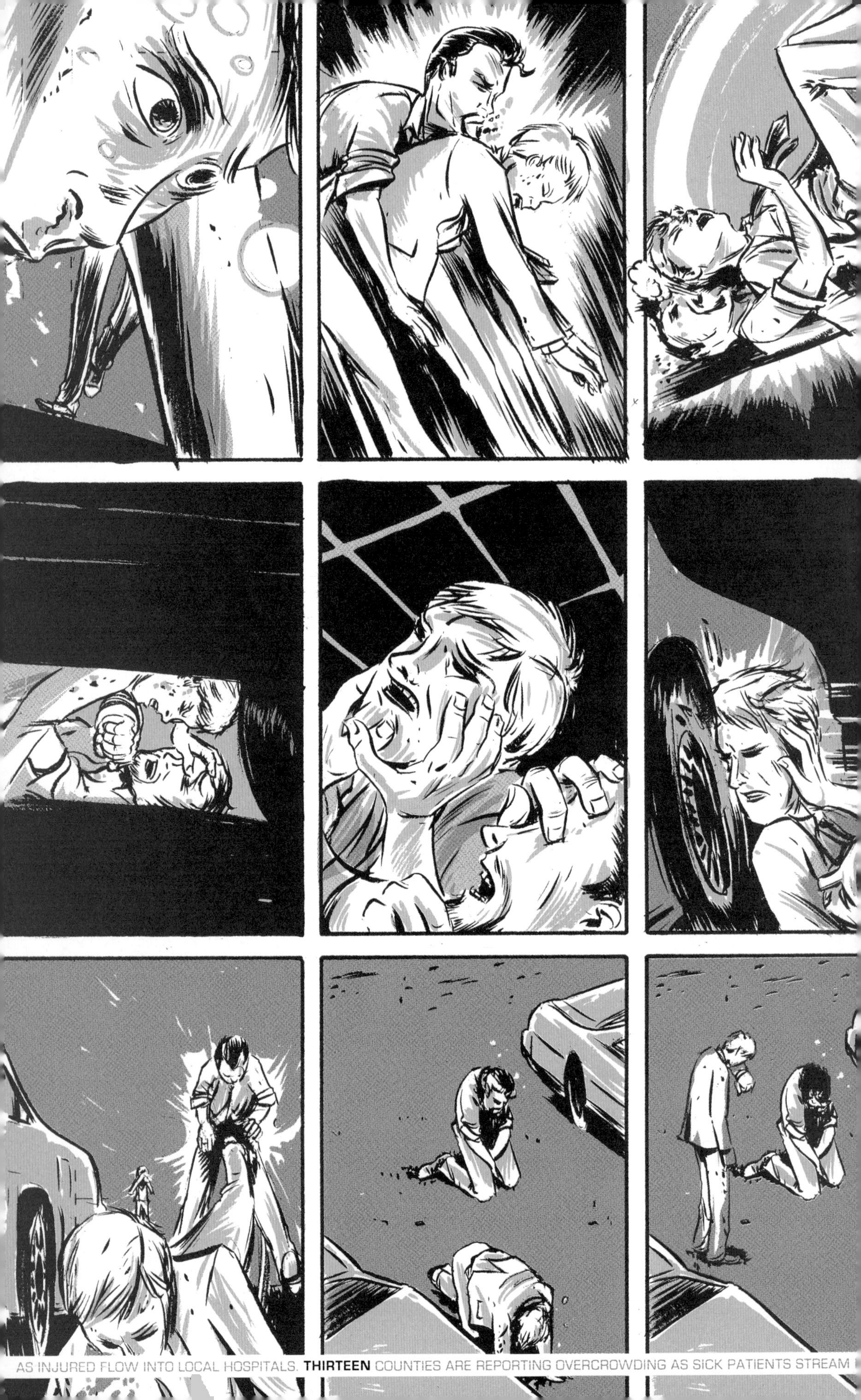
AS INJURED FLOW INTO LOCAL HOSPITALS. **THIRTEEN** COUNTIES ARE REPORTING OVERCROWDING AS SICK PATIENTS STREAM

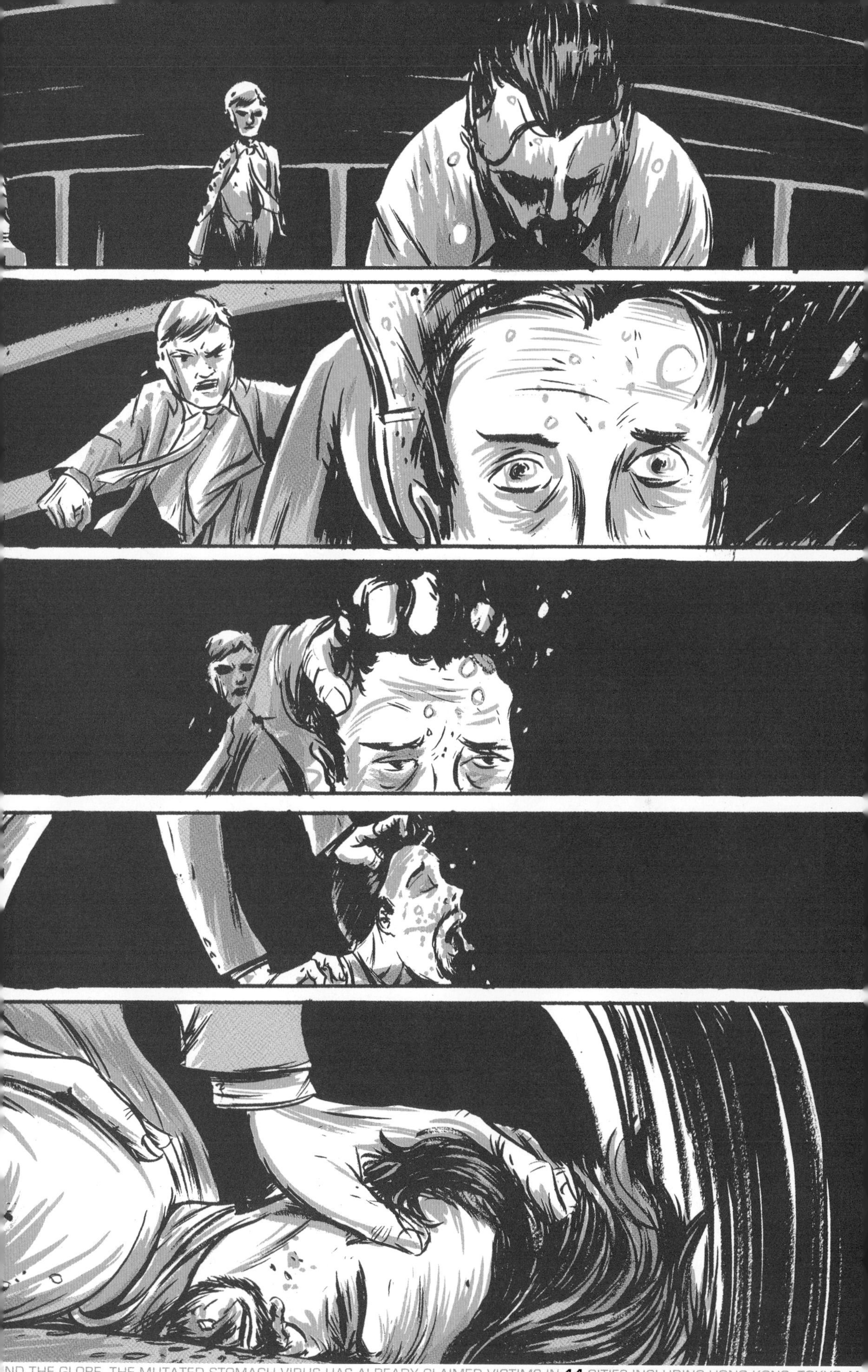

ND THE GLOBE. THE MUTATED STOMACH VIRUS HAS ALREADY CLAIMED VICTIMS IN **14** CITIES INCLUDING HONG KONG, TOKYO AN

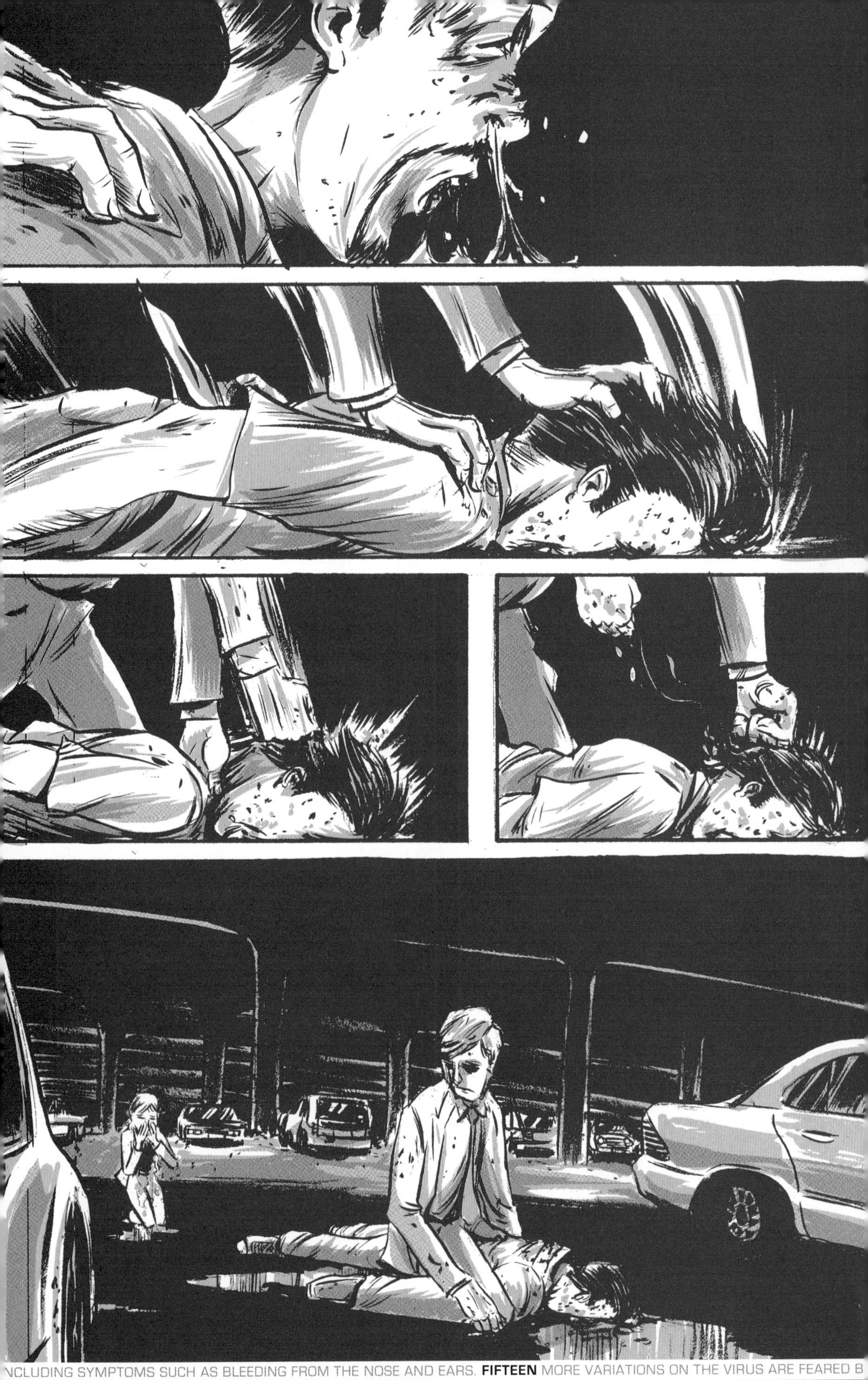

NCLUDING SYMPTOMS SUCH AS BLEEDING FROM THE NOSE AND EARS. **FIFTEEN** MORE VARIATIONS ON THE VIRUS ARE FEARED B

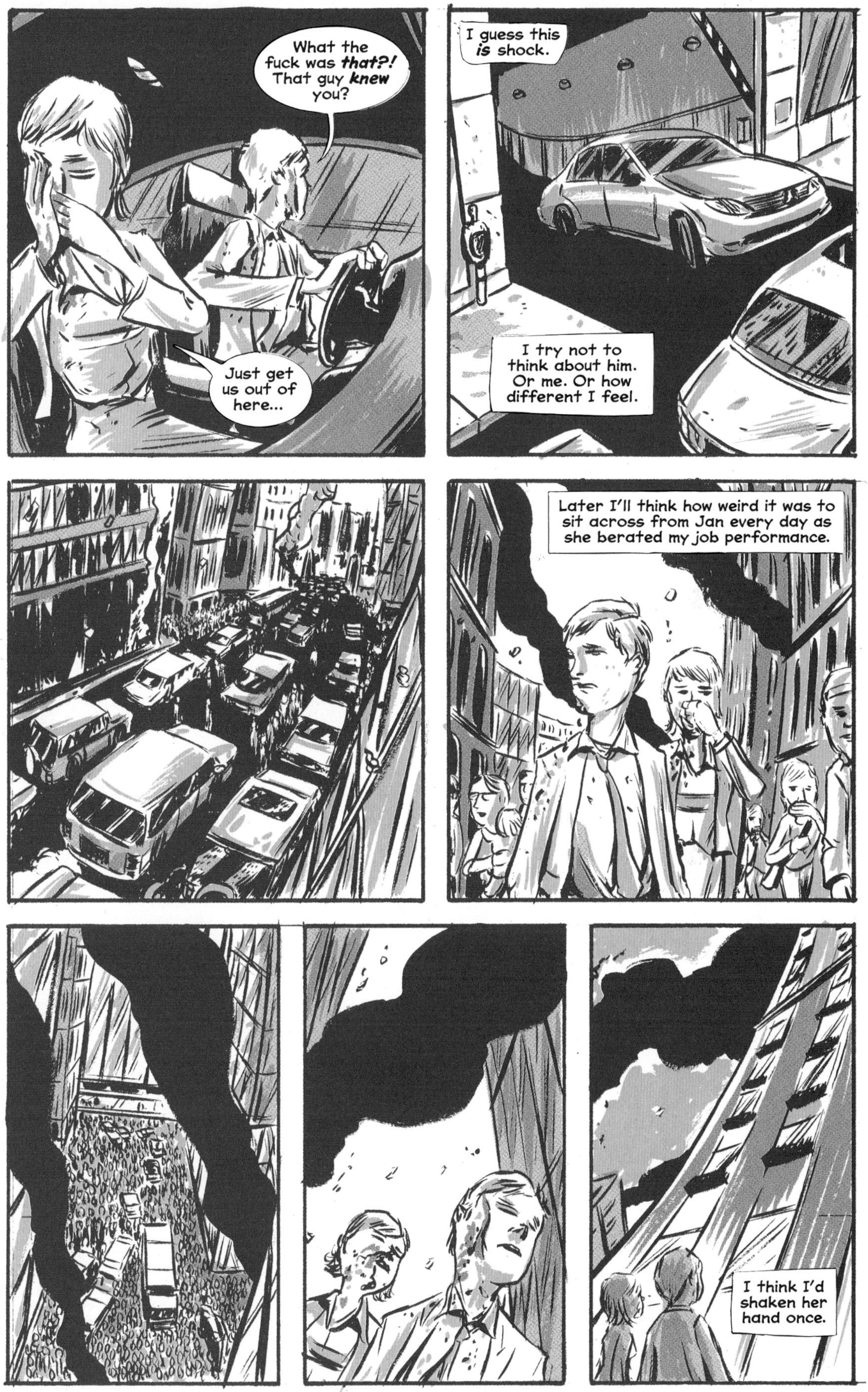
What the fuck was ***that?!*** That guy ***knew*** you?
Just get us out of here...
I guess this ***is*** shock.
I try not to think about him. Or me. Or how different I feel.
Later I'll think how weird it was to sit across from Jan every day as she berated my job performance.
I think I'd shaken her hand once.

RLY AND THE YOUNG ARE AT RISK. YOUNGEST VICTIM REPORTED IS A LOCAL **SIXTEEN**-YEAR-OLD GIRL WHO DIED EARLIER THIS MO

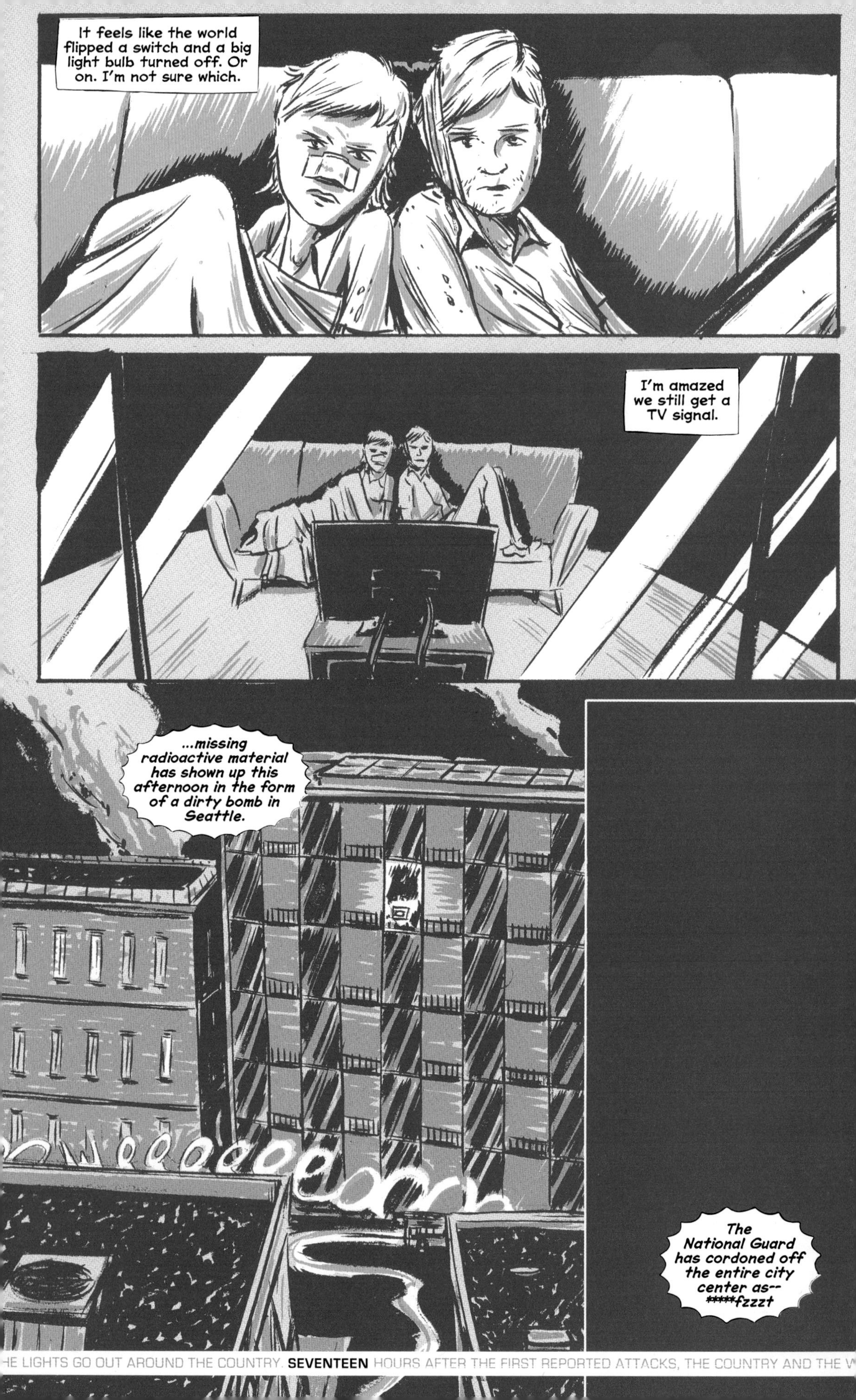
It feels like the world flipped a switch and a big light bulb turned off. Or on. I'm not sure which.
I'm amazed we still get a TV signal.
...missing radioactive material has shown up this afternoon in the form of a dirty bomb in Seattle.
The National Guard has cordoned off the entire city center as-- *****fzzzt
HE LIGHTS GO OUT AROUND THE COUNTRY. SEVENTEEN HOURS AFTER THE FIRST REPORTED ATTACKS, THE COUNTRY AND THE V

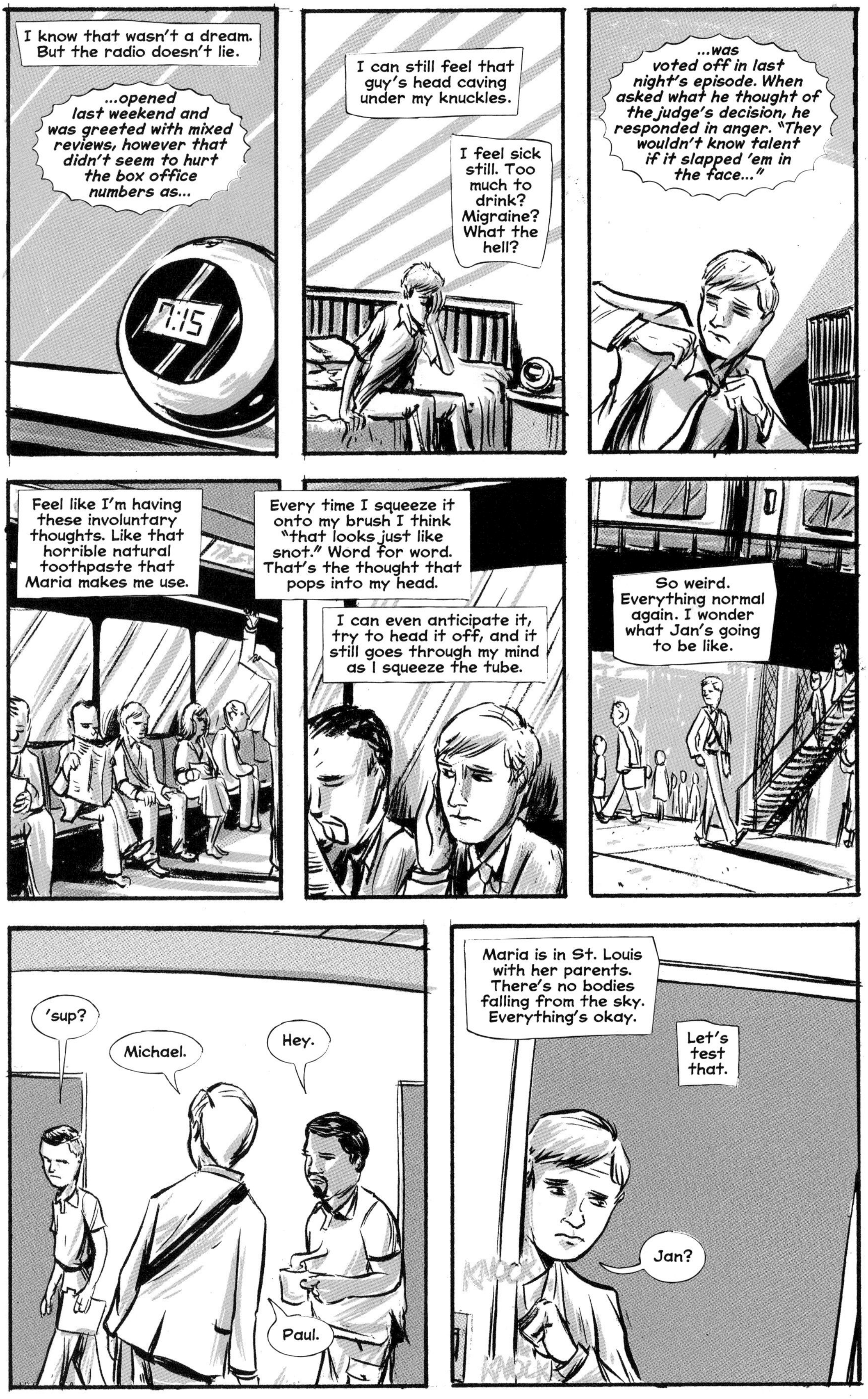
I know that wasn't a dream. But the radio doesn't lie.
...opened last weekend and was greeted with mixed reviews, however that didn't seem to hurt the box office numbers as...
I can still feel that guy's head caving under my knuckles.
I feel sick still. Too much to drink? Migraine? What the hell?
...was voted off in last night's episode. When asked what he thought of the judge's decision, he responded in anger. "They wouldn't know talent if it slapped 'em in the face..."
Feel like I'm having these involuntary thoughts. Like that horrible natural toothpaste that Maria makes me use.
Every time I squeeze it onto my brush I think "that looks just like snot." Word for word. That's the thought that pops into my head.
I can even anticipate it, try to head it off, and it still goes through my mind as I squeeze the tube.
So weird. Everything normal again. I wonder what Jan's going to be like.
'sup?
Michael.
Hey.
Paul.
Maria is in St. Louis with her parents. There's no bodies falling from the sky. Everything's okay.
Let's test that.
Jan?
KNOCK
KNOCK

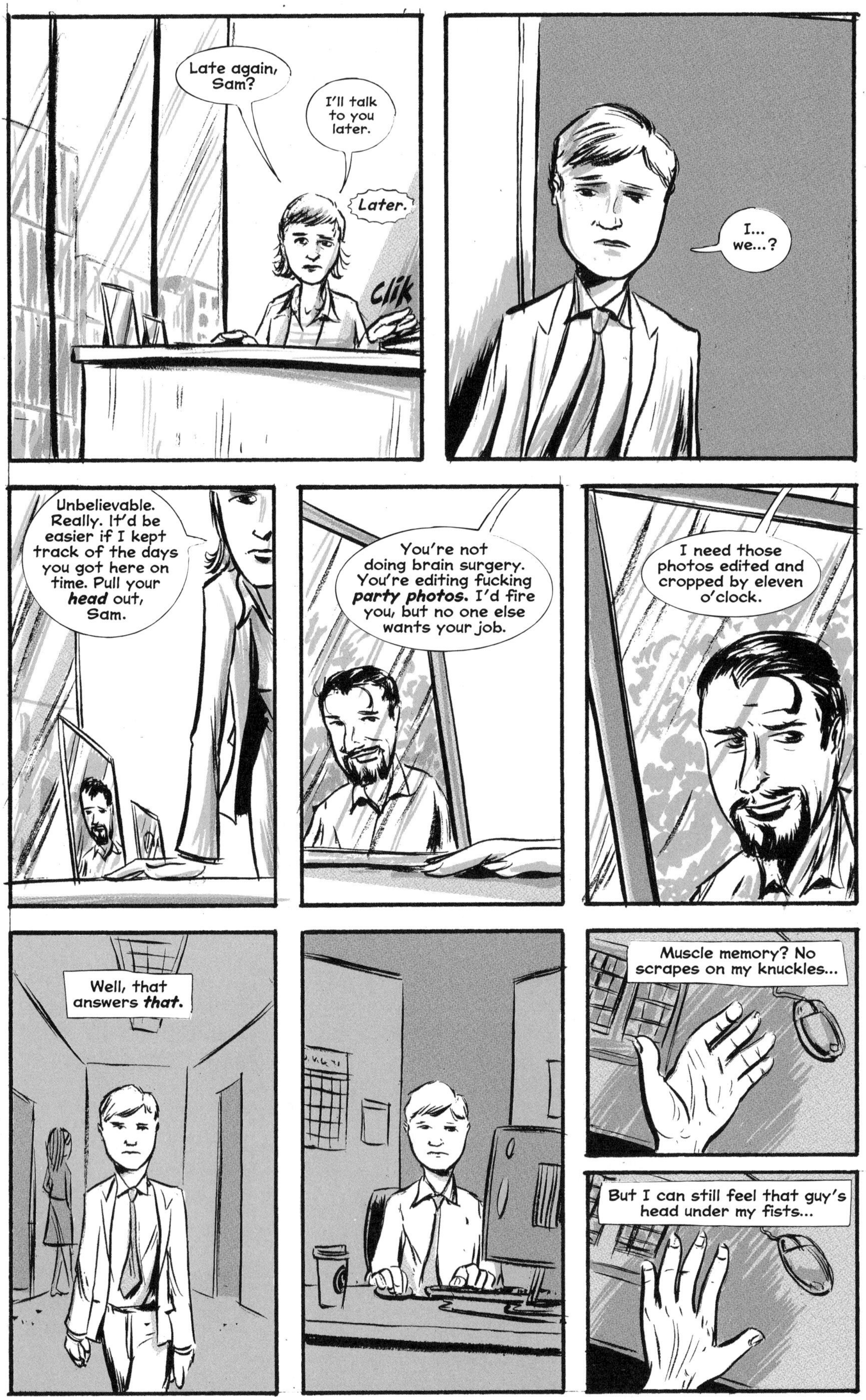
Late again, Sam?
I'll talk to you later.
Later.
Clik
I... we...?
Unbelievable. Really. It'd be easier if I kept track of the days you got here on time. Pull your **head** out, Sam.
You're not doing brain surgery. You're editing fucking **party photos.** I'd fire you, but no one else wants your job.
I need those photos edited and cropped by eleven o'clock.
Well, that answers ***that.***
Muscle memory? No scrapes on my knuckles...
But I can still feel that guy's head under my fists...

ATHER FORECAST FOR THE WEEKEND WILL MARK THE **19**TH STRAIGHT DAY OF SUN AS PERFECT WEATHER CONTINUES THROUGH

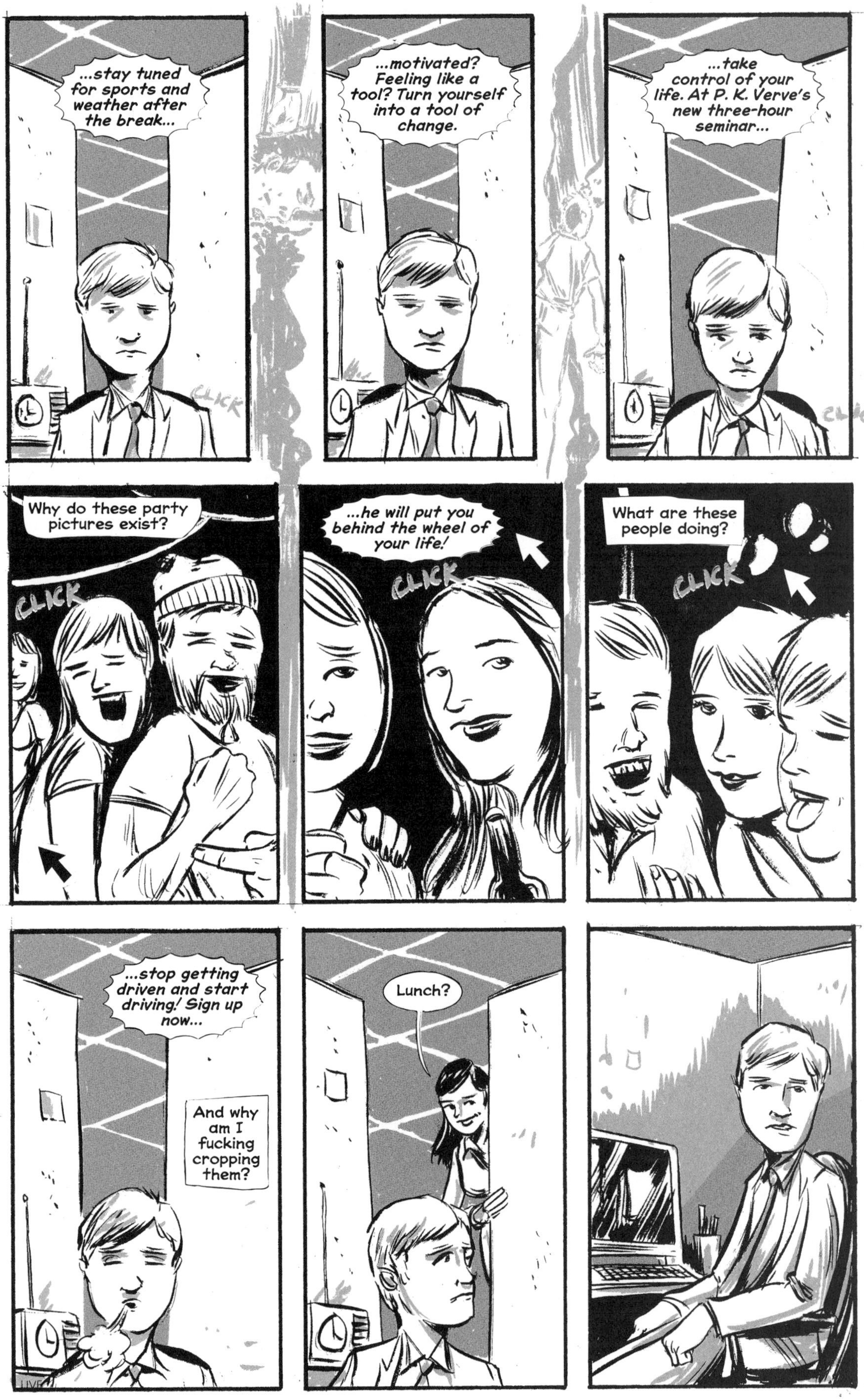
...stay tuned for sports and weather after the break...
CLICK
...motivated? Feeling like a tool? Turn yourself into a tool of change.
...take control of your life. At P. K. Verve's new three-hour seminar...
CLICK
Why do these party pictures exist?
CLICK
...he will put you behind the wheel of your life!
CLICK
What are these people doing?
CLICK
...stop getting driven and start driving! Sign up now...
And why am I fucking cropping them?
Lunch?

NED SPEAKER P. K. VERVE BOUGHT THE RIGHTS TO THE VINTAGE NOVEL FOR A MERE $20K AND PLANS TO RELEASE IT AS A HARD

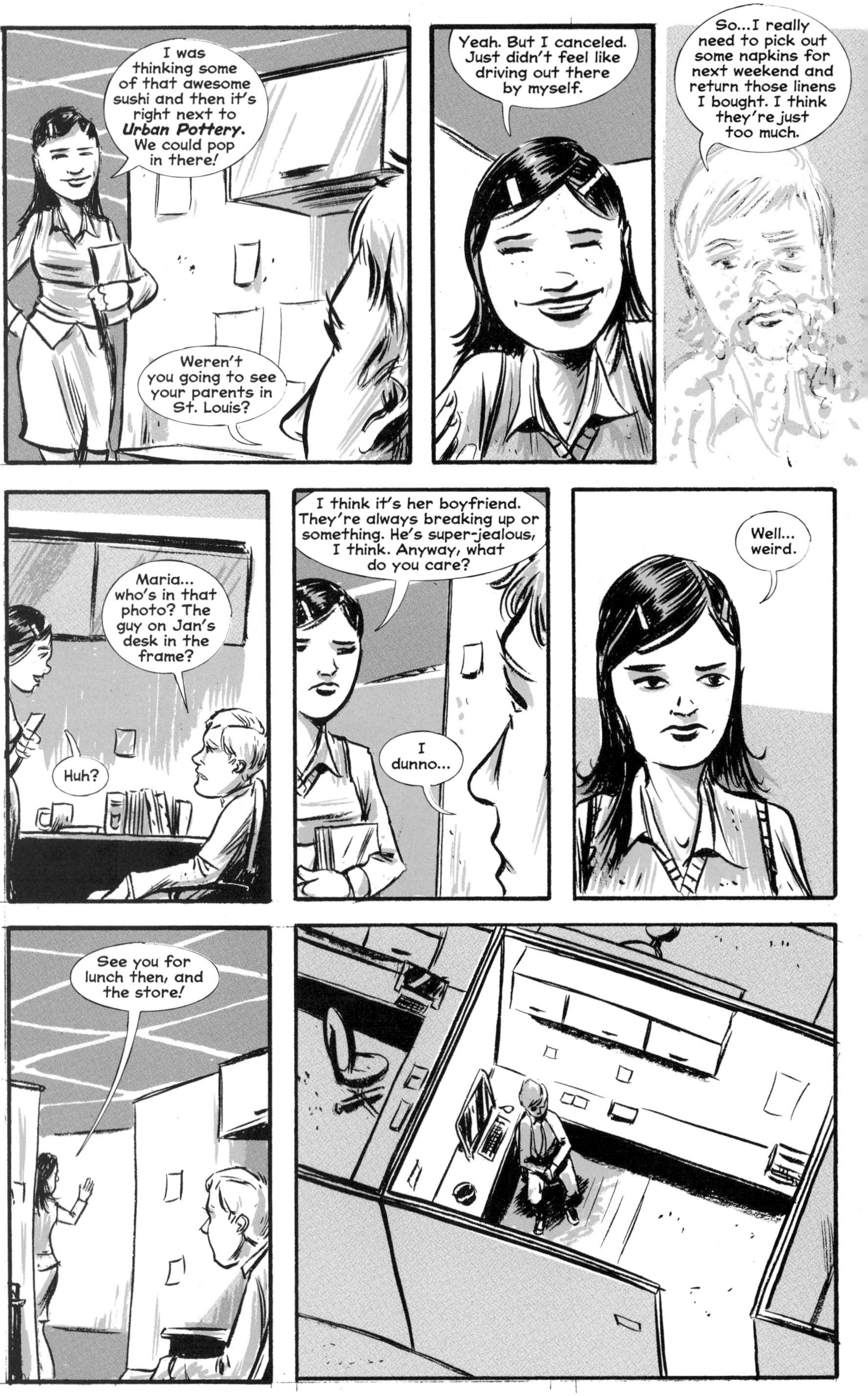
I was thinking some of that awesome sushi and then it's right next to **Urban Pottery.** We could pop in there!
Weren't you going to see your parents in St. Louis?
Yeah. But I canceled. Just didn't feel like driving out there by myself.
So...I really need to pick out some napkins for next weekend and return those linens I bought. I think they're just too much.
Maria... who's in that photo? The guy on Jan's desk in the frame?
Huh?
I think it's her boyfriend. They're always breaking up or something. He's super-jealous, I think. Anyway, what do you care?
I dunno...
Well... weird.
See you for lunch then, and the store!

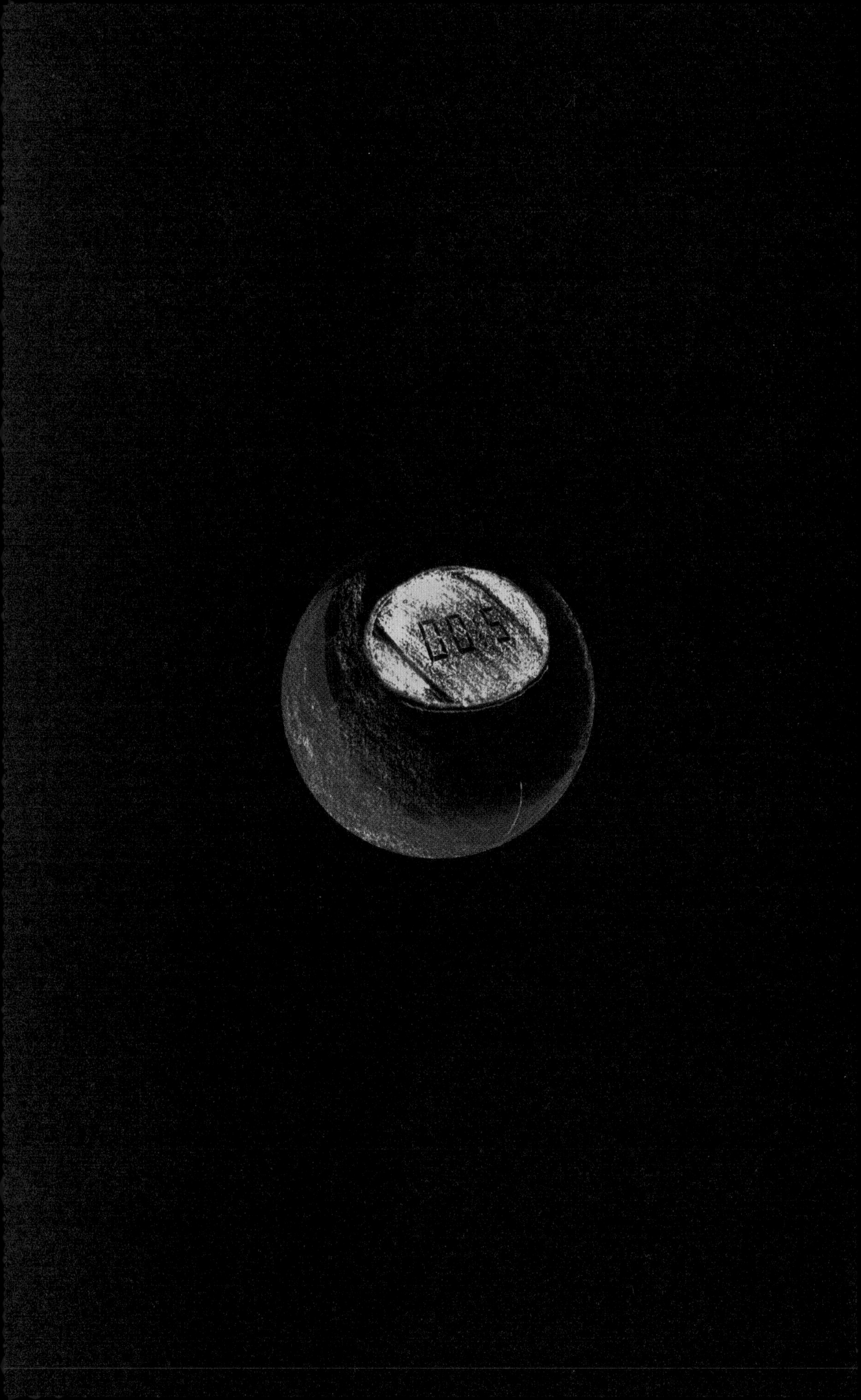

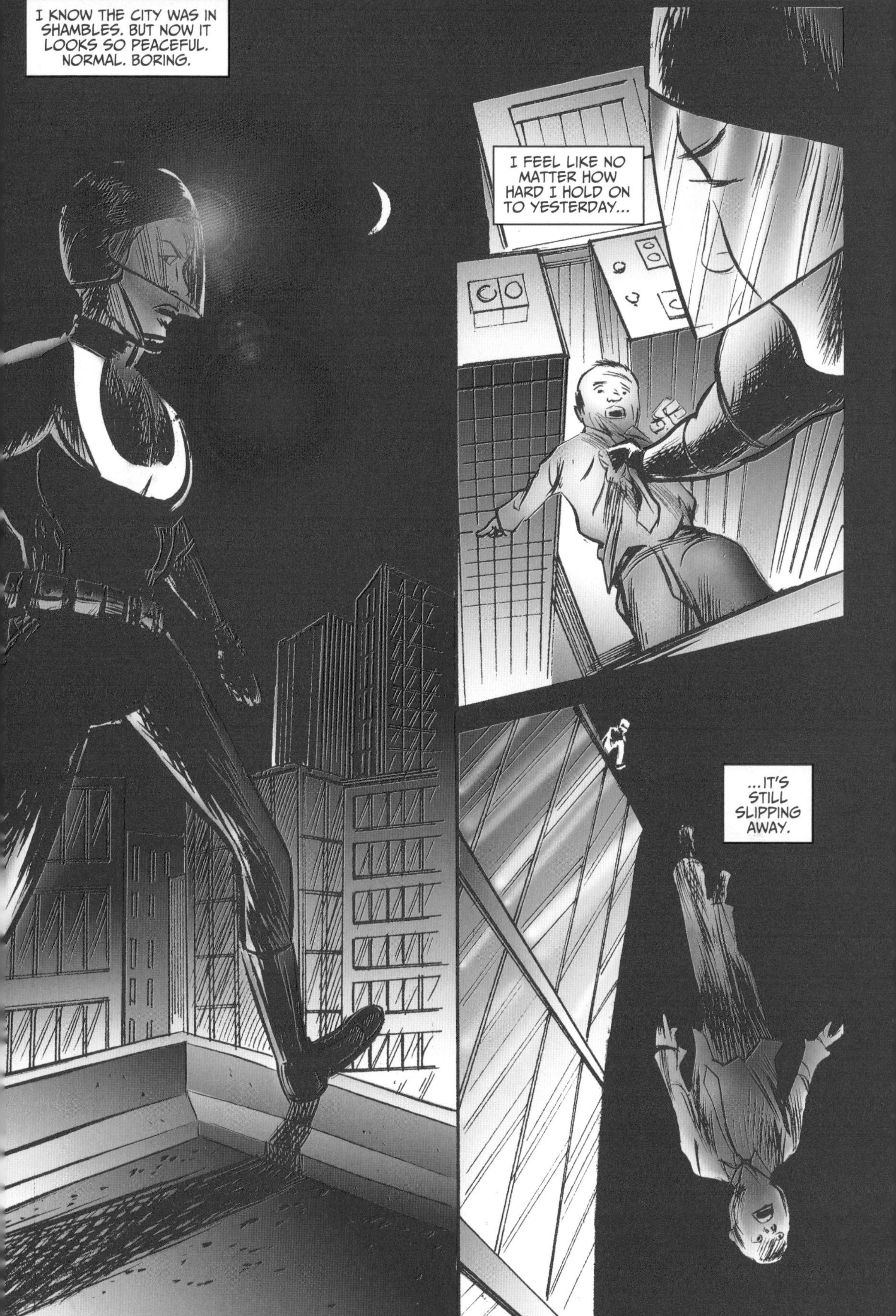
I KNOW THE CITY WAS IN SHAMBLES. BUT NOW IT LOOKS SO PEACEFUL. NORMAL. BORING.
I FEEL LIKE NO MATTER HOW HARD I HOLD ON TO YESTERDAY...
...IT'S STILL SLIPPING AWAY.

PLE EYEWITNESS REPORTS SAY THAT THE 22-YEAR-OLD SAVED THE LIVES OF EVERYONE IN THE HOUSE BY SHOUTING "FIRE" TO M

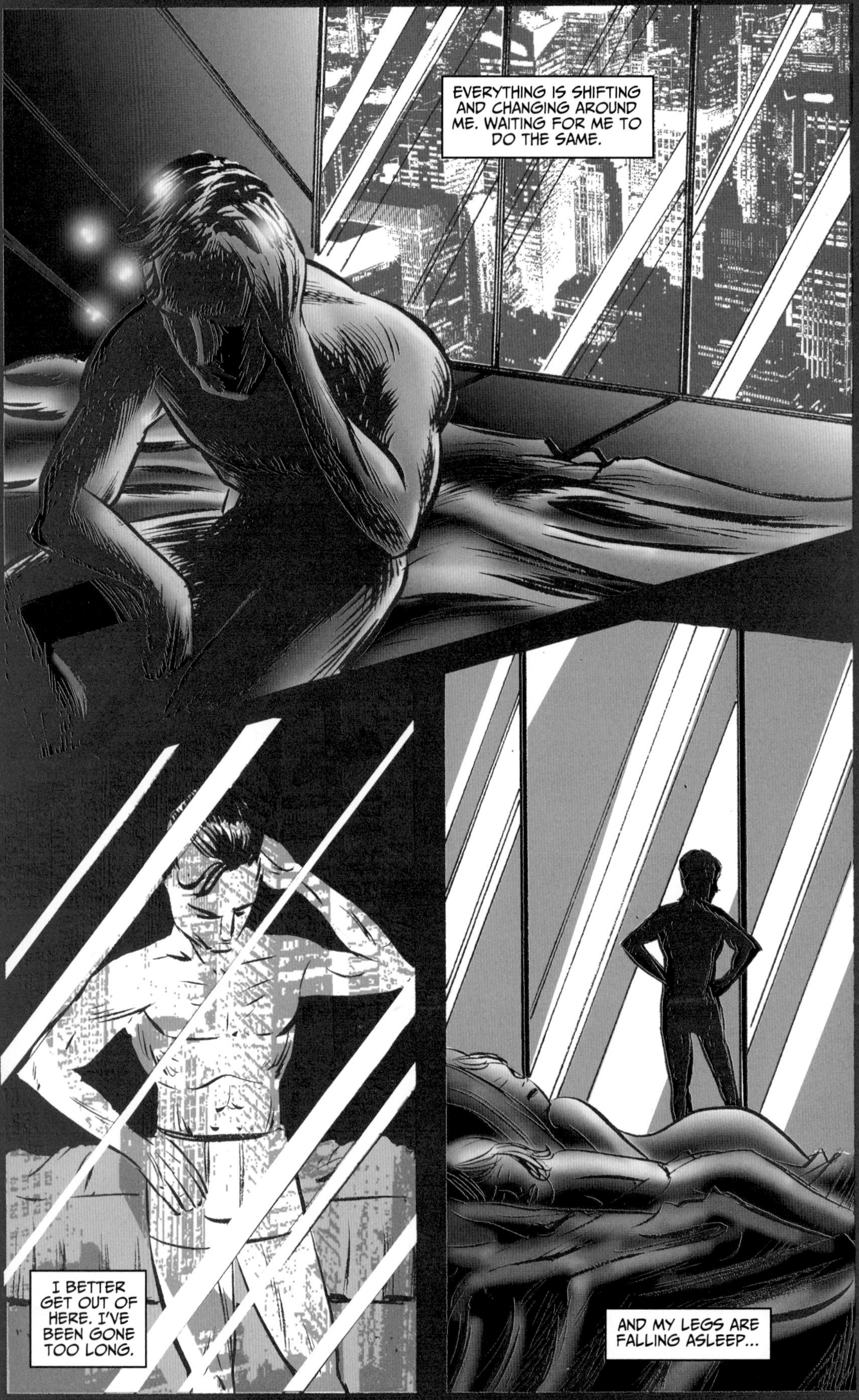
EVERYTHING IS SHIFTING AND CHANGING AROUND ME. WAITING FOR ME TO DO THE SAME.
I BETTER GET OUT OF HERE. I'VE BEEN GONE TOO LONG.
AND MY LEGS ARE FALLING ASLEEP...

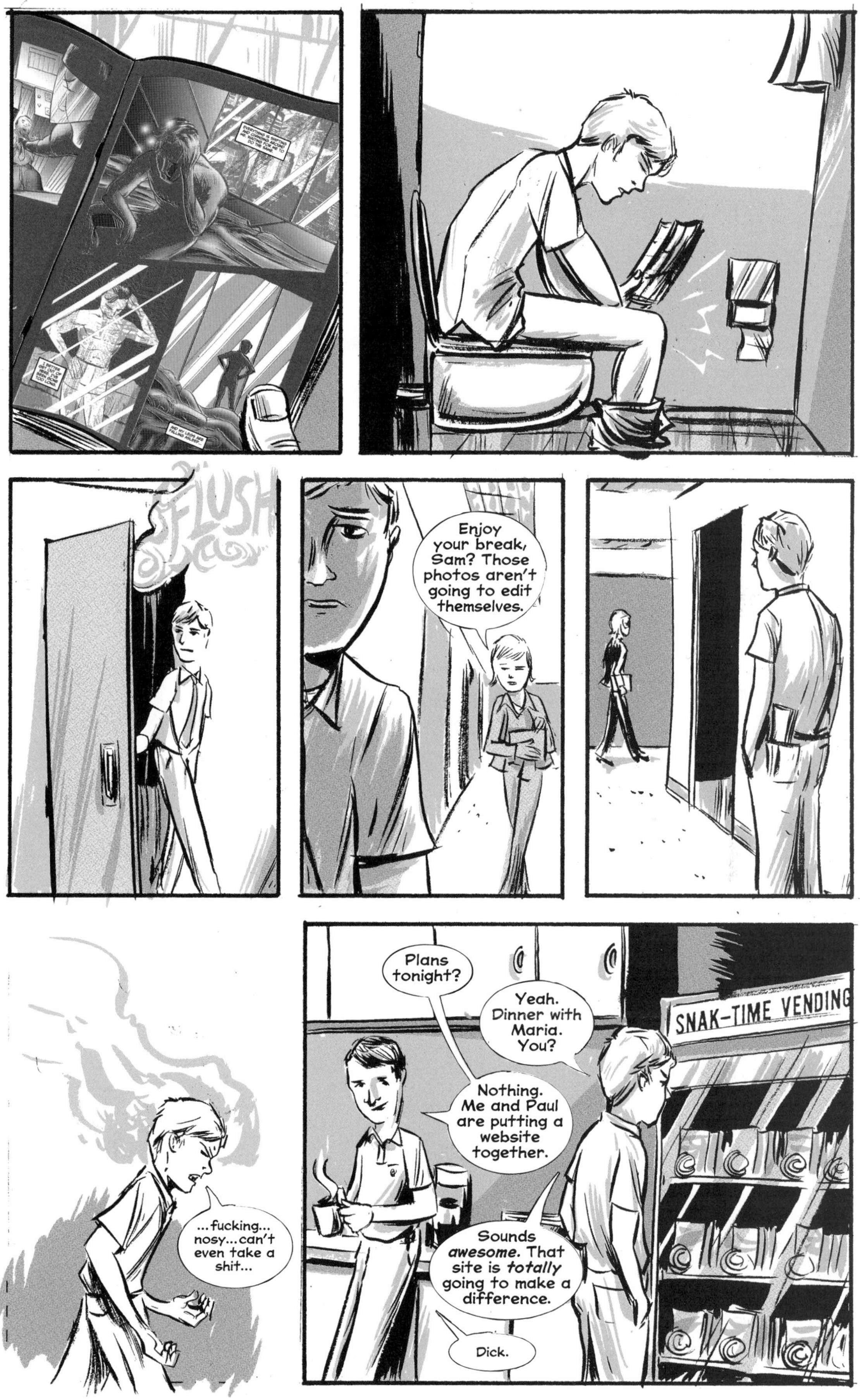
EVERYTHING IS SHIFTING AND CHANGING AROUND ME. WAITING FOR ME TO DO THE SAME.
I BETTER GET OUT OF HERE. I'VE BEEN GONE TOO LONG.
AND MY LEGS ARE FALLING ASLEEP...
FLUSH
Enjoy your break, Sam? Those photos aren't going to edit themselves.
...fucking... nosy...can't even take a shit...
Plans tonight?
Yeah. Dinner with Maria. You?
Nothing. Me and Paul are putting a website together.
Sounds *awesome.* That site is *totally* going to make a difference.
Dick.
SNAK-TIME VENDING

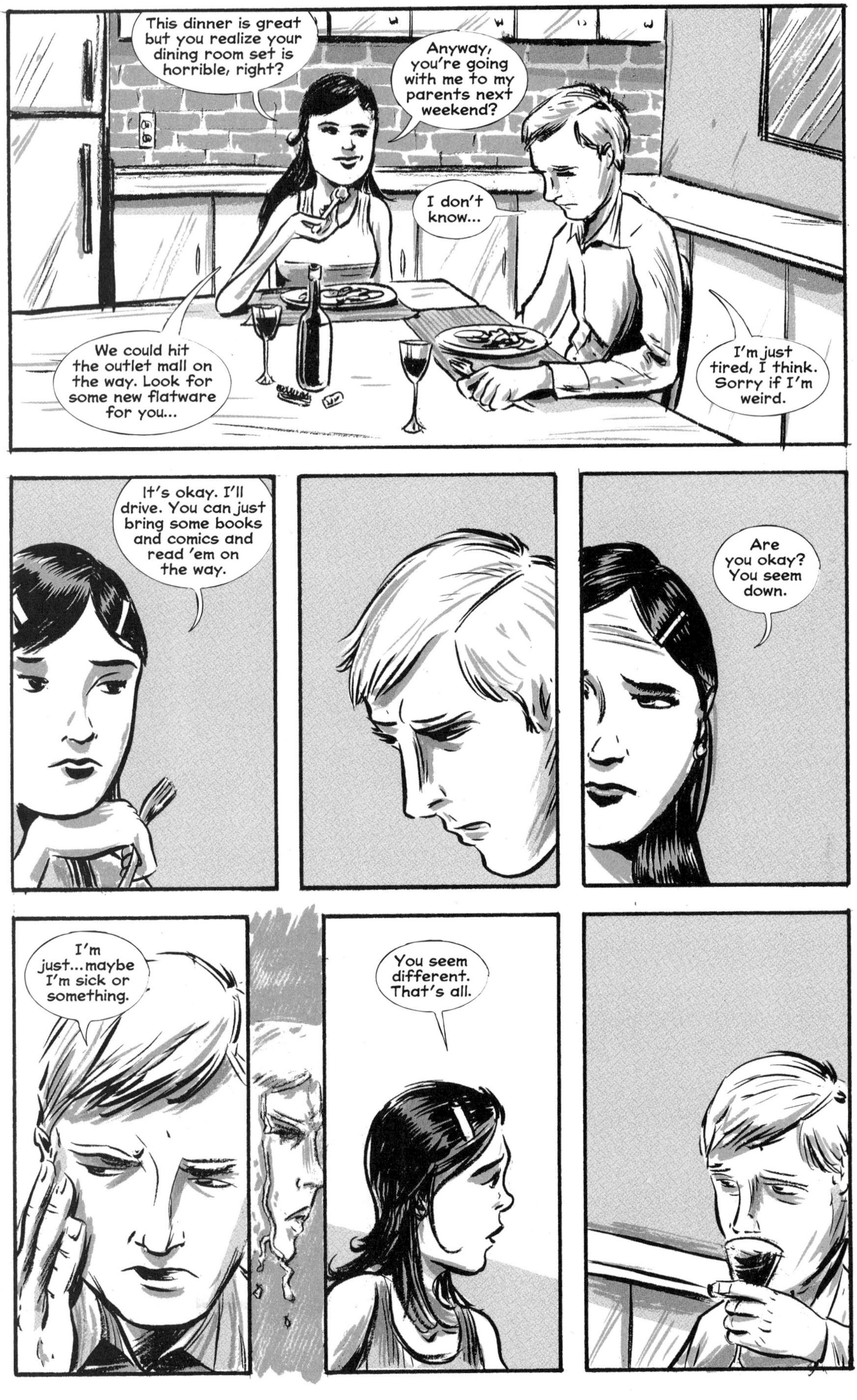
This dinner is great but you realize your dining room set is horrible, right?
Anyway, you're going with me to my parents next weekend?
I don't know...
We could hit the outlet mall on the way. Look for some new flatware for you...
I'm just tired, I think. Sorry if I'm weird.
It's okay. I'll drive. You can just bring some books and comics and read 'em on the way.
Are you okay? You seem down.
I'm just...maybe I'm sick or something.
You seem different. That's all.

RESTAURANT CHAIN. **TWENTY-FIVE** NEW LOCATIONS HAVE GRAND OPENINGS THIS WEEKEND WHICH ANALYSTS ATTRIBUTE TO TH

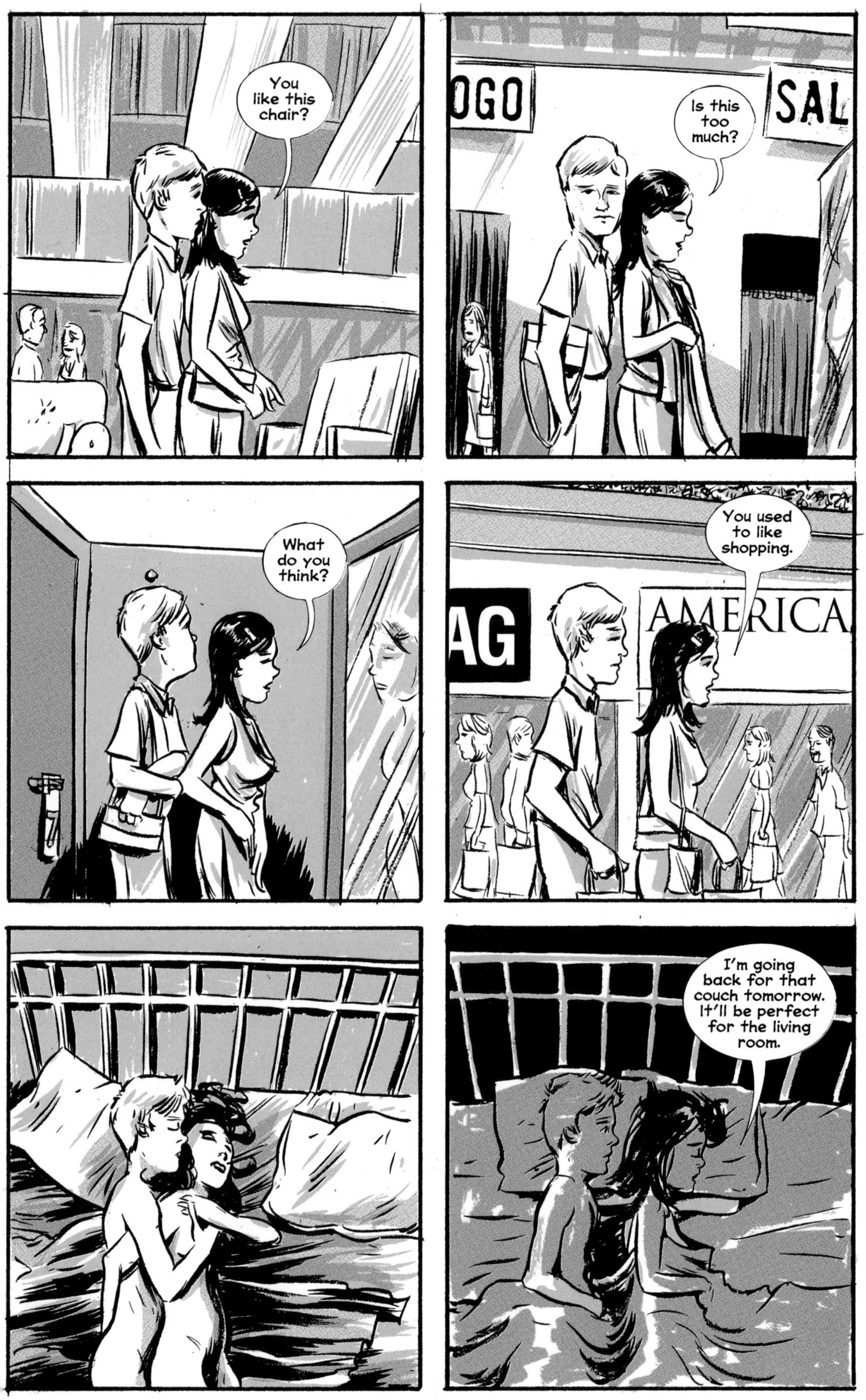
You like this chair?
OGO
SAL
Is this too much?
What do you think?
AG
AMERICA
You used to like shopping.
I'm going back for that couch tomorrow. It'll be perfect for the living room.

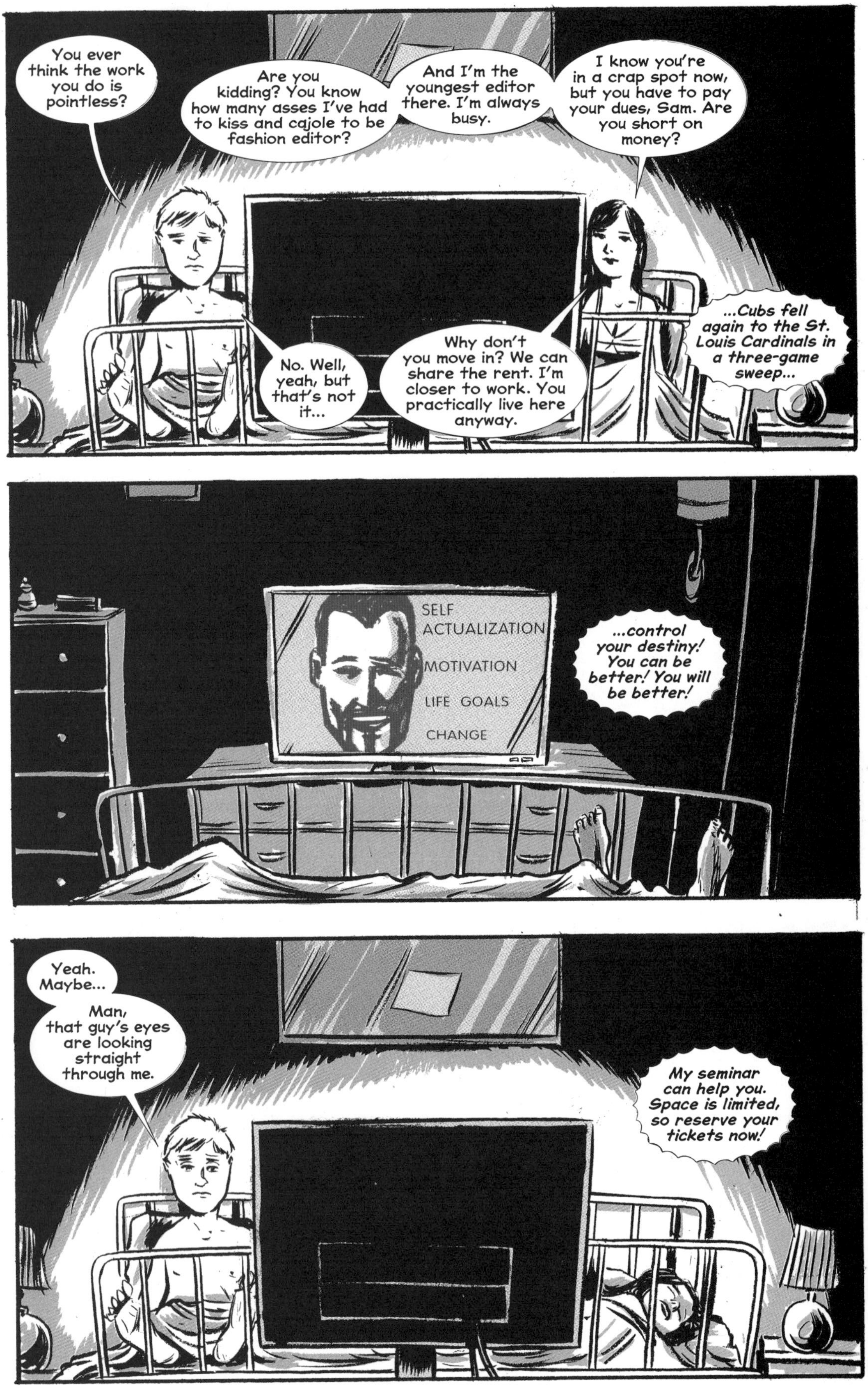
You ever think the work you do is pointless?
Are you kidding? You know how many asses I've had to kiss and cajole to be fashion editor?
And I'm the youngest editor there. I'm always busy.
I know you're in a crap spot now, but you have to pay your dues, Sam. Are you short on money?
No. Well, yeah, but that's not it...
Why don't you move in? We can share the rent. I'm closer to work. You practically live here anyway.
...Cubs fell again to the St. Louis Cardinals in a three-game sweep...
SELF ACTUALIZATION
MOTIVATION
LIFE GOALS
CHANGE
...control your destiny! You can be better! You will be better!
Yeah. Maybe...
Man, that guy's eyes are looking straight through me.
My seminar can help you. Space is limited, so reserve your tickets now!

INCREASE IN SALES AS THE REAL ESTATE INDUSTRY EXPLODES. **27**% OF RENTERS HAVE BECOME HOMEOWNERS IN THE LAST Q

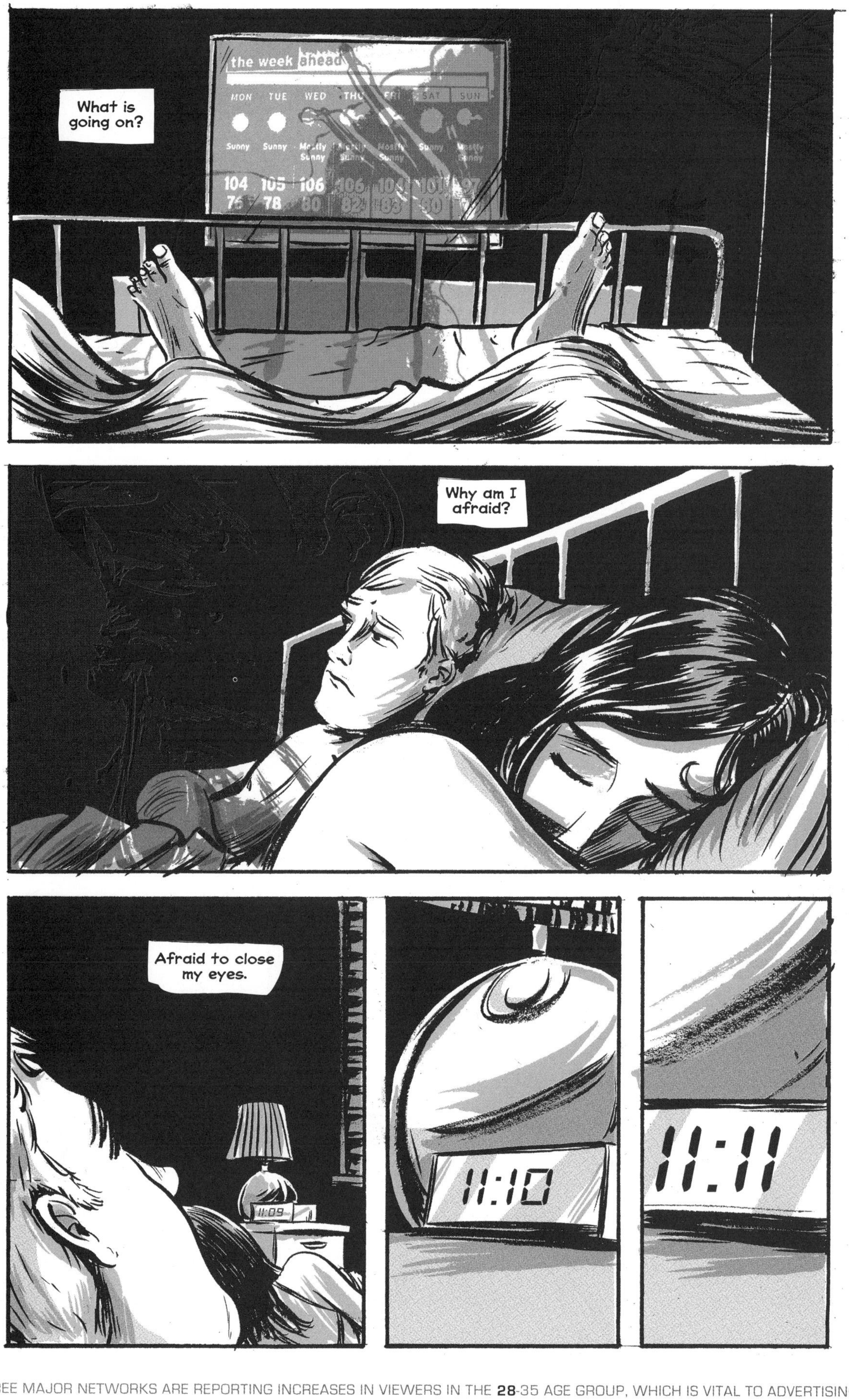
the week ahead
MON TUE WED
What is going on?
Why am I afraid?
Afraid to close my eyes.
11:09
11:10
11:11

HREE MAJOR NETWORKS ARE REPORTING INCREASES IN VIEWERS IN THE **28**-35 AGE GROUP, WHICH IS VITAL TO ADVERTISING DO

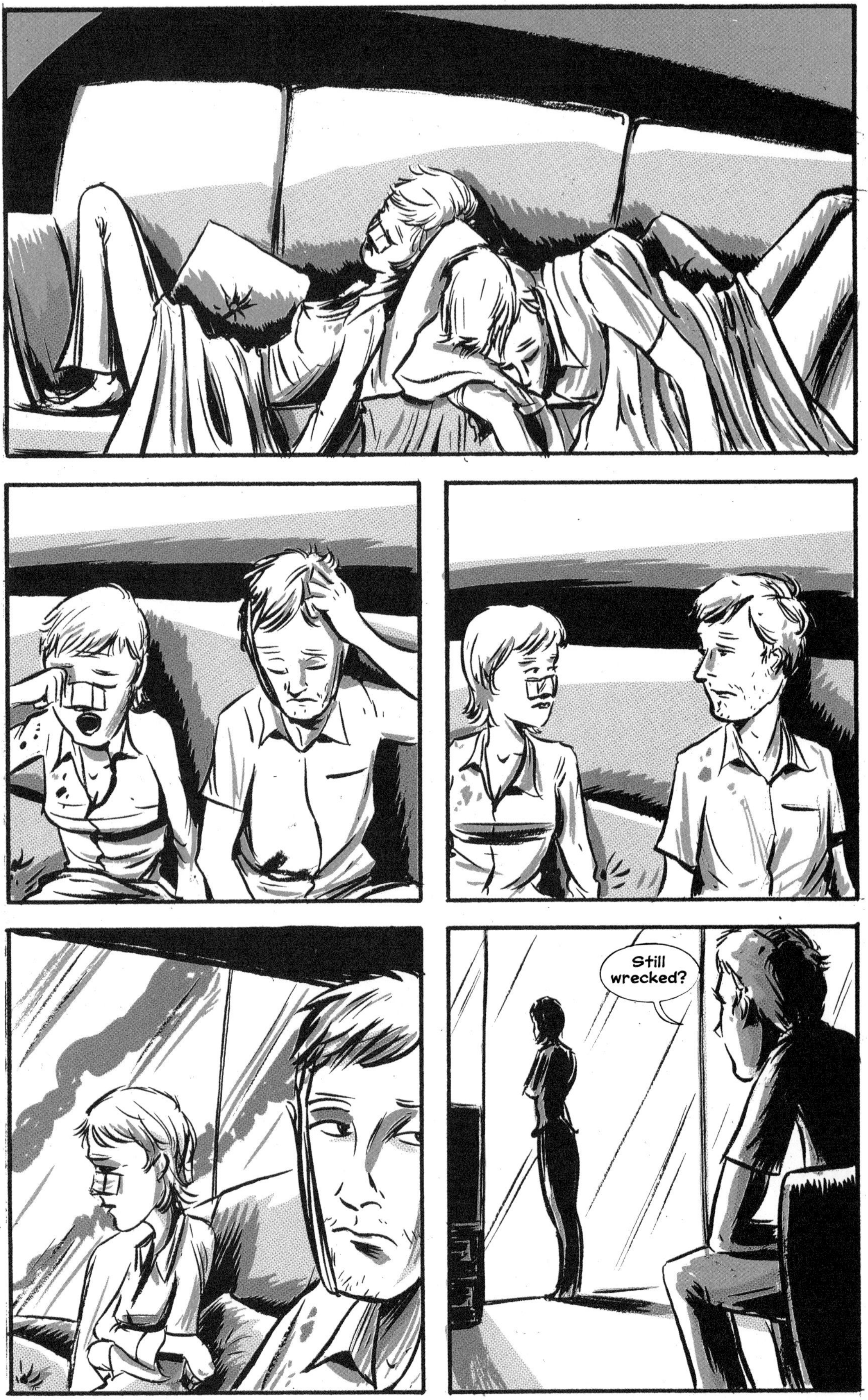
Still wrecked?

E ENTIRE COUNTRY HAS WOKEN UP TO A WORLD IN TURMOIL. MORE THAN **29** STATES HAVE REQUESTED FEDERAL DISASTER REL

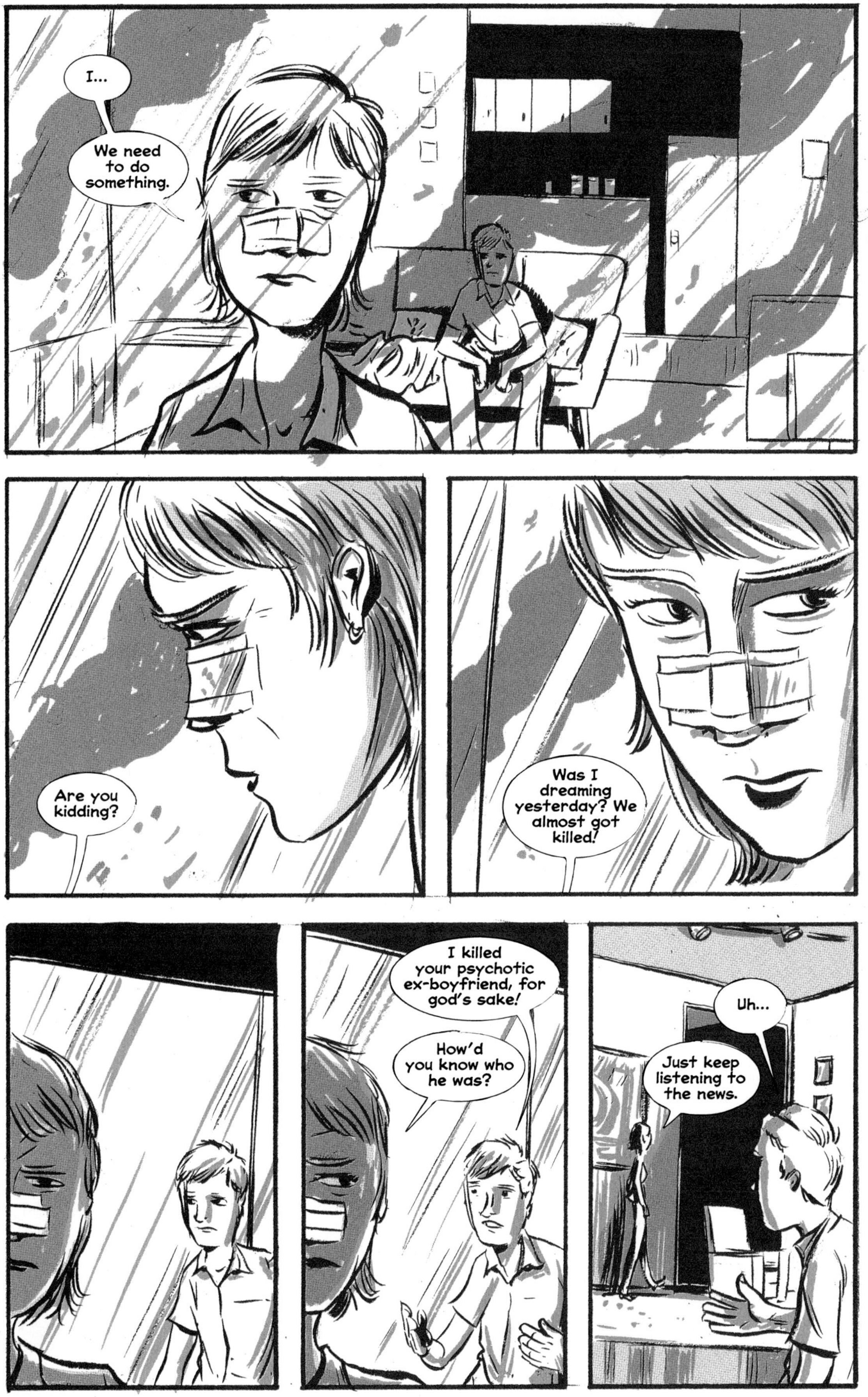
I...
We need to do something.
Are you kidding?
Was I dreaming yesterday? We almost got killed!
I killed your psychotic ex-boyfriend, for god's sake!
How'd you know who he was?
Uh...
Just keep listening to the news.

D IS IN JEOPARDY. NEWS OUTLETS ARE BLACKING OUT NATIONWIDE. **THIRTY** FLIGHTS ARE UNACCOUNTED FOR AS ALL AIR TRAF

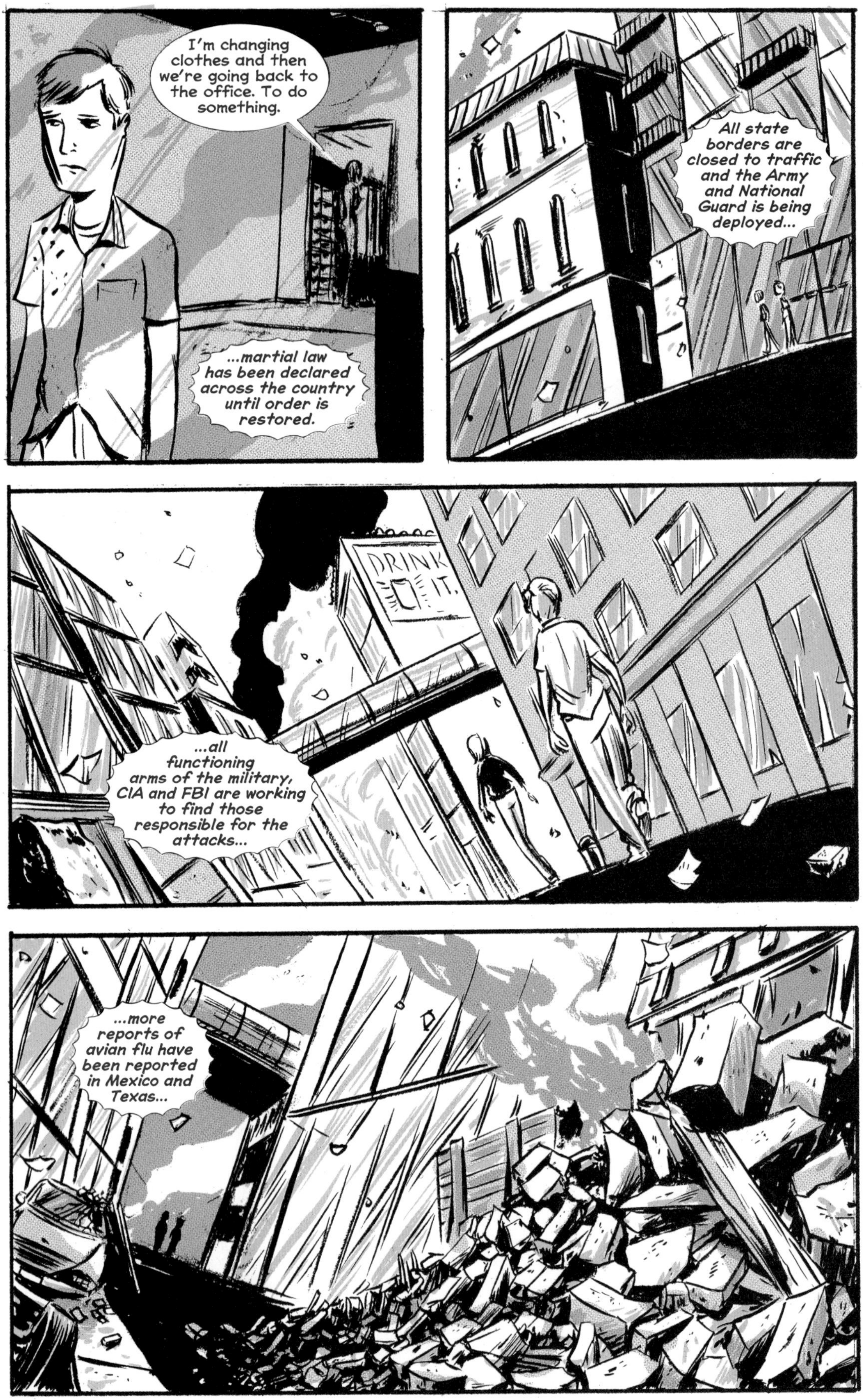
I'm changing clothes and then we're going back to the office. To do something.
...martial law has been declared across the country until order is restored.
All state borders are closed to traffic and the Army and National Guard is being deployed...
DRINK IT.
...all functioning arms of the military, CIA and FBI are working to find those responsible for the attacks...
...more reports of avian flu have been reported in Mexico and Texas...

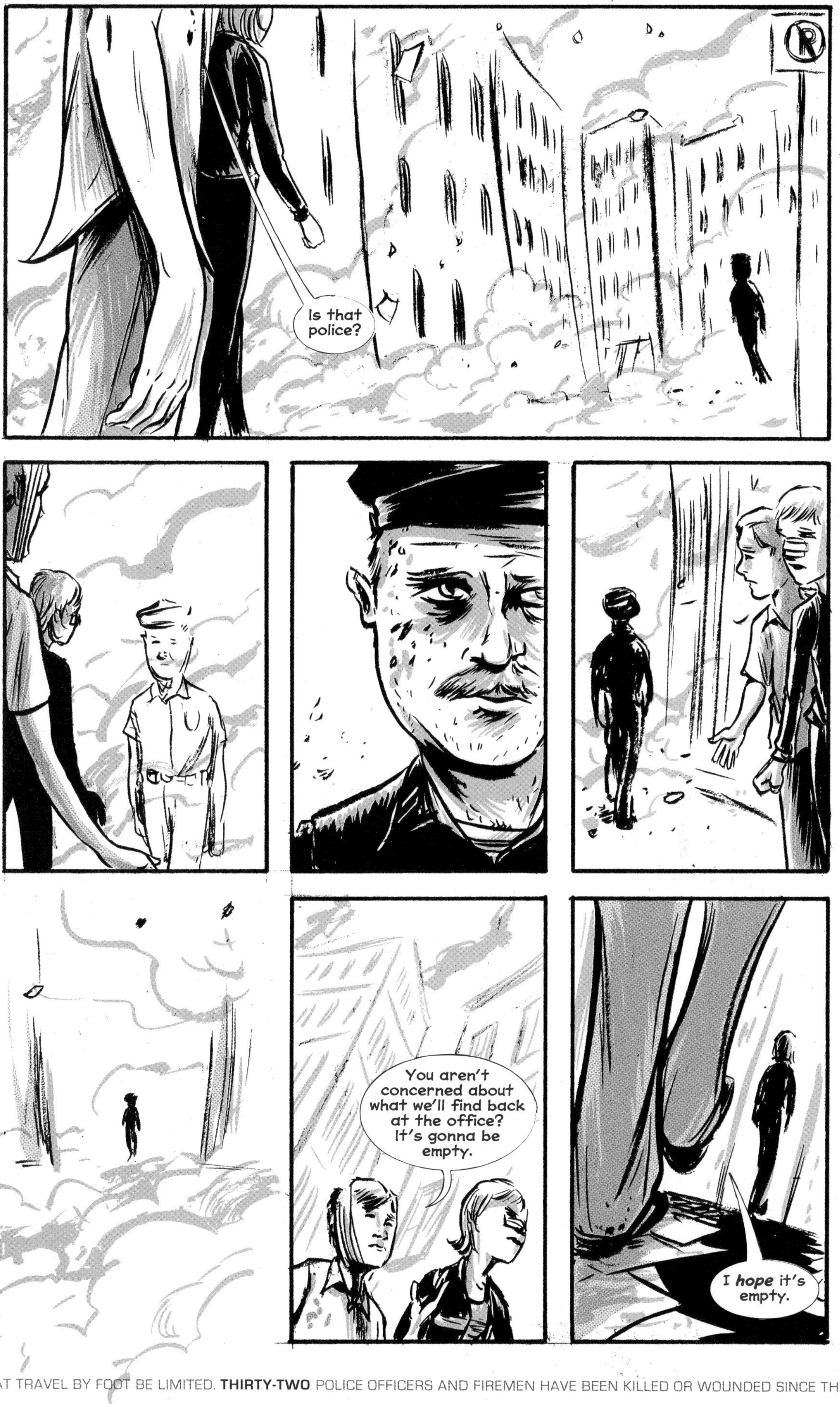
Is that police?
You aren't concerned about what we'll find back at the office? It's gonna be empty.
I *hope* it's empty.

IAT TRAVEL BY FOOT BE LIMITED. **THIRTY-TWO** POLICE OFFICERS AND FIREMEN HAVE BEEN KILLED OR WOUNDED SINCE THE CAT

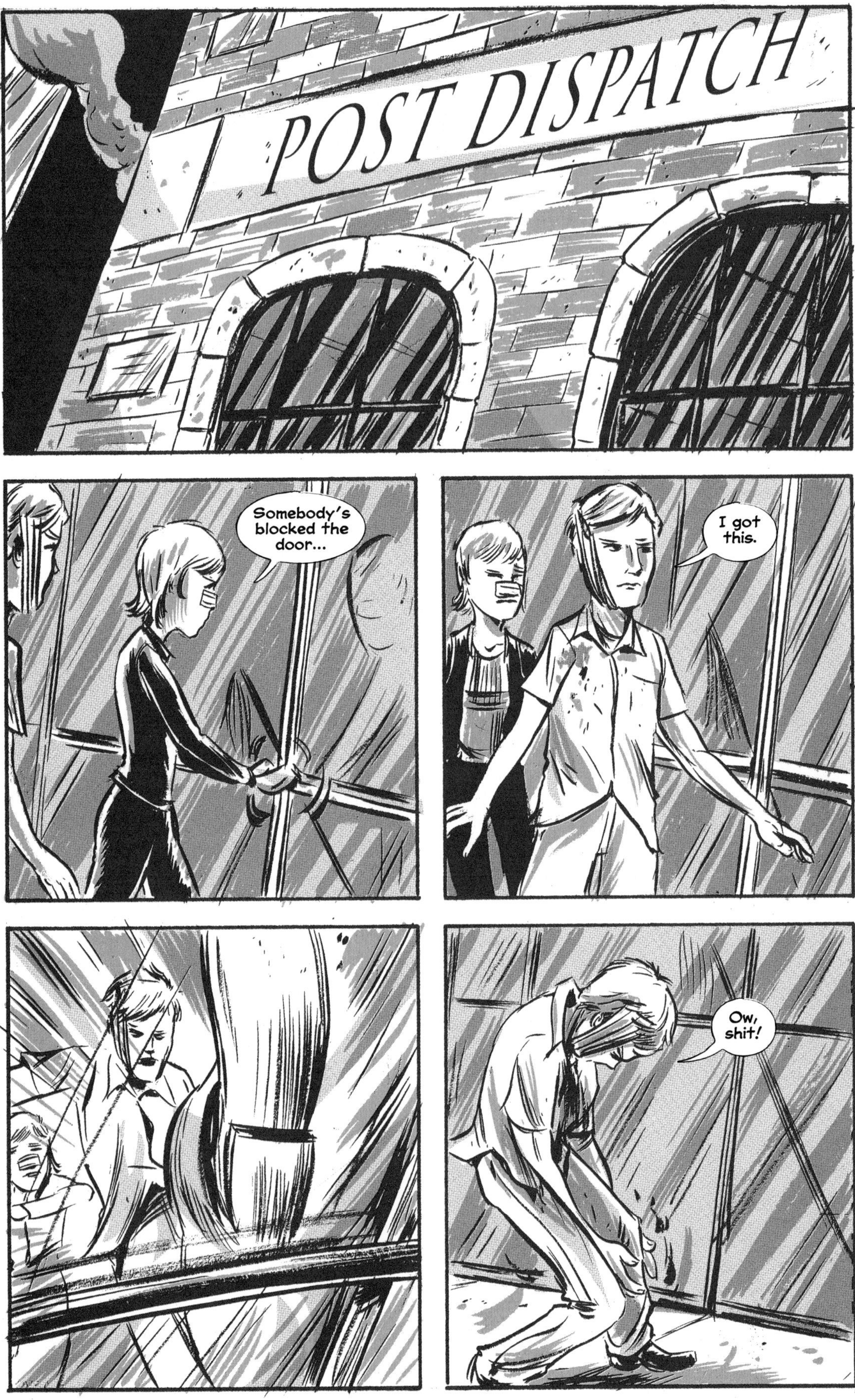
POST DISPATCH
Somebody's blocked the door...
I got this.
Ow, shit!

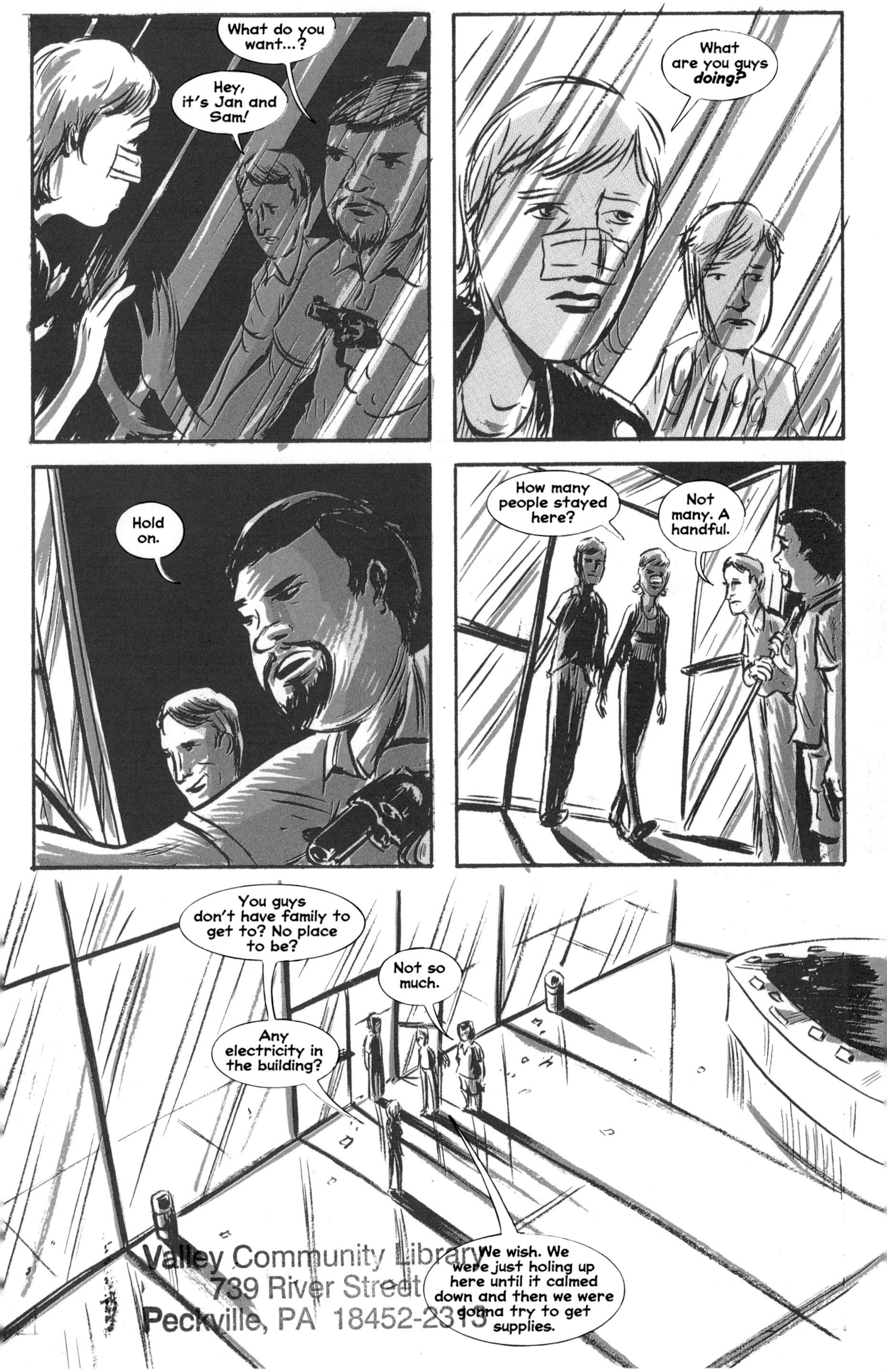
What do you want...?
Hey, it's Jan and Sam!
What are you guys *doing?*
Hold on.
How many people stayed here?
Not many. A handful.
You guys don't have family to get to? No place to be?
Not so much.
Any electricity in the building?
We wish. We were just holing up here until it calmed down and then we were gonna try to get supplies.

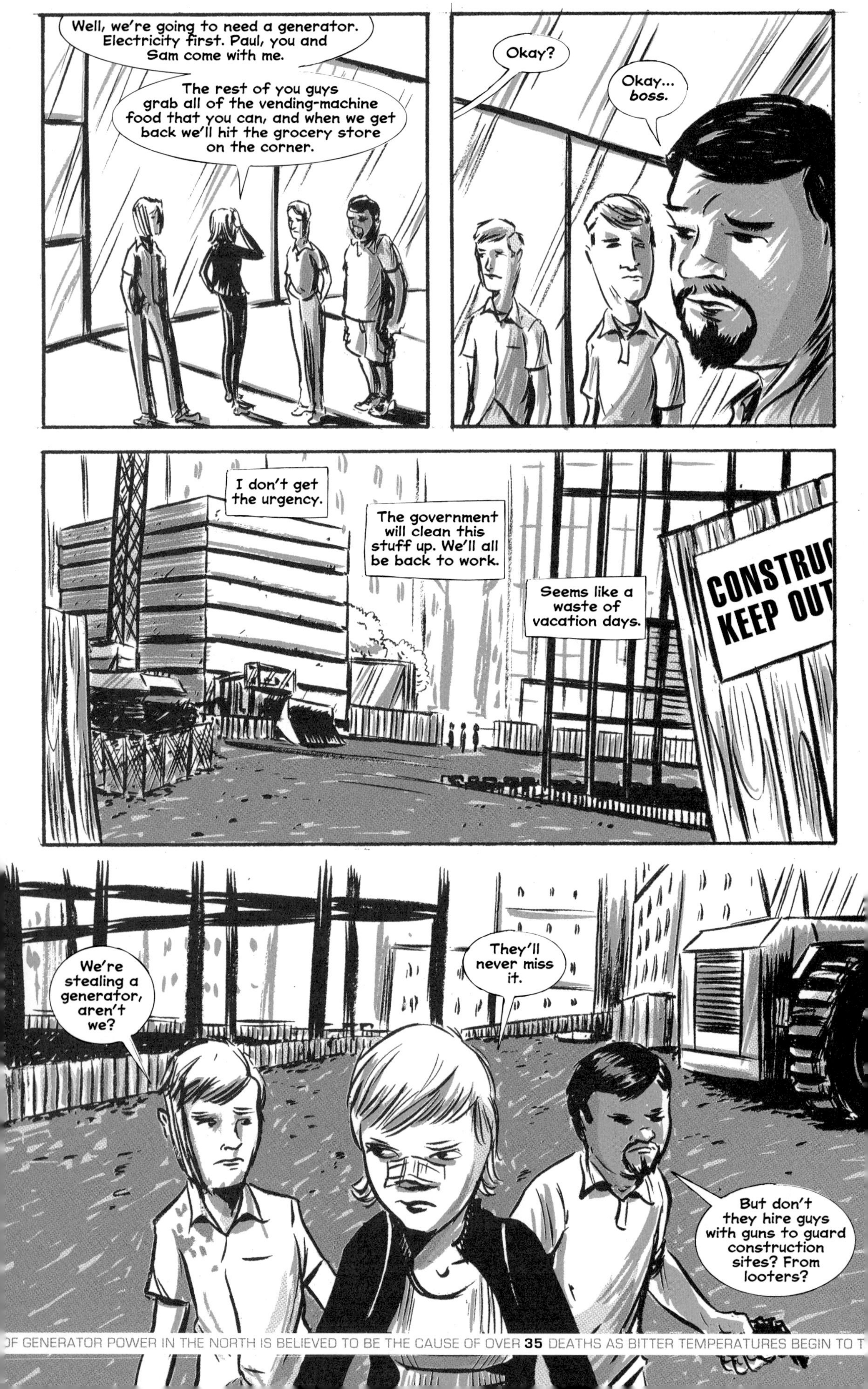

Well, we're going to need a generator. Electricity first. Paul, you and Sam come with me.
The rest of you guys grab all of the vending-machine food that you can, and when we get back we'll hit the grocery store on the corner.
Okay?
Okay... boss.
I don't get the urgency.
The government will clean this stuff up. We'll all be back to work.
Seems like a waste of vacation days.
KEEP OUT
We're stealing a generator, aren't we?
They'll never miss it.
But don't they hire guys with guns to guard construction sites? From looters?
GENERATOR POWER IN THE NORTH IS BELIEVED TO BE THE CAUSE OF OVER 35 DEATHS AS BITTER TEMPERATURES BEGIN TO

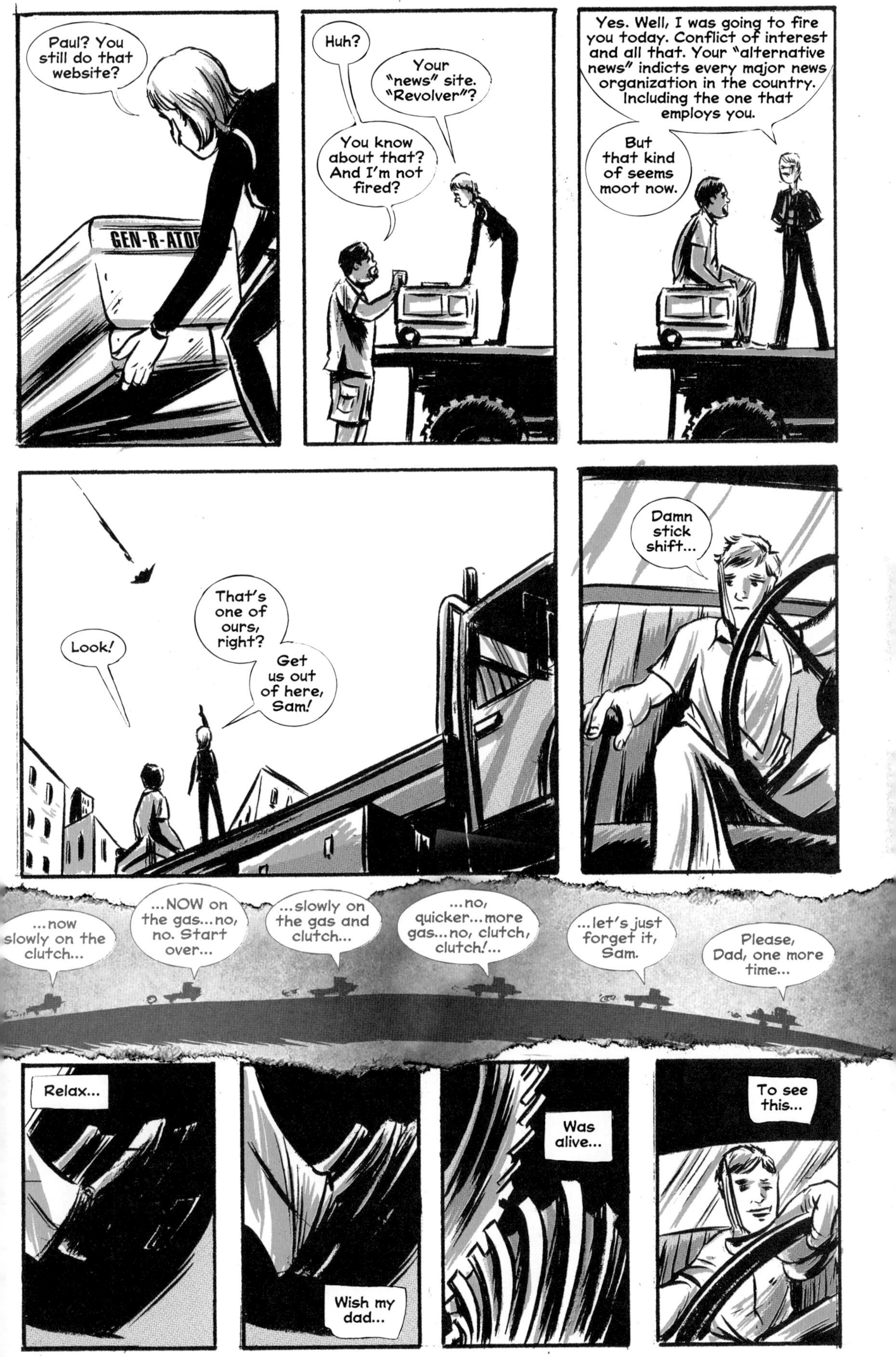
Paul? You still do that website?
Huh?
Your "news" site. "Revolver"?
You know about that? And I'm not fired?
Yes. Well, I was going to fire you today. Conflict of interest and all that. Your "alternative news" indicts every major news organization in the country. Including the one that employs you.
But that kind of seems moot now.
GEN-R-ATO
Look!
That's one of ours, right?
Get us out of here, Sam!
Damn stick shift...
...now slowly on the clutch...
...NOW on the gas...no, no. Start over...
...slowly on the gas and clutch...
...no, quicker...more gas...no, clutch, clutch!...
...let's just forget it, Sam.
Please, Dad, one more time...
Relax...
Wish my dad...
Was alive...
To see this...

DING SUCH STAPLES AS GASOLINE, WHICH IS FETCHING OVER $36 A GALLON. NUMEROUS ACCOUNTS OF LOOTERS BEING SHOT I

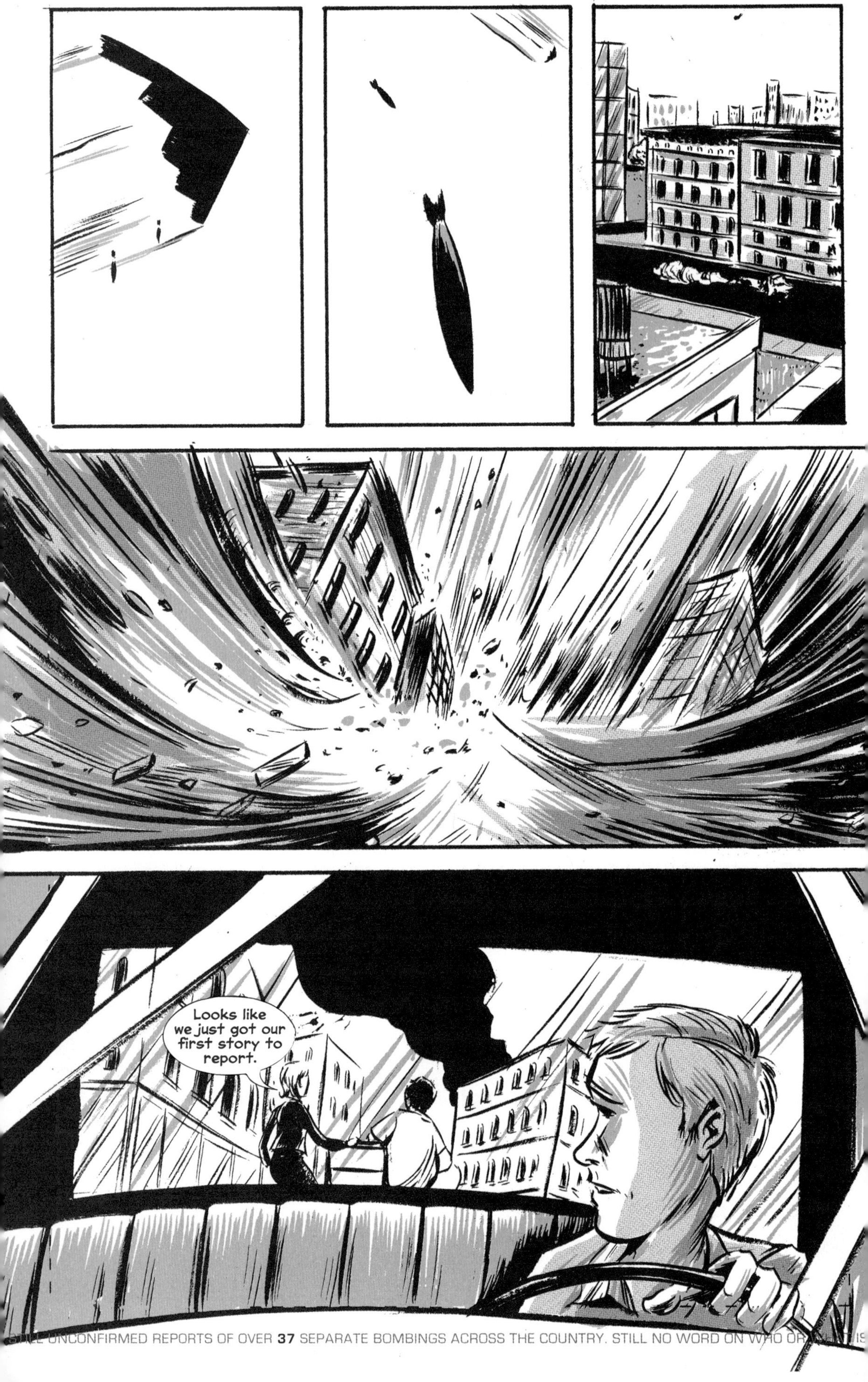
Looks like we just got our first story to report.
UNCONFIRMED REPORTS OF OVER 37 SEPARATE BOMBINGS ACROSS THE COUNTRY. STILL NO WORD ON WHO OR

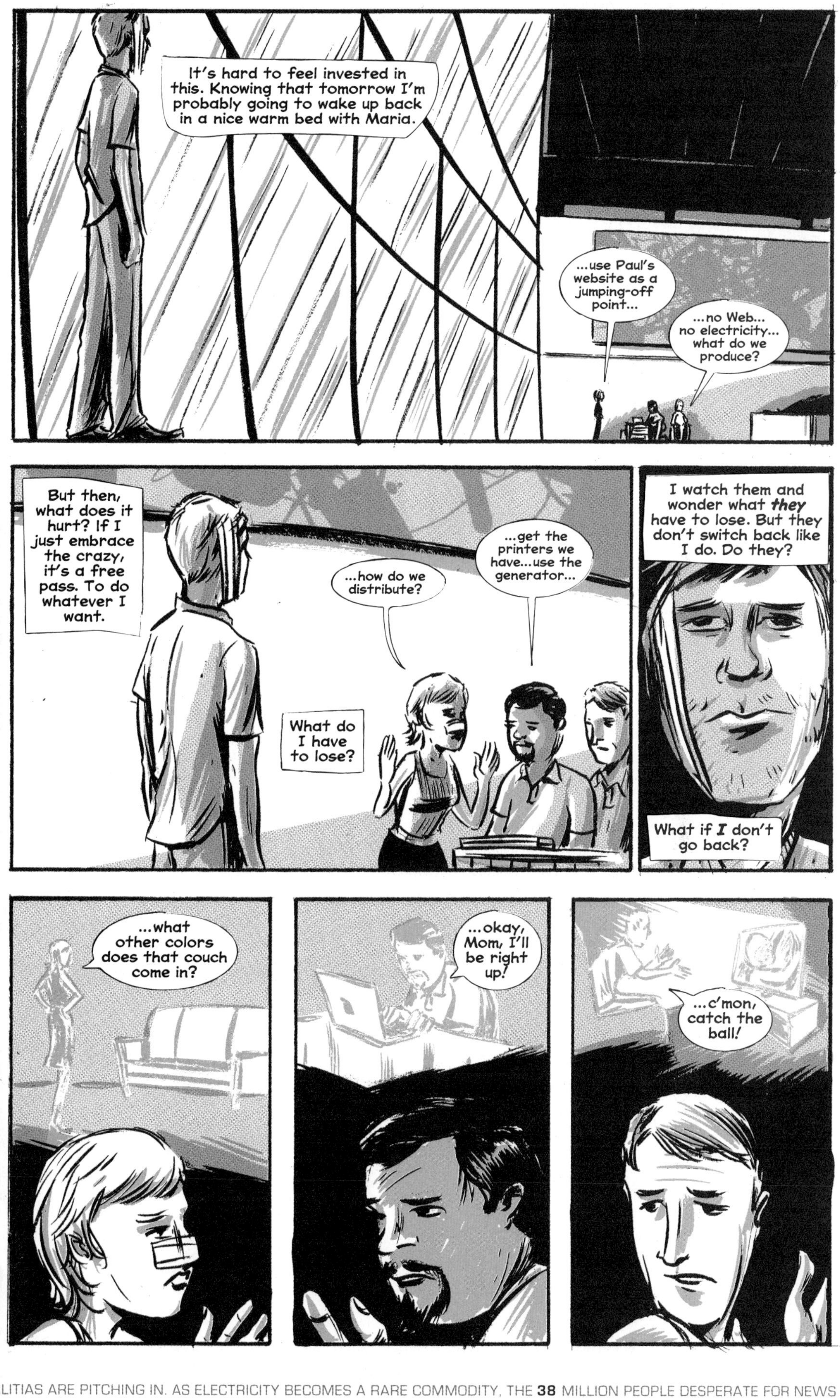
It's hard to feel invested in this. Knowing that tomorrow I'm probably going to wake up back in a nice warm bed with Maria.
...use Paul's website as a jumping-off point...
...no Web... no electricity... what do we produce?
But then, what does it hurt? If I just embrace the crazy, it's a free pass. To do whatever I want.
...how do we distribute?
...get the printers we have...use the generator...
What do I have to lose?
I watch them and wonder what *they* have to lose. But they don't switch back like I do. Do they?
What if *I* don't go back?
...what other colors does that couch come in?
...okay, Mom, I'll be right up!
...c'mon, catch the ball!

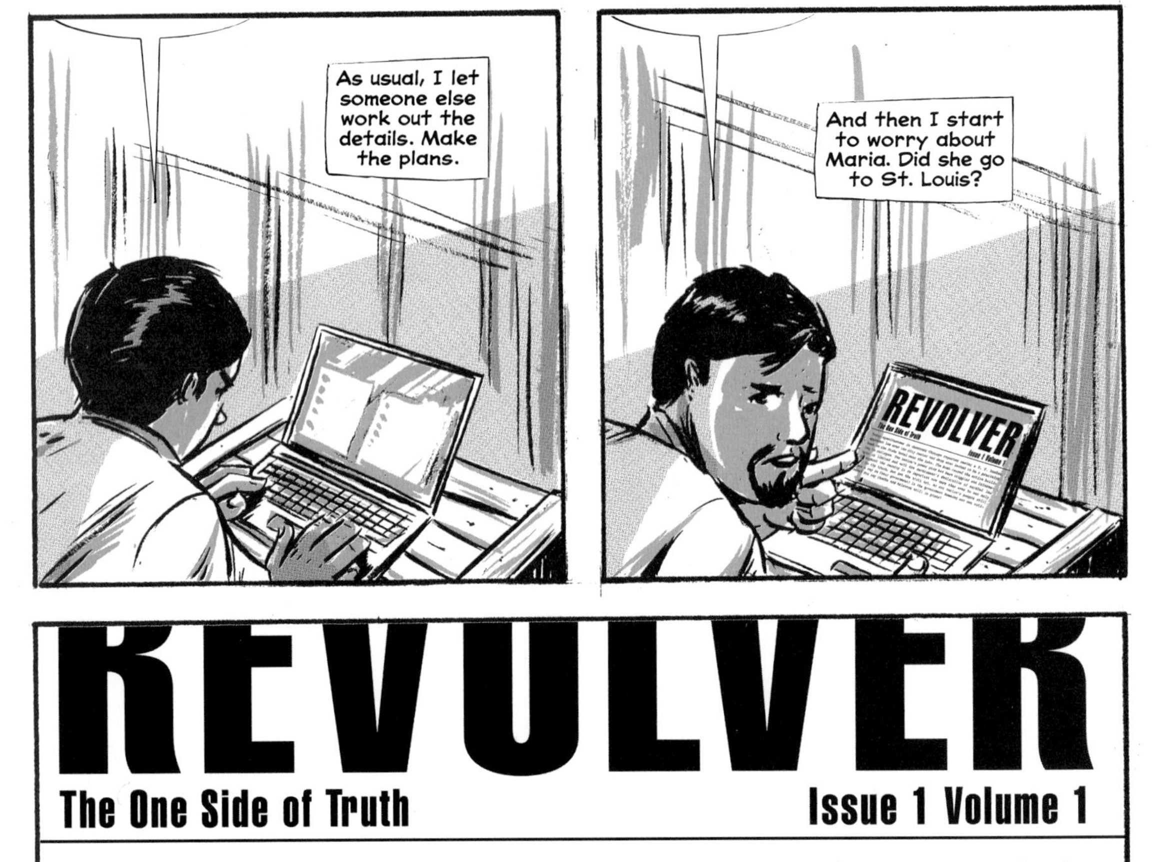
As usual, I let someone else work out the details. Make the plans.
And then I start to worry about Maria. Did she go to St. Louis?
REVOLVER

REVOLVER

The One Side of Truth **Issue 1 Volume 1**

Today eyewitnesses in downtown Chicago reported seeing a U. S. bomber approach low over the city center and drop what looked to be a precision bomb on the Drake hotel near the lake. The bomb caused the entire building to collapse. The nation's power grid has been crippled and information is limited and with the government's declaration of martial law throughout the country it is important now more than ever to not only get to the truth, but get the truth out. Do our nation's people still have a say in their government? Is the government bombing its own citizens? Are any checks and balances still in place?

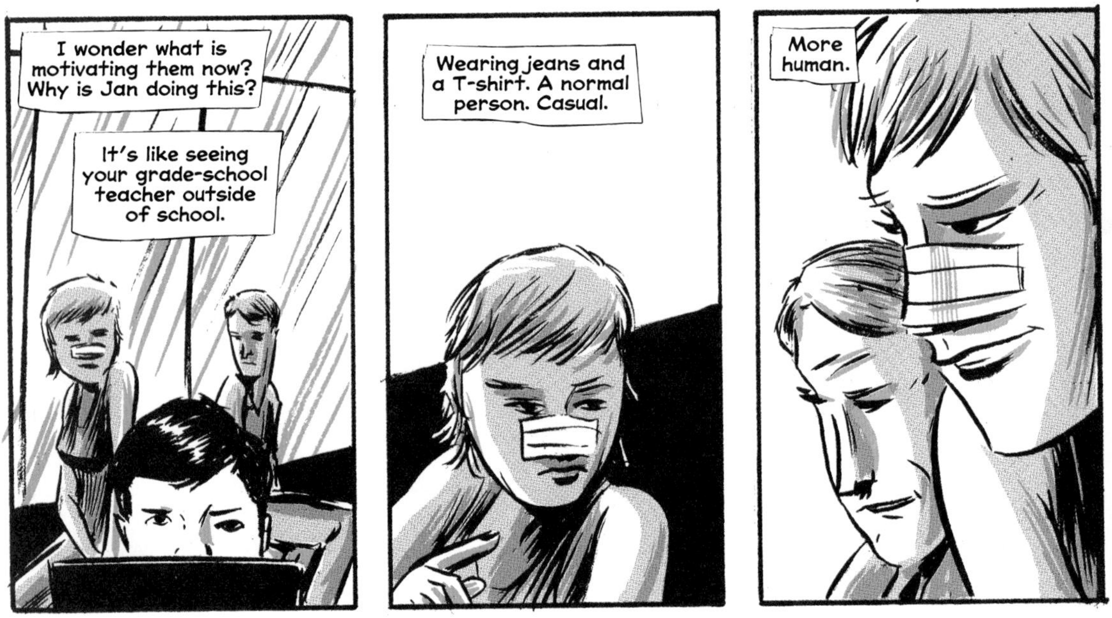
I wonder what is motivating them now? Why is Jan doing this?
It's like seeing your grade-school teacher outside of school.
Wearing jeans and a T-shirt. A normal person. Casual.
More human.

OCALLY-RUN WEBSITES TO DISTRIBUTE NEWS AND INFORMATION ON RELIEF EFFORTS. **THIRTY-NINE** ARE REPORTED MISSING IN A

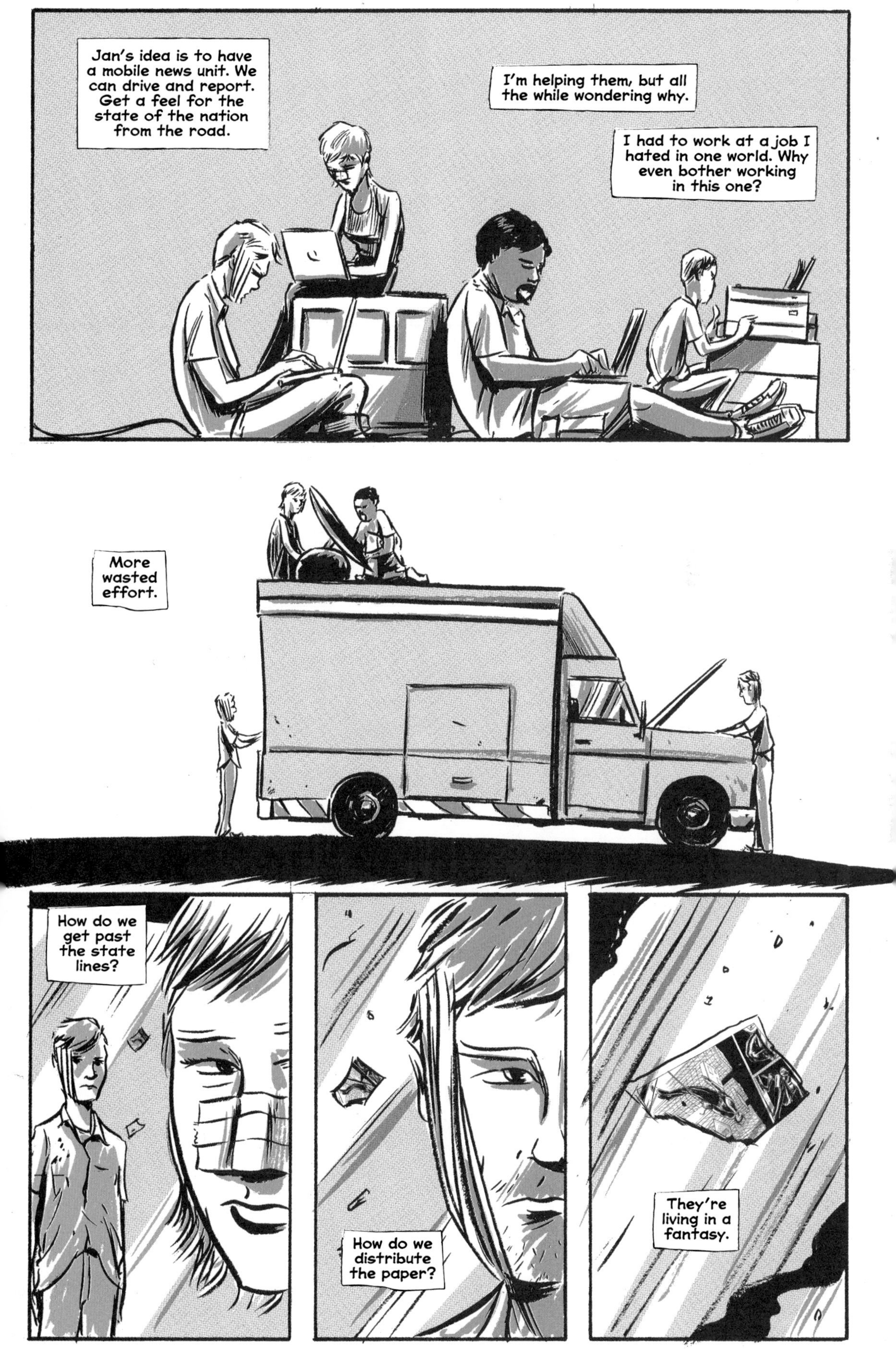
Jan's idea is to have a mobile news unit. We can drive and report. Get a feel for the state of the nation from the road.
I'm helping them, but all the while wondering why.
I had to work at a job I hated in one world. Why even bother working in this one?
More wasted effort.
How do we get past the state lines?
How do we distribute the paper?
They're living in a fantasy.

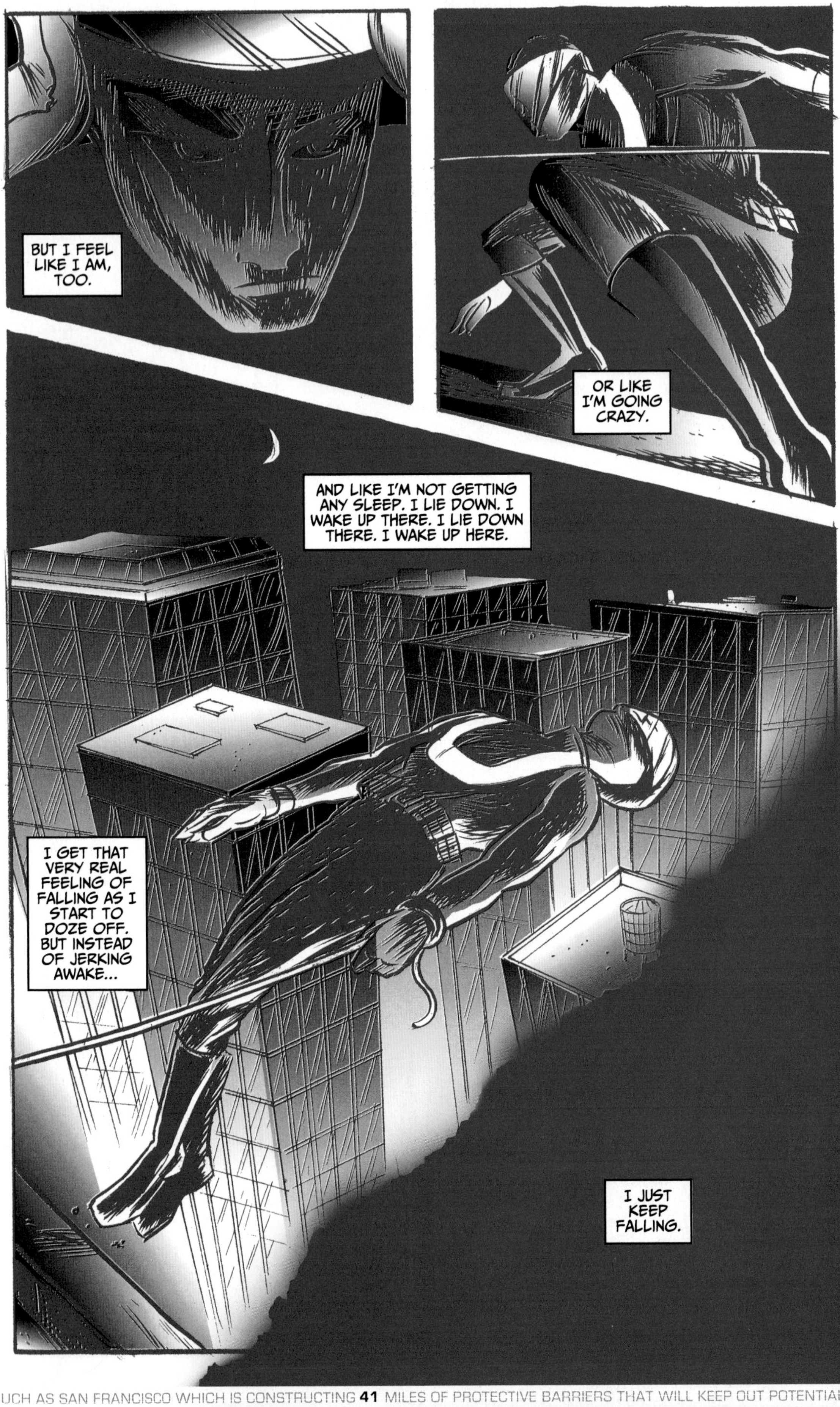
BUT I FEEL LIKE I AM, TOO.
OR LIKE I'M GOING CRAZY.
AND LIKE I'M NOT GETTING ANY SLEEP. I LIE DOWN. I WAKE UP THERE. I LIE DOWN THERE. I WAKE UP HERE.
I GET THAT VERY REAL FEELING OF FALLING AS I START TO DOZE OFF. BUT INSTEAD OF JERKING AWAKE...
I JUST KEEP FALLING.

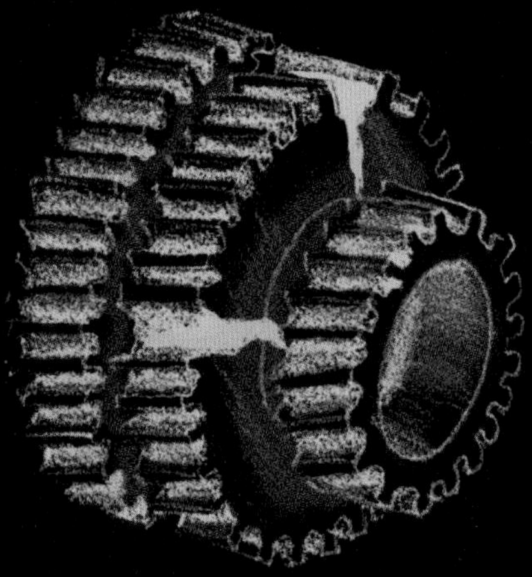

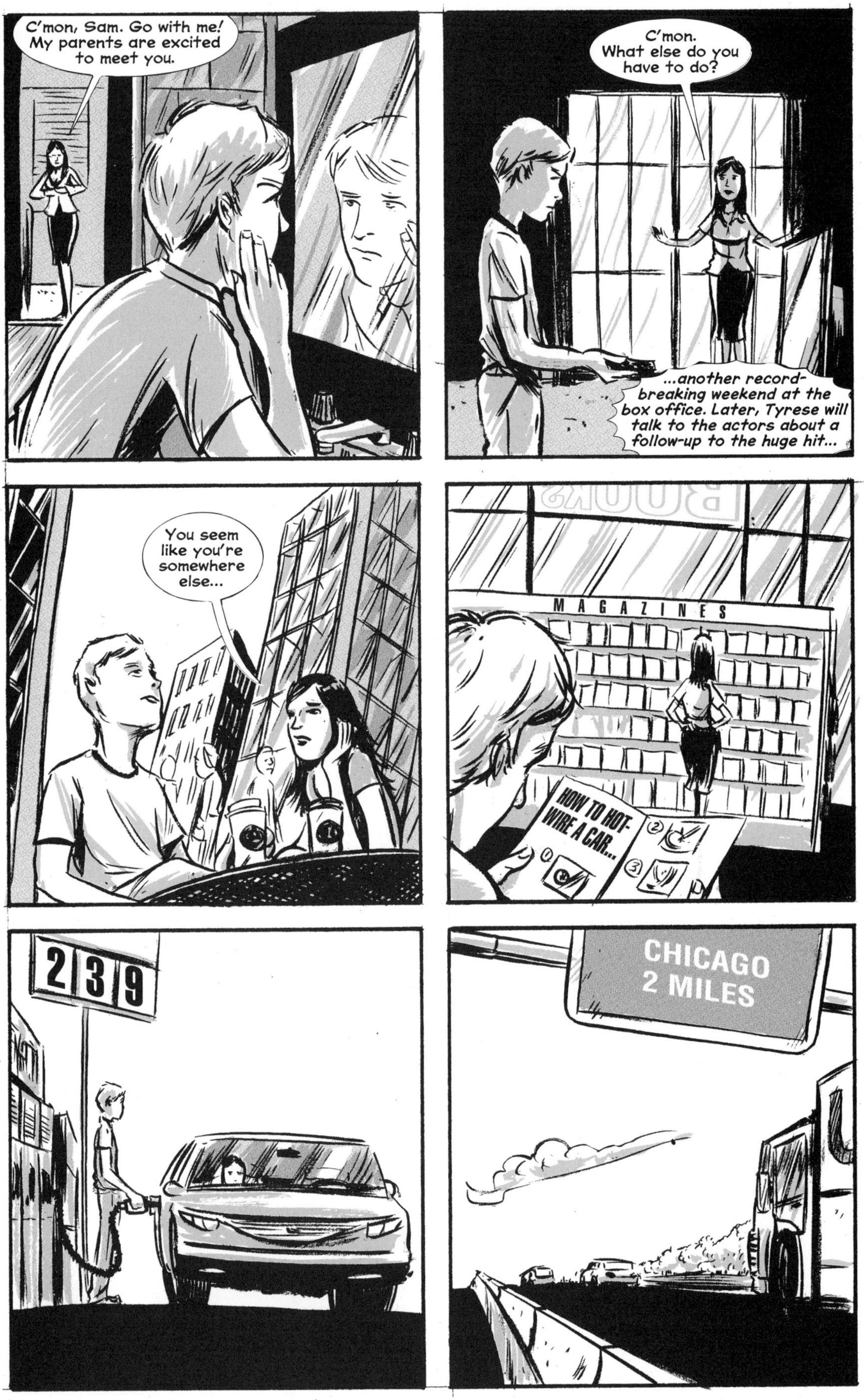
C'mon, Sam. Go with me! My parents are excited to meet you.
C'mon. What else do you have to do?
...another record-breaking weekend at the box office. Later, Tyrese will talk to the actors about a follow-up to the huge hit...
You seem like you're somewhere else...
BOOKS
MAGAZINES
HOW TO HOT-WIRE A CAR...
239
CHICAGO 2 MILES

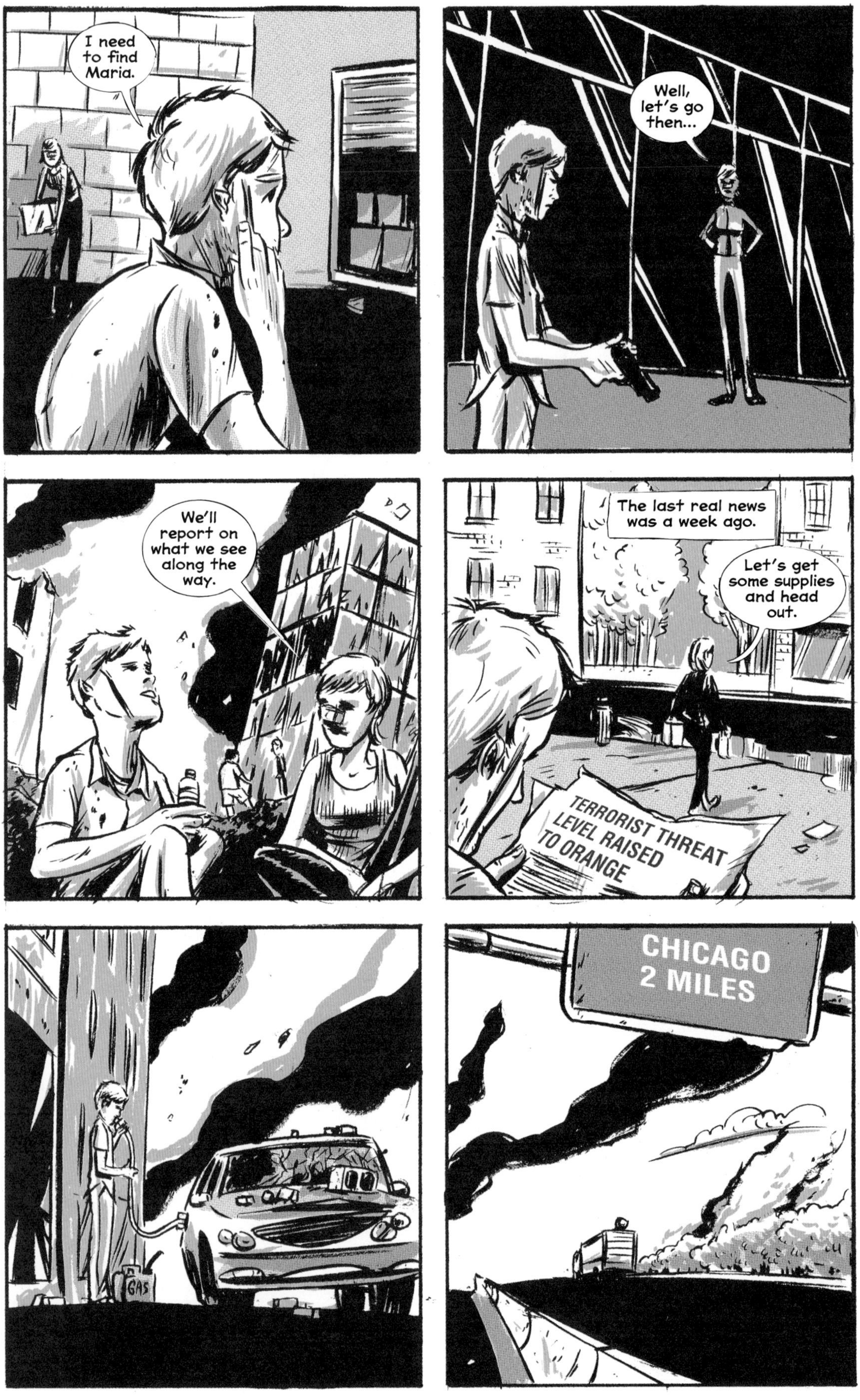
I need to find Maria.
Well, let's go then...
We'll report on what we see along the way.
The last real news was a week ago.
Let's get some supplies and head out.
TERRORIST THREAT LEVEL RAISED TO ORANGE
CHICAGO 2 MILES
GAS

ONTINUE TO TRANSMIT NEWS REPORTS. **FORTY-THREE** NEWS STATIONS ARE STILL BROADCASTING ALTHOUGH MOST WON'T BE

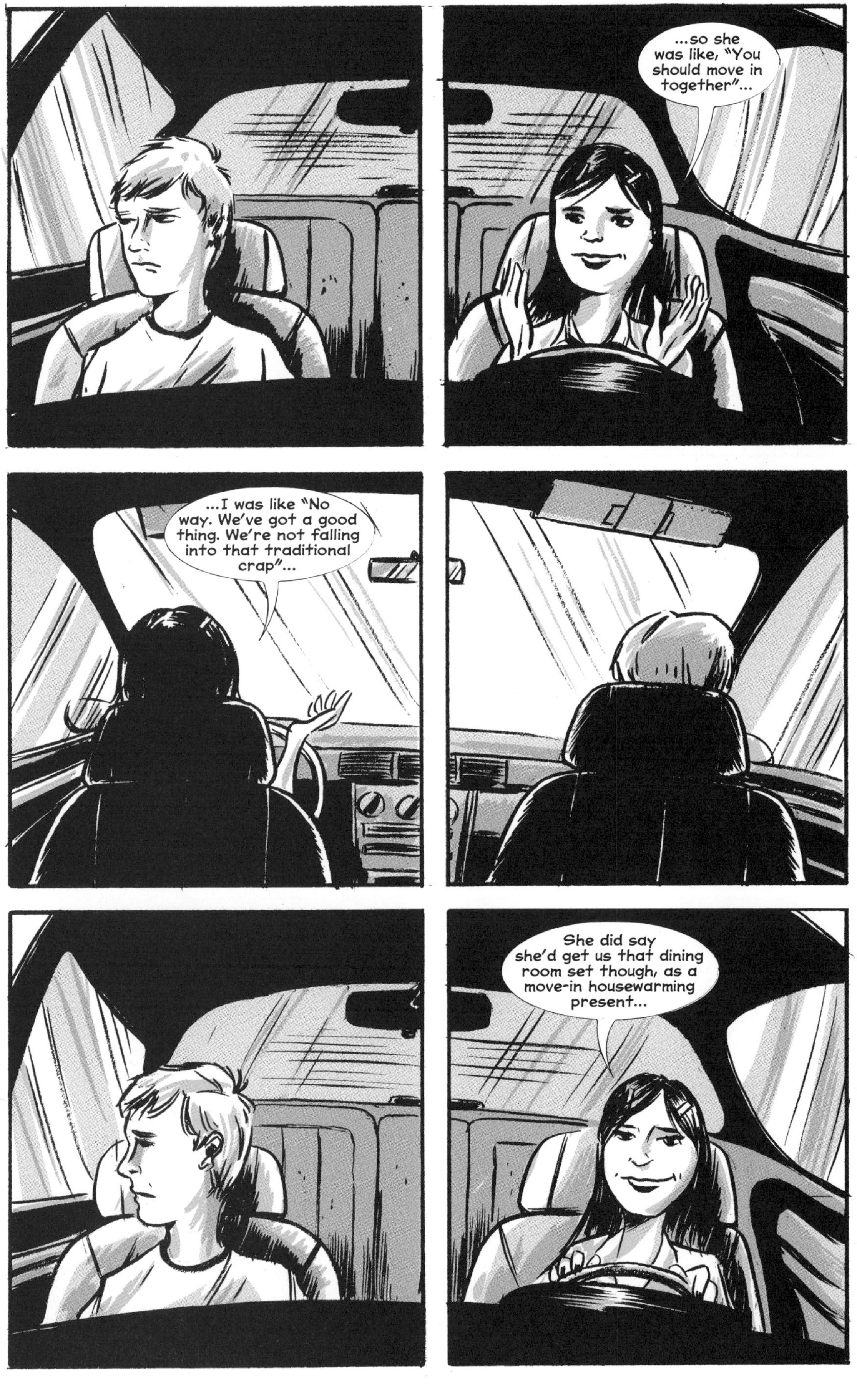
...so she was like, "You should move in together"...
...I was like "No way. We've got a good thing. We're not falling into that traditional crap"...
She did say she'd get us that dining room set though, as a move-in housewarming present...

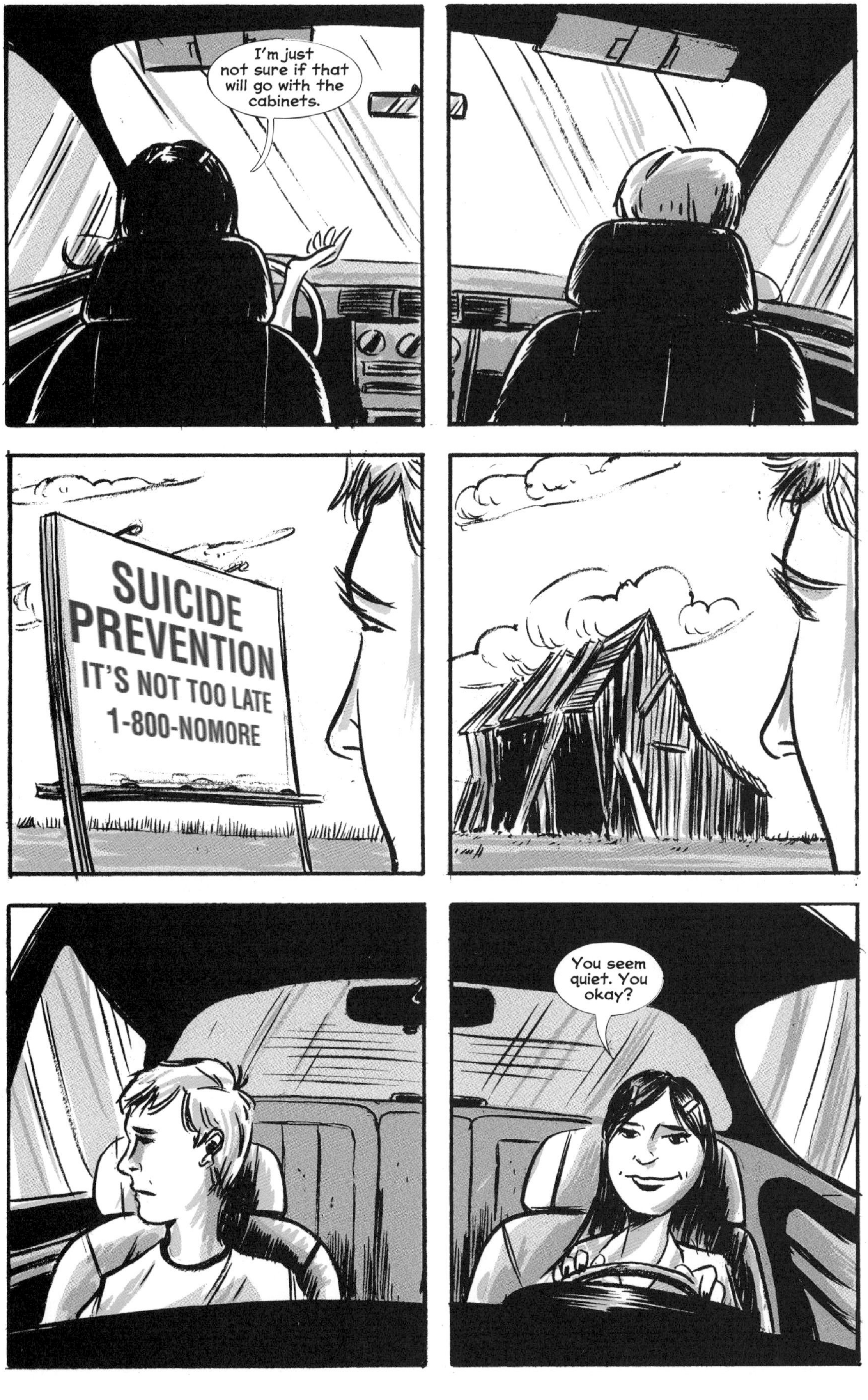
I'm just not sure if that will go with the cabinets.
SUICIDE PREVENTION
IT'S NOT TOO LATE
1-800-NOMORE
You seem quiet. You okay?

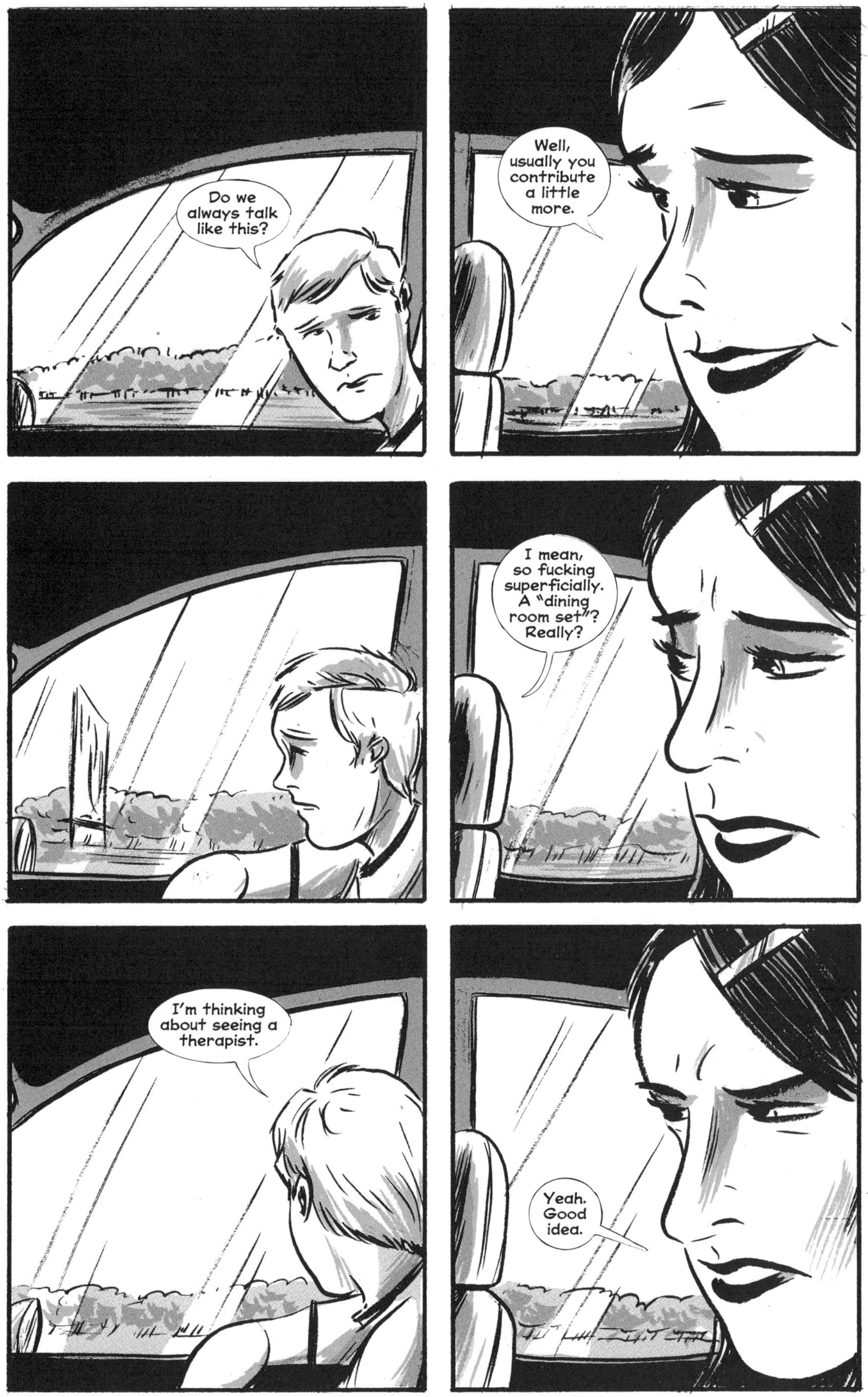
Do we always talk like this?
Well, usually you contribute a little more.
I mean, so fucking superficially. A "dining room set"? Really?
I'm thinking about seeing a therapist.
Yeah. Good idea.

HAT WITH MORE HOURS WORKED, MORE MONEY IS INJECTED INTO THE ECONOMY. **46**% OF THOSE POLLED AGREED THAT THEY W

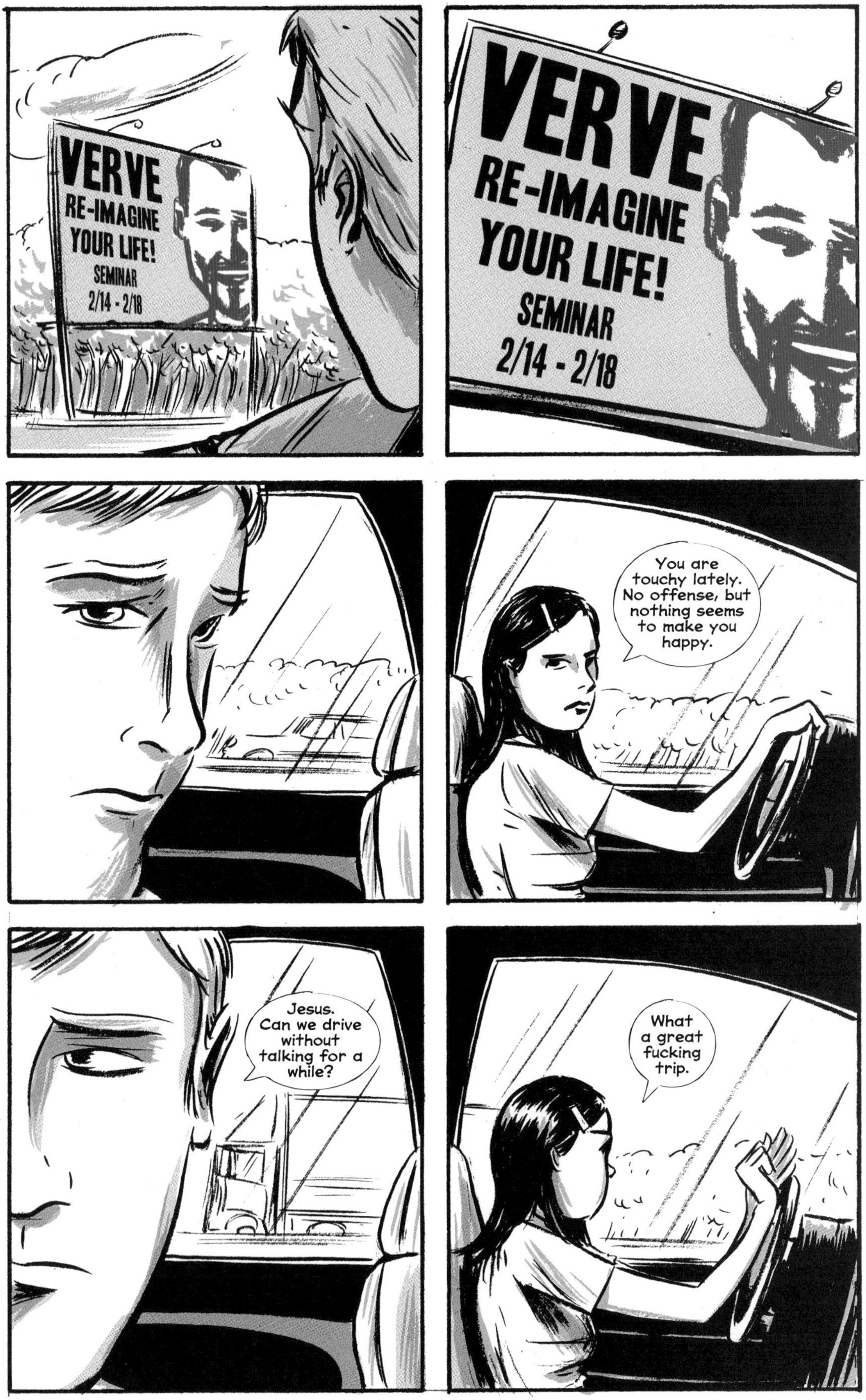
VERVE
RE-IMAGINE
YOUR LIFE!
SEMINAR
2/14 - 2/18
VERVE
RE-IMAGINE
YOUR LIFE!
SEMINAR
2/14 - 2/18
You are touchy lately. No offense, but nothing seems to make you happy.
Jesus. Can we drive without talking for a while?
What a great fucking trip.

THAT ON AVERAGE NEARLY **47** MILLION PEOPLE WILL BE TRAVELING BY CAR, AIR, AND TRAIN DURING THIS HOLIDAY SEASON WH

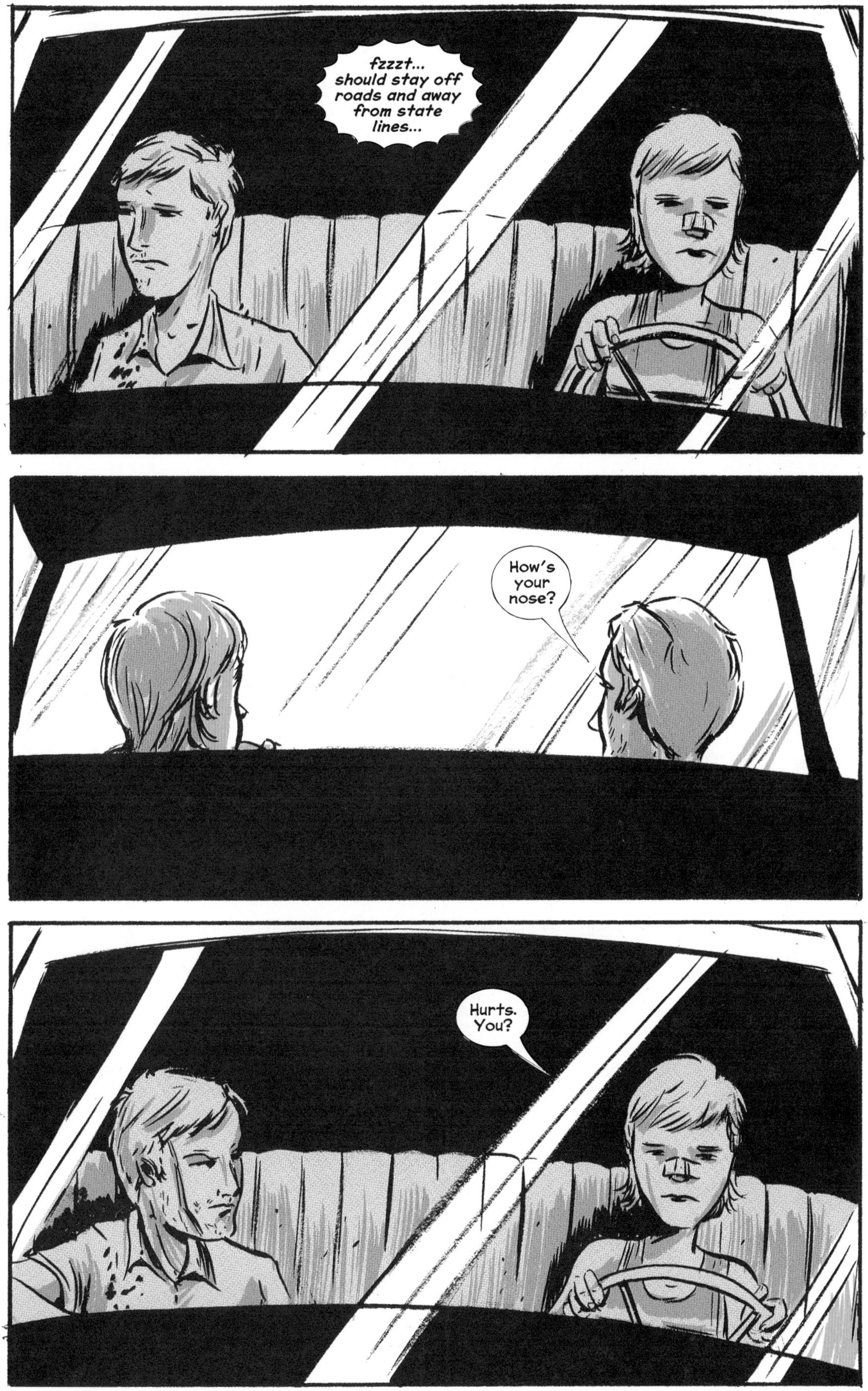
fzzzt... should stay off roads and away from state lines...
How's your nose?
Hurts. You?

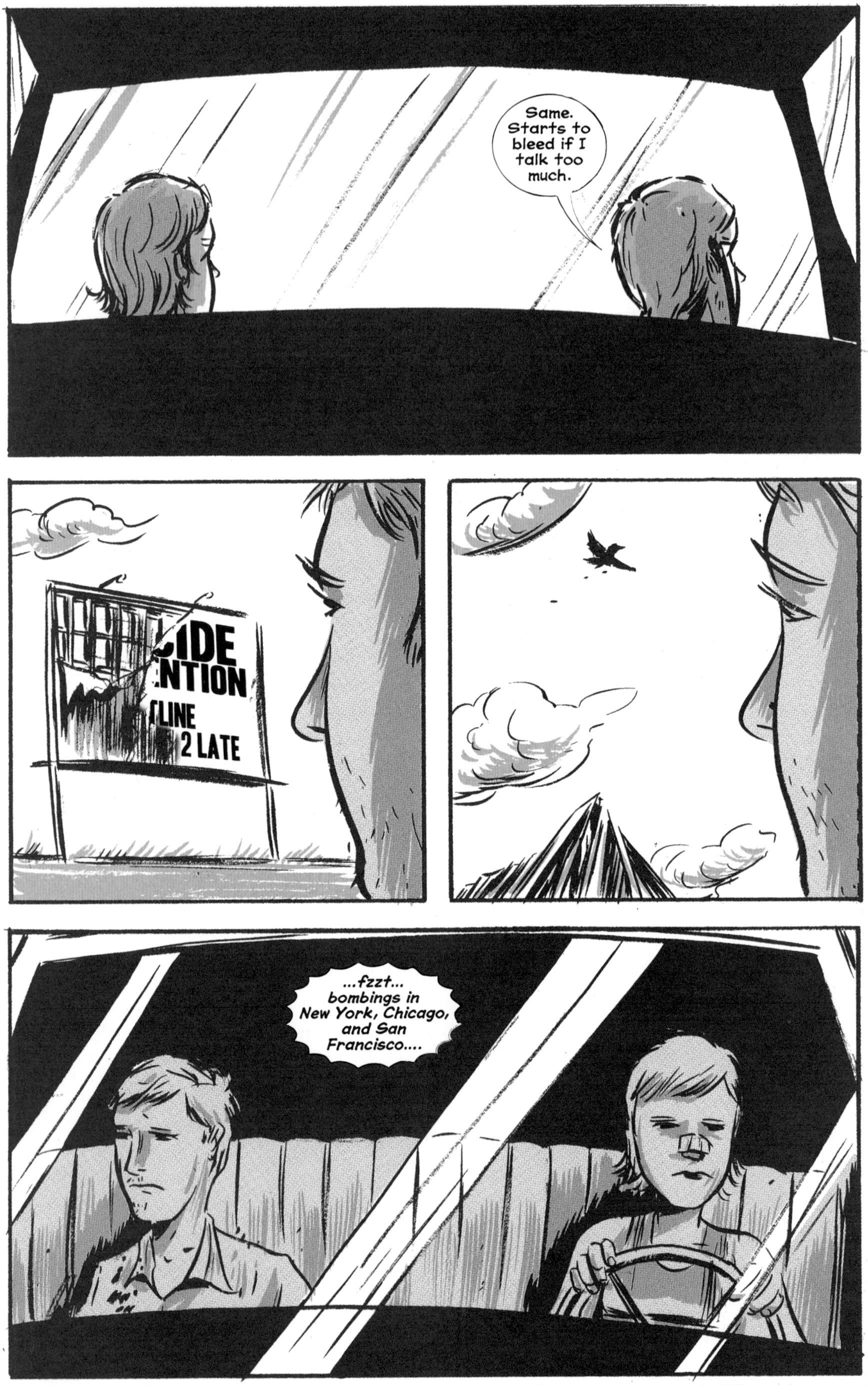
Same. Starts to bleed if I talk too much.
CIDE
NTION
CLINE
2 LATE
...fzzt... bombings in New York, Chicago, and San Francisco....

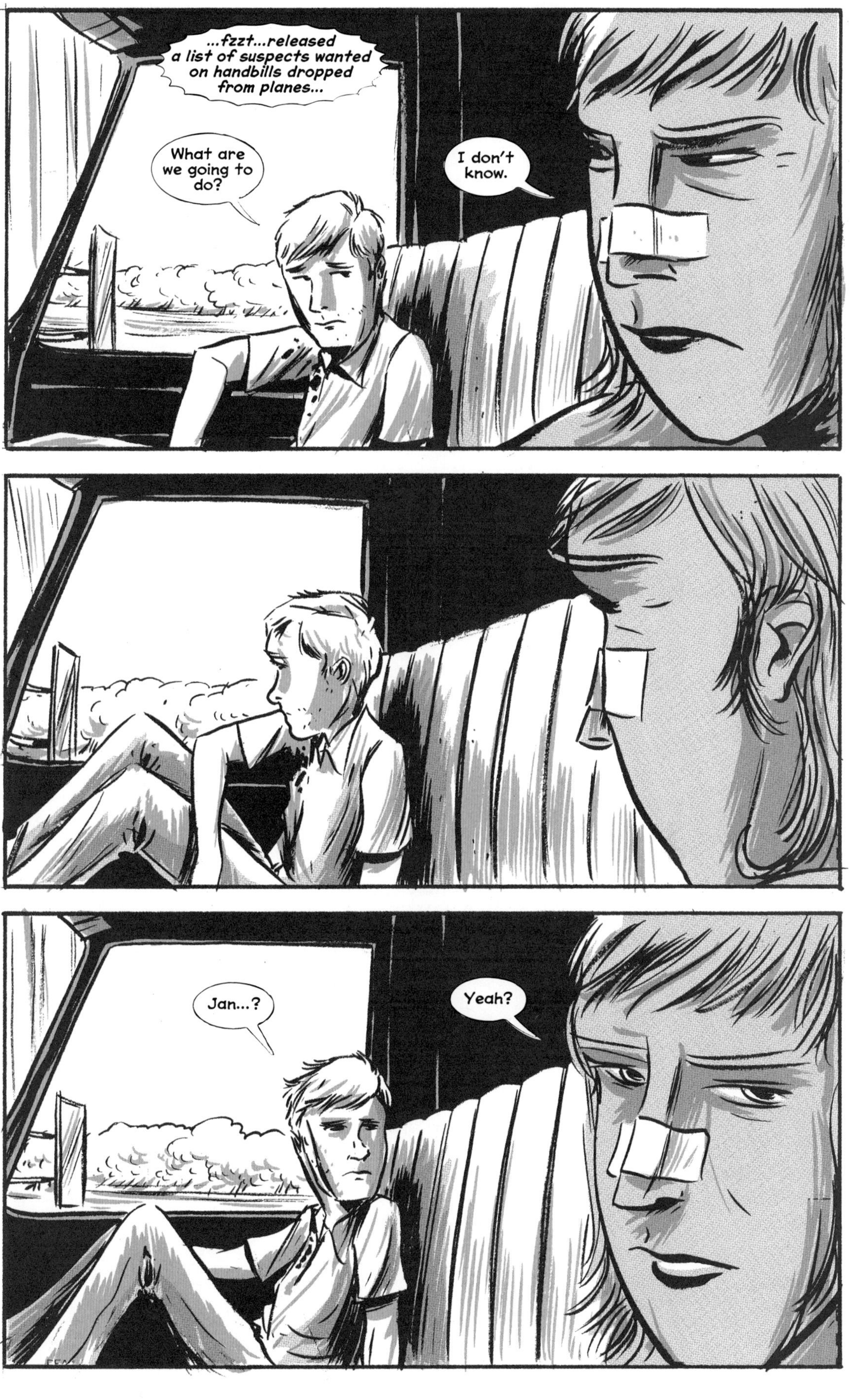
...fzzt...released a list of suspects wanted on handbills dropped from planes...
What are we going to do?
I don't know.
Jan...?
Yeah?

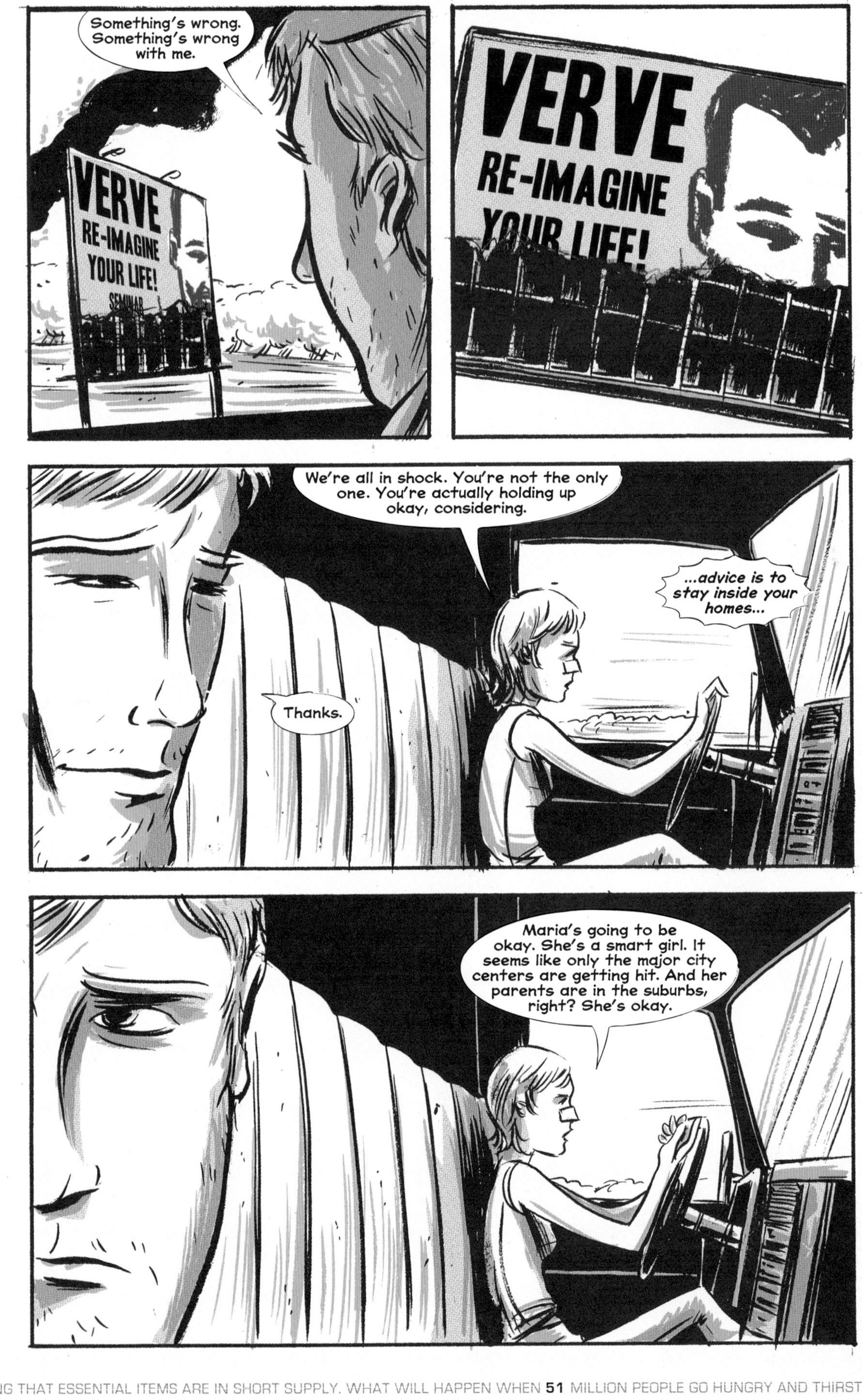
Something's wrong. Something's wrong with me.
VERVE
RE-IMAGINE
YOUR LIFE!
SEMINAR
VERVE
RE-IMAGINE
YOUR LIFE!
We're all in shock. You're not the only one. You're actually holding up okay, considering.
...advice is to stay inside your homes...
Thanks.
Maria's going to be okay. She's a smart girl. It seems like only the major city centers are getting hit. And her parents are in the suburbs, right? She's okay.

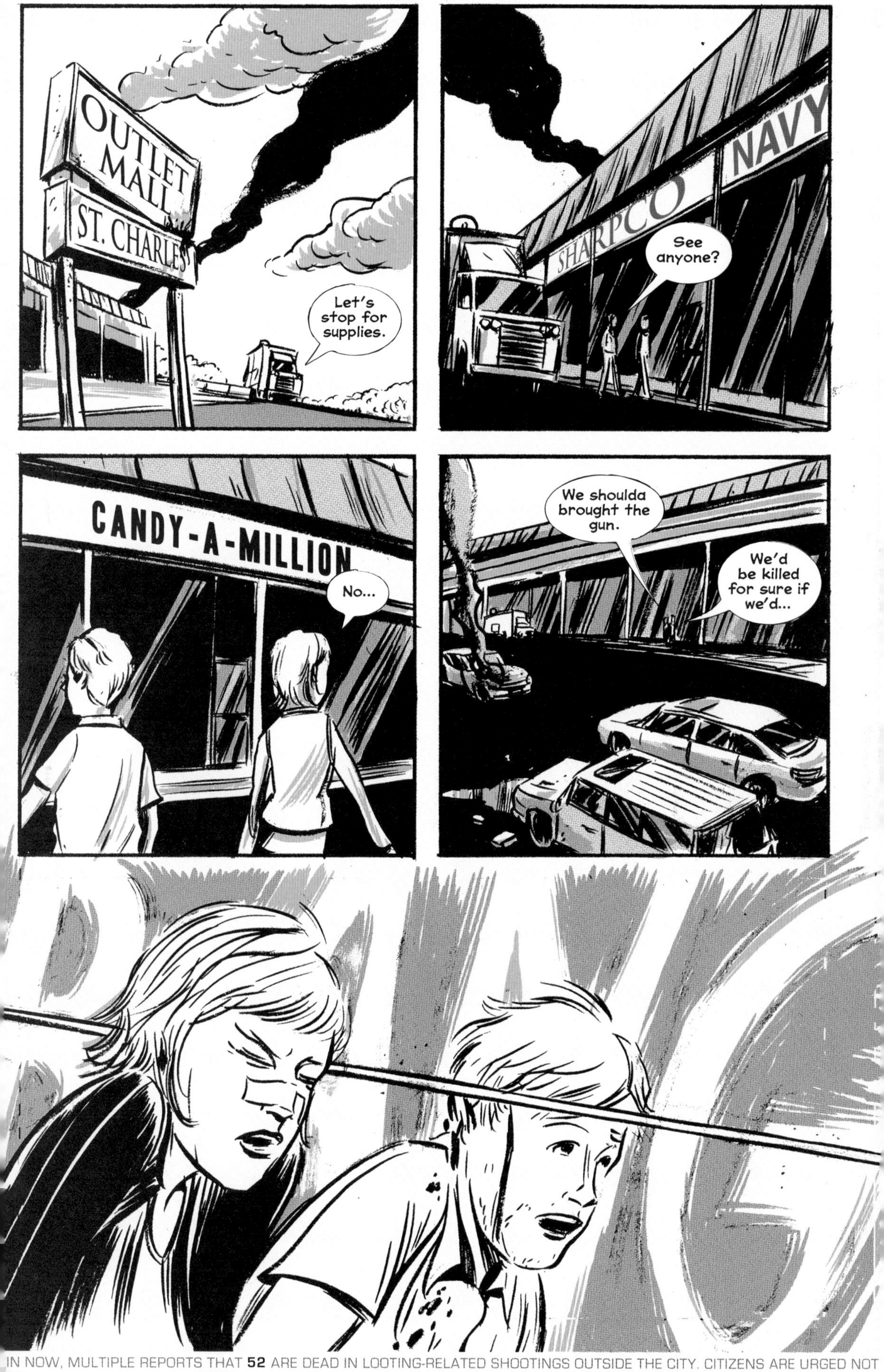
OUTLET MALL
ST. CHARLES
Let's stop for supplies.
SHARPCO
NAVY
See anyone?
CANDY-A-MILLION
No...
We shoulda brought the gun.
We'd be killed for sure if we'd...

IN NOW, MULTIPLE REPORTS THAT **52** ARE DEAD IN LOOTING-RELATED SHOOTINGS OUTSIDE THE CITY. CITIZENS ARE URGED NOT

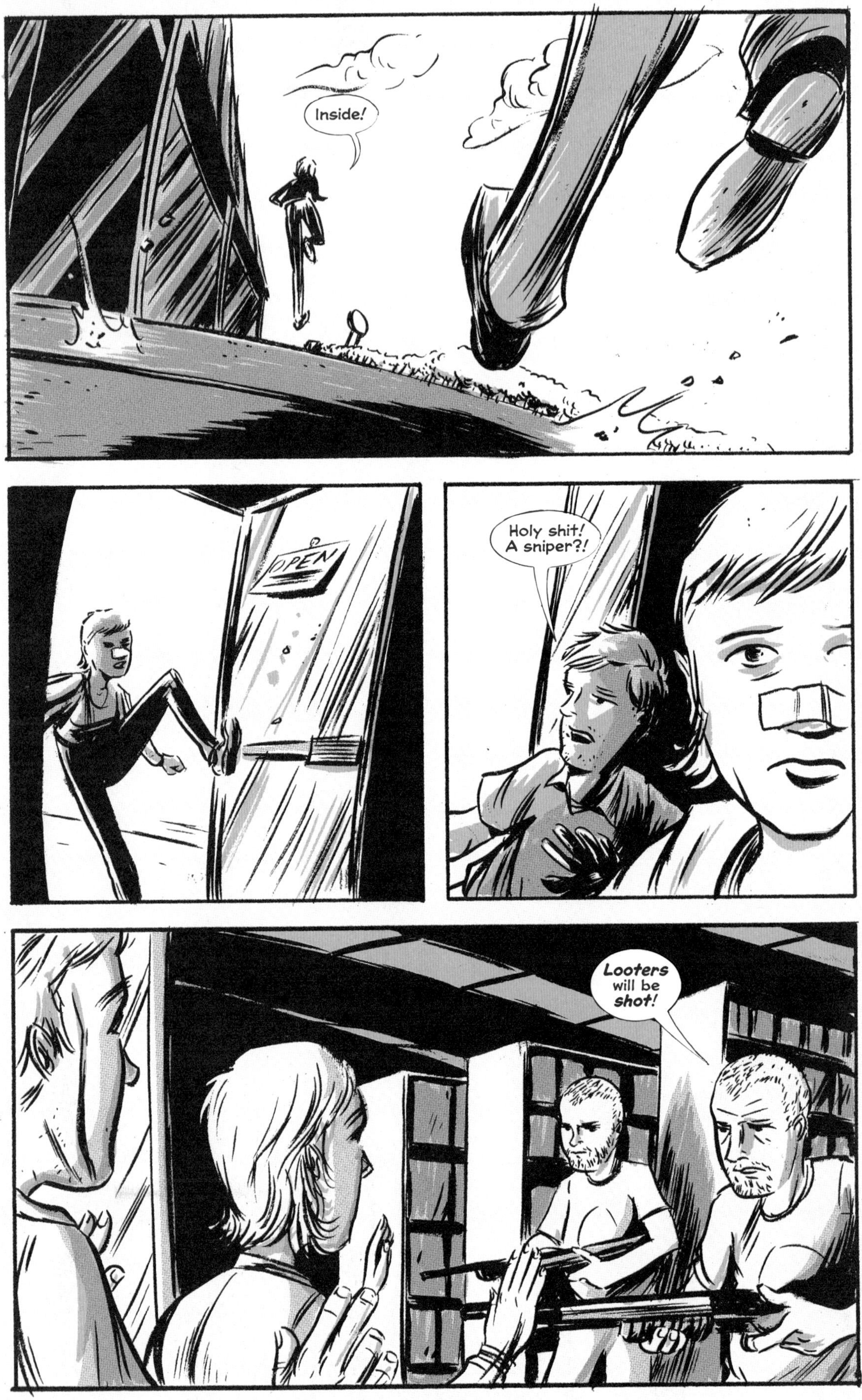
Inside!
Holy shit! A sniper?!
Looters will be shot!

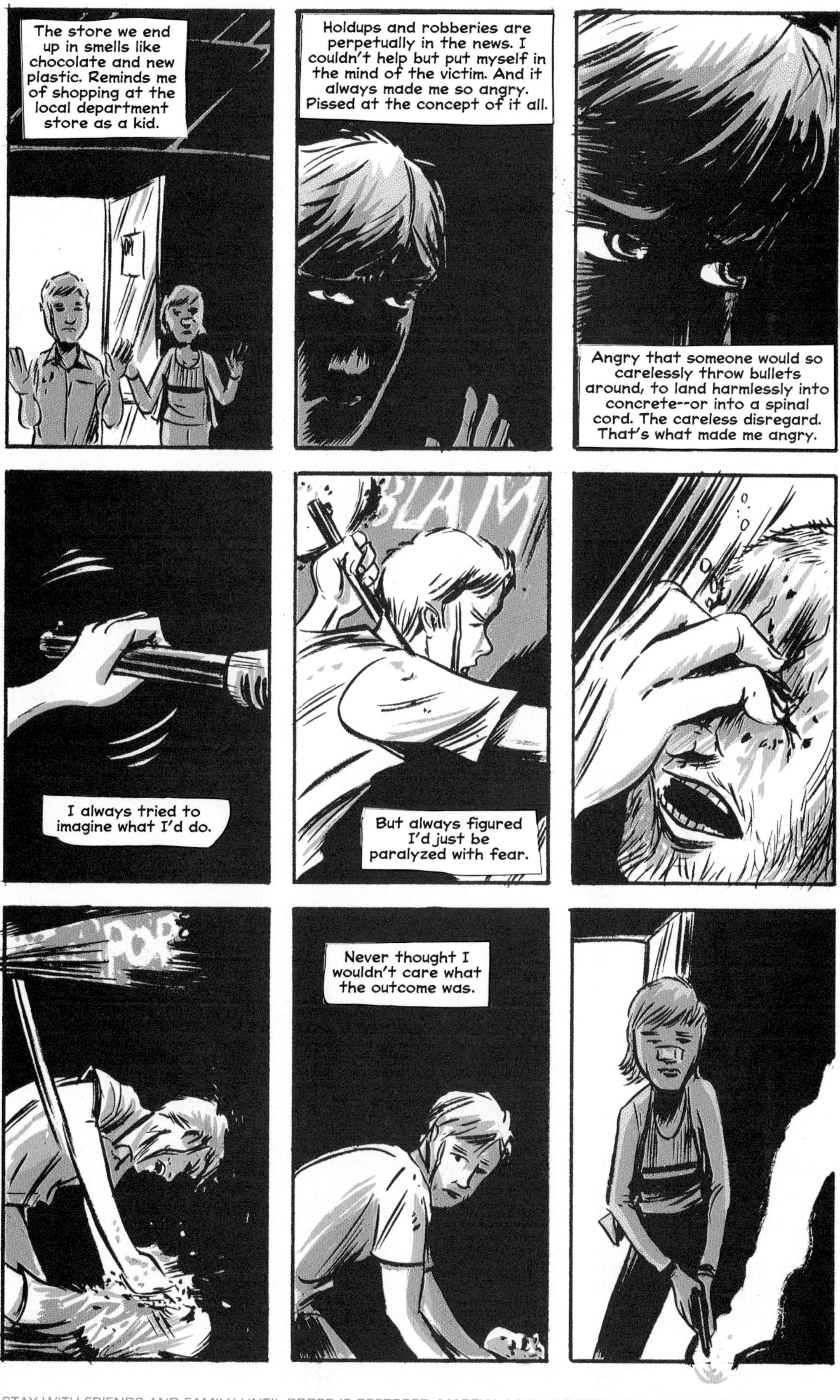
The store we end up in smells like chocolate and new plastic. Reminds me of shopping at the local department store as a kid.
Holdups and robberies are perpetually in the news. I couldn't help but put myself in the mind of the victim. And it always made me so angry. Pissed at the concept of it all.
Angry that someone would so carelessly throw bullets around, to land harmlessly into concrete--or into a spinal cord. The careless disregard. That's what made me angry.
I always tried to imagine what I'd do.
BLAM
But always figured I'd just be paralyzed with fear.
POP
Never thought I wouldn't care what the outcome was.

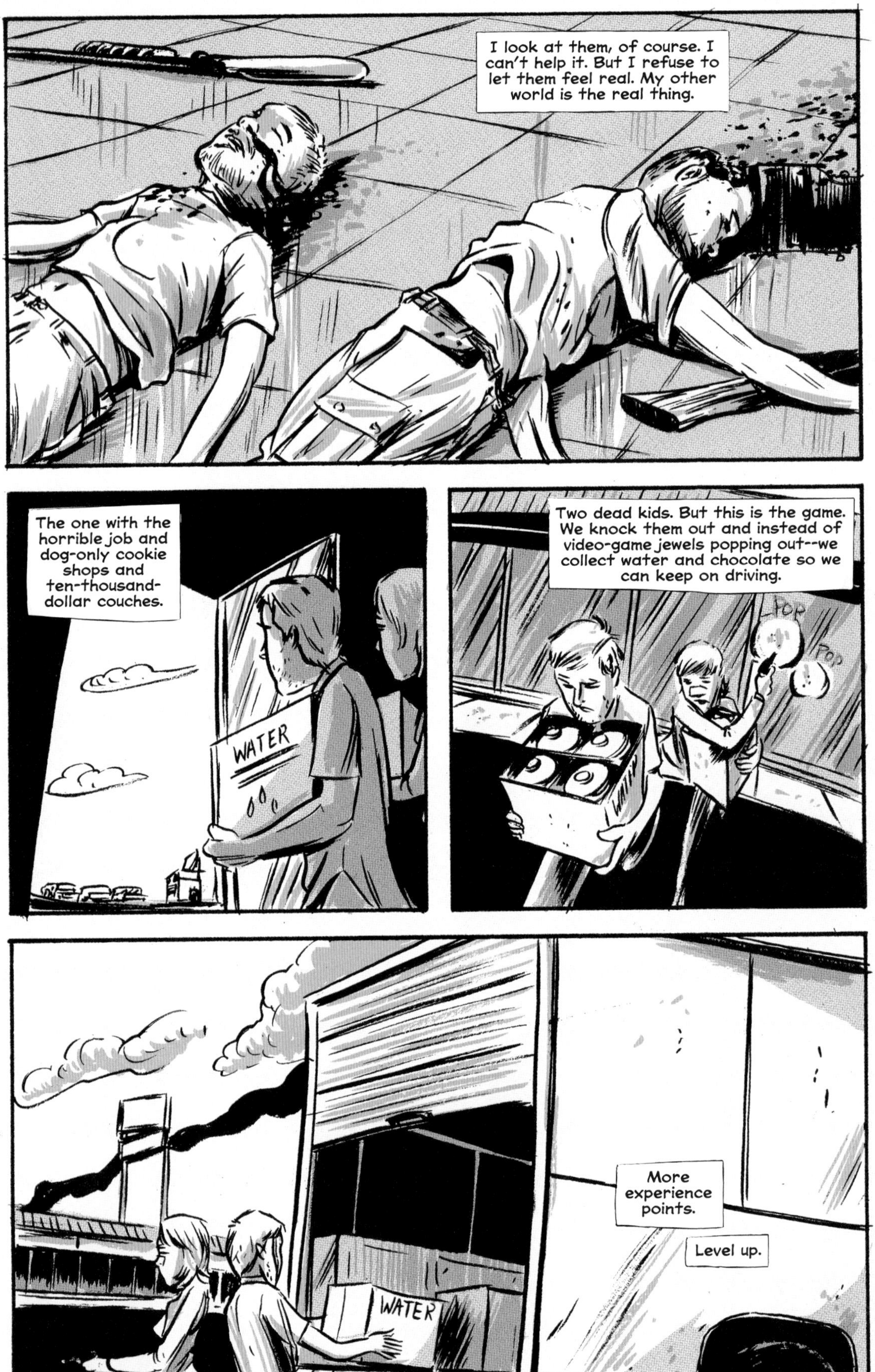
I look at them, of course. I can't help it. But I refuse to let them feel real. My other world is the real thing.
The one with the horrible job and dog-only cookie shops and ten-thousand-dollar couches.
WATER
Two dead kids. But this is the game. We knock them out and instead of video-game jewels popping out--we collect water and chocolate so we can keep on driving.
POP
POP
WATER
More experience points.
Level up.

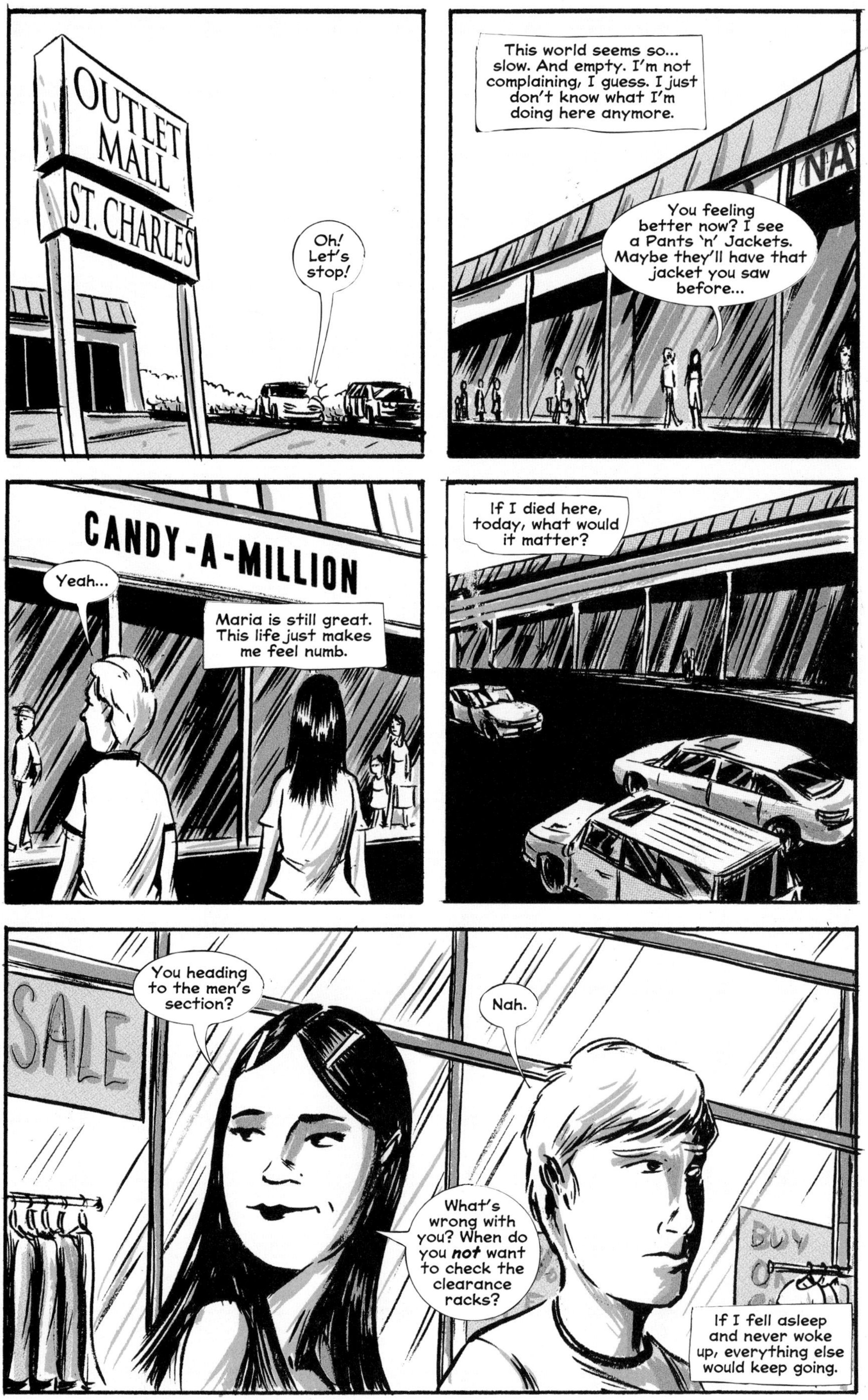
OUTLET MALL
ST. CHARLES
Oh! Let's stop!
This world seems so... slow. And empty. I'm not complaining, I guess. I just don't know what I'm doing here anymore.
You feeling better now? I see a Pants 'n' Jackets. Maybe they'll have that jacket you saw before...
CANDY-A-MILLION
Yeah...
Maria is still great. This life just makes me feel numb.
If I died here, today, what would it matter?
SALE
You heading to the men's section?
Nah.
What's wrong with you? When do you ***not*** want to check the clearance racks?
If I fell asleep and never woke up, everything else would keep going.

RS FLOOD THE CITY. **FIFTY-SIX** DIFFERENT MAPS WILL BE PROVIDED AS TOURISTS THRONG TO LOCAL ATTRACTIONS, INCLUDING

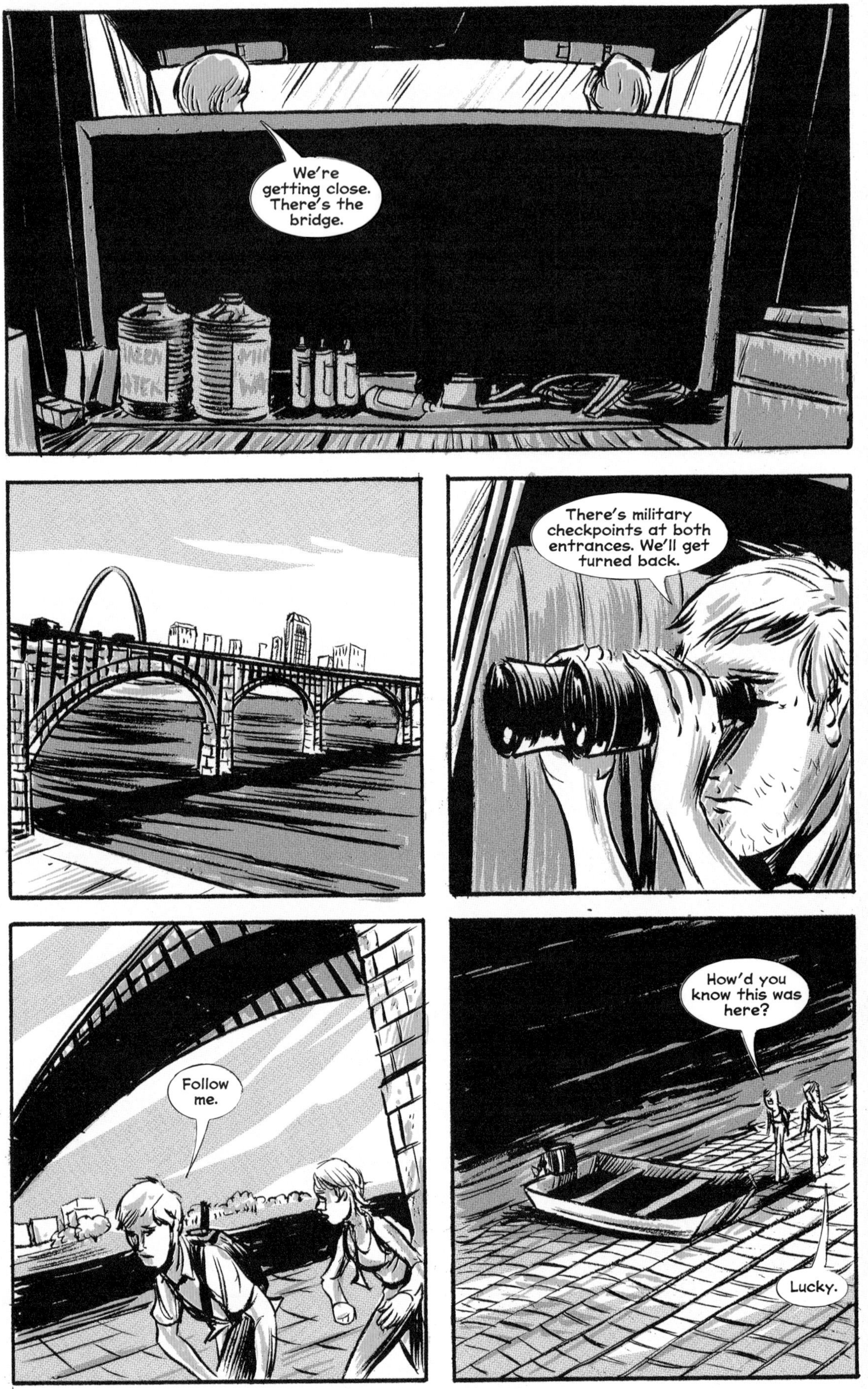
We're getting close. There's the bridge.
There's military checkpoints at both entrances. We'll get turned back.
Follow me.
How'd you know this was here?
Lucky.

BEING ASKED TO CONSERVE GASOLINE UNTIL FURTHER NOTICE. **FIFTY-SEVEN** CITIES HAVE NOW DECLARED MARTIAL LAW AS MO

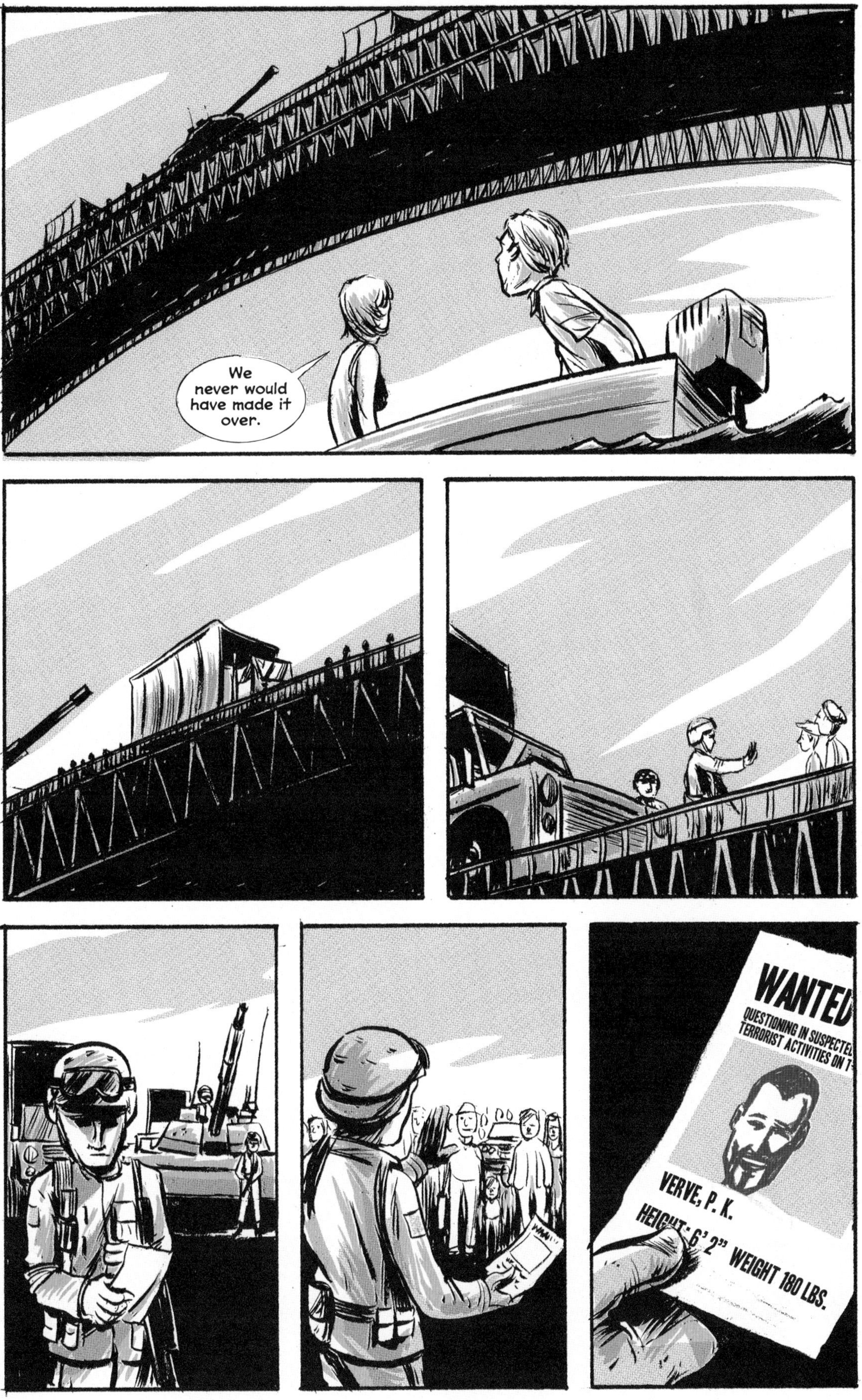
We never would have made it over.
WANTED
QUESTIONING IN SUSPECTE
TERRORIST ACTIVITIES ON T
VERVE, P. K.
HEIGHT: 6' 2" WEIGHT 180 LBS.

TIMATED **58**,000 TROOPS ARE STILL ON ACTIVE DUTY GUARDING BRIDGES AND BLOCKING THE FLOW OF TRAFFIC IN AND OUT OF

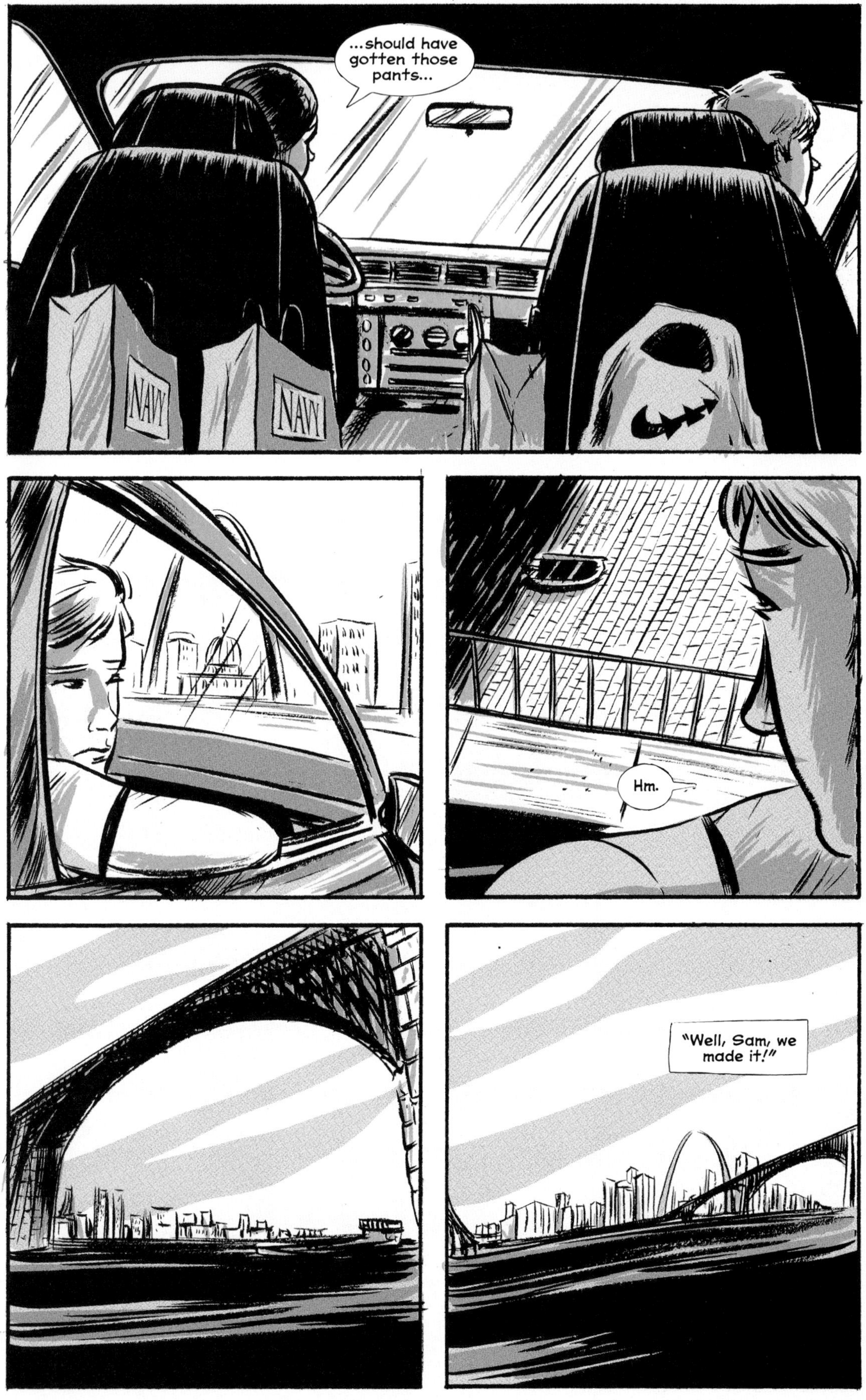
...should have gotten those pants...
NAVY
NAVY
Hm.
"Well, Sam, we made it!"

E CLAIMING THAT THE ACTRESS WAS STOPPED WHILE INTOXICATED AND WILL HAVE TO PAY OVER $**5.9** MILLION IN DAMAGES IN

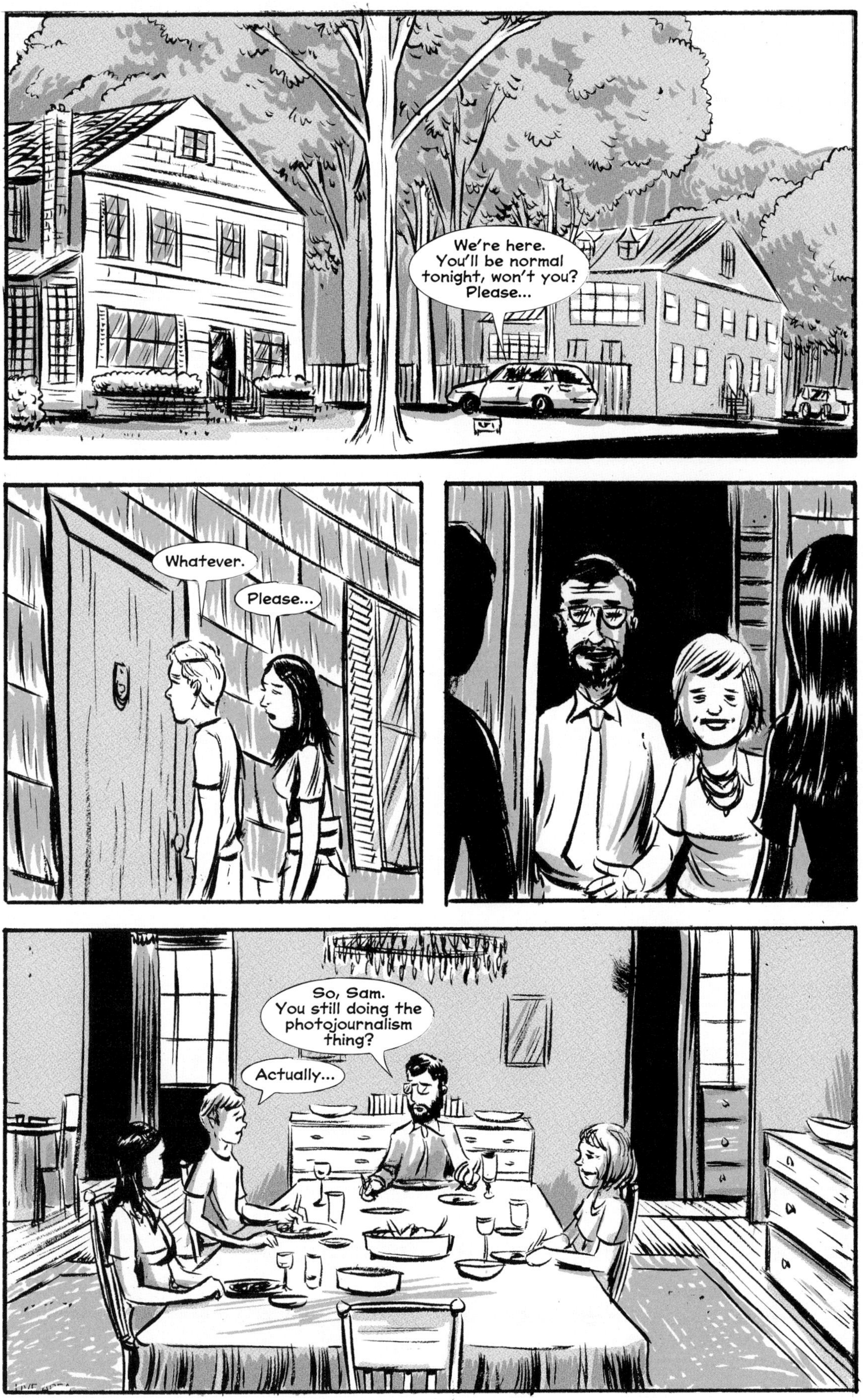
We're here. You'll be normal tonight, won't you? Please...
Whatever.
Please...
So, Sam. You still doing the photojournalism thing?
Actually...

TO COMMEMORATE THE **60**TH ANNIVERSARY OF THE WAR. VETERANS OF ALL FOREIGN WARS ARE GATHERING IN REMEMBRAN

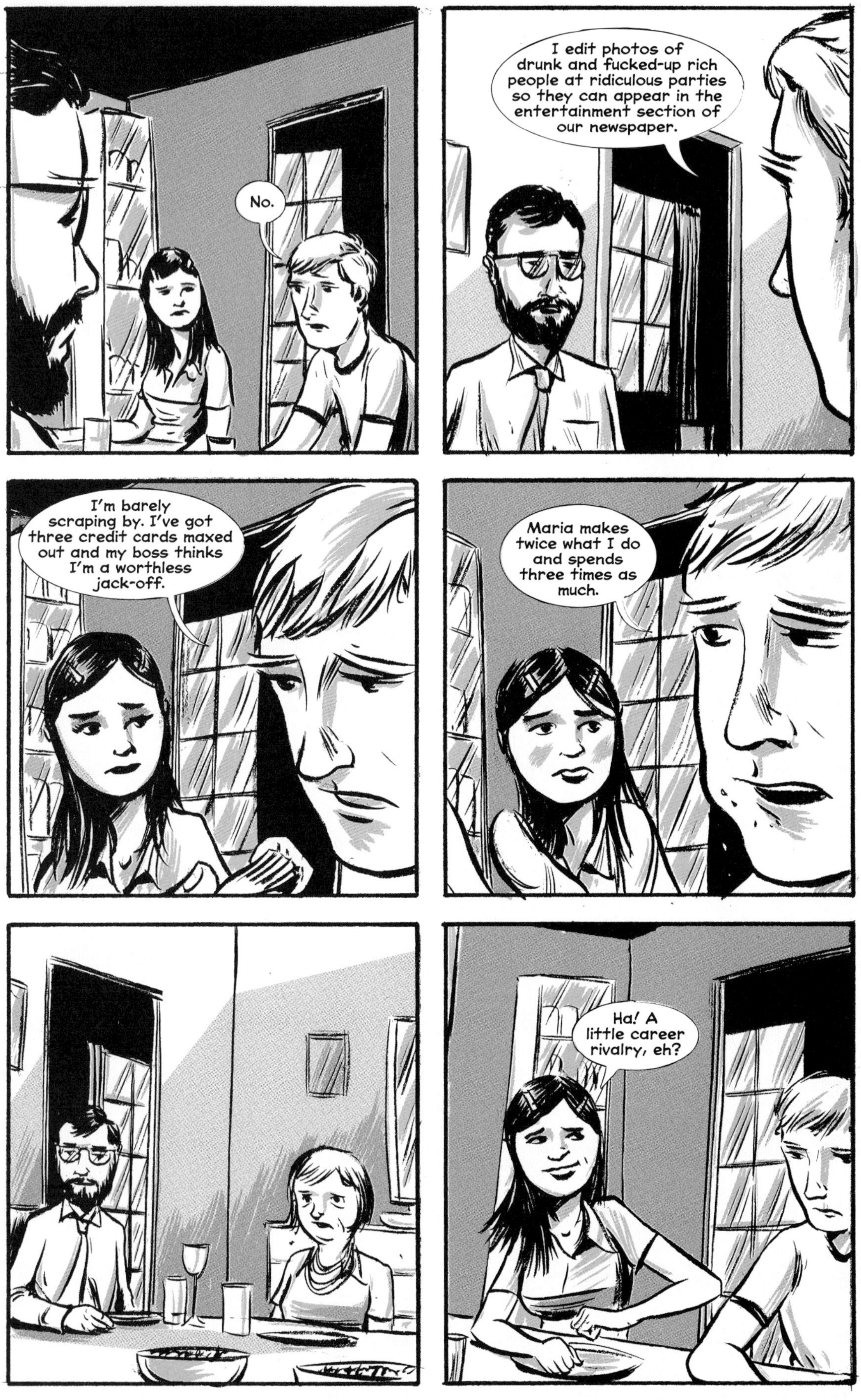
No.
I edit photos of drunk and fucked-up rich people at ridiculous parties so they can appear in the entertainment section of our newspaper.
I'm barely scraping by. I've got three credit cards maxed out and my boss thinks I'm a worthless jack-off.
Maria makes twice what I do and spends three times as much.
Ha! A little career rivalry, eh?

TODAY AS THE ORIGINAL CANDID PHOTOS ARE EXPECTED TO FETCH OVER $61,000 EACH AS FANS CLAMOR TO GET COPIES OF T

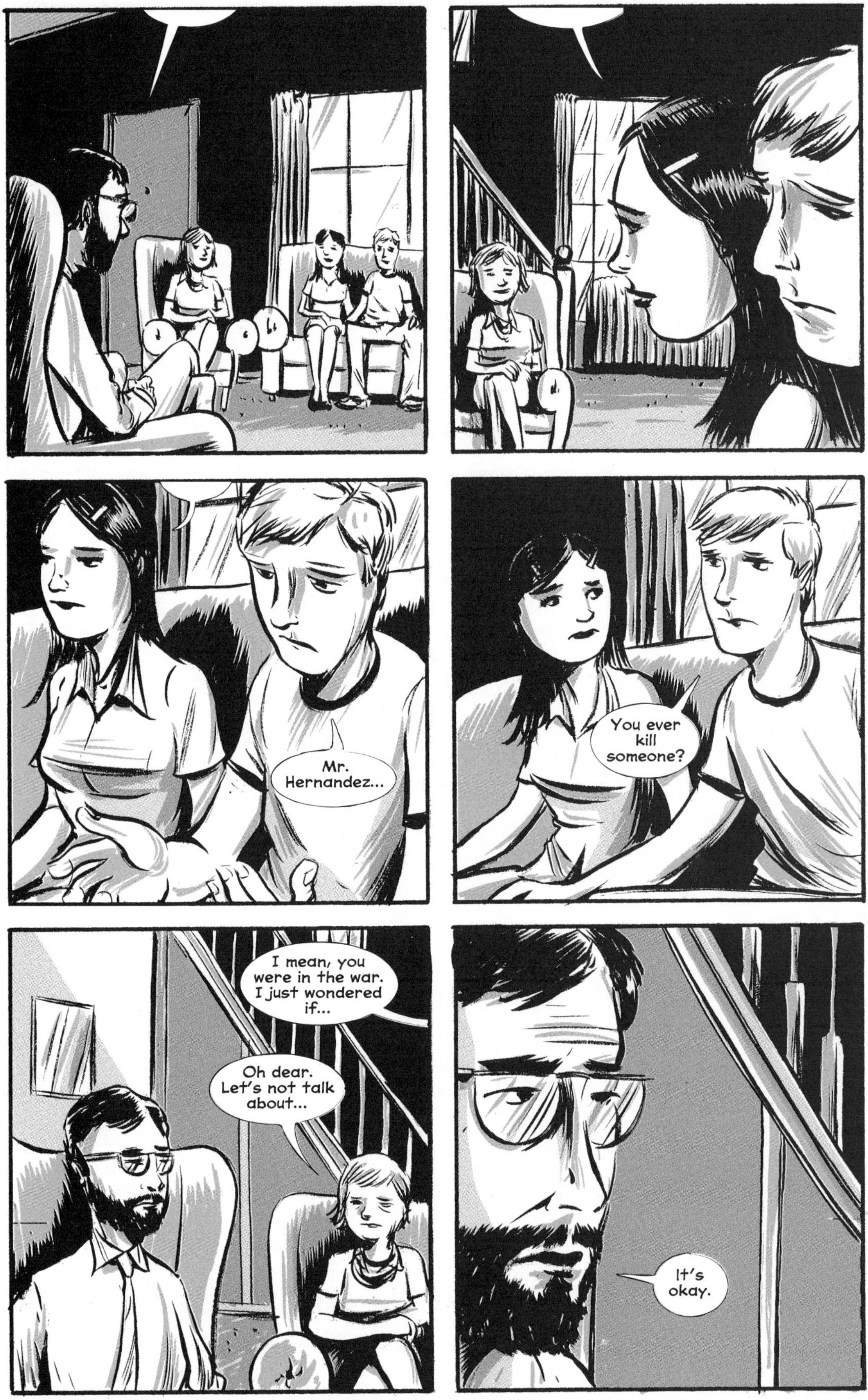
Mr. Hernandez...
You ever kill someone?
I mean, you were in the war. I just wondered if...
Oh dear. Let's not talk about...
It's okay.

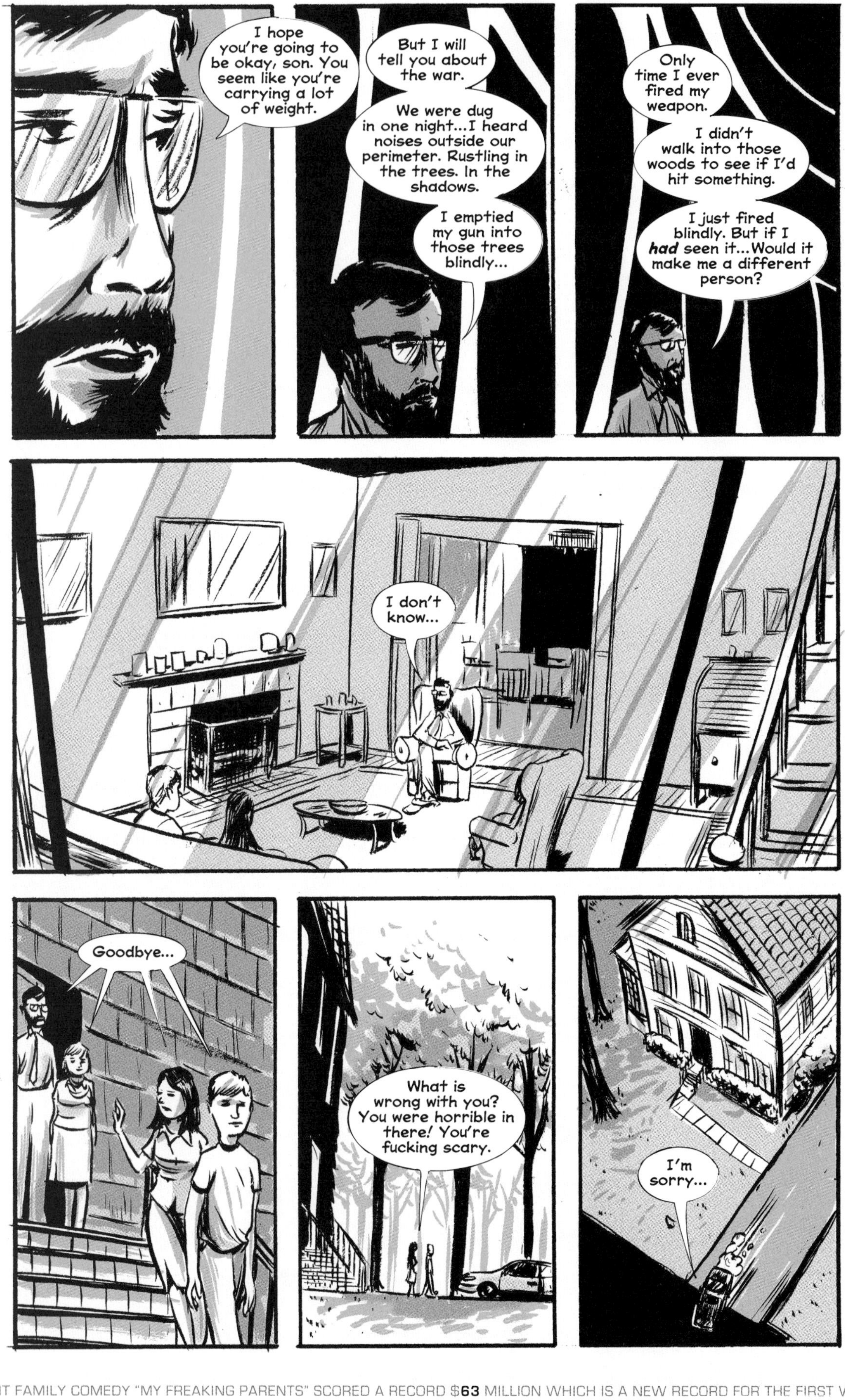
I hope you're going to be okay, son. You seem like you're carrying a lot of weight.
But I will tell you about the war.
We were dug in one night...I heard noises outside our perimeter. Rustling in the trees. In the shadows.
I emptied my gun into those trees blindly...
Only time I ever fired my weapon.
I didn't walk into those woods to see if I'd hit something.
I just fired blindly. But if I ***had*** seen it...Would it make me a different person?
I don't know...
Goodbye...
What is wrong with you? You were horrible in there! You're fucking scary.
I'm sorry...

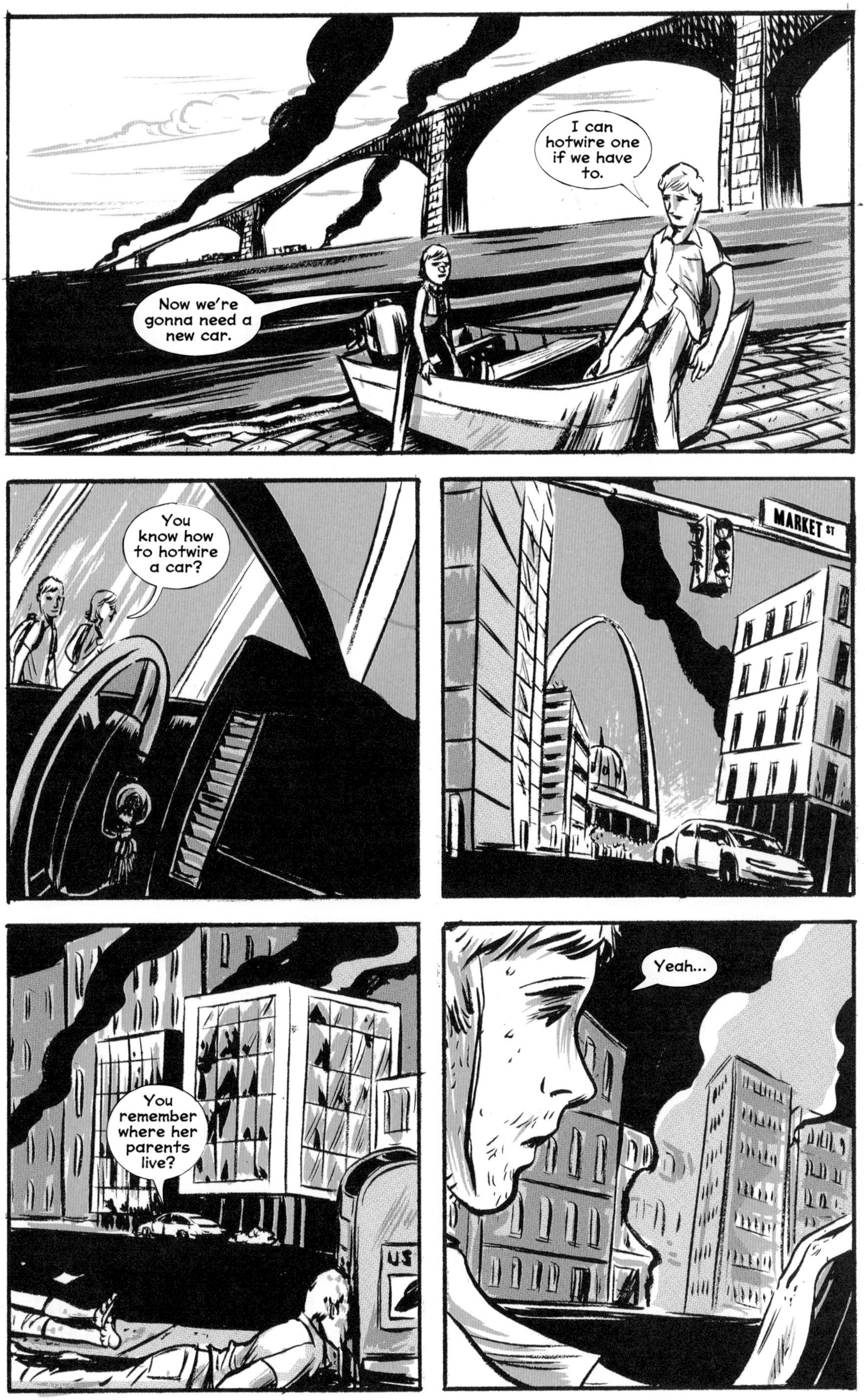
I can hotwire one if we have to.
Now we're gonna need a new car.
You know how to hotwire a car?
MARKET ST
You remember where her parents live?
US
Yeah...

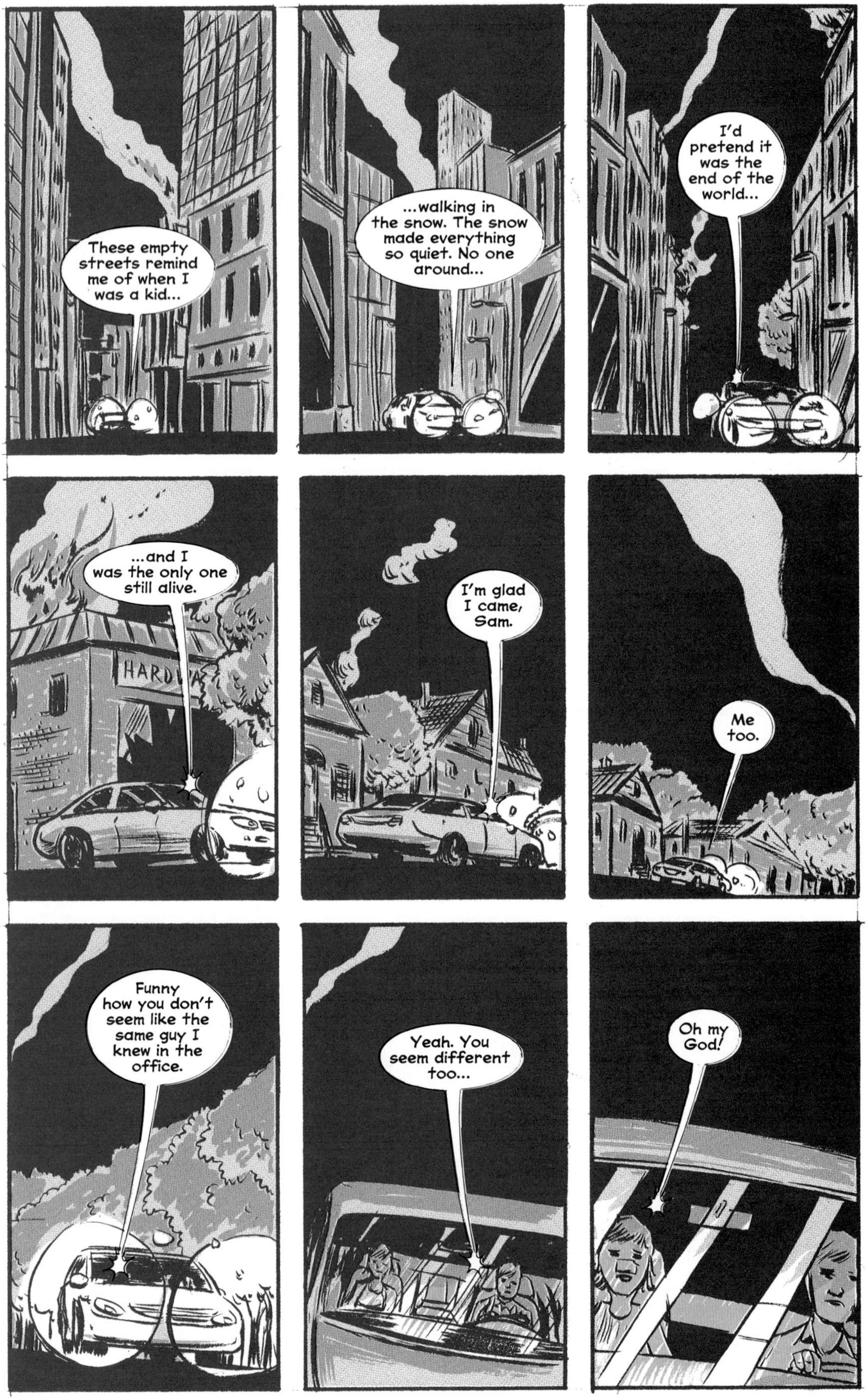
These empty streets remind me of when I was a kid...
...walking in the snow. The snow made everything so quiet. No one around...
I'd pretend it was the end of the world...
...and I was the only one still alive.
HARDWA
I'm glad I came, Sam.
Me too.
Funny how you don't seem like the same guy I knew in the office.
Yeah. You seem different too...
Oh my God!

AYING THAT THE COORDINATED ATTACKS BEGAN AT **6:5**0 AM ON WHAT PEOPLE ARE NOW REFERRING TO AS "DAY ZERO". THE C

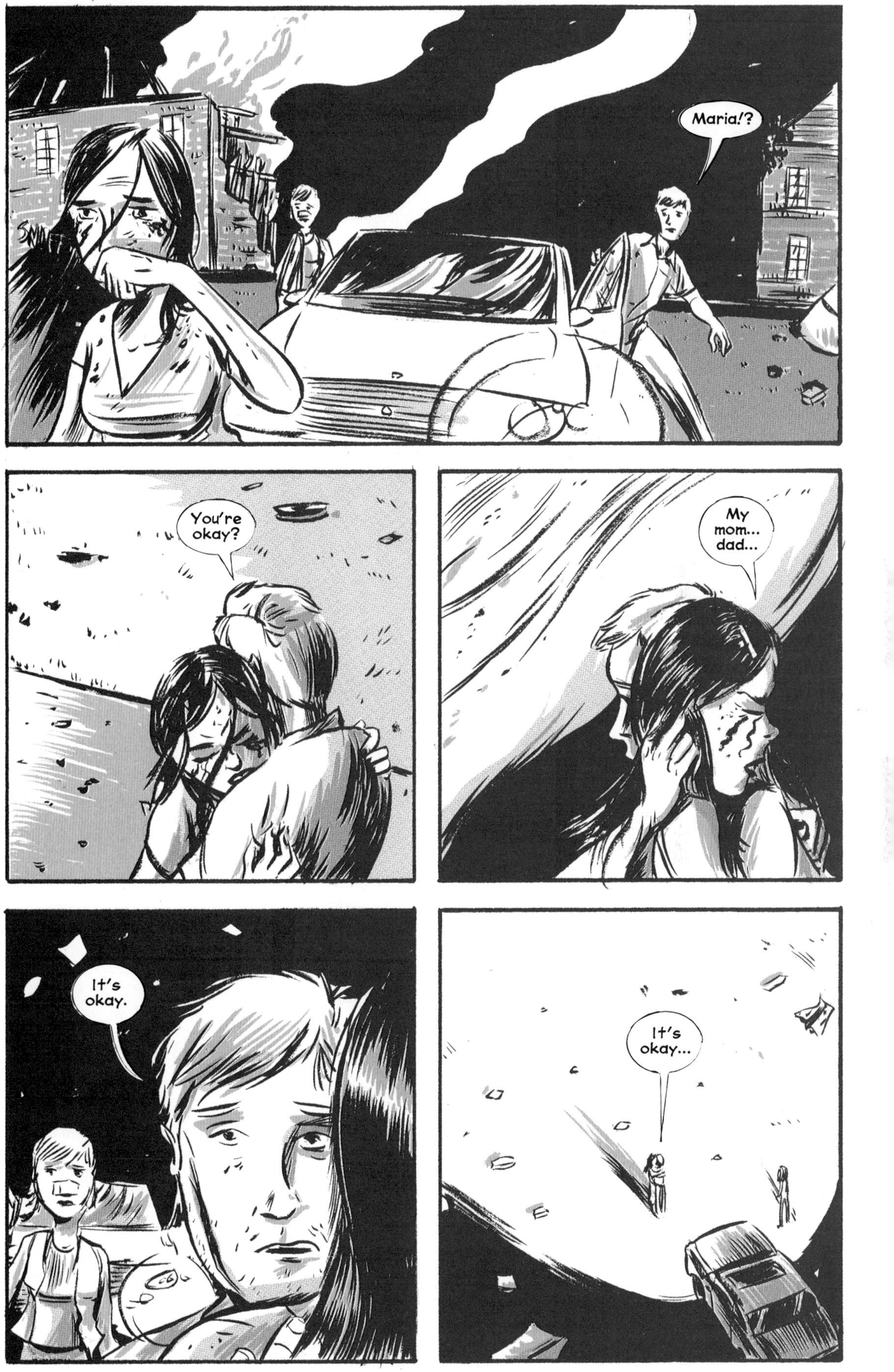
Maria!?
You're okay?
My mom... dad...
It's okay.
It's okay...

ESIDENT REGARDING THE SAFETY OF HIS FAMILY. IT IS BELIEVED THAT BOMBS FELL NEAR THE ADDRESS OF NEWPORT BUT NO

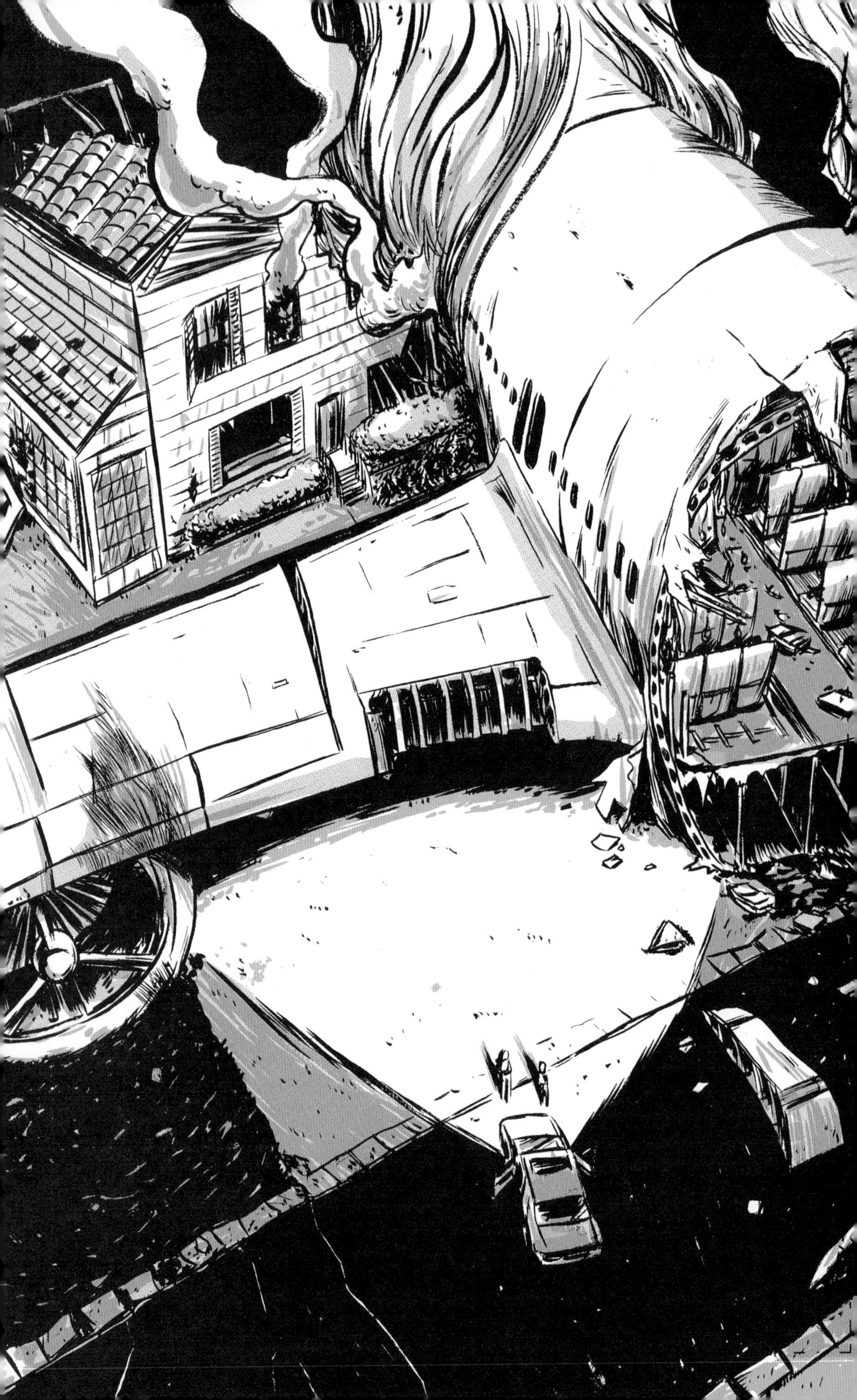

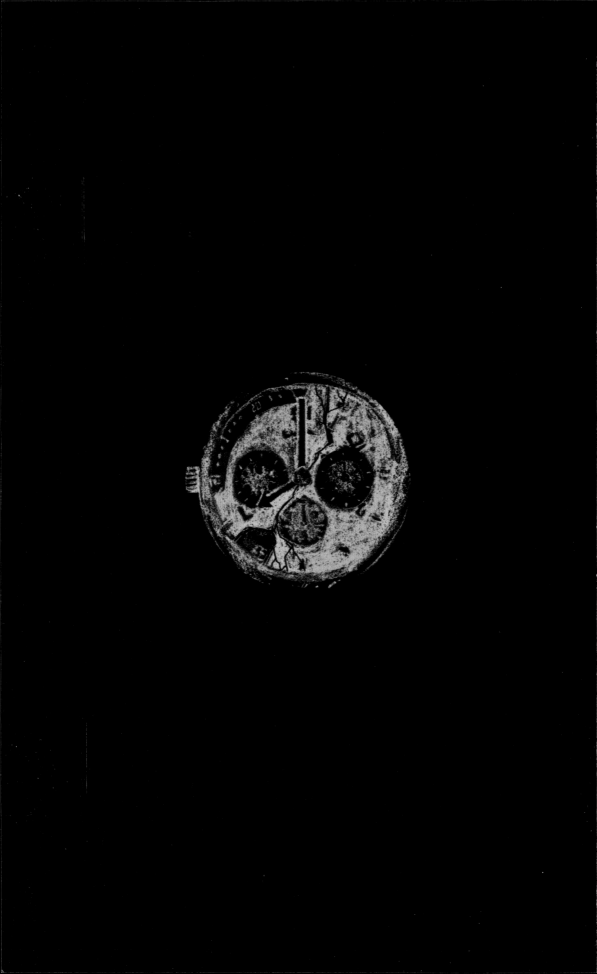

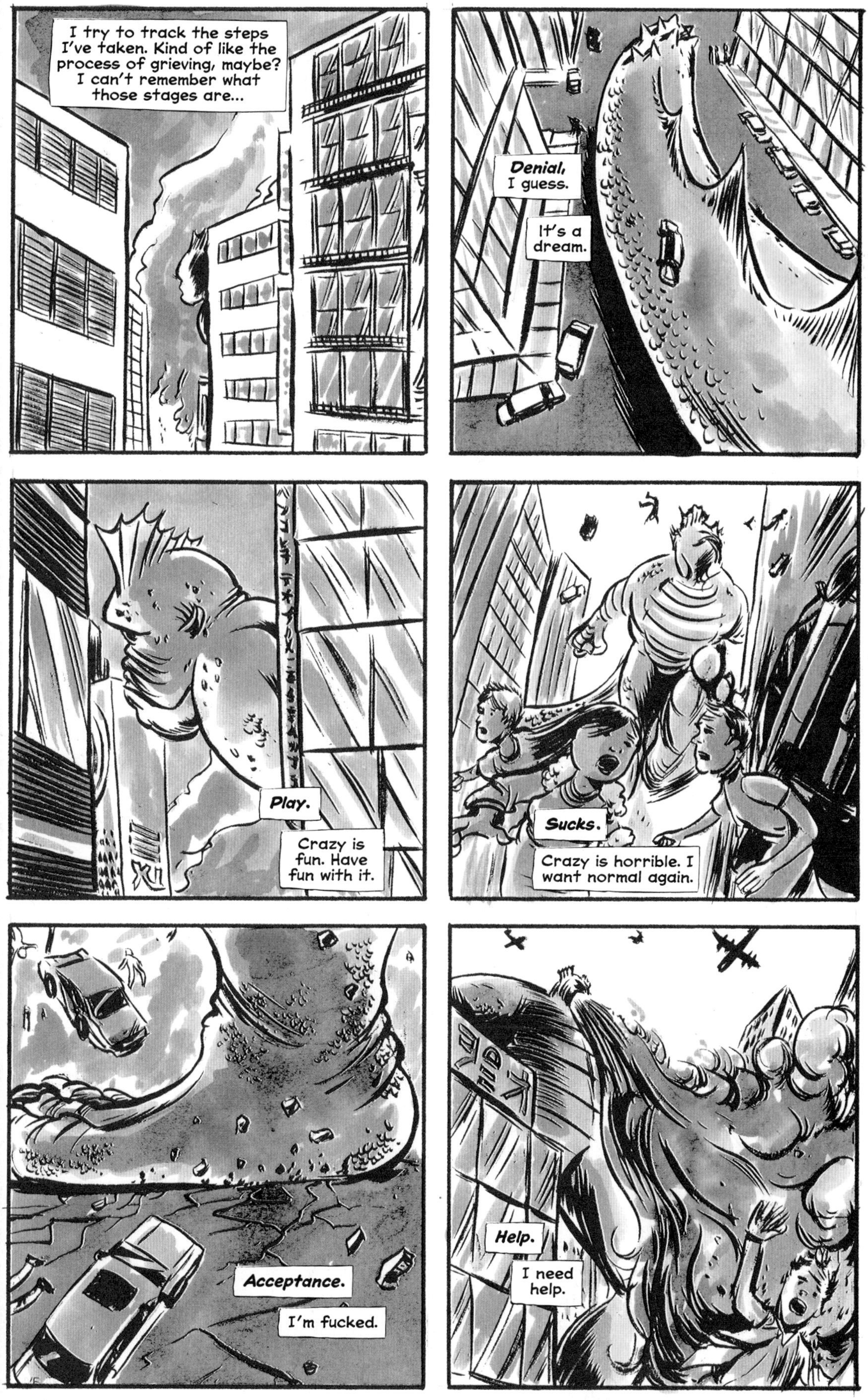
I try to track the steps I've taken. Kind of like the process of grieving, maybe? I can't remember what those stages are...
Denial, I guess.
It's a dream.
Play.
Crazy is fun. Have fun with it.
Sucks.
Crazy is horrible. I want normal again.
Acceptance.
I'm fucked.
Help.
I need help.

) FANS PRAISE THE MONSTER HIT AND **68**TH FILM FROM THE ACCLAIMED STUDIO. "LORD LIZARD," WHILE RECEIVING RAVE REVIE

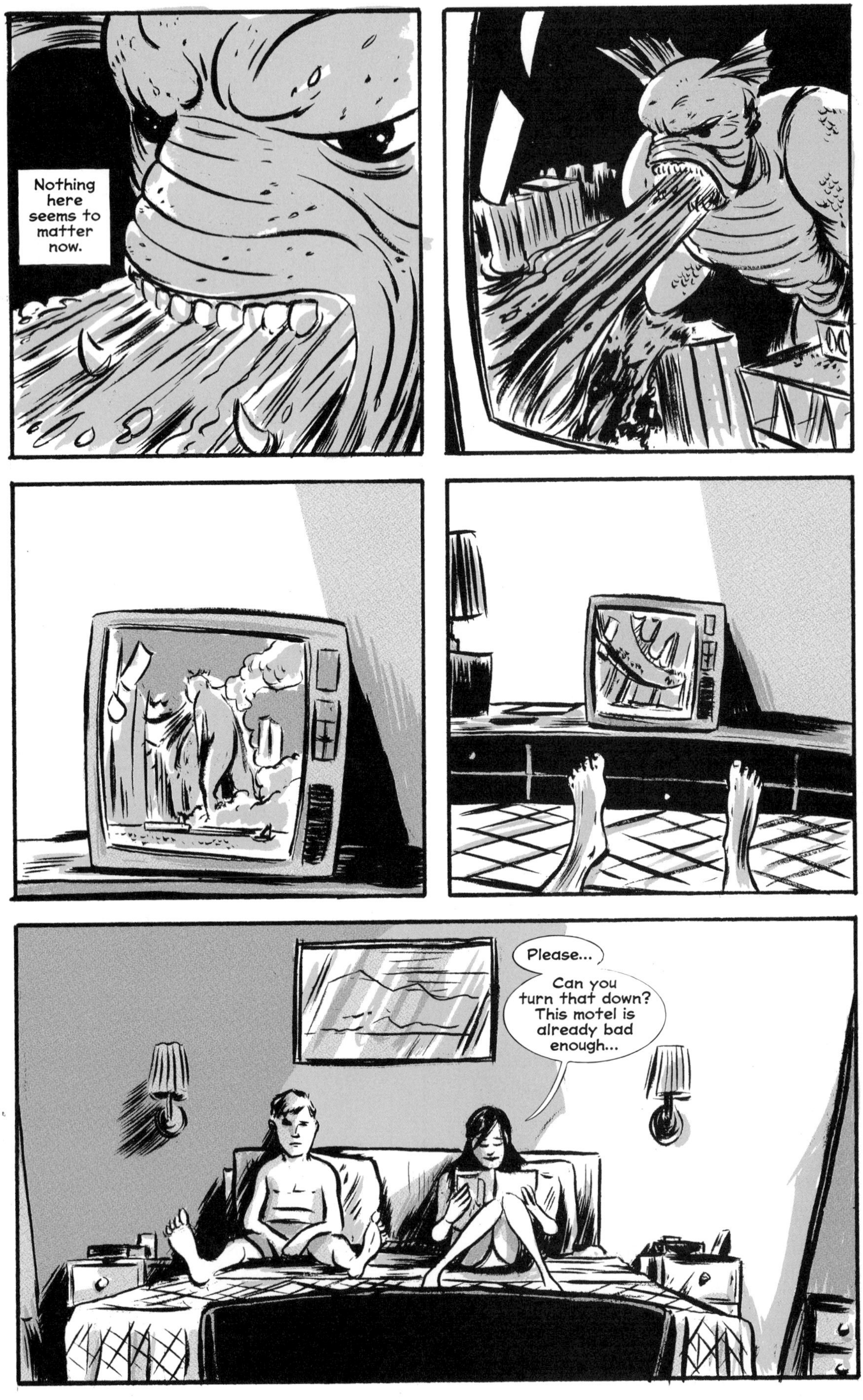
Nothing here seems to matter now.
Please...
Can you turn that down? This motel is already bad enough...

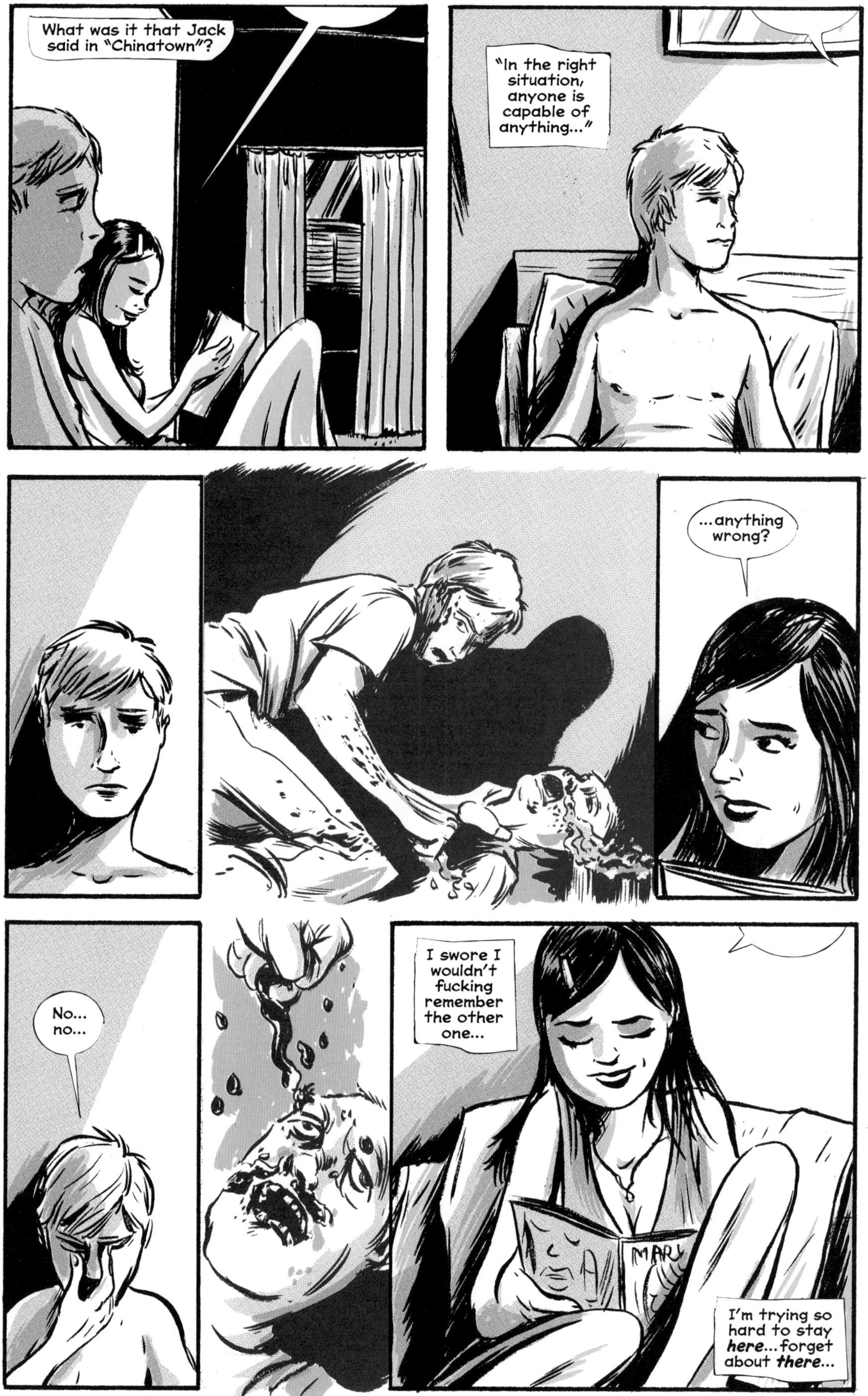
What was it that Jack said in "Chinatown"?
"In the right situation, anyone is capable of anything..."
...anything wrong?
No... no...
I swore I wouldn't fucking remember the other one...
I'm trying so hard to stay *here*... forget about *there*...

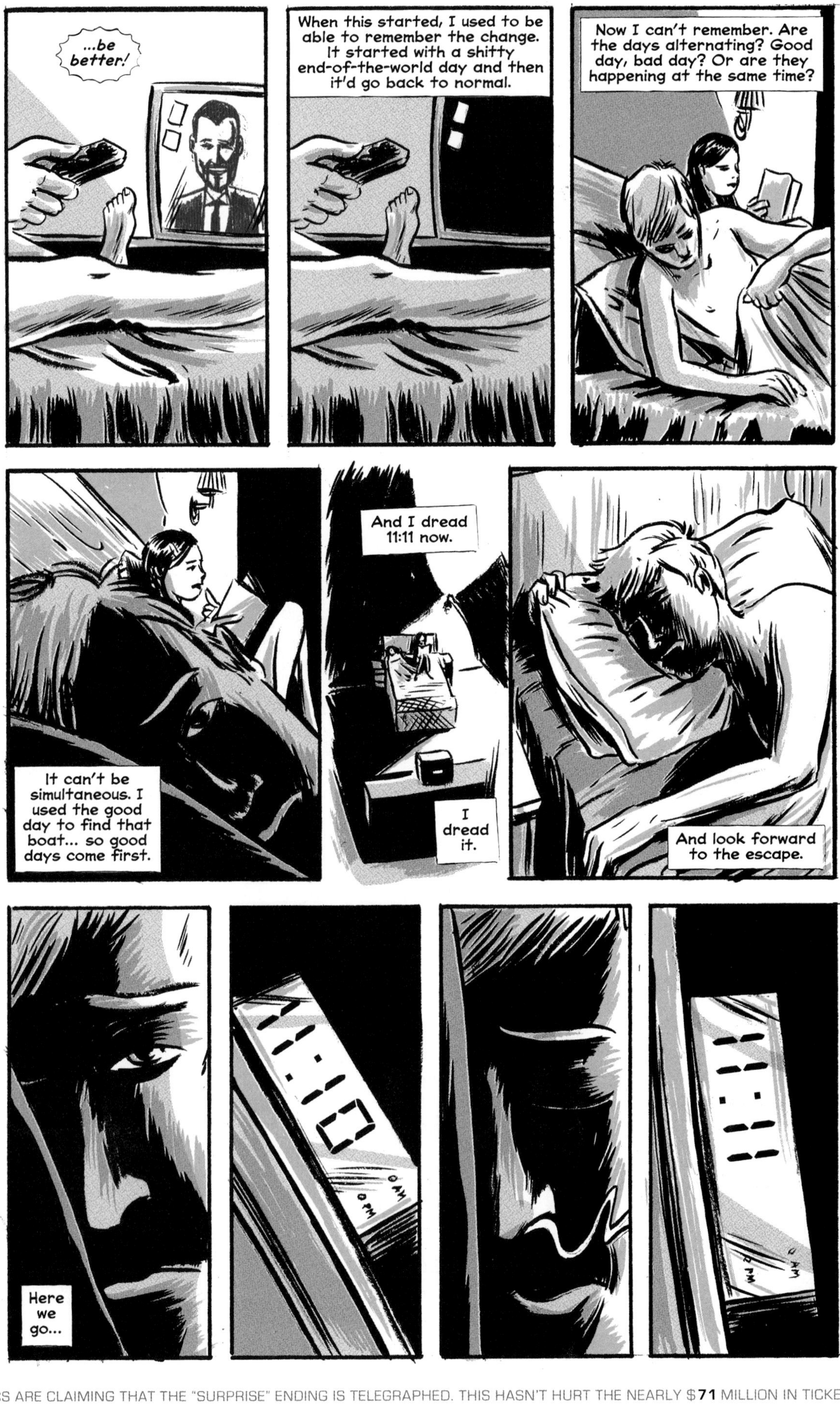
...be better!
When this started, I used to be able to remember the change. It started with a shitty end-of-the-world day and then it'd go back to normal.
Now I can't remember. Are the days alternating? Good day, bad day? Or are they happening at the same time?
It can't be simultaneous. I used the good day to find that boat... so good days come first.
And I dread 11:11 now.
I dread it.
And look forward to the escape.
Here we go...
AM
PM
AM
PM

CRITICS ARE CLAIMING THAT THE "SURPRISE" ENDING IS TELEGRAPHED. THIS HASN'T HURT THE NEARLY $71 MILLION IN TICKET

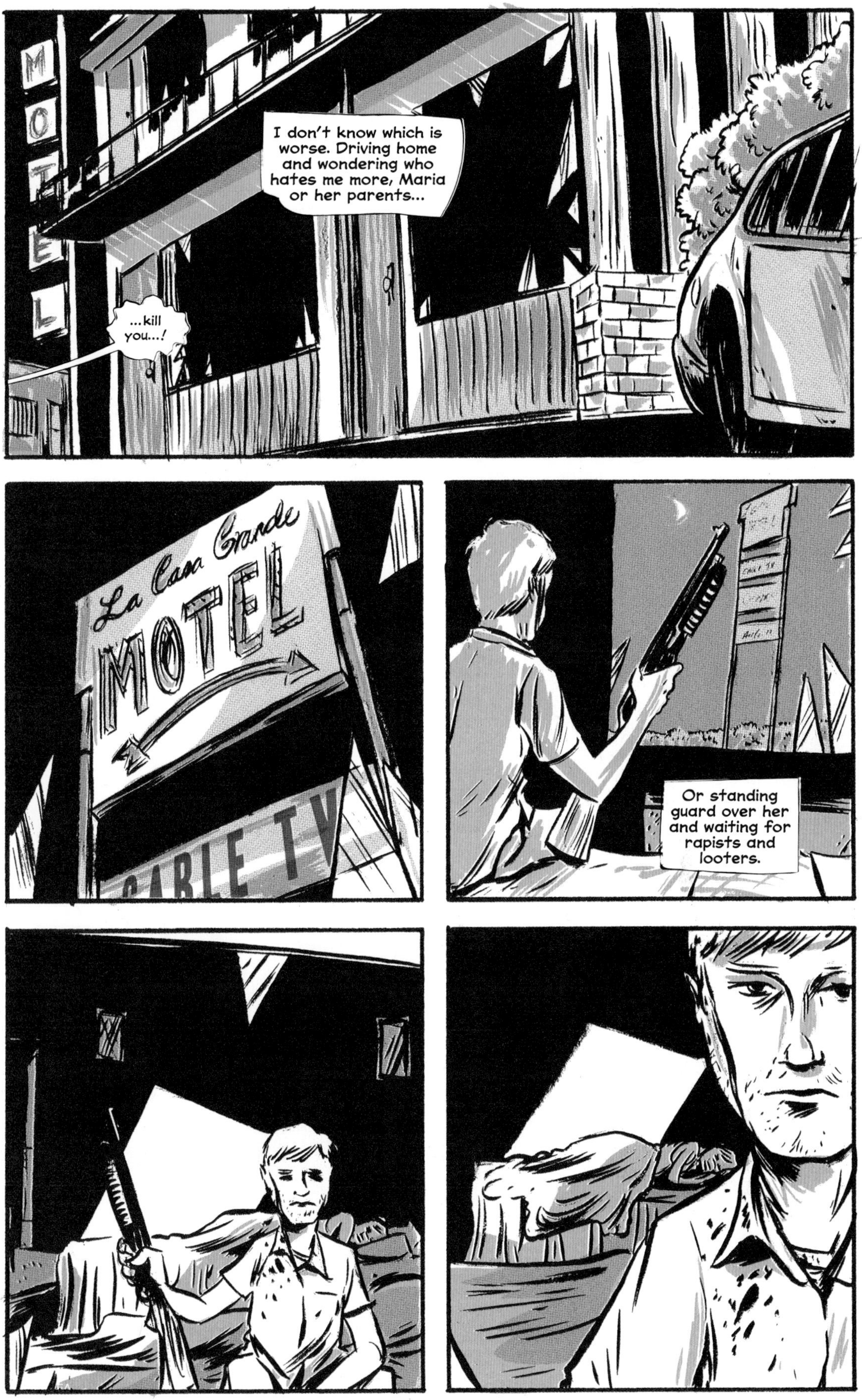
MOTEL
I don't know which is worse. Driving home and wondering who hates me more, Maria or her parents...
...kill you...!
La Casa Grande
MOTEL
Or standing guard over her and waiting for rapists and looters.

AINST TRAVEL. IN LOCAL NEWS, A **72**-YEAR-OLD WOMAN WAS FOUND DEAD IN HER CONDO, APPARENTLY ATTACKED BY A ROVIN

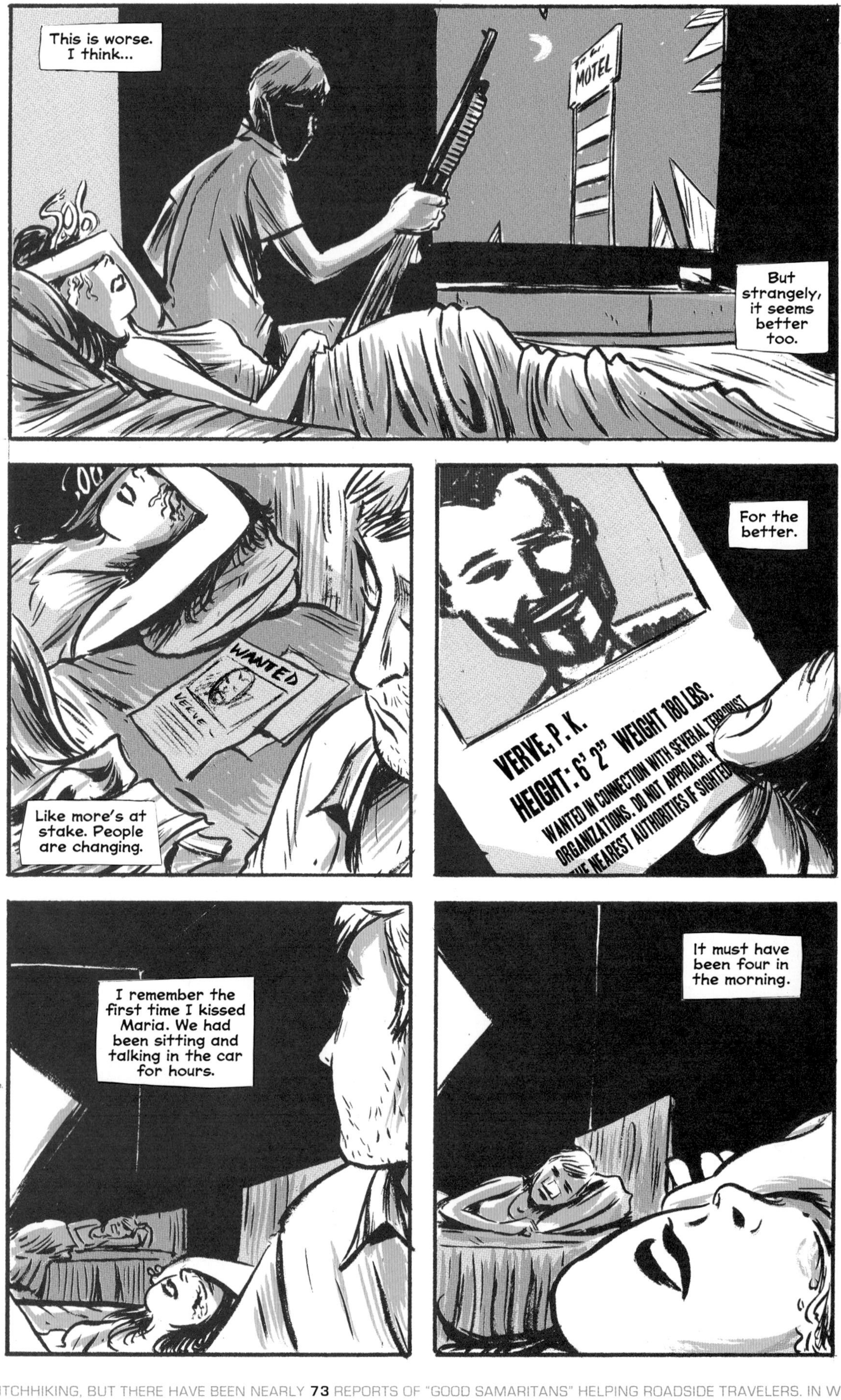
This is worse. I think...
MOTEL
But strangely, it seems better too.
WANTED
VERVE
Like more's at stake. People are changing.
For the better.
VERVE, P. K.
HEIGHT: 6' 2" WEIGHT 180 LBS.
WANTED IN CONNECTION WITH SEVERAL TERRORIST
ORGANIZATIONS. DO NOT APPROACH.
NEAREST AUTHORITIES IF SIGHTED
I remember the first time I kissed Maria. We had been sitting and talking in the car for hours.
It must have been four in the morning.

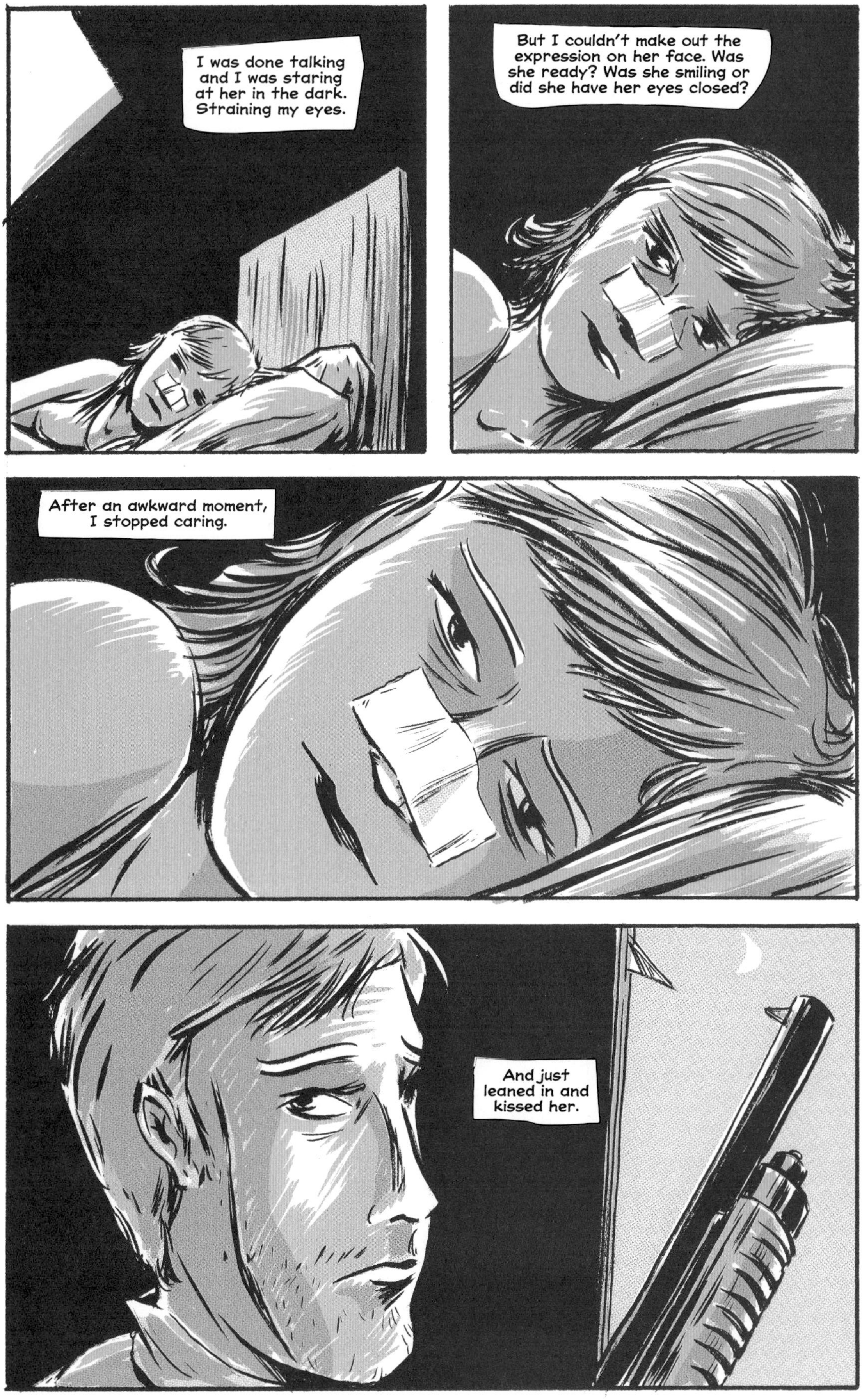
I was done talking and I was staring at her in the dark. Straining my eyes.
But I couldn't make out the expression on her face. Was she ready? Was she smiling or did she have her eyes closed?
After an awkward moment, I stopped caring.
And just leaned in and kissed her.

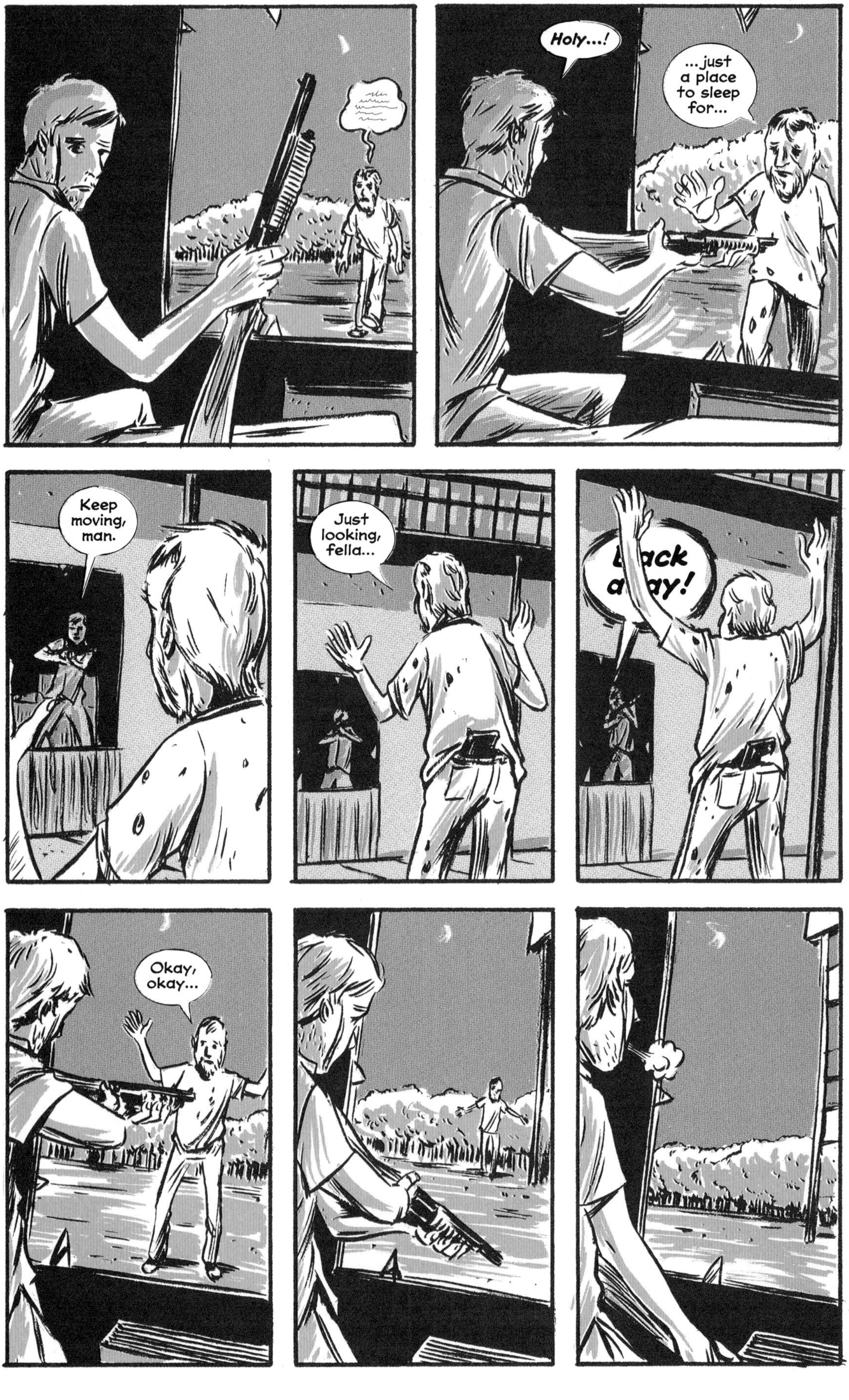
Holy...!
...just a place to sleep for...
Keep moving, man.
Just looking, fella...
Back away!
Okay, okay...

IMPOSSIBLE TO ESTIMATE BUT OVER **75** MILLION PEOPLE IN THE UNITED STATES AND EUROPE ARE HOMELESS AFTER ANOTHER

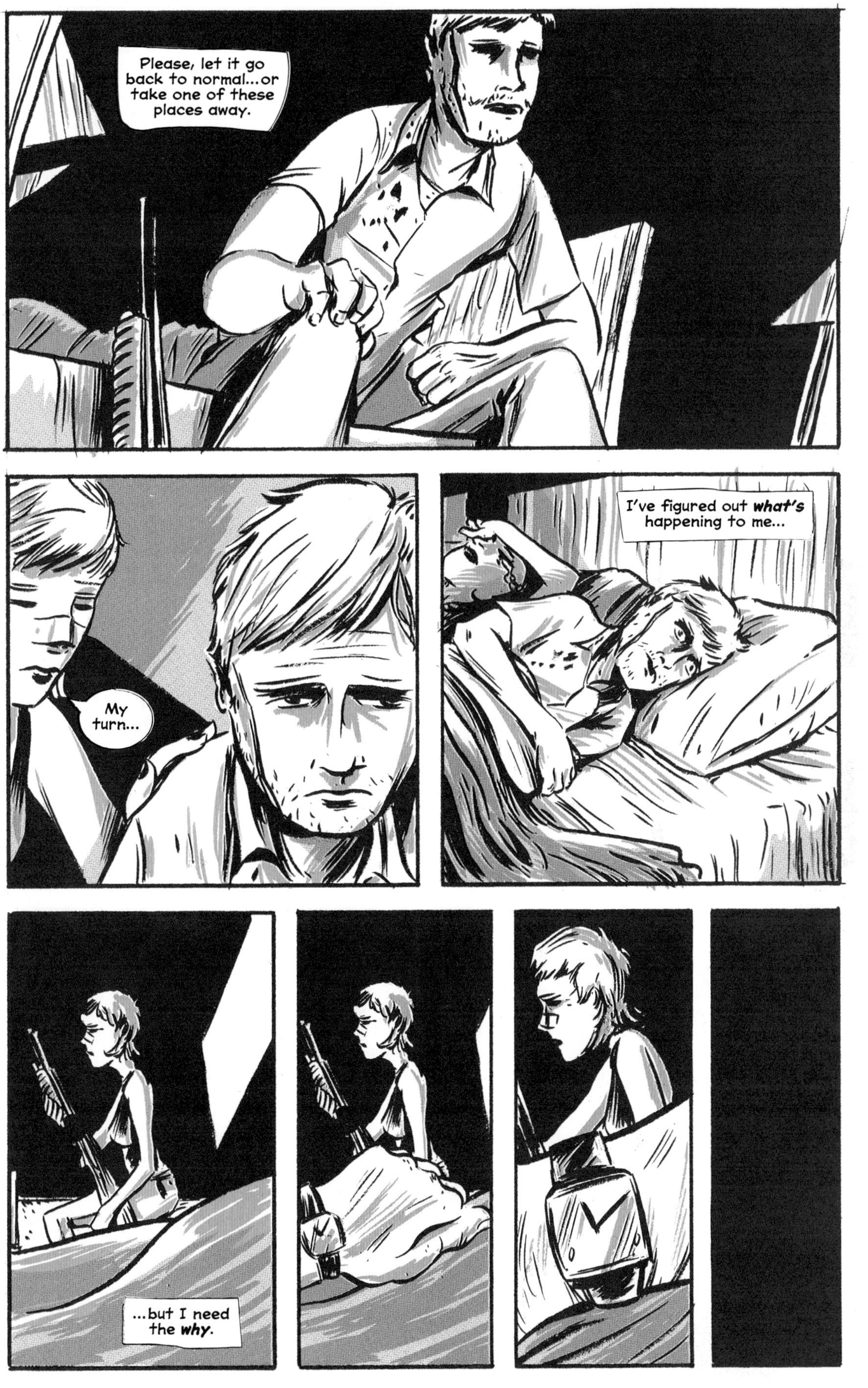
Please, let it go back to normal...or take one of these places away.
My turn...
I've figured out ***what's*** happening to me...
...but I need the ***why***.

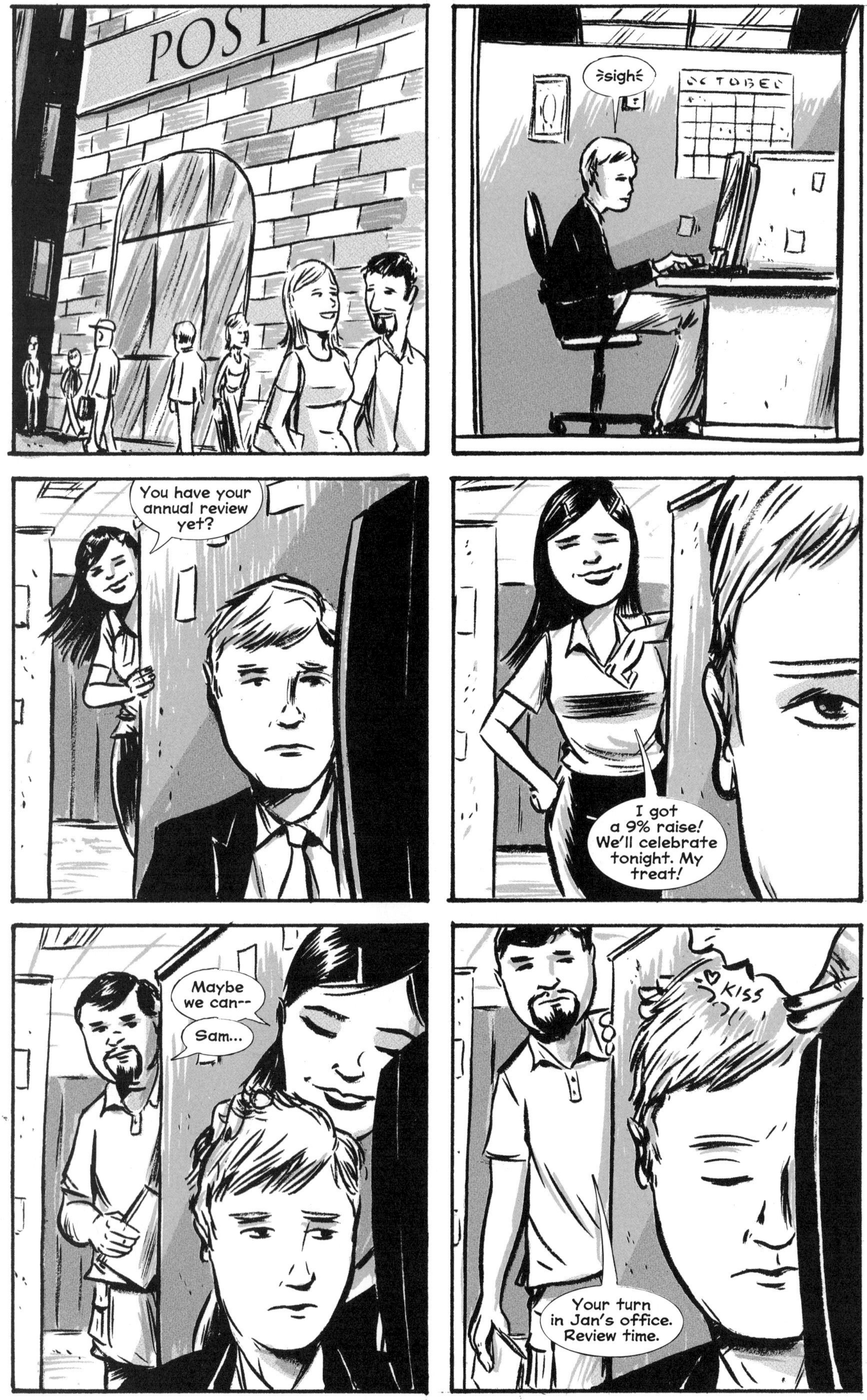
POST
sigh
OCTOBER
You have your annual review yet?
I got a 9% raise! We'll celebrate tonight. My treat!
Maybe we can--
Sam...
KISS
Your turn in Jan's office. Review time.

HER BOOST EXPECTED AS TAX RETURN MONEY COMES IN; RETAILERS ARE ENCOURAGING THE ESTIMATED $77 MILLION BE SPEN

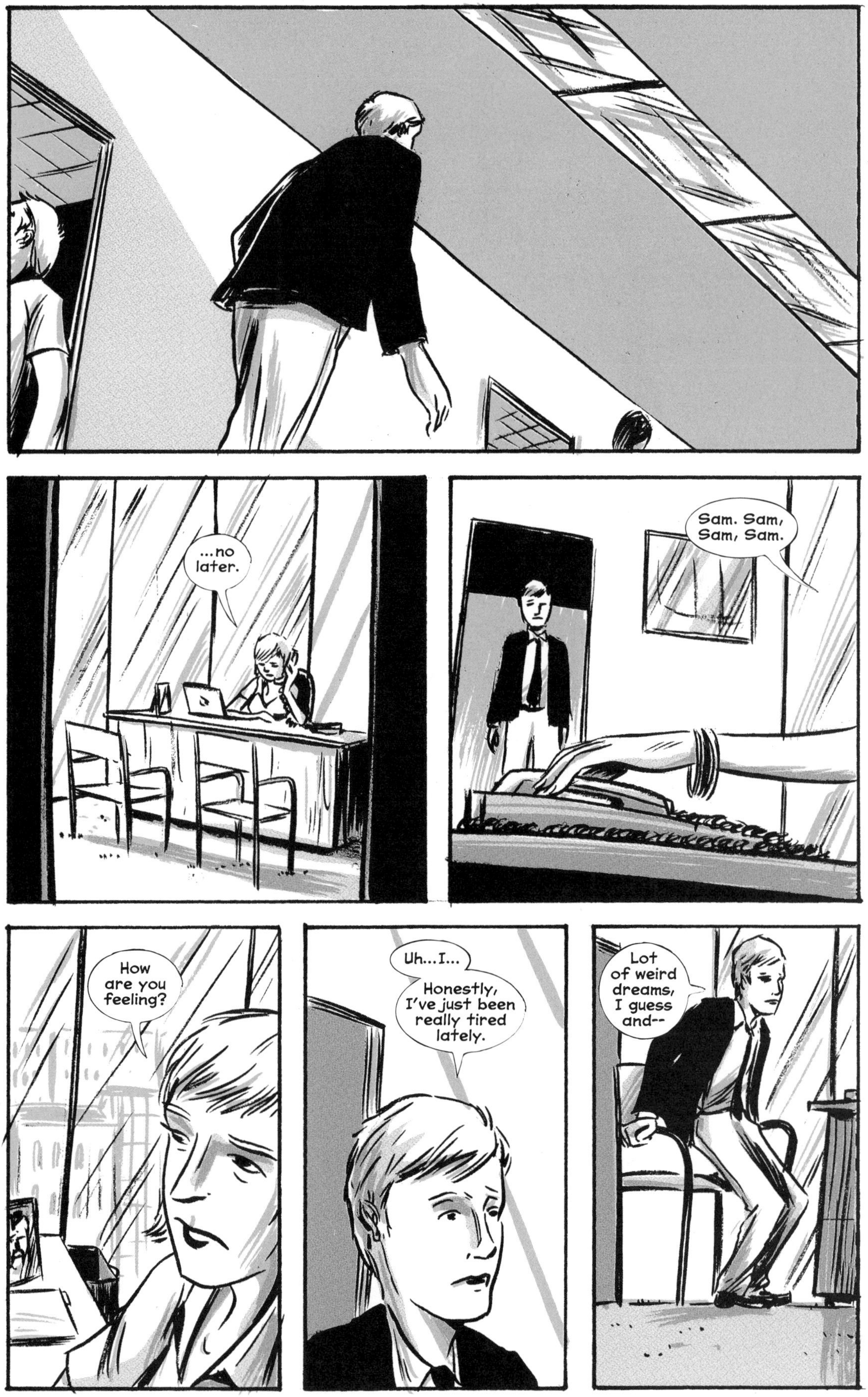
...no later.
Sam. Sam, Sam, Sam.
How are you feeling?
Uh...I...
Honestly, I've just been really tired lately.
Lot of weird dreams, I guess and--

LES ARE MUCH HIGHER THAN EXPECTED. THE **78**,000 CAPACITY HALL IS SOLD OUT IN ANTICIPATION OF "THE BOSS"'S NEW ALBU

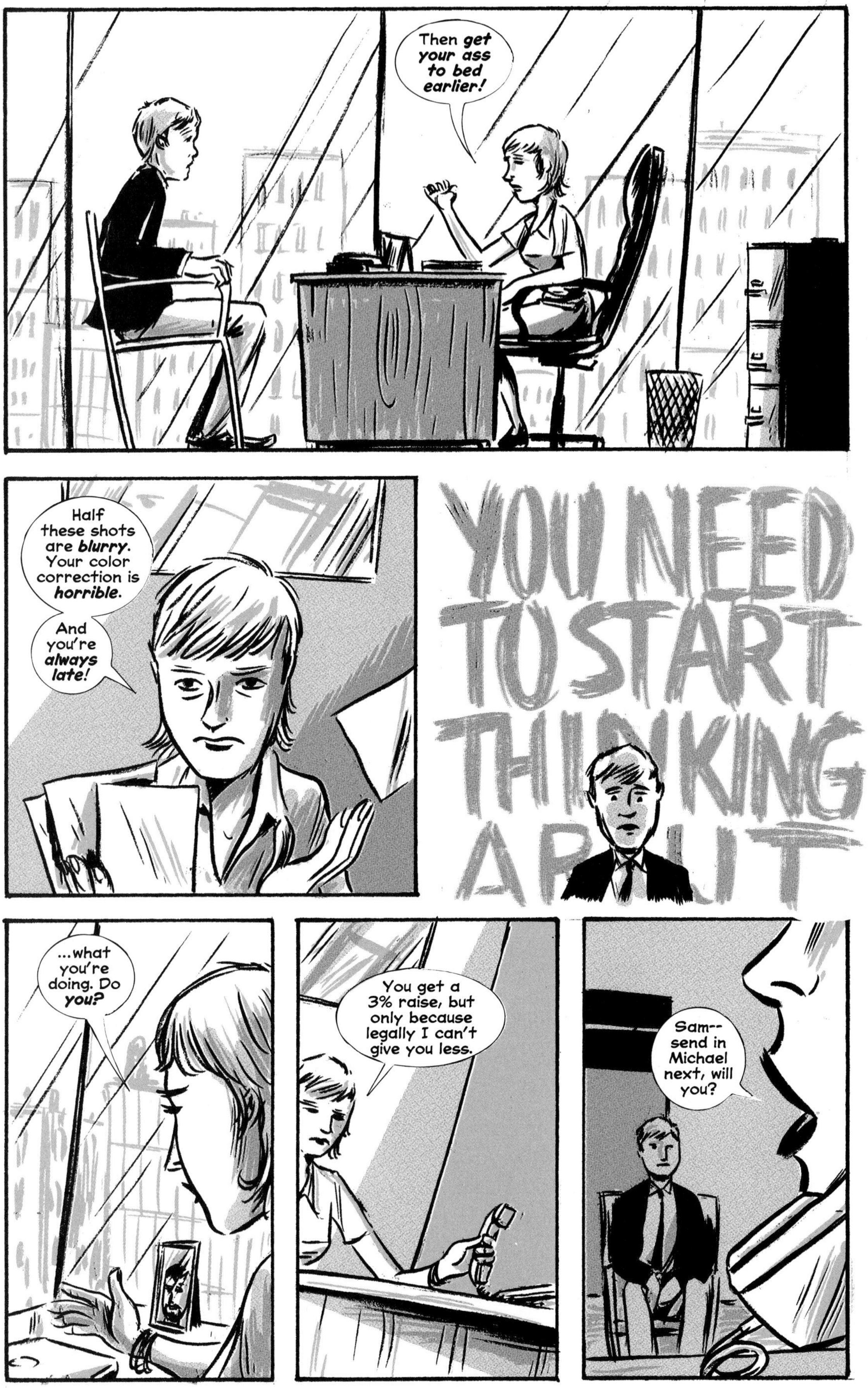
Then get your ass to bed earlier!
Half these shots are blurry. Your color correction is horrible.
And you're always late!
YOU NEED TO START THINKING AB
...what you're doing. Do you?
You get a 3% raise, but only because legally I can't give you less.
Sam-- send in Michael next, will you?

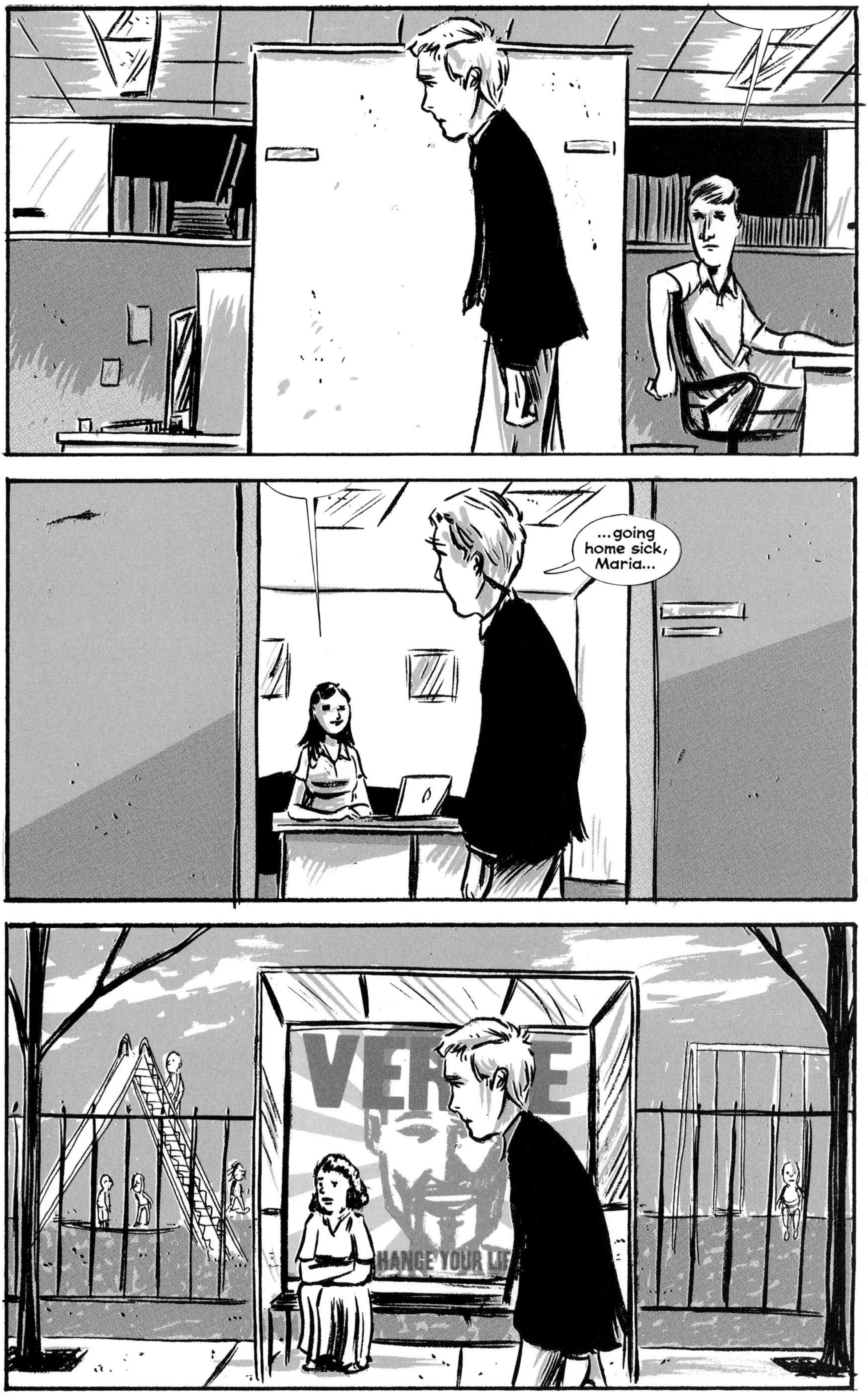
...going home sick, Maria...

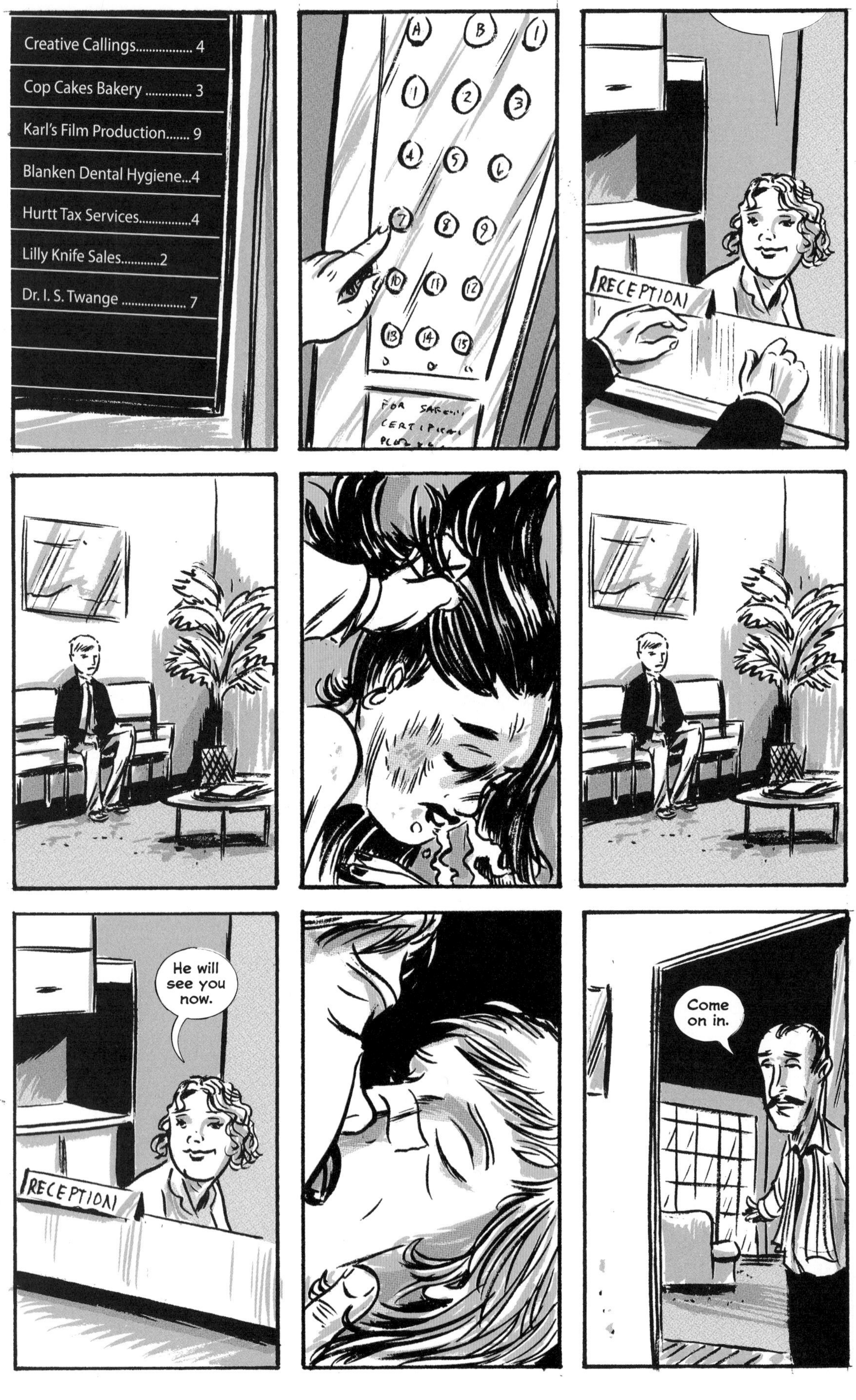
Creative Callings................. 4
Cop Cakes Bakery 3
Karl's Film Production....... 9
Blanken Dental Hygiene...4
Hurtt Tax Services................4
Lilly Knife Sales............2
Dr. I. S. Twange 7
RECEPTION
RECEPTION
He will see you now.
Come on in.

EDY ACTOR JUST TURNING **81** IS STILL ACTIVE. HIS LATEST HIT COMEDY "IS THERE A DOCTOR IN THE MADHOUSE" IS STILL PACK

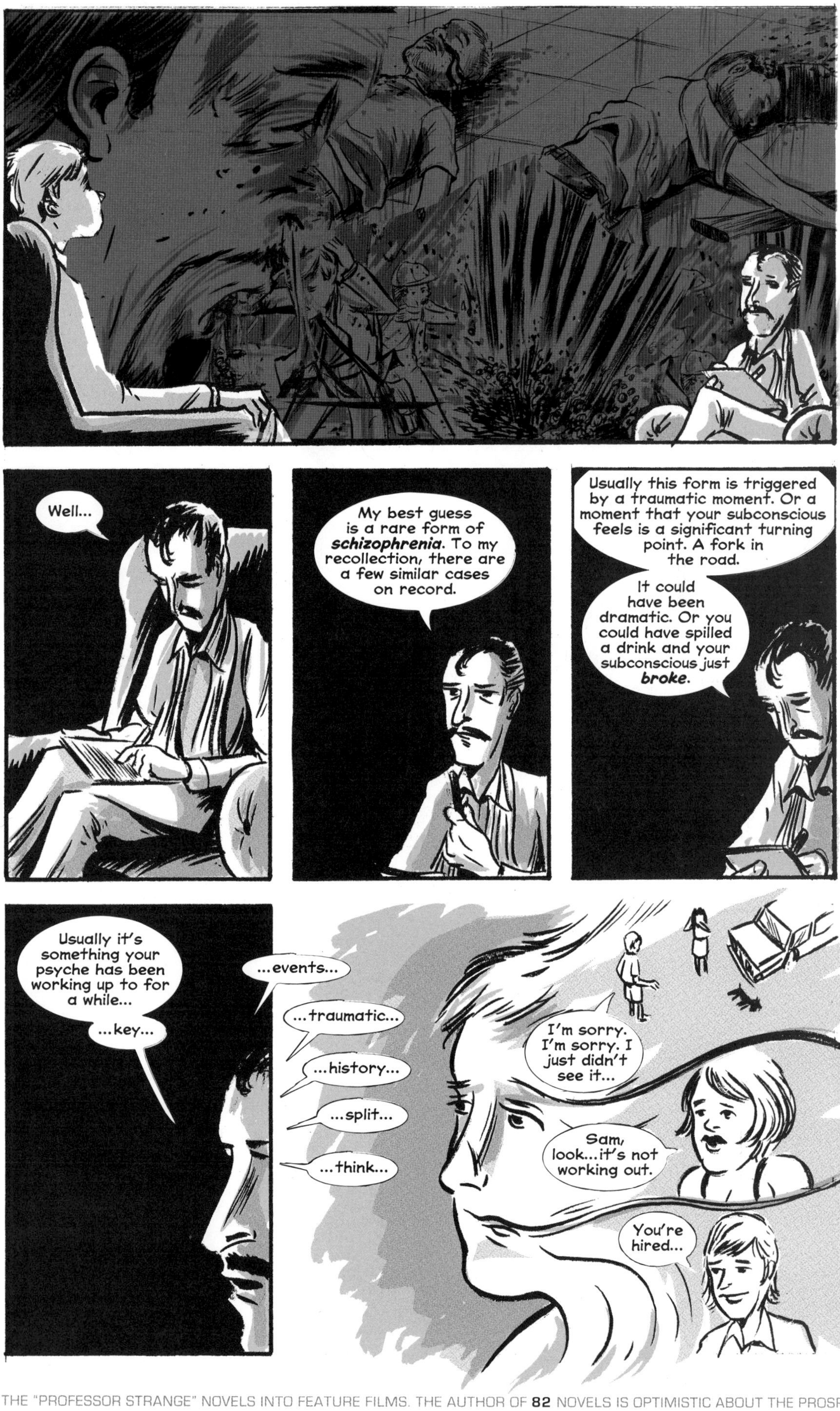
Well...
My best guess is a rare form of ***schizophrenia***. To my recollection, there are a few similar cases on record.
Usually this form is triggered by a traumatic moment. Or a moment that your subconscious feels is a significant turning point. A fork in the road.
It could have been dramatic. Or you could have spilled a drink and your subconscious just **broke**.
Usually it's something your psyche has been working up to for a while...
...key...
...events...
...traumatic...
...history...
...split...
...think...
I'm sorry. I'm sorry. I just didn't see it...
Sam, look...it's not working out.
You're hired...

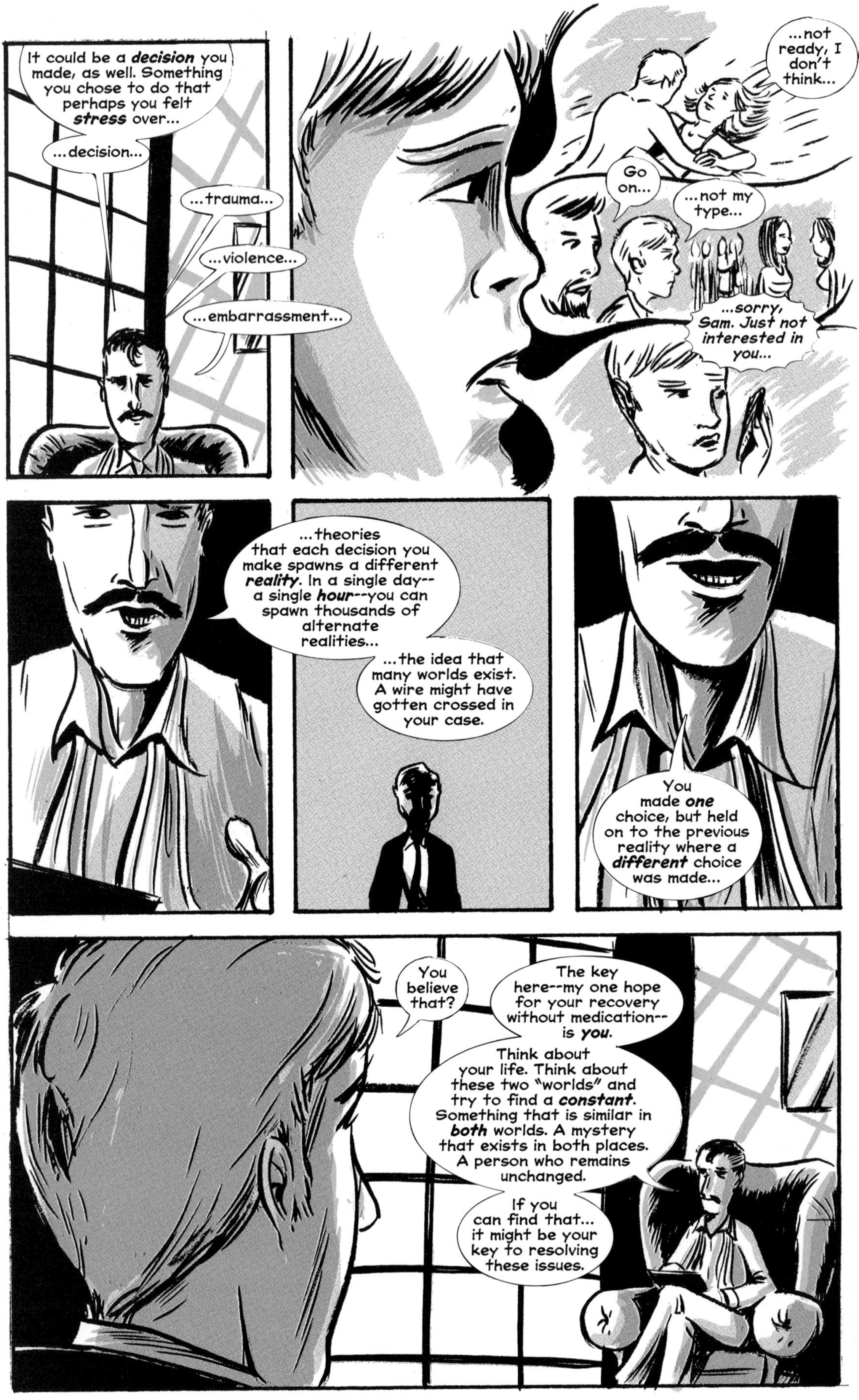

It could be a *decision* you made, as well. Something you chose to do that perhaps you felt *stress* over...
...decision...
...trauma...
...violence...
...embarrassment...
...not ready, I don't think...
Go on...
...not my type...
...sorry, Sam. Just not interested in you...
...theories that each decision you make spawns a different *reality*. In a single day--a single *hour*--you can spawn thousands of alternate realities...
...the idea that many worlds exist. A wire might have gotten crossed in your case.
You made *one* choice, but held on to the previous reality where a *different* choice was made...
You believe that?
The key here--my one hope for your recovery without medication--is *you*.
Think about your life. Think about these two "worlds" and try to find a *constant*. Something that is similar in *both* worlds. A mystery that exists in both places. A person who remains unchanged.
If you can find that... it might be your key to resolving these issues.

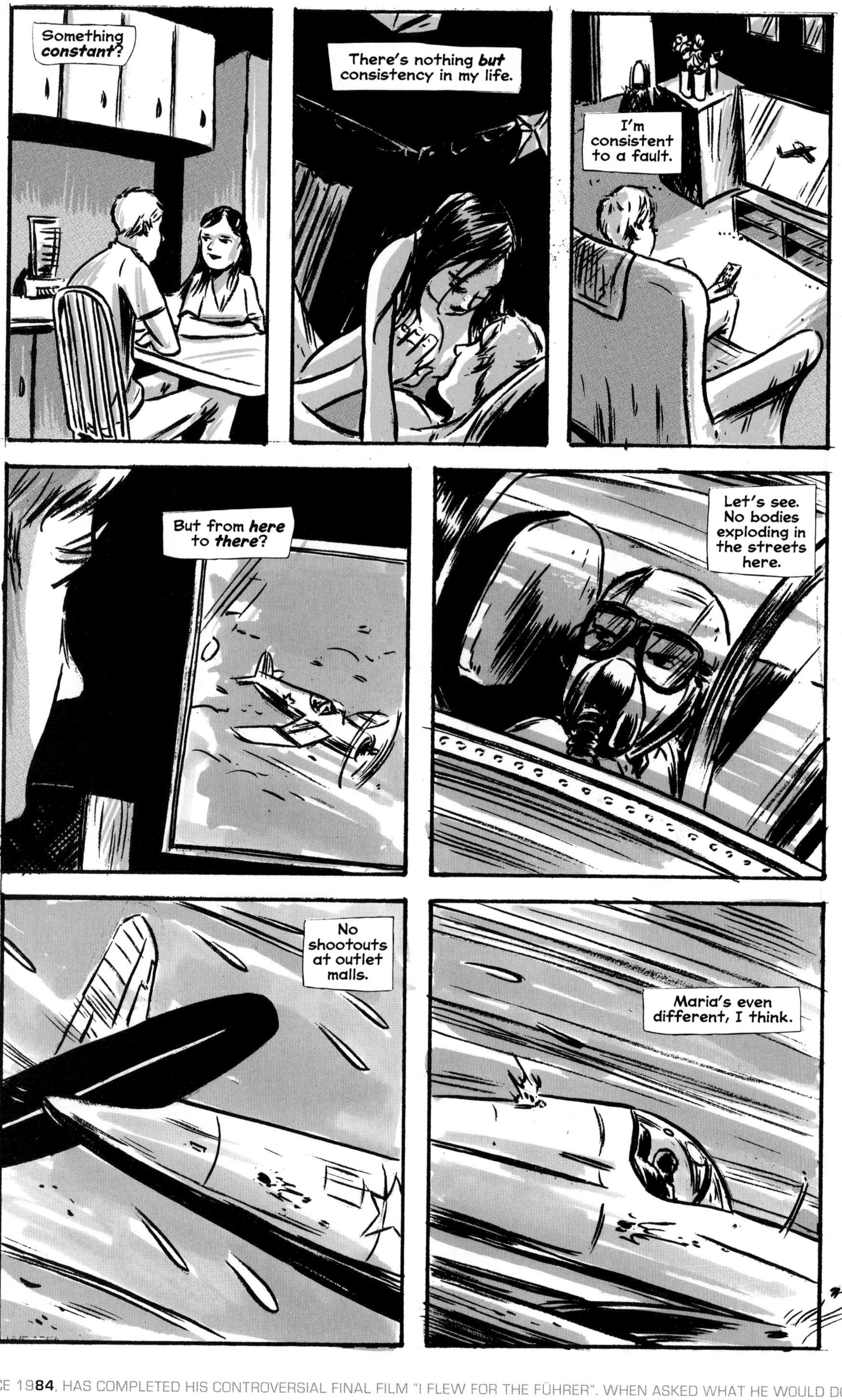
Something *constant*?
There's nothing *but* consistency in my life.
I'm consistent to a fault.
But from *here* to *there*?
Let's see. No bodies exploding in the streets here.
No shootouts at outlet malls.
Maria's even different, I think.

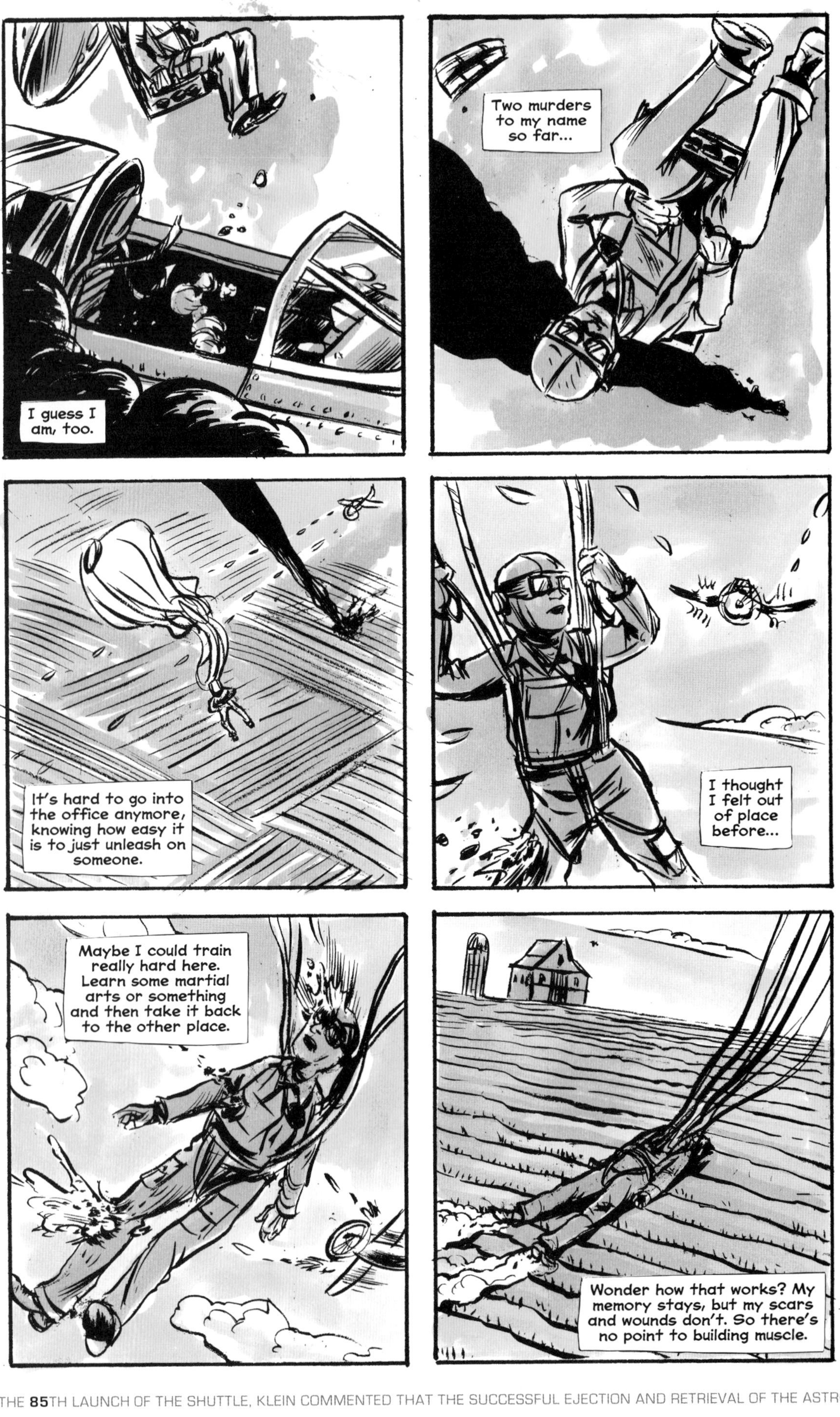
I guess I am, too.
Two murders to my name so far...
It's hard to go into the office anymore, knowing how easy it is to just unleash on someone.
I thought I felt out of place before...
Maybe I could train really hard here. Learn some martial arts or something and then take it back to the other place.
Wonder how that works? My memory stays, but my scars and wounds don't. So there's no point to building muscle.

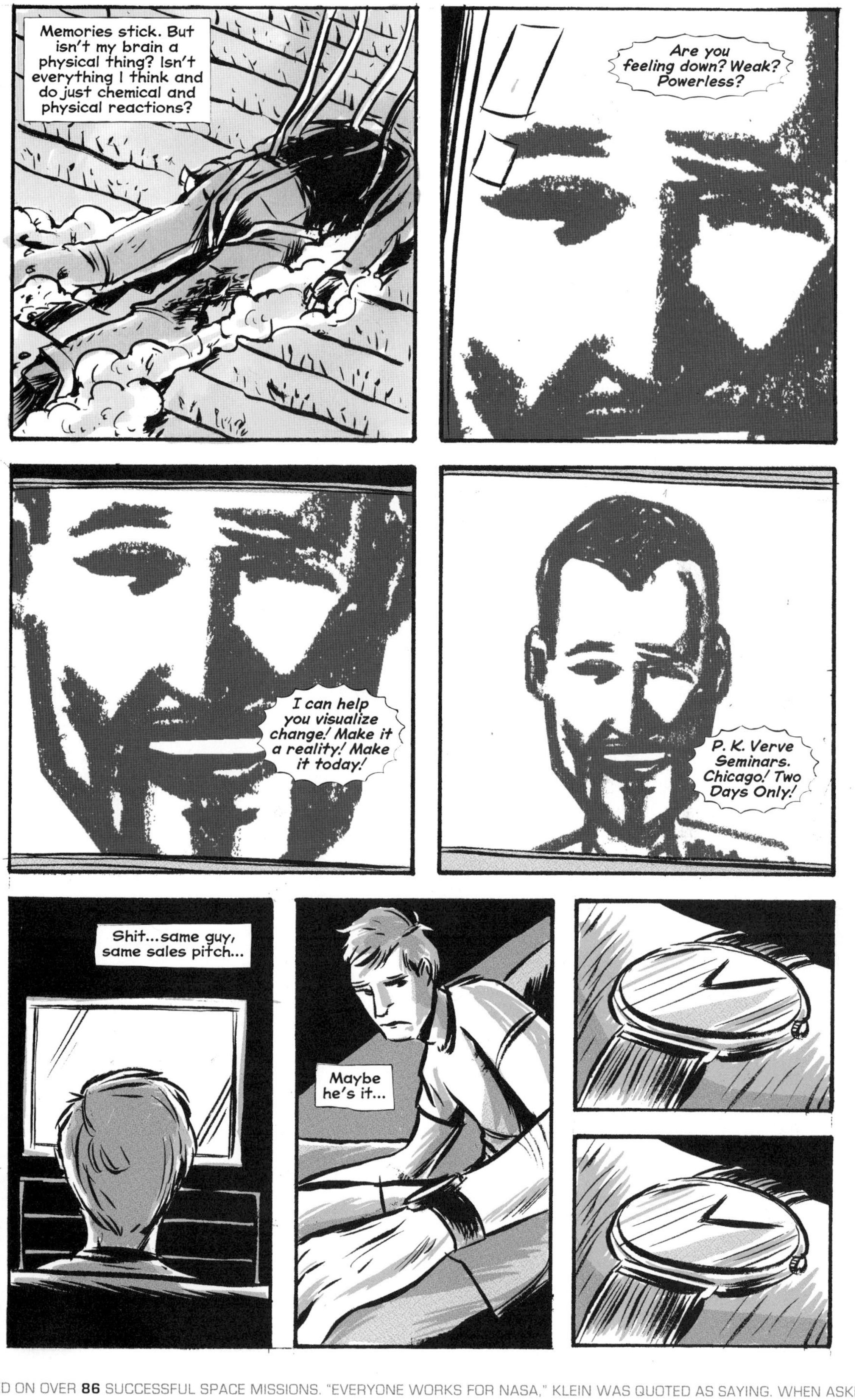
Memories stick. But isn't my brain a physical thing? Isn't everything I think and do just chemical and physical reactions?
Are you feeling down? Weak? Powerless?
I can help you visualize change! Make it a reality! Make it today!
P. K. Verve Seminars. Chicago! Two Days Only!
Shit...same guy, same sales pitch...
Maybe he's it...

ED ON OVER 86 SUCCESSFUL SPACE MISSIONS. "EVERYONE WORKS FOR NASA," KLEIN WAS QUOTED AS SAYING. WHEN ASKED TO

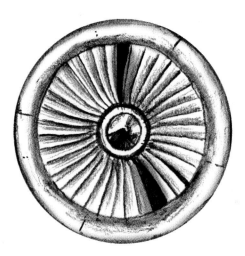

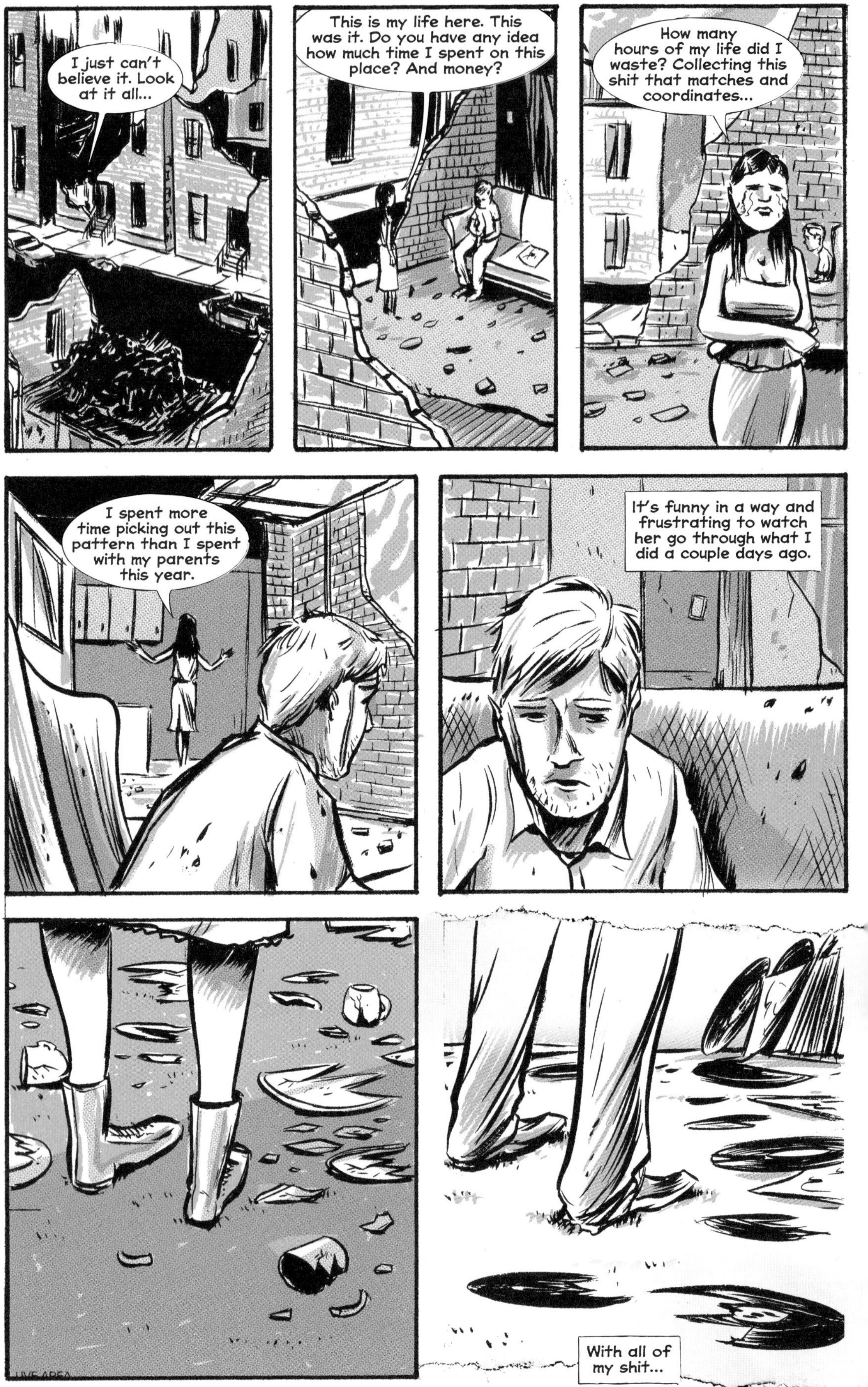
I just can't believe it. Look at it all...
This is my life here. This was it. Do you have any idea how much time I spent on this place? And money?
How many hours of my life did I waste? Collecting this shit that matches and coordinates...
I spent more time picking out this pattern than I spent with my parents this year.
It's funny in a way and frustrating to watch her go through what I did a couple days ago.
With all of my shit...

NS WORRIED THAT THE ANARCHY WILL LEAD TO AN INVASION. HOWEVER, WITH **87** COUNTRIES NOW SUFFERING FROM NATUR

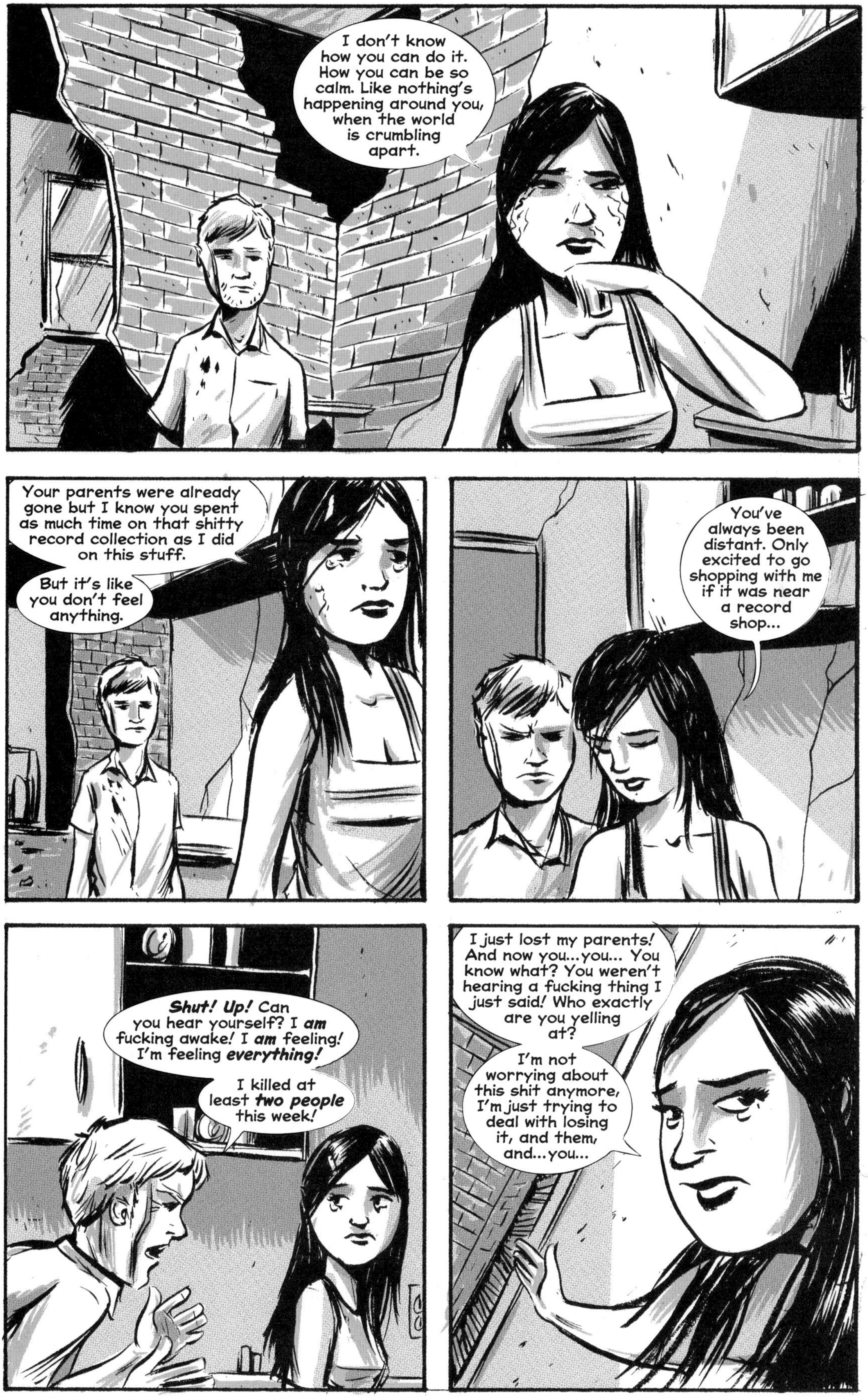
I don't know how you can do it. How you can be so calm. Like nothing's happening around you, when the world is crumbling apart.
Your parents were already gone but I know you spent as much time on that shitty record collection as I did on this stuff.
But it's like you don't feel anything.
You've always been distant. Only excited to go shopping with me if it was near a record shop...
Shut! Up! Can you hear yourself? I am fucking awake! I am feeling! I'm feeling everything!
I killed at least two people this week!
I just lost my parents! And now you...you... You know what? You weren't hearing a fucking thing I just said! Who exactly are you yelling at?
I'm not worrying about this shit anymore, I'm just trying to deal with losing it, and them, and...you...

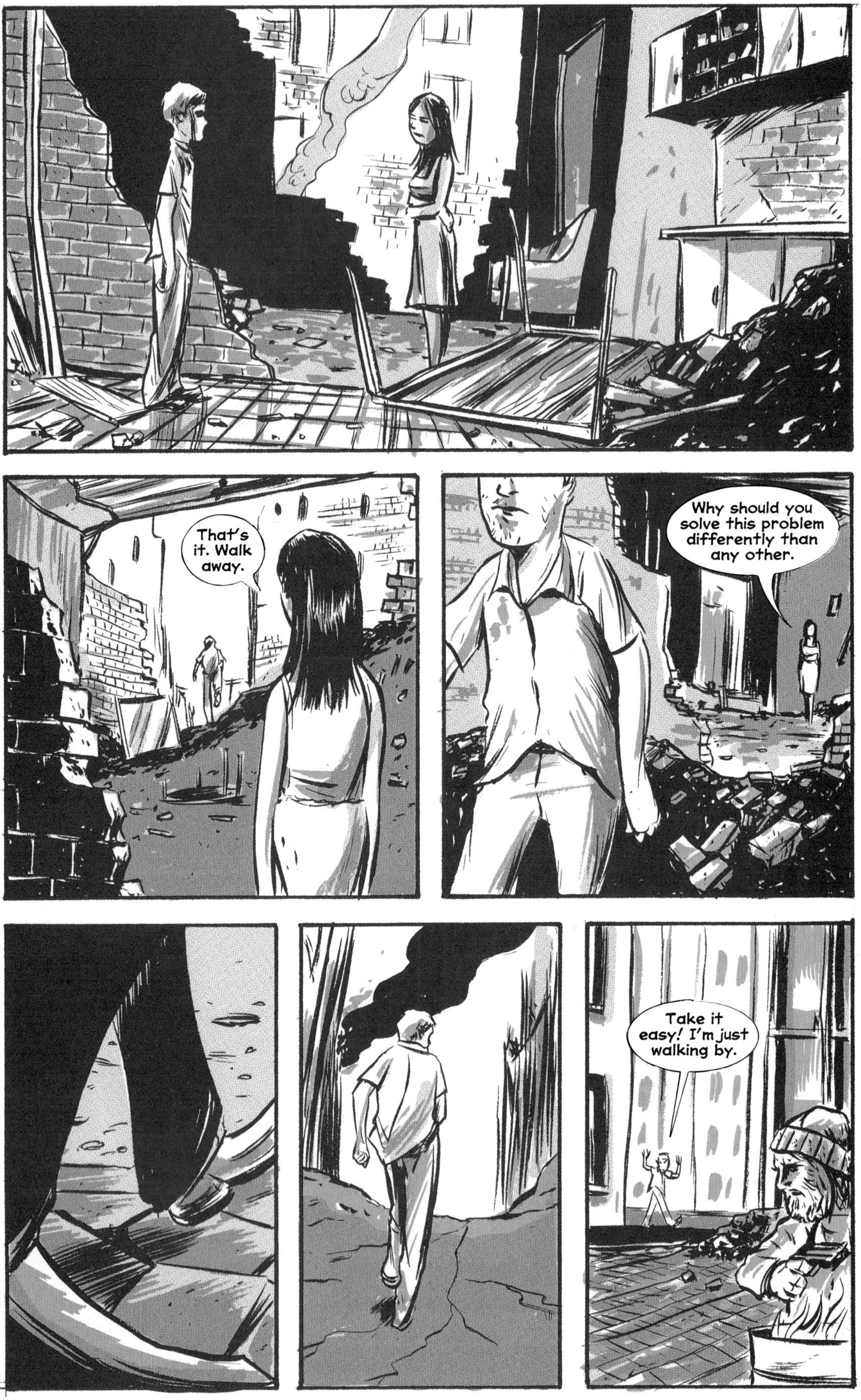
That's it. Walk away.
Why should you solve this problem differently than any other.
Take it easy! I'm just walking by.

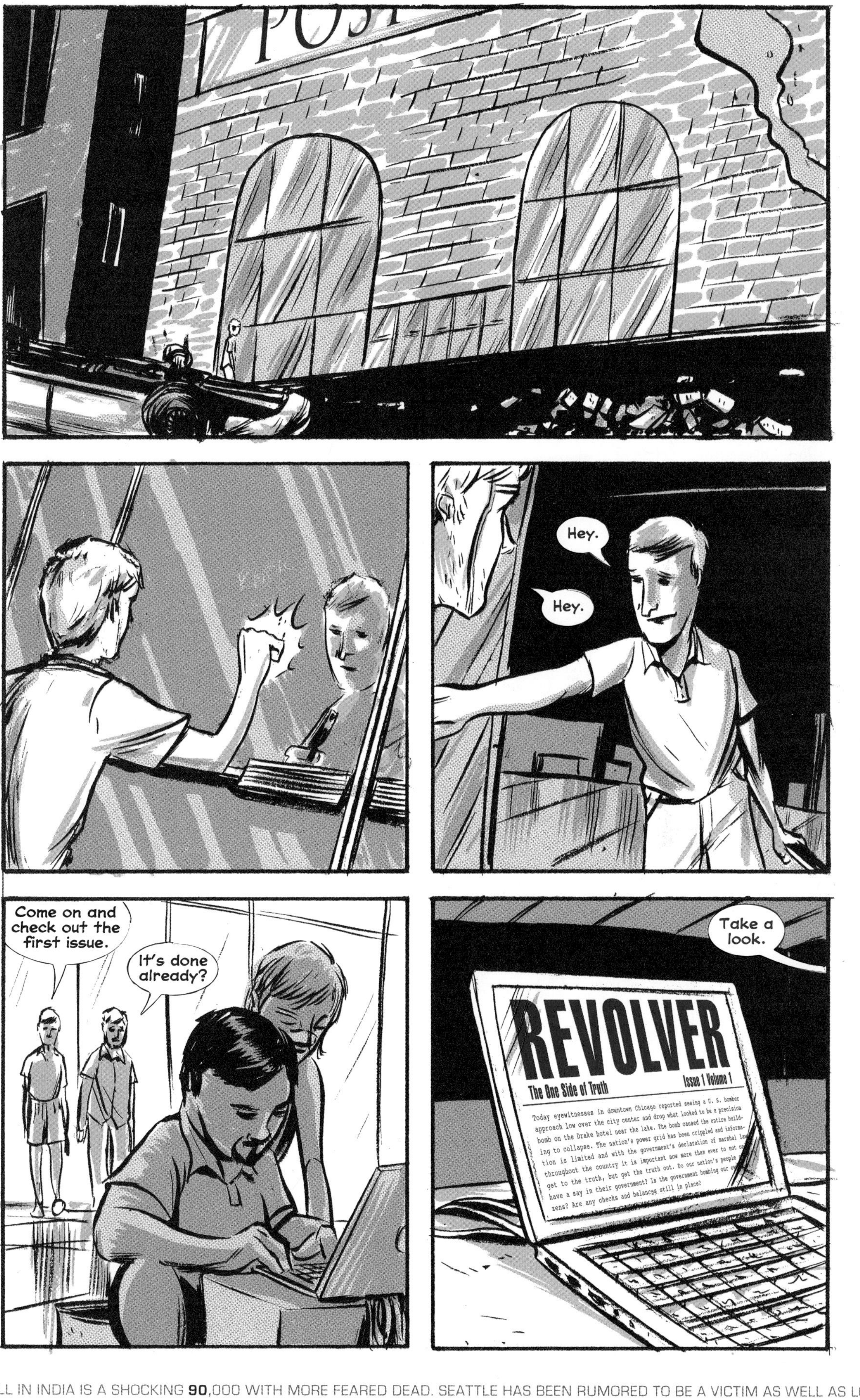
POS
Hey.
Hey.
Come on and check out the first issue.
It's done already?
Take a look.
REVOLVER
The One Side of Truth
Issue 1 Volume 1
Today eyewitnesses in downtown Chicago reported seeing a U. S. bomber
approach low over the city center and drop what looked to be a precision
bomb on the Drake hotel near the lake. The bomb caused the entire build-
ing to collapse. The nation's power grid has been crippled and informa-
tion is limited and with the government's declaration of marshal law
throughout the country it is important now more than ever to not on
get to the truth, but get the truth out. Do our nation's people
have a say in their government? Is the government bombing our ow
zens? Are any checks and balances still in place?

TOLL IN INDIA IS A SHOCKING **90**,000 WITH MORE FEARED DEAD. SEATTLE HAS BEEN RUMORED TO BE A VICTIM AS WELL AS LON

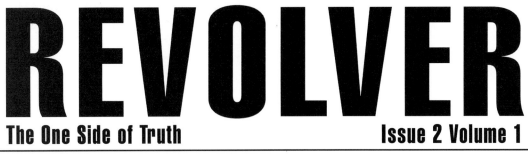

REVOLVER

The One Side of Truth   Issue 2 Volume 1

MARTIAL LAW?

In a nation where martial law is imposed, what does this mean exactly? We sent several reporters cross-country to check on the state of the nation. What we found was non-existent police forces and very little military presence, be it the National Guard, Coast Guard or Army.

State borders seem to be the only places where that military presence is visible. However, it seemed as if the barricades were in place not to restrict the movement of citizens but rather, to gather information regarding P. K. Verve. A man previously known for his inspirational seminars, Verve has mysteriously ascended to the top of the FBI's Most Wanted List. In fact,

the list that is currently being distributed via old-fashioned flyers and leaflets contains only one name: Verve.

With the nation and the world in turmoil it seems unlikely that one man is responsible for everything, and without a way for our commander-in-chief to address the nation directly we're left to wonder: Who is in charge?

WHO IS P. K. VERVE?

One of the nation's best-known inspirational speakers had humble beginnings. The son of Algerian immigrants, Verve excelled in science and math and eventually found work in Silicon Valley. Verve and his brother, Robert Lilly Verve, soon created a start-up technology company and became millionaires virtually overnight.

With their newfound clout in the industry, the brothers rose to prominence not only in the technology world but also asserted

political power in Washington - putting all of their money and resources behind projects and initiatives that suited their bottom line and, some would say, radical political views.

Government agencies soon cracked down on the Verves and they became embroiled in a host of legal battles. It appeared as if they had become too powerful. Too influential. Everything ended the following year as Robert Lilly Verve nearly died in an ultra-light airplane crash.

-cont. on page 27

SUBURBS NEXT TARGET?

Scattered reporting and some eyewitness accounts, as well as the last few radio and TV broadcasts heard before the grid's crash, would suggest that major city centers were the primary targets for the first wave of attacks. But what does this mean? Is it over? Or is there a second wave coming? Certainly the nation and the world will be dealing with the fallout and clean-up from the attacks, as well as the devastation of the resulting natural disasters, for years. And certainly the avian flu epidemics will continue to spread without an infrastructure to distribute vaccines. But as the cities are deserted, overcrowding in suburban areas will create new population-rich targets. With the government preoccupied with the capture of one man, it is up to us to defend ourselves. For more information on ways to prepare and safeguard overpopulated suburban areas, turn to page 3.

SAN FRANCISCO SAFE HAVEN?

Recently an amateur pilot flying out of San Francisco arrived in St. Louis to refuel and gave us an update on the city. According to his eyewitness report, the city is cordoning itself off from the surrounding areas. Giant earth-moving equipment is being utilized to create a defensive border, and it appears as if the city is protecting its inhabitants by keeping all military presence out of San Francisco. It

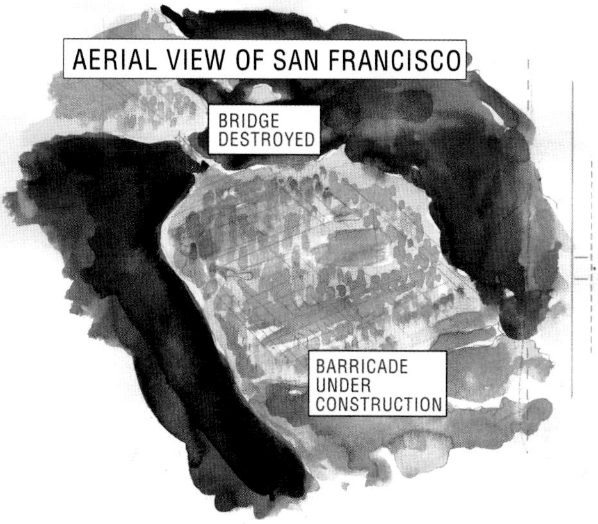

AERIAL VIEW OF SAN FRANCISCO
BRIDGE DESTROYED
BARRICADE UNDER CONSTRUCTION

is still unclear what the situation is for those citizens intent on entering the city; defense perimeters were still being put into place as

(continued on page 6)

BEWARE LOOTERS

With the increased lawlessness, looting is a very real and everyday problem. Indeed, this poses dangers to those protecting their property as well as those attempting to travel and peacefully gather supplies for their journeys. It is recommended when approaching any inhabited area to move slowly and with hands in the air to avoid unnecessary conflict when

(continued on page 6)

SEATTLE GONE?

We have yet to receive reports post-nuclear attack on Seattle, but if the final radio and TV reports were correct regarding estimated amount of radioactive nuclear material detonated in the city center, it could be 40 or more years before the city center is inhabitable. We're sending reporters to the scene as quickly as possible to assess the

(continued on page 4)

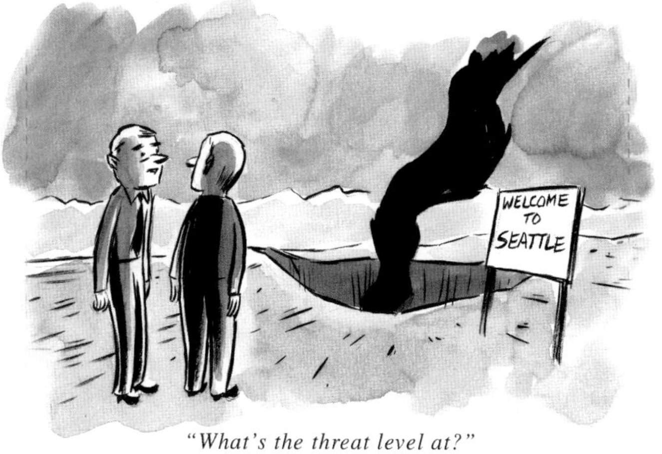

WELCOME TO SEATTLE

"What's the threat level at?"

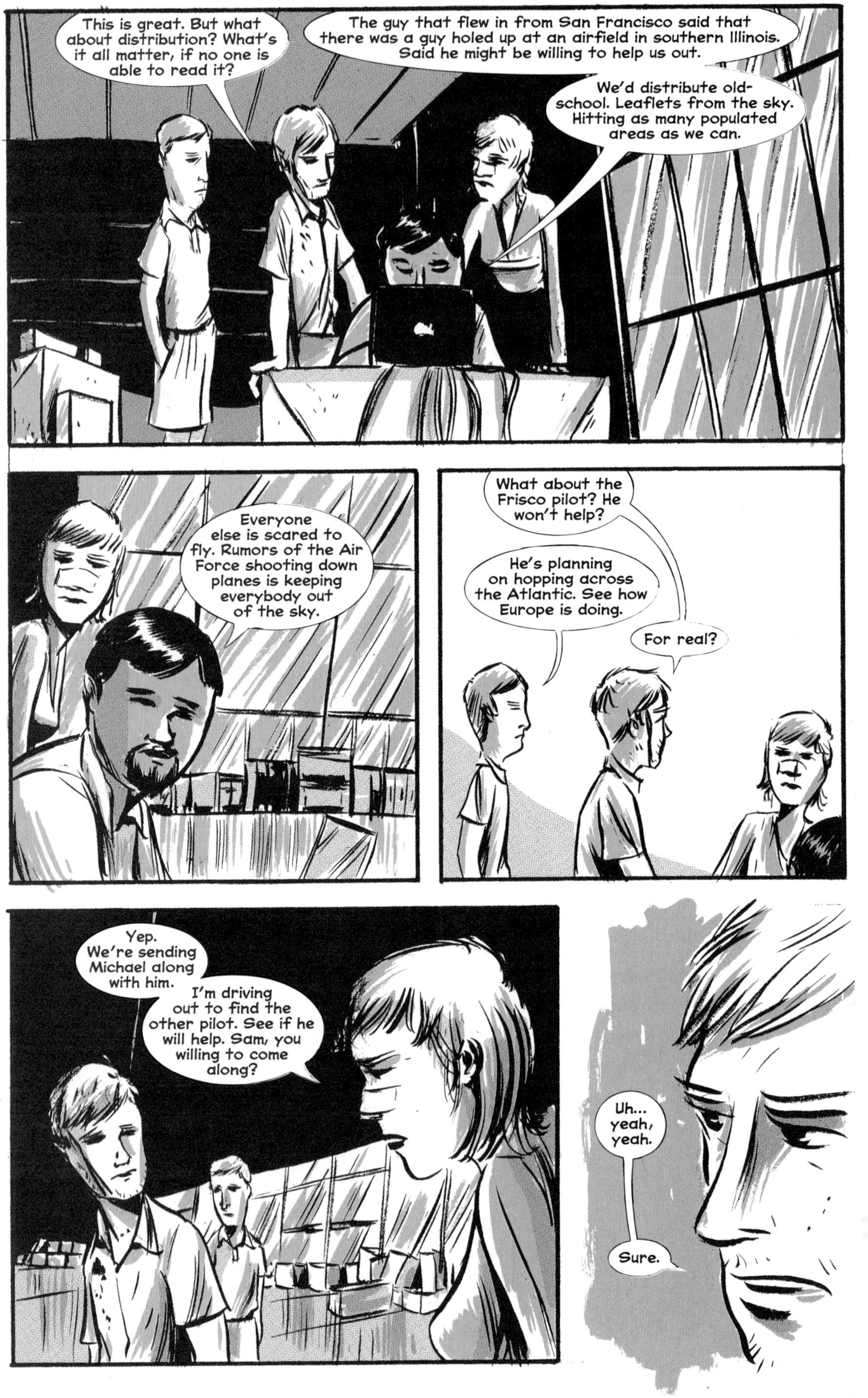
This is great. But what about distribution? What's it all matter, if no one is able to read it?
The guy that flew in from San Francisco said that there was a guy holed up at an airfield in southern Illinois. Said he might be willing to help us out.
We'd distribute old-school. Leaflets from the sky. Hitting as many populated areas as we can.
Everyone else is scared to fly. Rumors of the Air Force shooting down planes is keeping everybody out of the sky.
What about the Frisco pilot? He won't help?
He's planning on hopping across the Atlantic. See how Europe is doing.
For real?
Yep. We're sending Michael along with him.
I'm driving out to find the other pilot. See if he will help. Sam, you willing to come along?
Uh... yeah, yeah.
Sure.

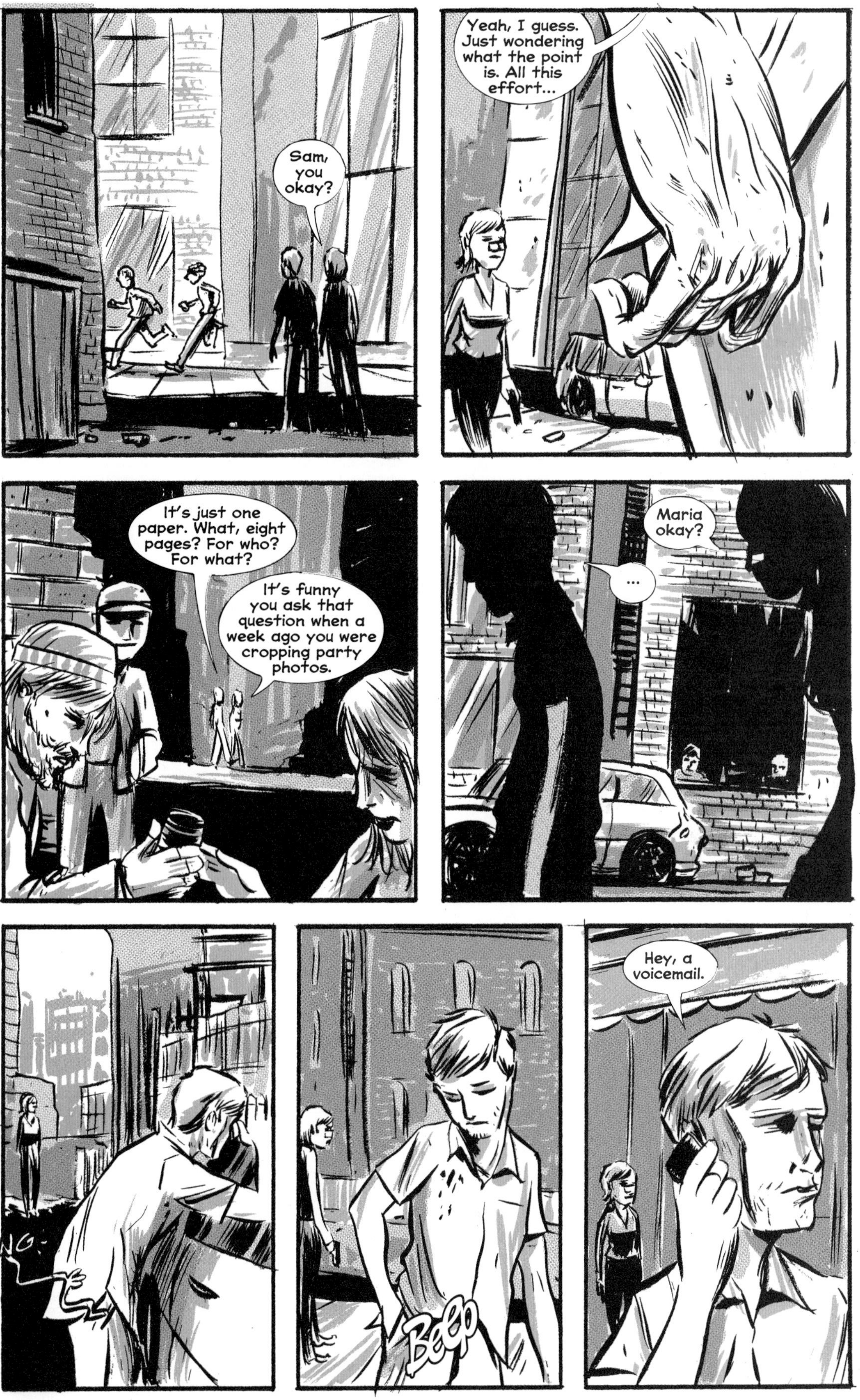
Sam, you okay?
Yeah, I guess. Just wondering what the point is. All this effort...
It's just one paper. What, eight pages? For who? For what?
It's funny you ask that question when a week ago you were cropping party photos.
Maria okay?
...
BEEP
Hey, a voicemail.

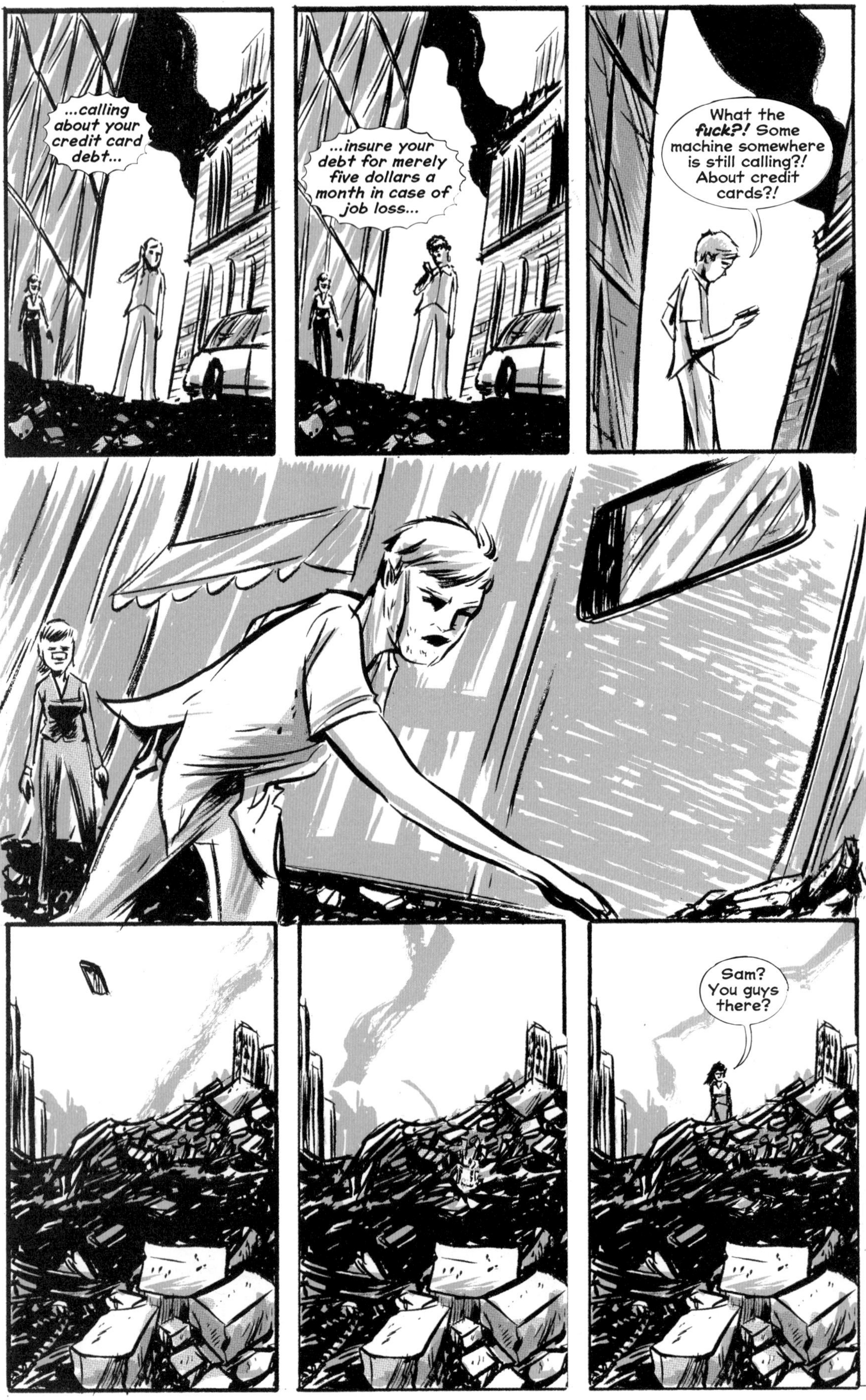
...calling about your credit card debt...
...insure your debt for merely five dollars a month in case of job loss...
What the *fuck?!* Some machine somewhere is still calling?! About credit cards?!
Sam? You guys there?

LITTLE STATISTICAL EVIDENCE. BUT EXPERTS BELIEVE THAT THERE HAVE BEEN OVER **95**,000 SUICIDES NATIONWIDE. THIS DOES N

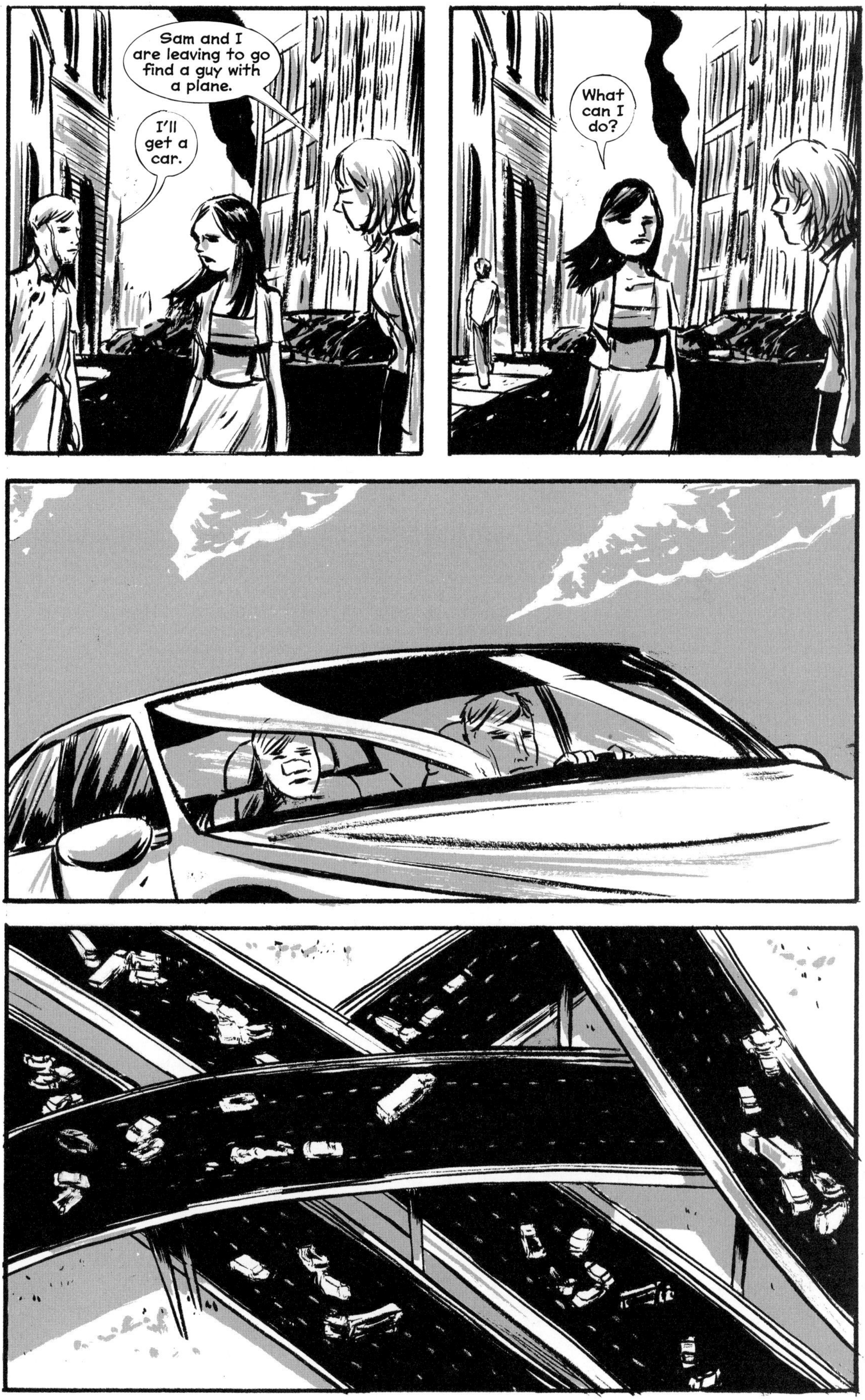
Sam and I are leaving to go find a guy with a plane.
I'll get a car.
What can I do?

URGING WOMEN NOT TO TRAVEL ALONE. IN THE PAST 24 HOURS THERE HAVE BEEN **96** REPORTS OF RAPE OR ATTEMPTED RAP

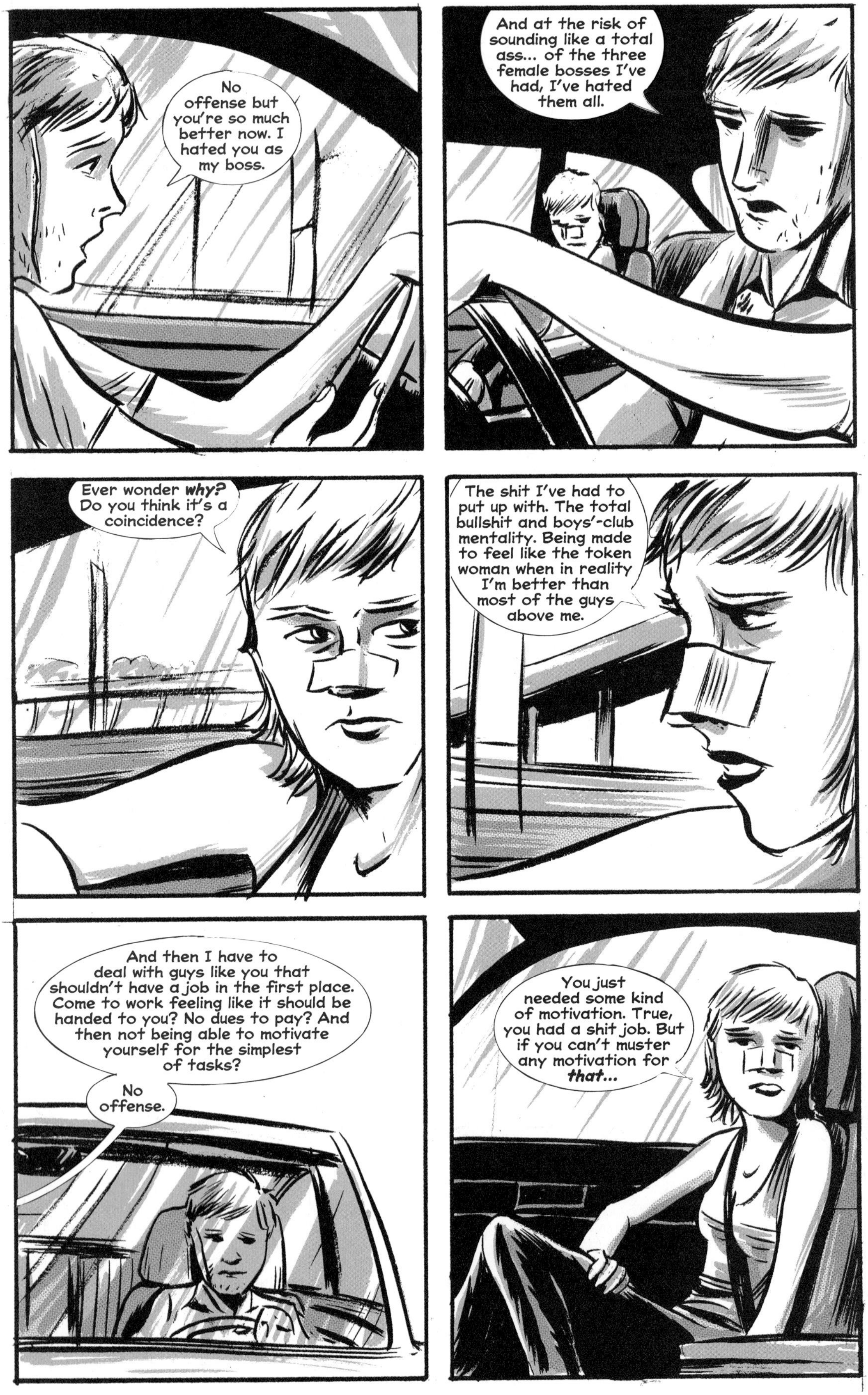
No offense but you're so much better now. I hated you as my boss.
And at the risk of sounding like a total ass... of the three female bosses I've had, I've hated them all.
Ever wonder *why?* Do you think it's a coincidence?
The shit I've had to put up with. The total bullshit and boys'-club mentality. Being made to feel like the token woman when in reality I'm better than most of the guys above me.
And then I have to deal with guys like you that shouldn't have a job in the first place. Come to work feeling like it should be handed to you? No dues to pay? And then not being able to motivate yourself for the simplest of tasks?
No offense.
You just needed some kind of motivation. True, you had a shit job. But if you can't muster any motivation for *that...*

NG THAT WHILE GAS SKYROCKETED THE POWER OF CURRENCY HAS FALLEN. WHILE A $**97** GALLON OF GAS SEEMS RIDICULOUS,

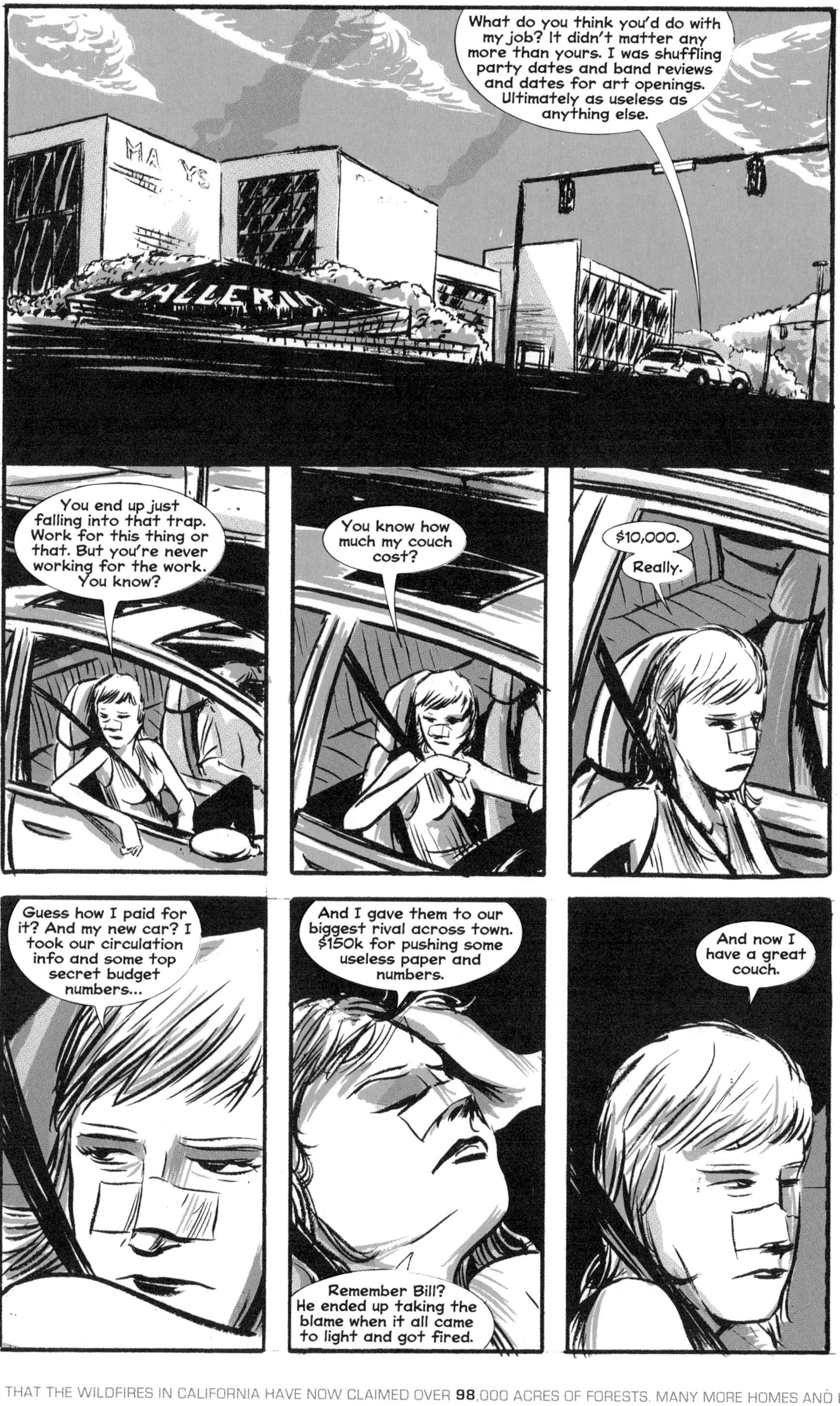
What do you think you'd do with my job? It didn't matter any more than yours. I was shuffling party dates and band reviews and dates for art openings. Ultimately as useless as anything else.
You end up just falling into that trap. Work for this thing or that. But you're never working for the work. You know?
You know how much my couch cost?
$10,000.
Really.
Guess how I paid for it? And my new car? I took our circulation info and some top secret budget numbers...
And I gave them to our biggest rival across town. $150k for pushing some useless paper and numbers.
Remember Bill? He ended up taking the blame when it all came to light and got fired.
And now I have a great couch.

G THAT THE WILDFIRES IN CALIFORNIA HAVE NOW CLAIMED OVER **98**,000 ACRES OF FORESTS. MANY MORE HOMES AND LIVES

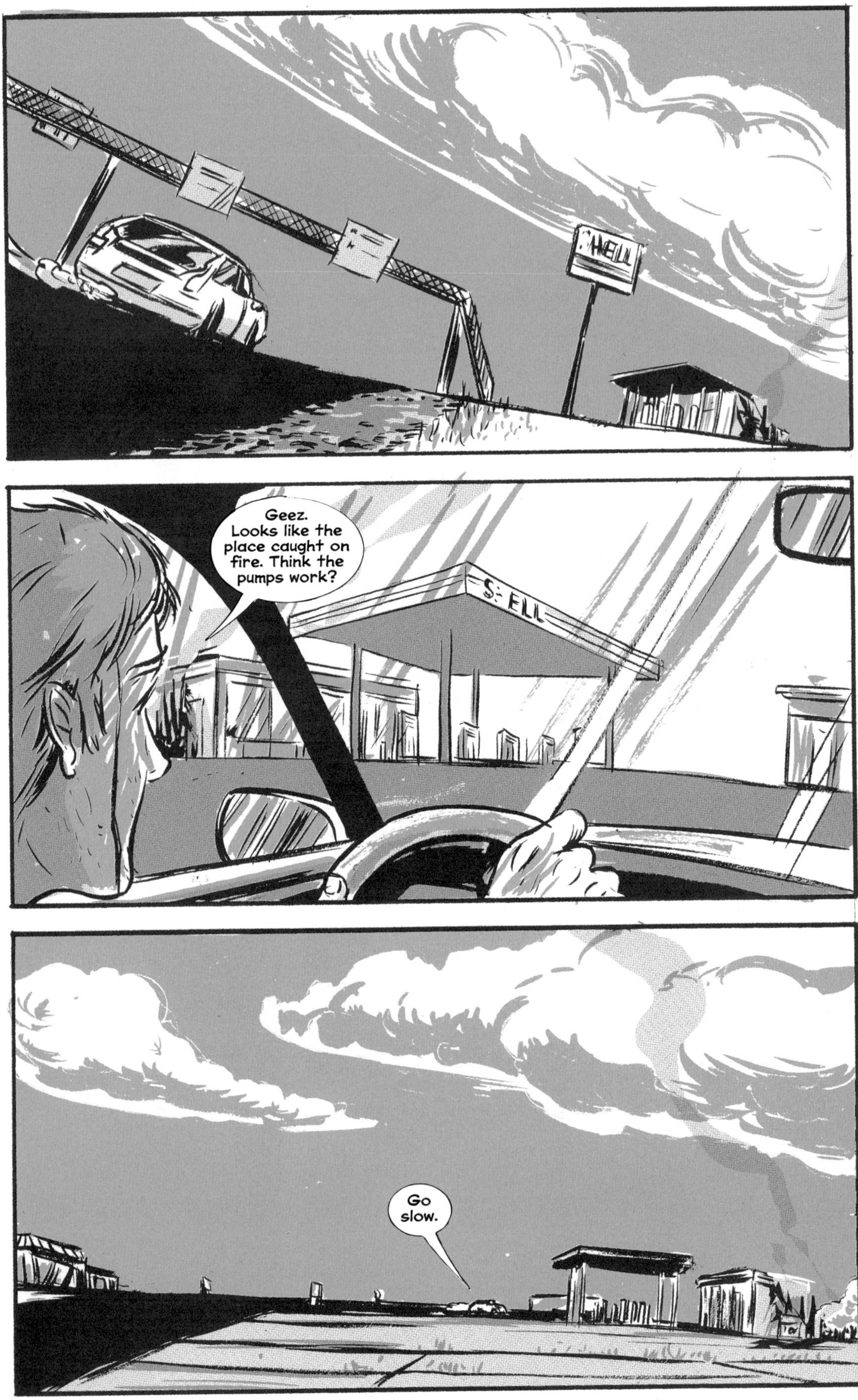
Geez. Looks like the place caught on fire. Think the pumps work?
Go slow.

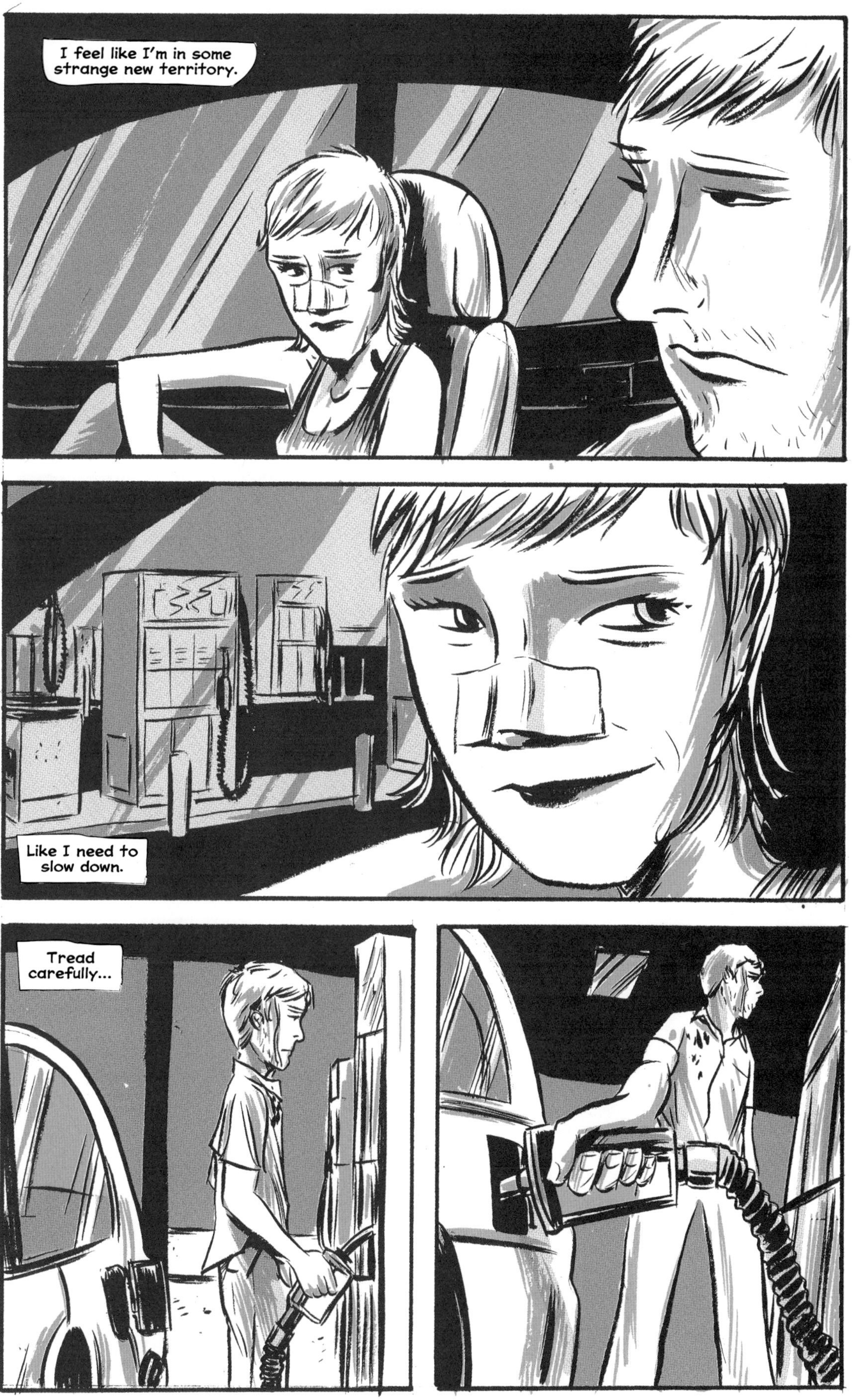
I feel like I'm in some strange new territory.
Like I need to slow down.
Tread carefully...

ACKS OF WILD DOGS. EXPERTS ARE SAYING THE CATASTROPHE HAS CLAIMED MORE LIVES THIS **CENTURY** THAN IN ANY OTHER

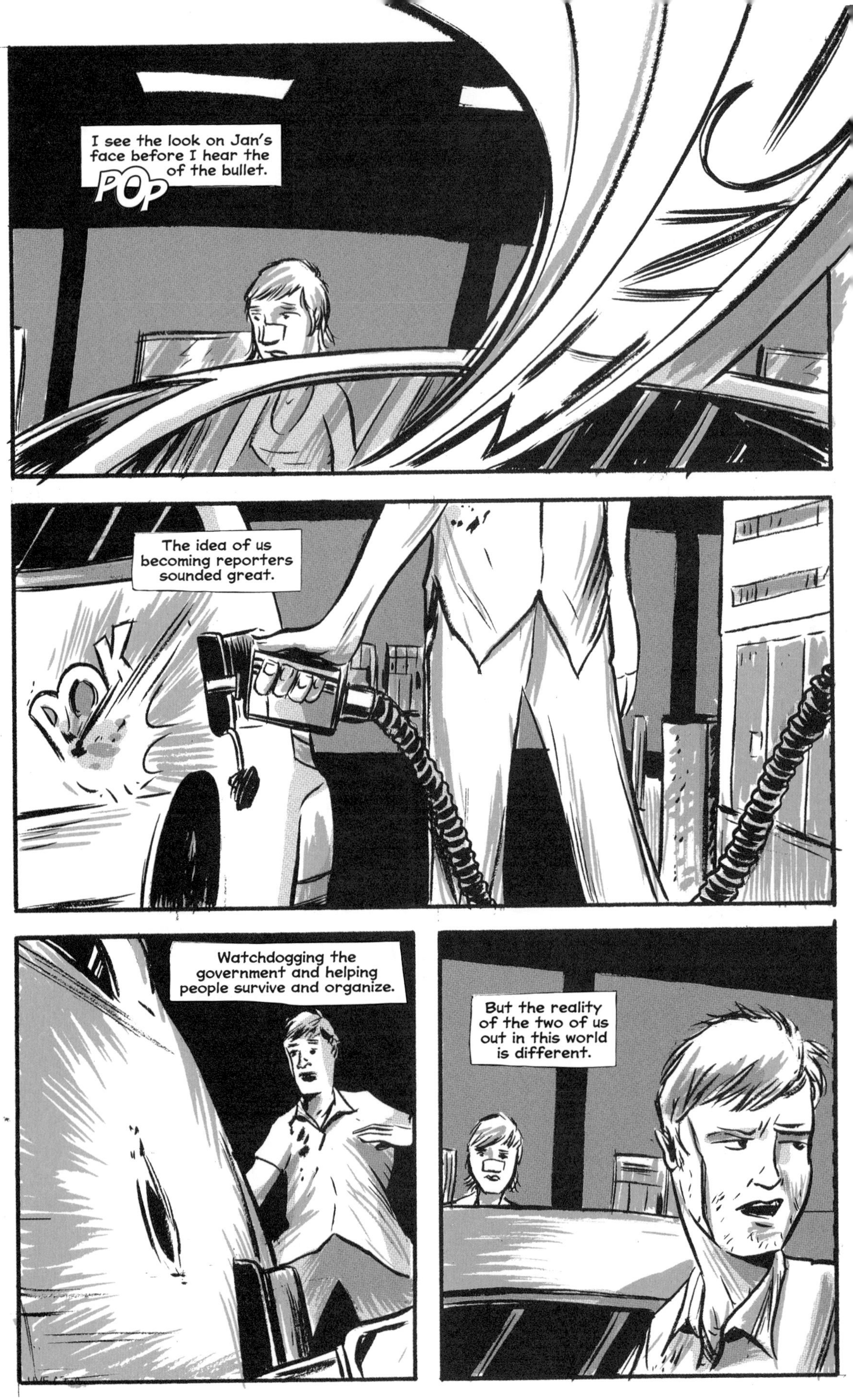
I see the look on Jan's face before I hear the
POP
of the bullet.
The idea of us becoming reporters sounded great.
BOOK
Watchdogging the government and helping people survive and organize.
But the reality of the two of us out in this world is different.

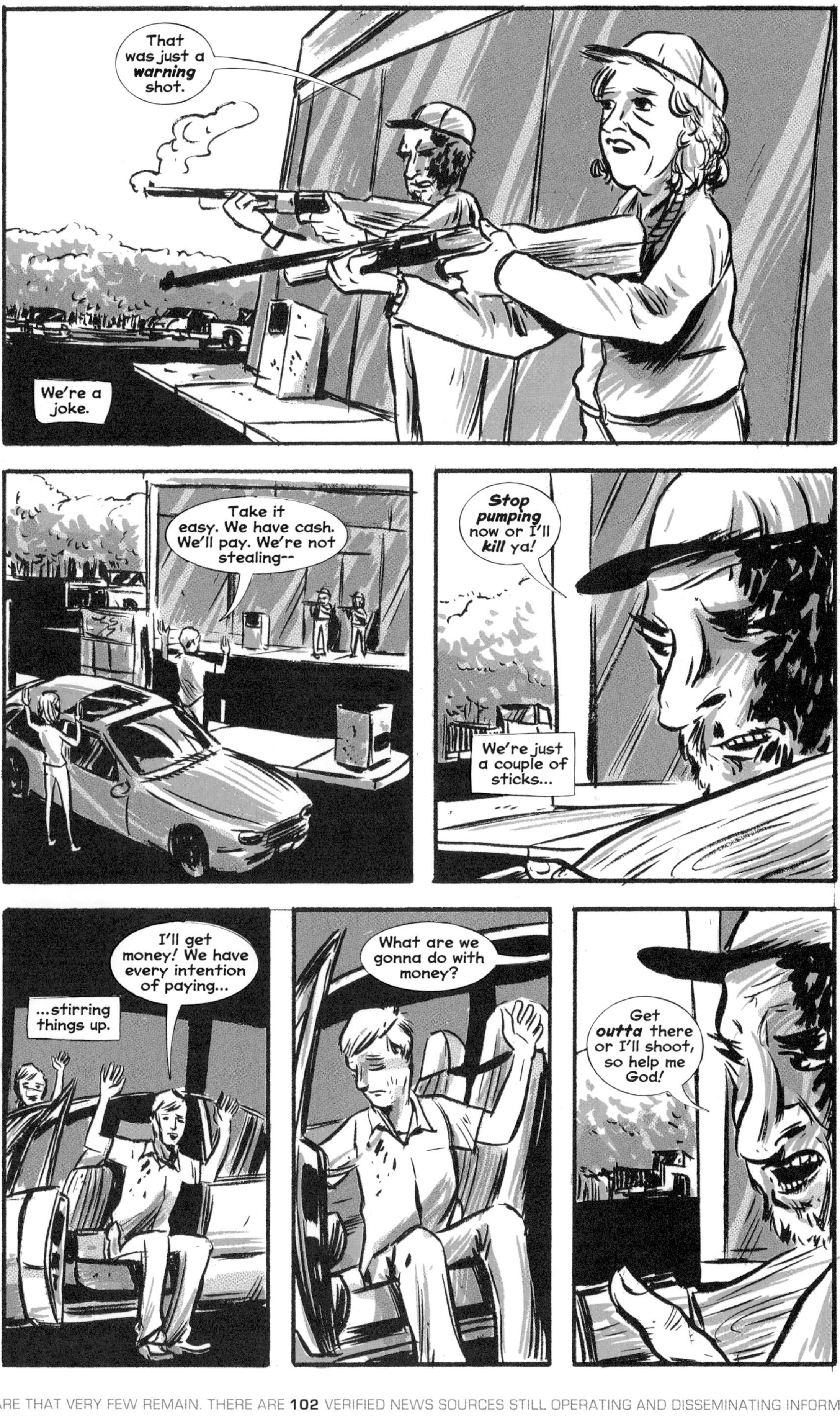

That was just a *warning* shot.
We're a joke.
Take it easy. We have cash. We'll pay. We're not stealing--
Stop pumping now or I'll *kill* ya!
We're just a couple of sticks...
...stirring things up.
I'll get money! We have every intention of paying...
What are we gonna do with money?
Get *outta* there or I'll shoot, so help me God!

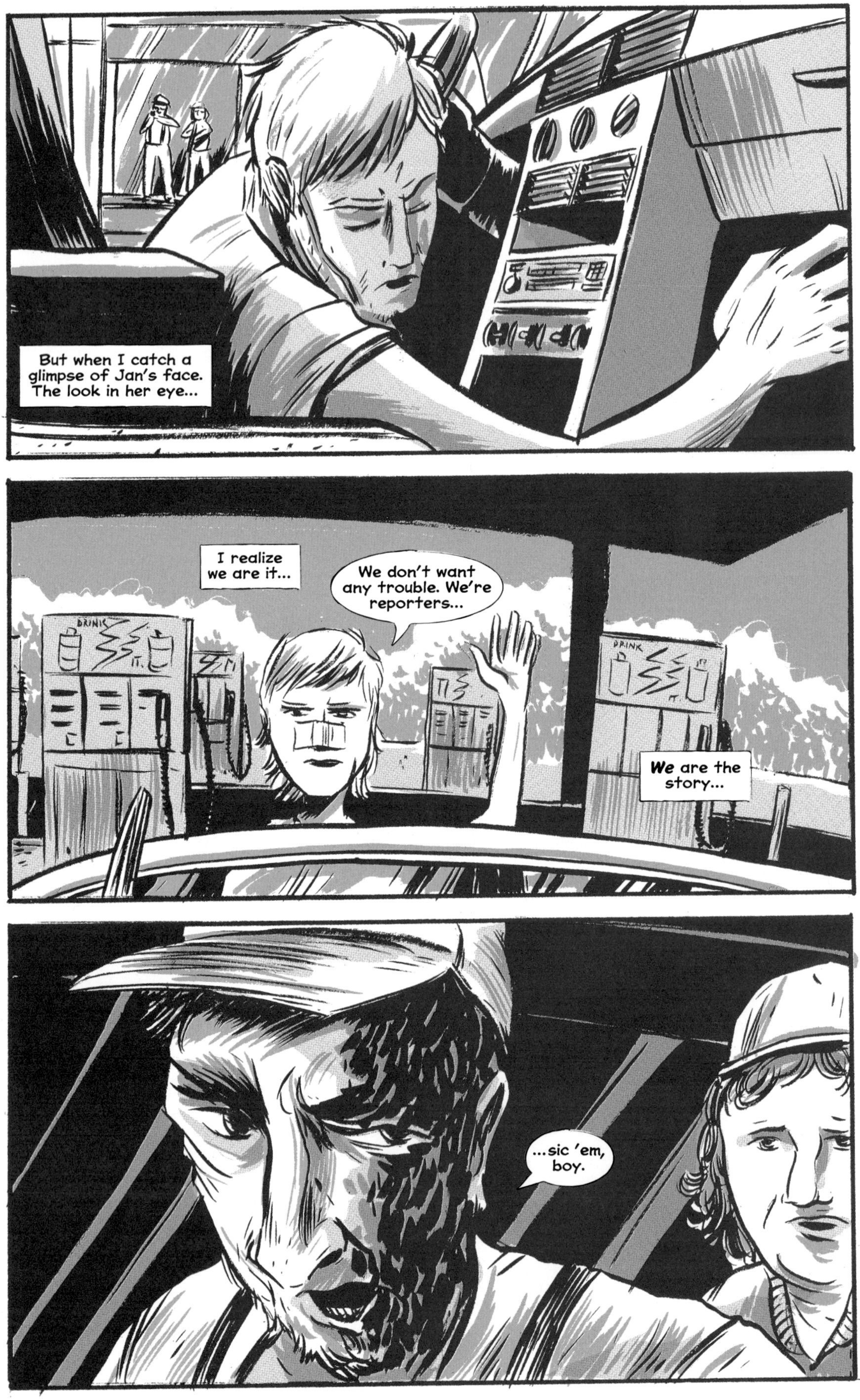
But when I catch a glimpse of Jan's face. The look in her eye...
I realize we are it...
We don't want any trouble. We're reporters...
DRINK
We are the story...
...sic 'em, boy.

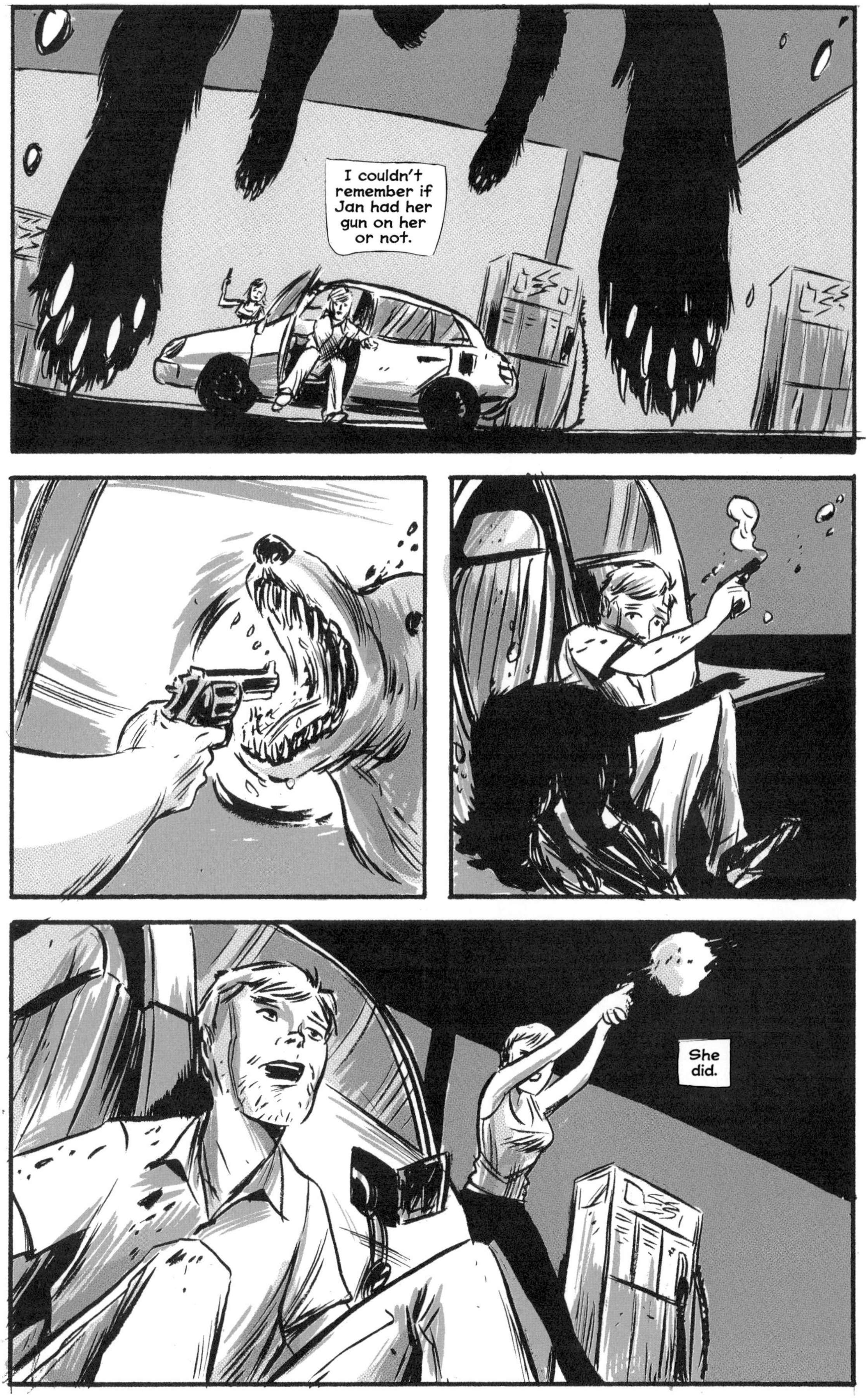
I couldn't remember if Jan had her gun on her or not.
She did.

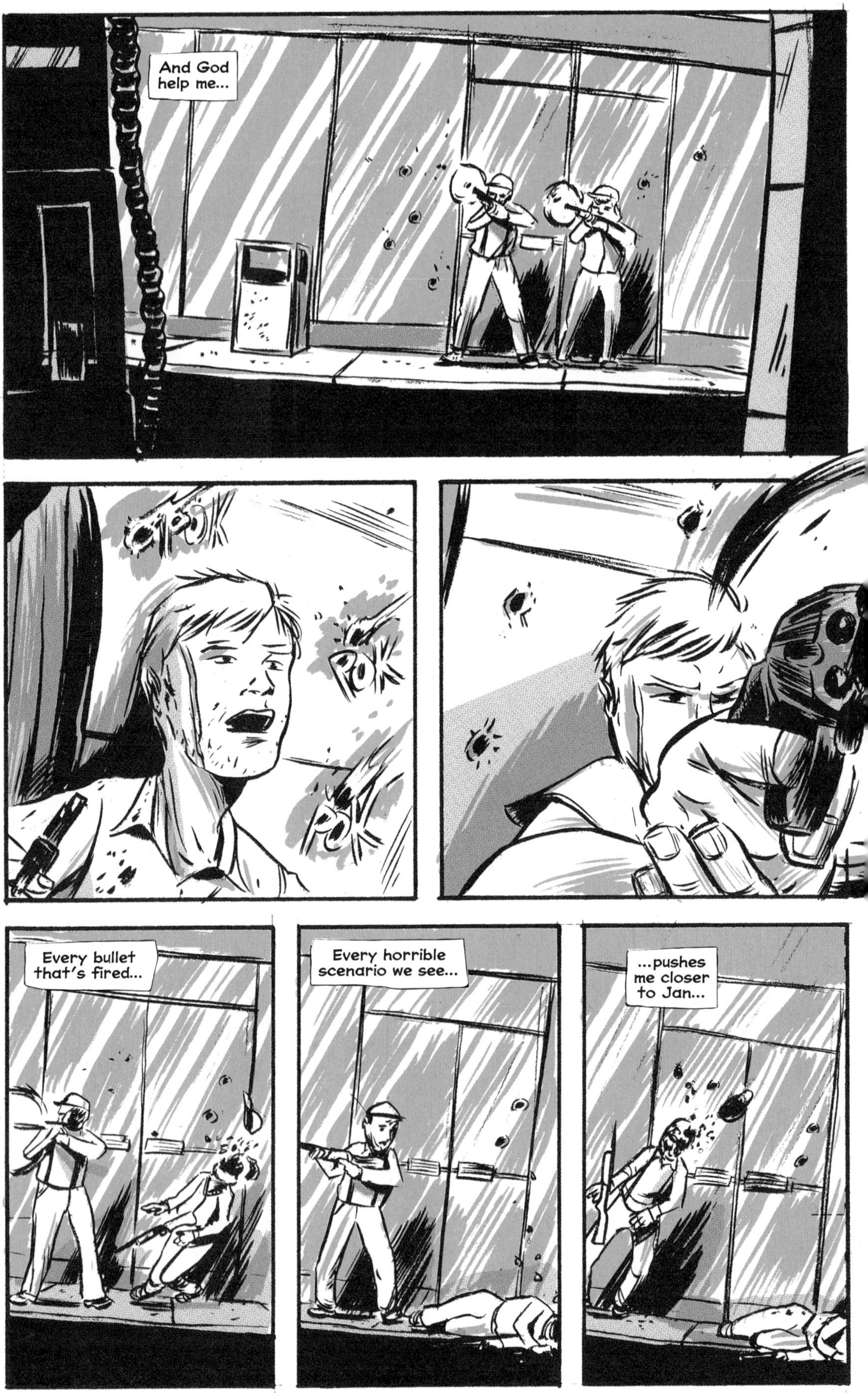
And God help me...
POK
POK
Every bullet that's fired...
Every horrible scenario we see...
...pushes me closer to Jan...

ISING THAT AS TIME PASSES. FOOD WITH A DATE EARLIER THAN **10/5** SHOULD BE AVOIDED. ALTHOUGH CANNED GOODS ARE US

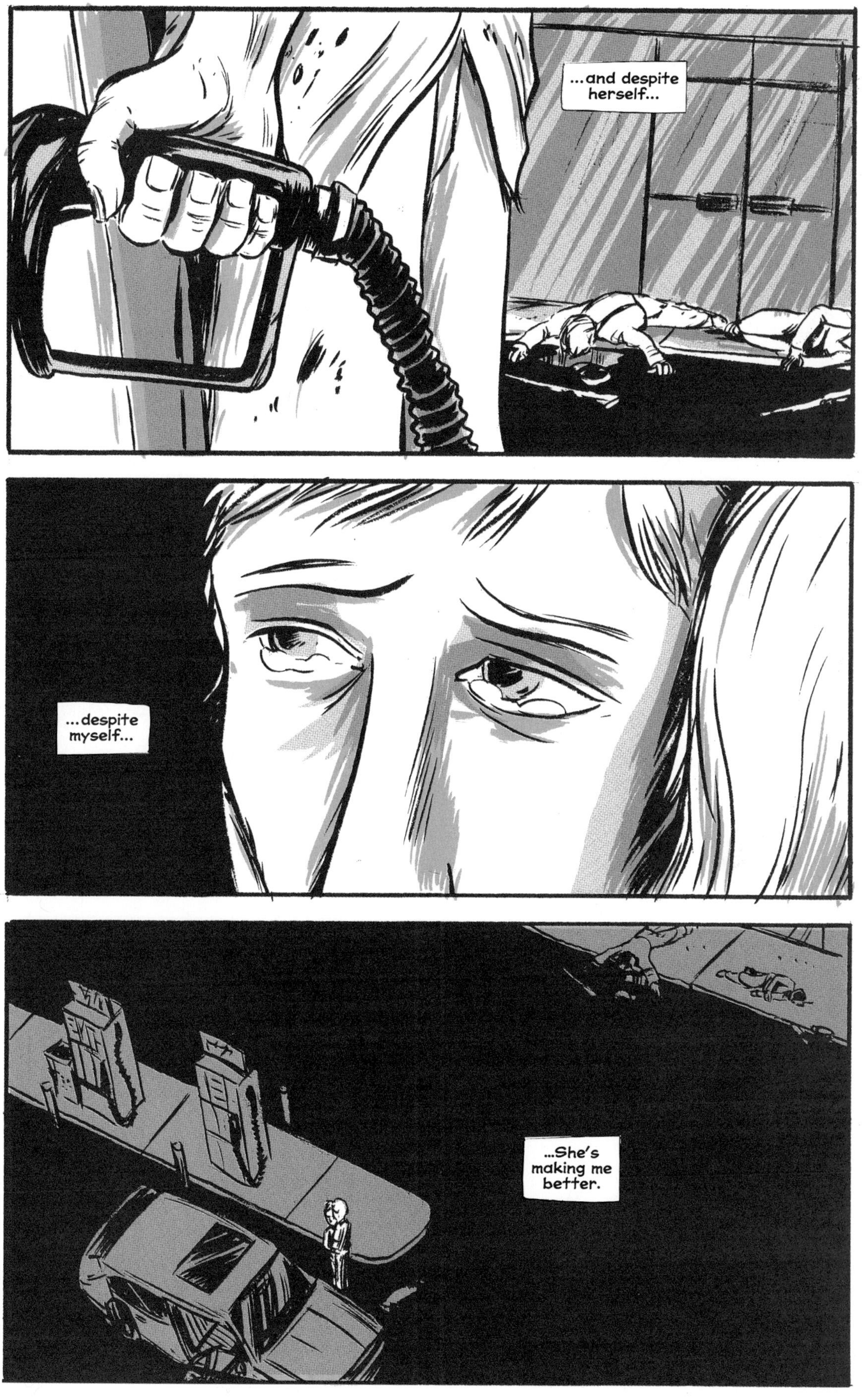
...and despite herself...
...despite myself...
...She's making me better.

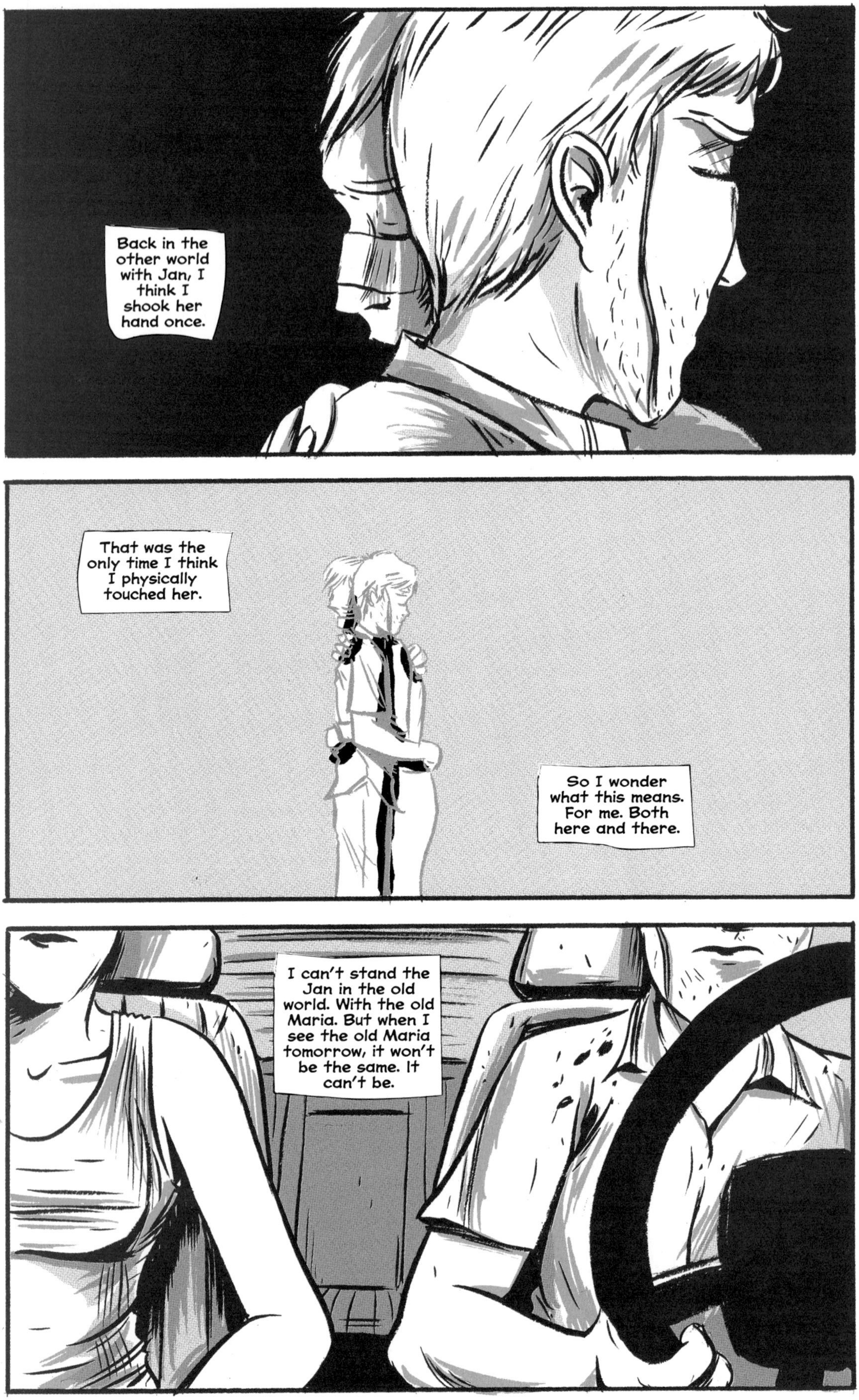
Back in the other world with Jan, I think I shook her hand once.
That was the only time I think I physically touched her.
So I wonder what this means. For me. Both here and there.
I can't stand the Jan in the old world. With the old Maria. But when I see the old Maria tomorrow, it won't be the same. It can't be.

EPORTING SHORTAGES OF FUEL SUPPLIES. OVER **107**,000 GALLONS OF FUEL HAVE GONE MISSING. ALTERNATIVE FUEL SOURCES

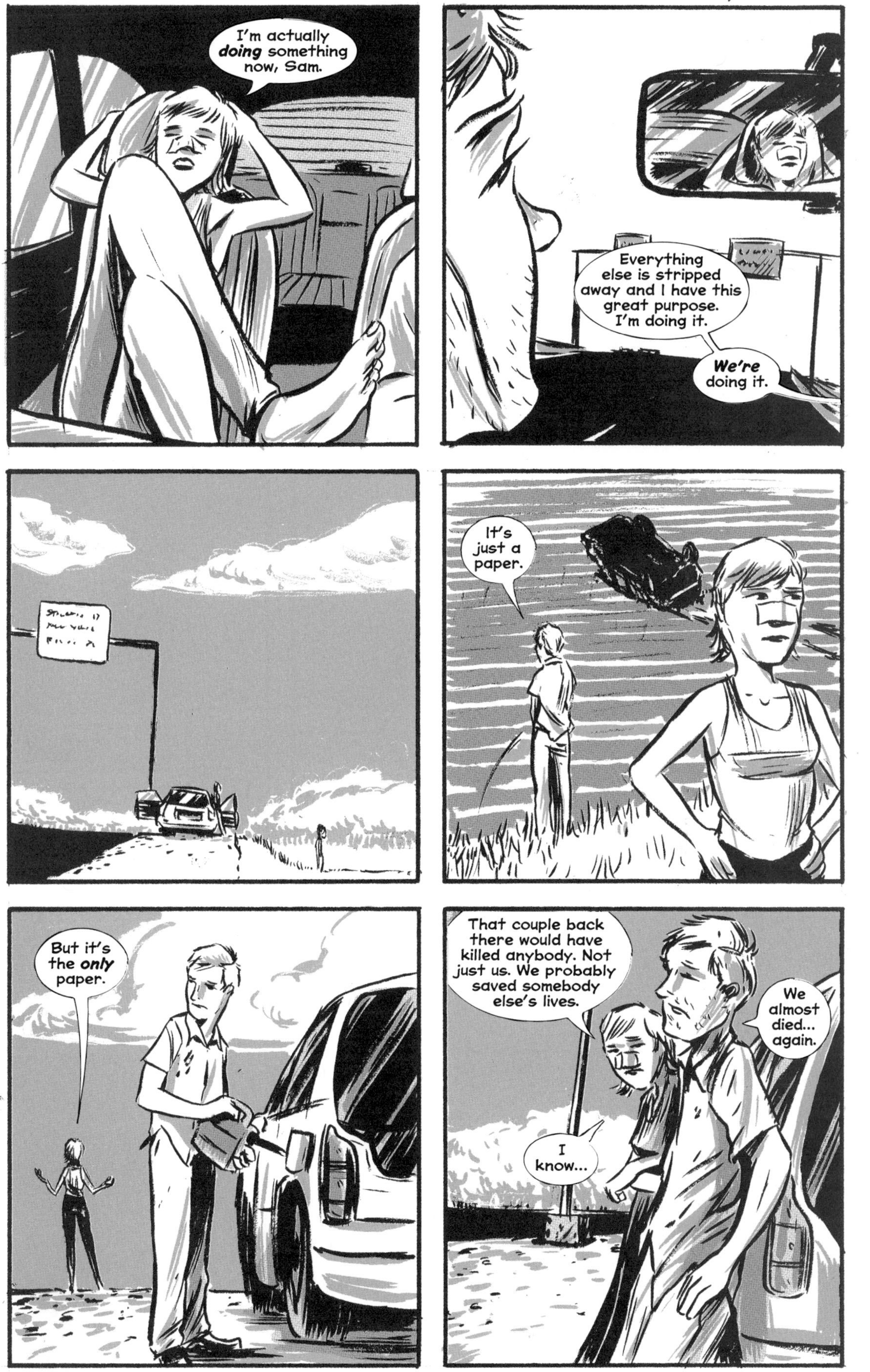
I'm actually *doing* something now, Sam.
Everything else is stripped away and I have this great purpose. I'm doing it.
We're doing it.
It's just a paper.
But it's the *only* paper.
That couple back there would have killed anybody. Not just us. We probably saved somebody else's lives.
We almost died... again.
I know...

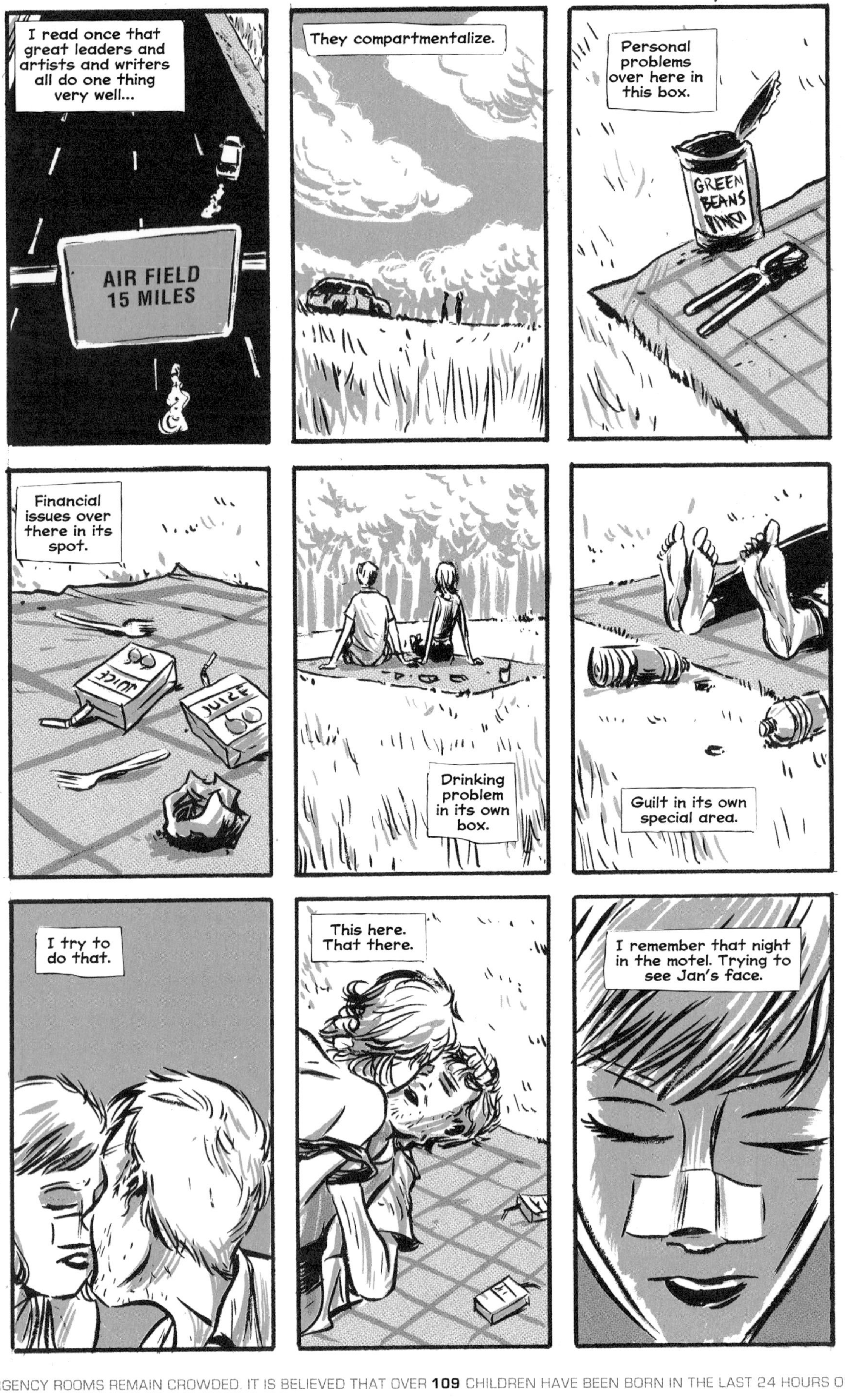
I read once that great leaders and artists and writers all do one thing very well...
AIR FIELD 15 MILES
They compartmentalize.
Personal problems over here in this box.
GREEN BEANS
Financial issues over there in its spot.
JUICE
JUICE
Drinking problem in its own box.
Guilt in its own special area.
I try to do that.
This here. That there.
I remember that night in the motel. Trying to see Jan's face.

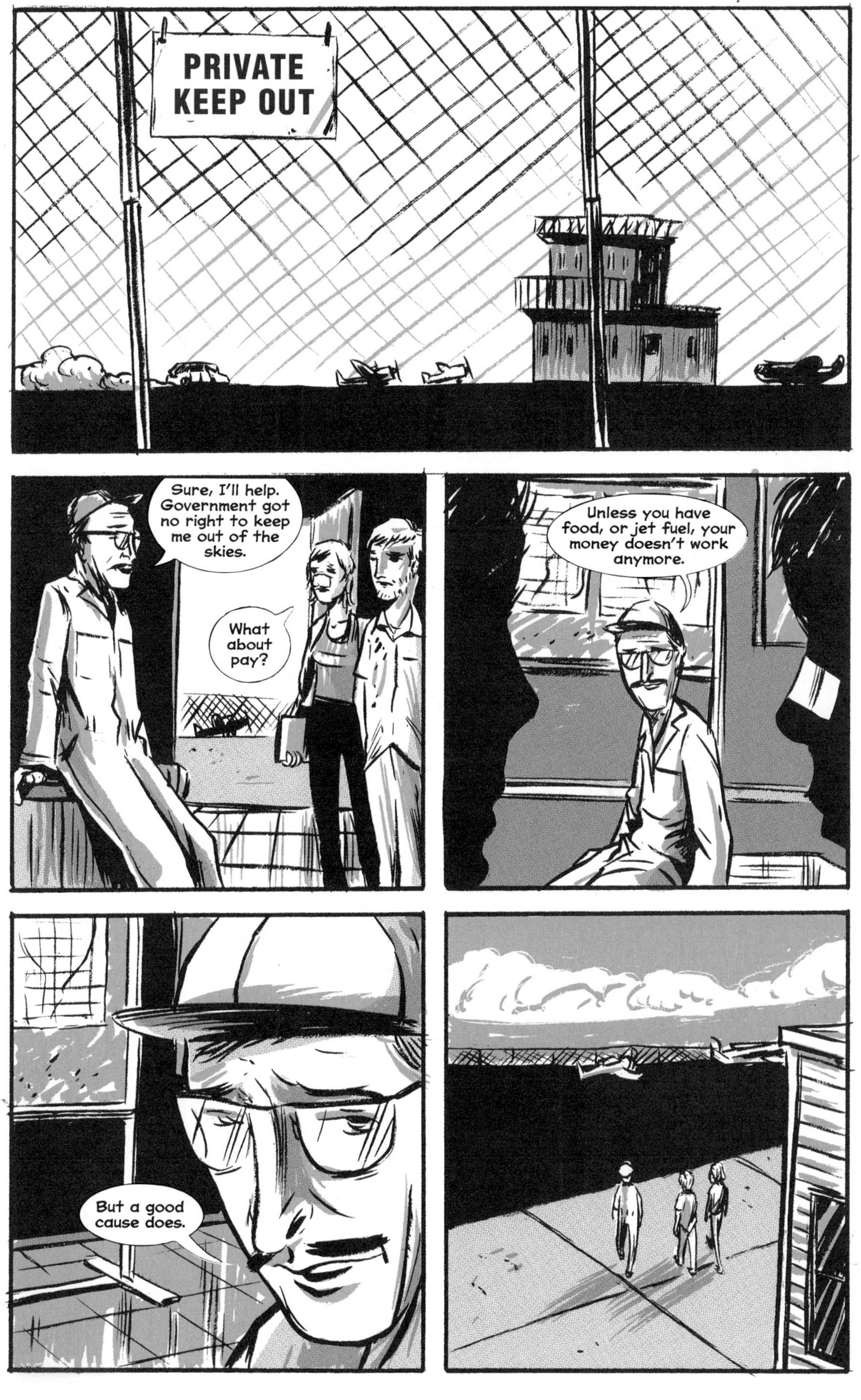
PRIVATE
KEEP OUT
Sure, I'll help. Government got no right to keep me out of the skies.
What about pay?
Unless you have food, or jet fuel, your money doesn't work anymore.
But a good cause does.

TS REMAIN RESTRICTED, THE **110**TH AIRBORNE DIVISION – A SPECIALTY TASK FORCE SET UP FOR INVASION SCENARIOS -- HAS BE

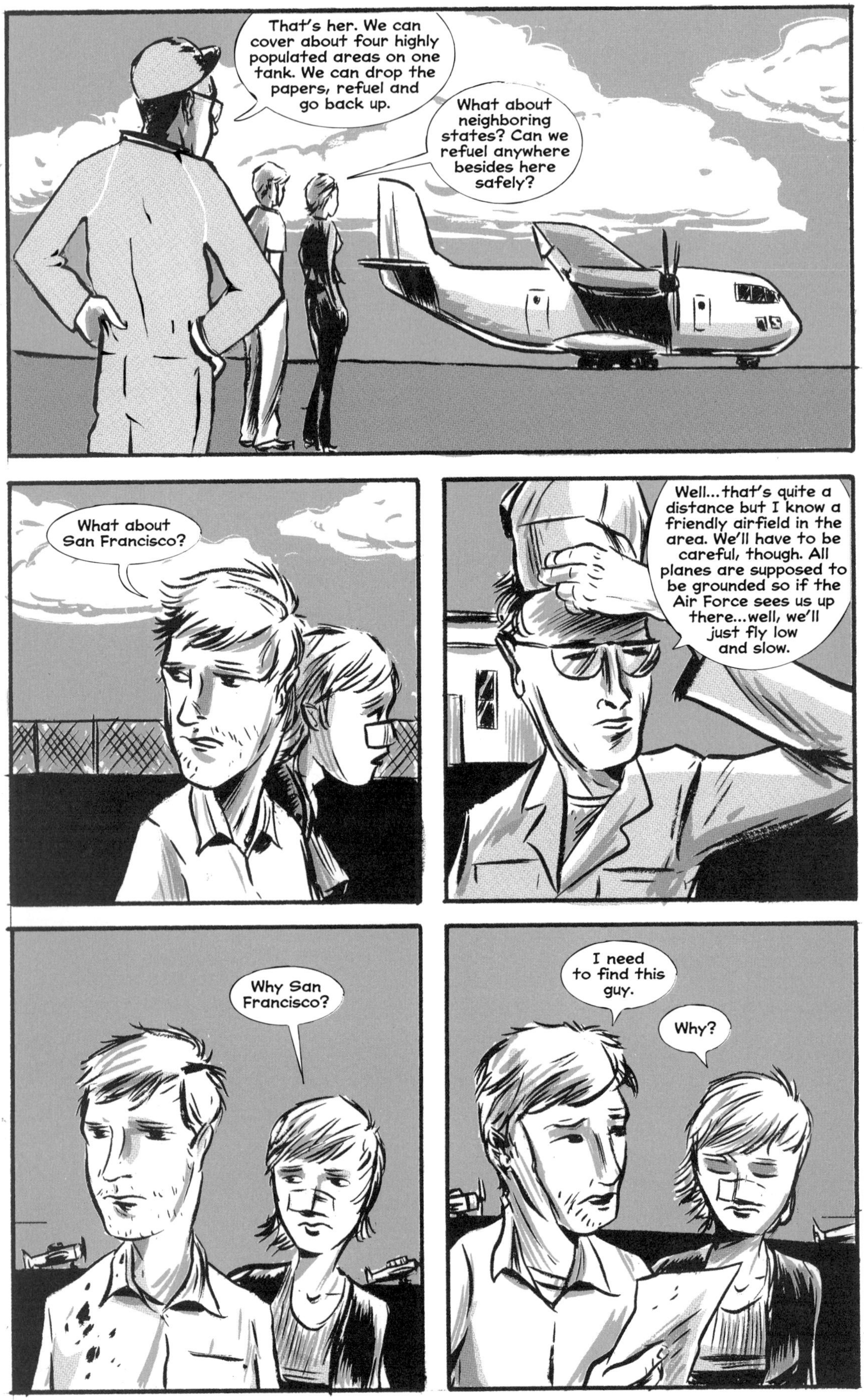
That's her. We can cover about four highly populated areas on one tank. We can drop the papers, refuel and go back up.
What about neighboring states? Can we refuel anywhere besides here safely?
What about San Francisco?
Well...that's quite a distance but I know a friendly airfield in the area. We'll have to be careful, though. All planes are supposed to be grounded so if the Air Force sees us up there...well, we'll just fly low and slow.
Why San Francisco?
I need to find this guy.
Why?

TERRORIST CZAR RUDY MONTGOMERY III IS CHASING P.K. VERVE. HE'S BEEN QUOTED AS SAYING "I'LL BE INSTRUMENTAL IN TUR

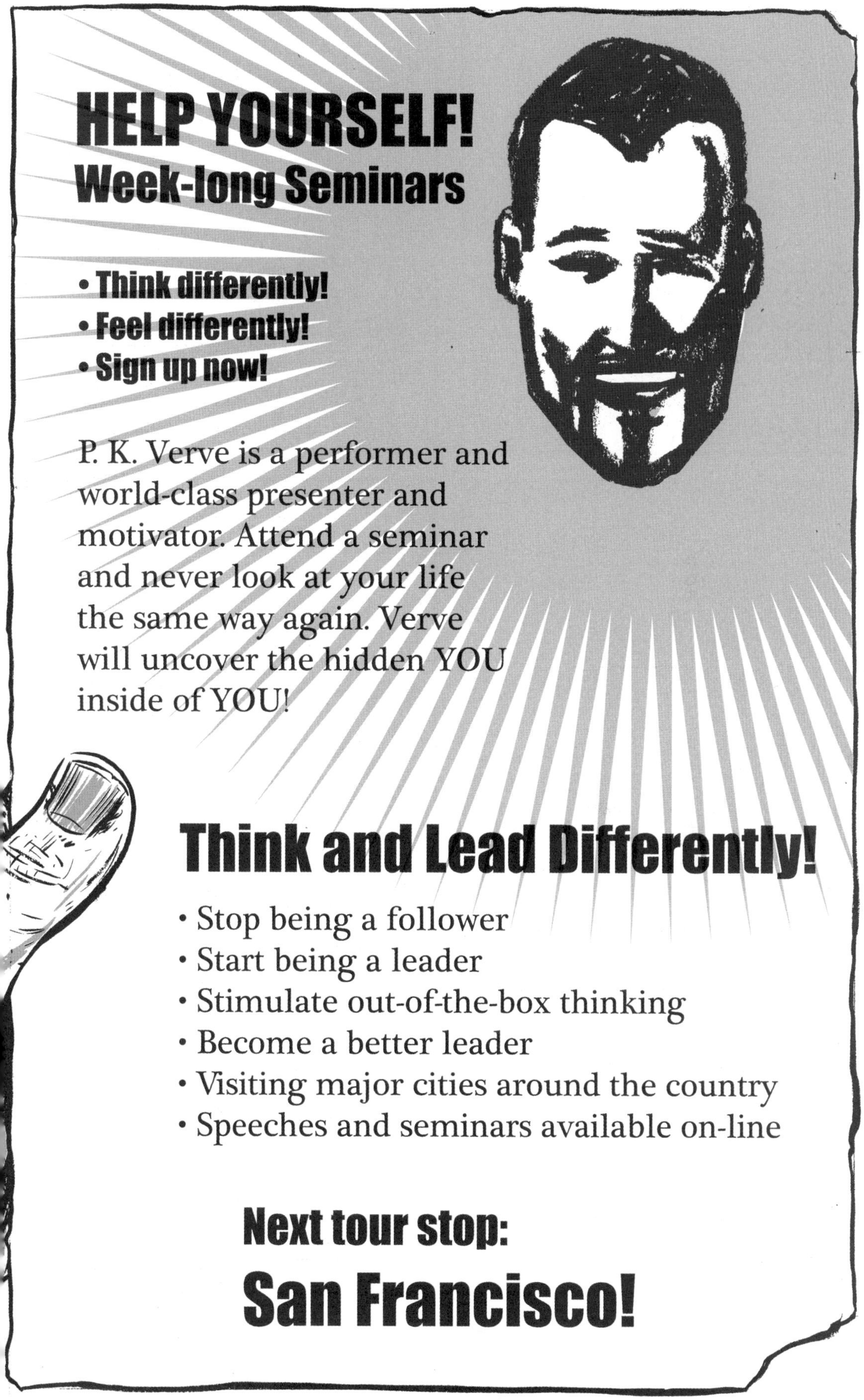
HELP YOURSELF!
Week-long Seminars
• Think differently!
• Feel differently!
• Sign up now!
P. K. Verve is a performer and world-class presenter and motivator. Attend a seminar and never look at your life the same way again. Verve will uncover the hidden YOU inside of YOU!
Think and Lead Differently!
• Stop being a follower
• Start being a leader
• Stimulate out-of-the-box thinking
• Become a better leader
• Visiting major cities around the country
• Speeches and seminars available on-line
Next tour stop:
San Francisco!

'S COMING IN THAT SAN FRANCISCO HAS CLAIMED INDEPENDENCE. IT IS ONE OF **112** CITIES TO DATE THAT HAVE REJECTED THE

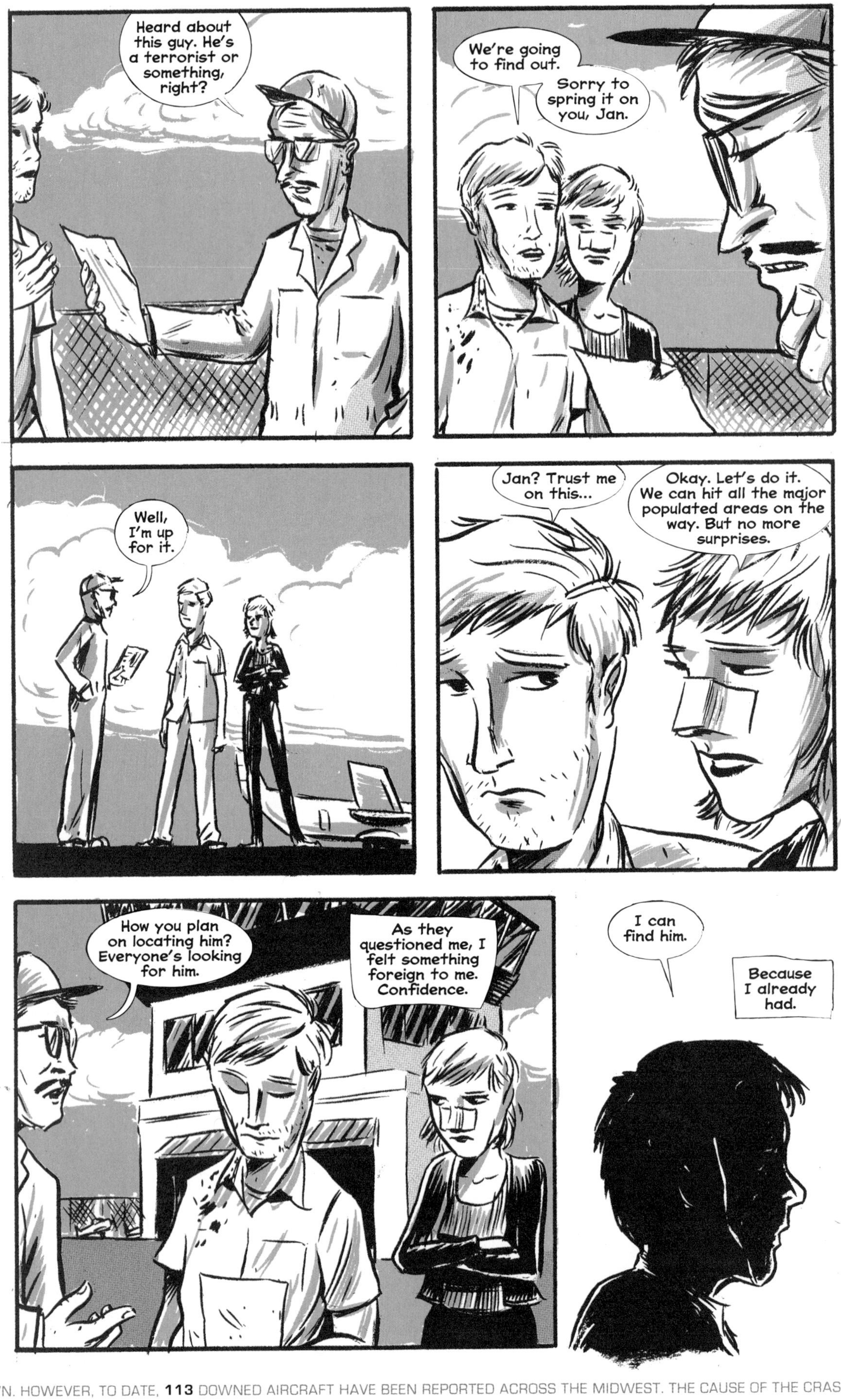
Heard about this guy. He's a terrorist or something, right?
We're going to find out.
Sorry to spring it on you, Jan.
Well, I'm up for it.
Jan? Trust me on this...
Okay. Let's do it. We can hit all the major populated areas on the way. But no more surprises.
How you plan on locating him? Everyone's looking for him.
As they questioned me, I felt something foreign to me. Confidence.
I can find him.
Because I already had.

NOWN. HOWEVER, TO DATE, **113** DOWNED AIRCRAFT HAVE BEEN REPORTED ACROSS THE MIDWEST. THE CAUSE OF THE CRASHE

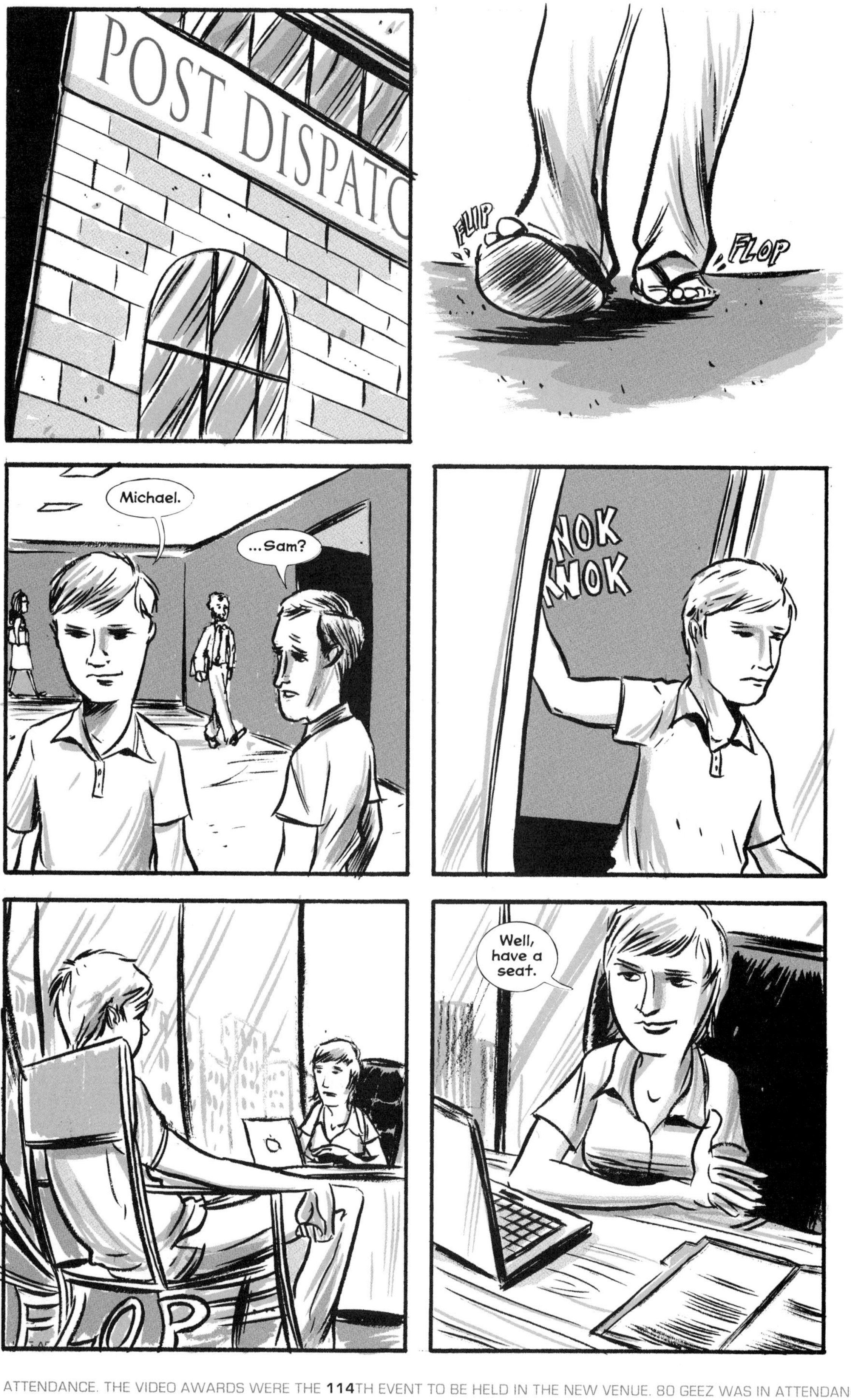
POST DISPATC
FLIP
FLOP
Michael.
...Sam?
NOK
NOK
FLOP
Well, have a seat.

N ATTENDANCE. THE VIDEO AWARDS WERE THE **114**TH EVENT TO BE HELD IN THE NEW VENUE. 80 GEEZ WAS IN ATTENDANCE

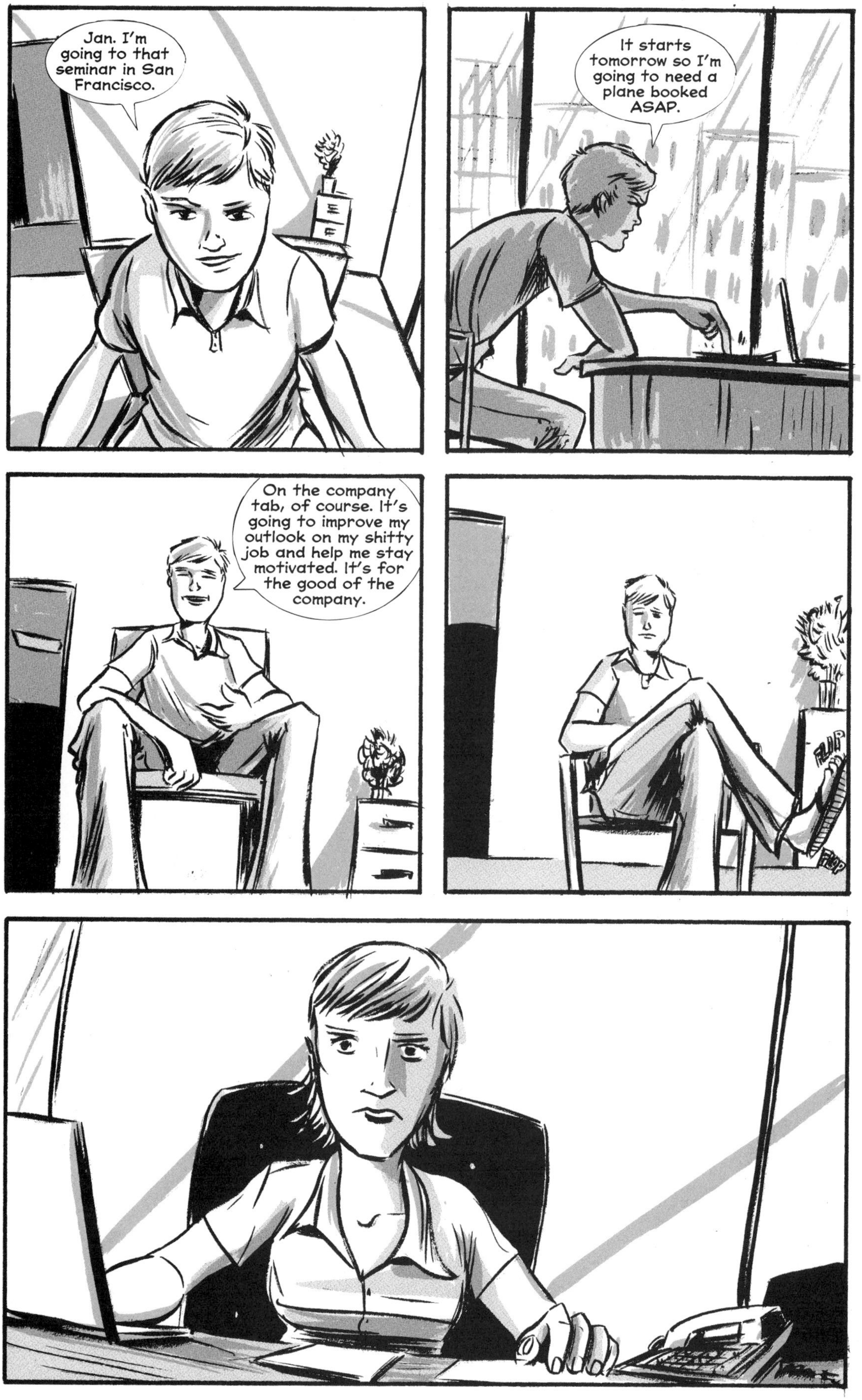
Jan. I'm going to that seminar in San Francisco.
It starts tomorrow so I'm going to need a plane booked ASAP.
On the company tab, of course. It's going to improve my outlook on my shitty job and help me stay motivated. It's for the good of the company.

LATEST OF NEARLY **116** GROUPS ON THE GOVERNMENT'S WATCH LIST. "I MISSED TV," IS WHAT MOST OF THE MEMBERS WERE

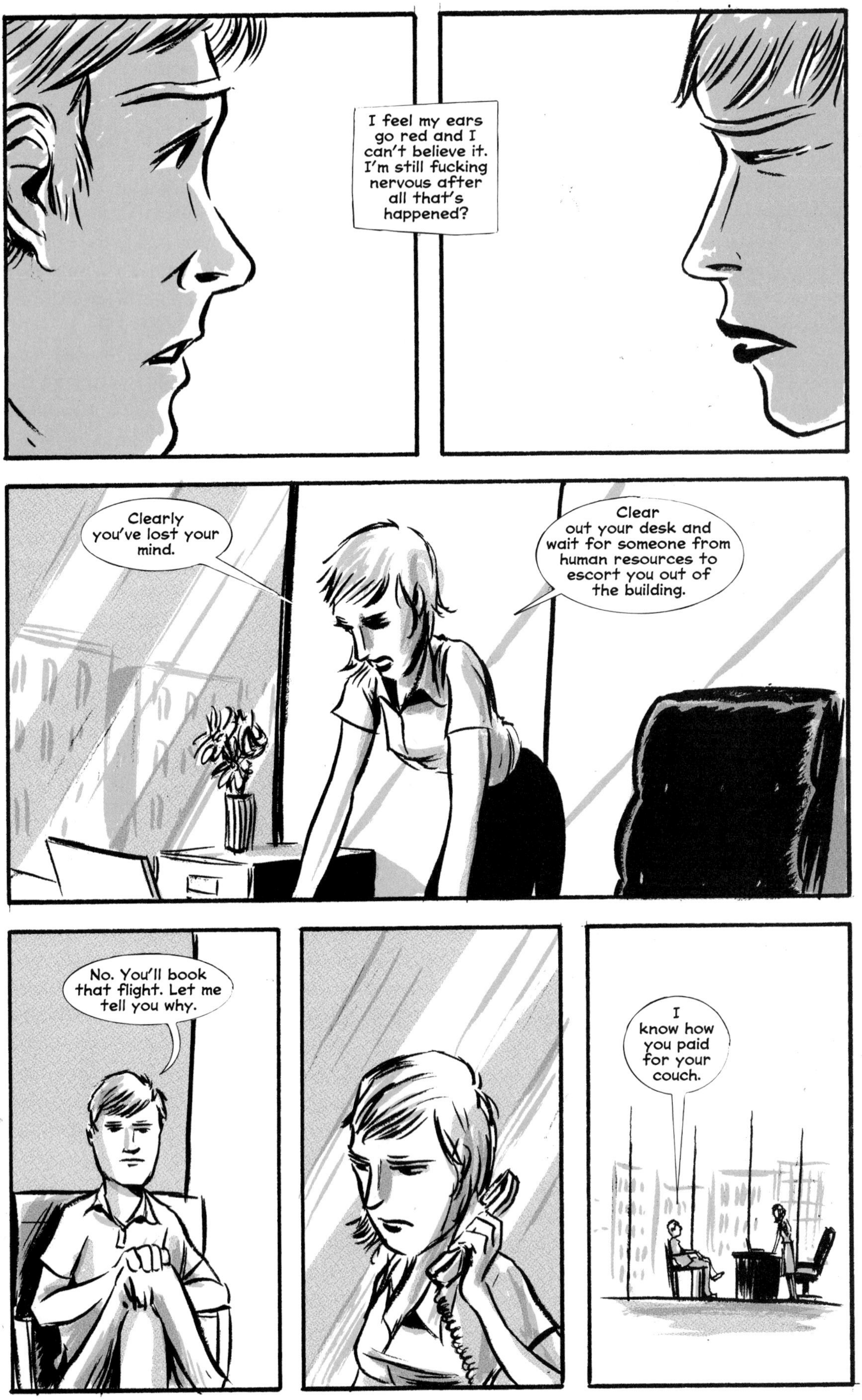
I feel my ears go red and I can't believe it. I'm still fucking nervous after all that's happened?
Clearly you've lost your mind.
Clear out your desk and wait for someone from human resources to escort you out of the building.
No. You'll book that flight. Let me tell you why.
I know how you paid for your couch.

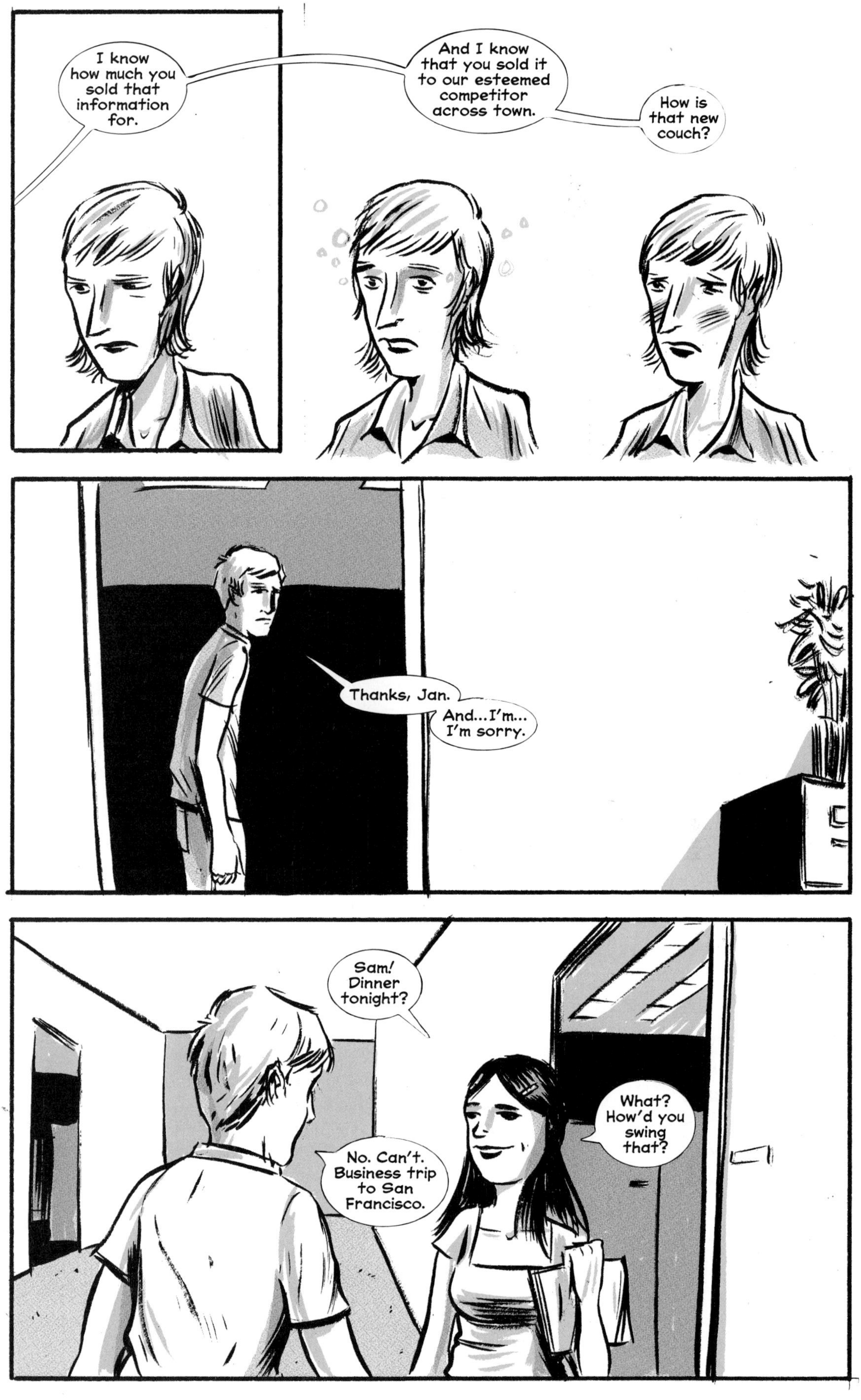
I know how much you sold that information for.
And I know that you sold it to our esteemed competitor across town.
How is that new couch?
Thanks, Jan.
And...I'm... I'm sorry.
Sam! Dinner tonight?
No. Can't. Business trip to San Francisco.
What? How'd you swing that?

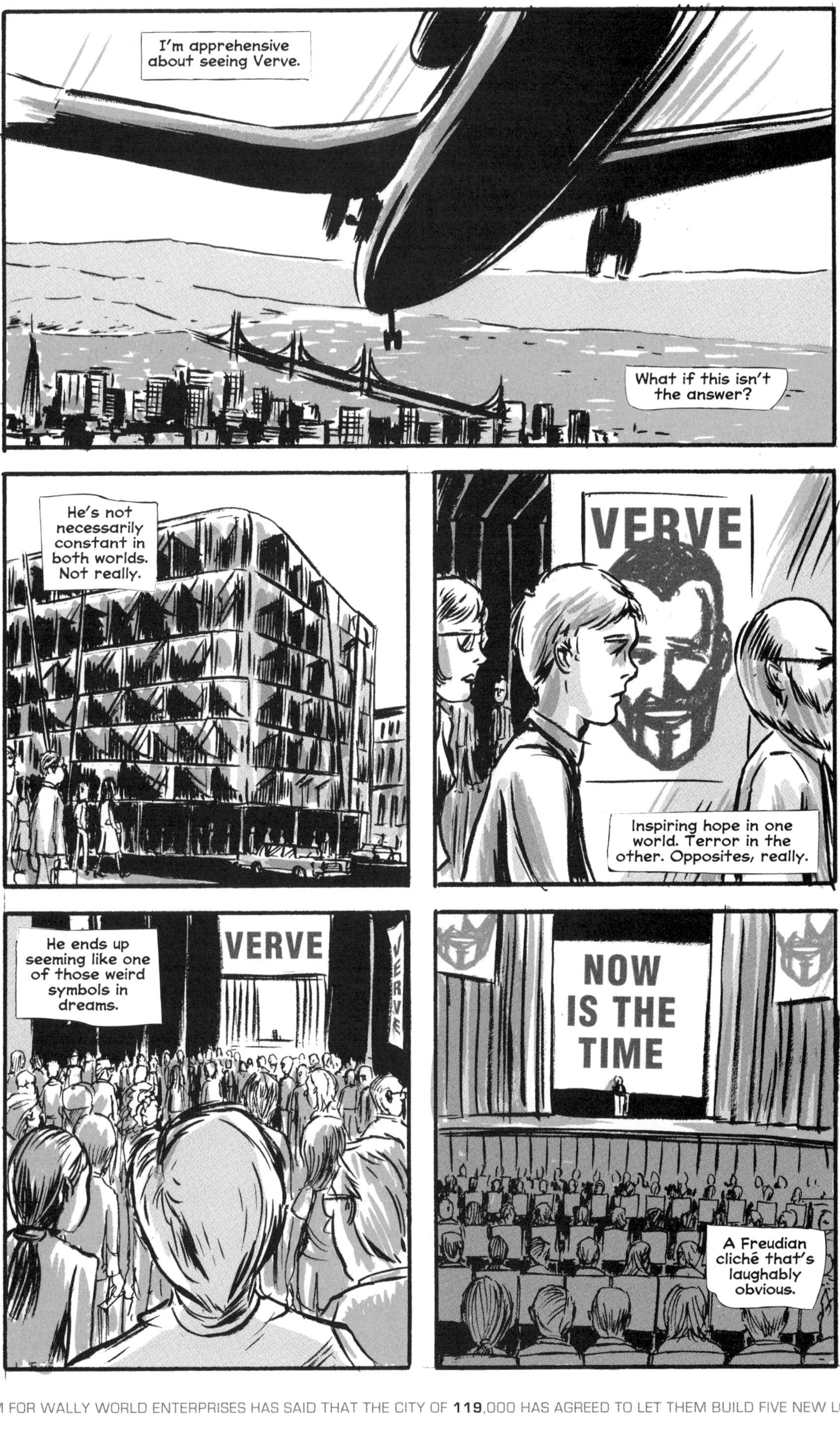
I'm apprehensive about seeing Verve.
What if this isn't the answer?
He's not necessarily constant in both worlds. Not really.
VERVE
Inspiring hope in one world. Terror in the other. Opposites, really.
He ends up seeming like one of those weird symbols in dreams.
VERVE
VERVE
NOW IS THE TIME
A Freudian cliché that's laughably obvious.

L TEAM FOR WALLY WORLD ENTERPRISES HAS SAID THAT THE CITY OF **119**,000 HAS AGREED TO LET THEM BUILD FIVE NEW LO

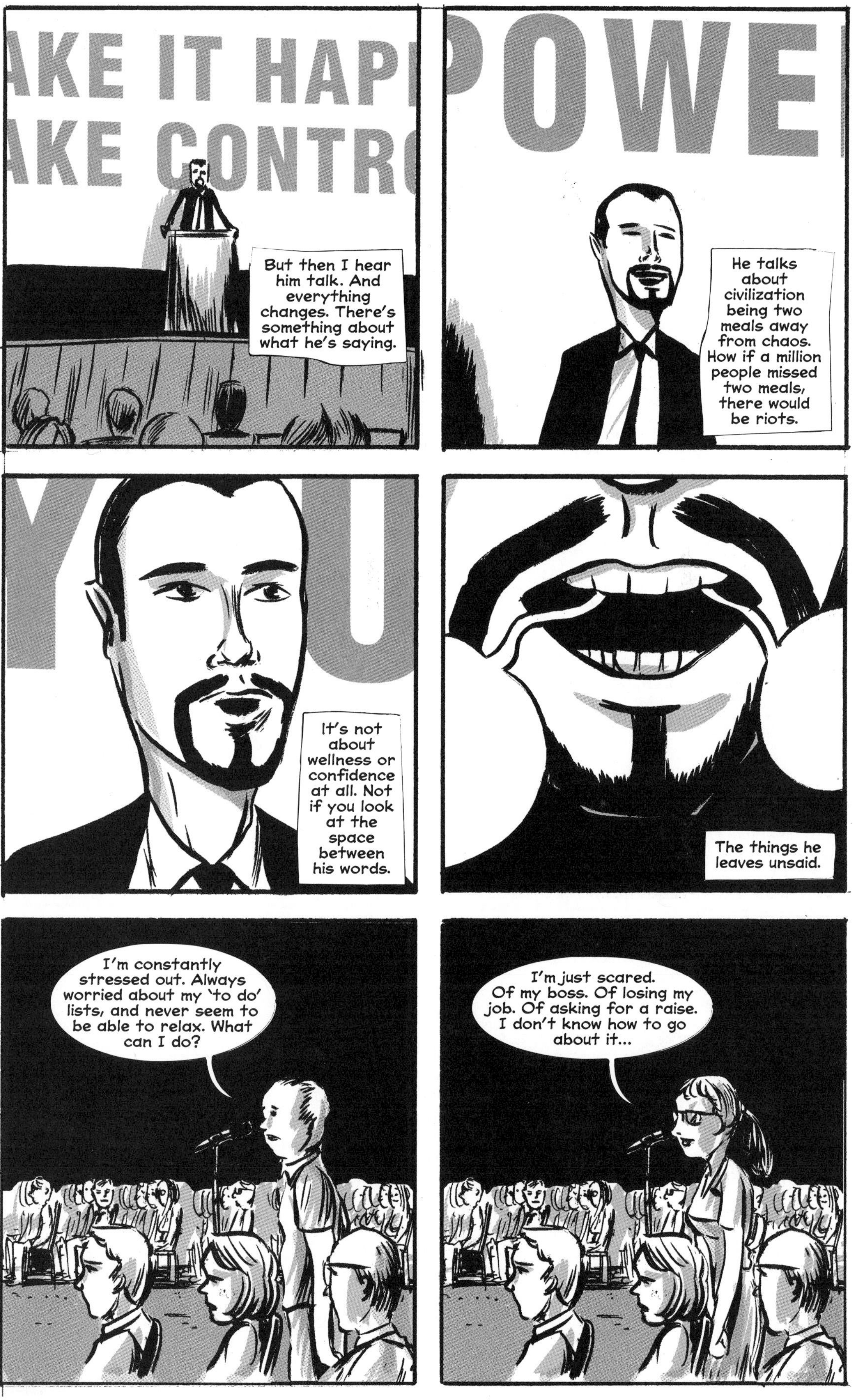
But then I hear him talk. And everything changes. There's something about what he's saying.
He talks about civilization being two meals away from chaos. How if a million people missed two meals, there would be riots.
It's not about wellness or confidence at all. Not if you look at the space between his words.
The things he leaves unsaid.
I'm constantly stressed out. Always worried about my 'to do' lists, and never seem to be able to relax. What can I do?
I'm just scared. Of my boss. Of losing my job. Of asking for a raise. I don't know how to go about it...

BACK BY THE DEAD AUTHOR, "BEAST WITH 1,000 FACES," HAS REEMERGED, SELLING OVER **120**,000 COPIES IN AN UNPRECEDEN

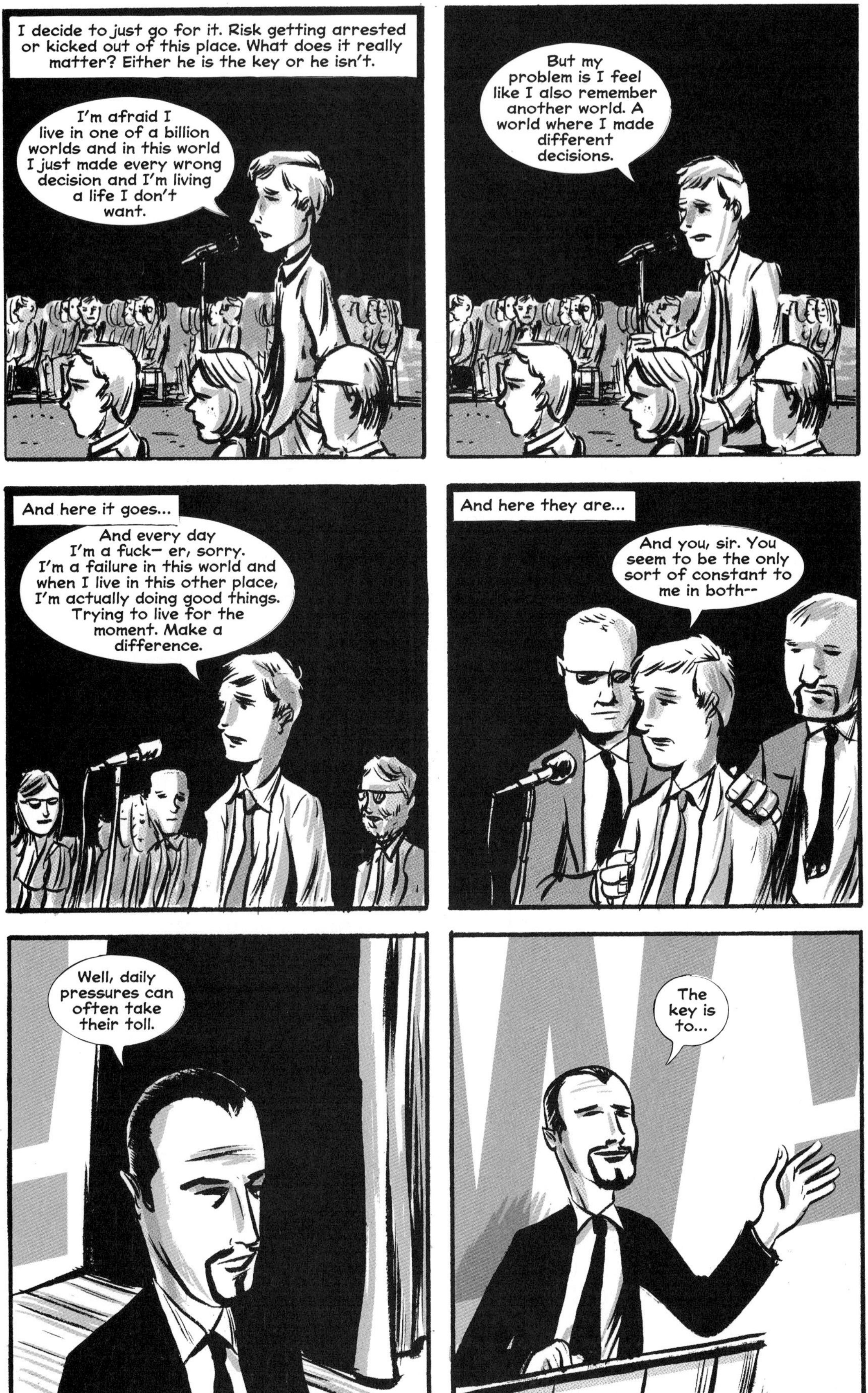
I decide to just go for it. Risk getting arrested or kicked out of this place. What does it really matter? Either he is the key or he isn't.
I'm afraid I live in one of a billion worlds and in this world I just made every wrong decision and I'm living a life I don't want.
But my problem is I feel like I also remember another world. A world where I made different decisions.
And here it goes...
And every day I'm a fuck— er, sorry. I'm a failure in this world and when I live in this other place, I'm actually doing good things. Trying to live for the moment. Make a difference.
And here they are...
And you, sir. You seem to be the only sort of constant to me in both--
Well, daily pressures can often take their toll.
The key is to...

VIEWS FOR THE BOOK HAVE BEEN MIXED. "A CONFUSING MUDDLE." HOWEVER IT STILL REMAINS #**1. 21** WEEKS ON THE BESTSEL

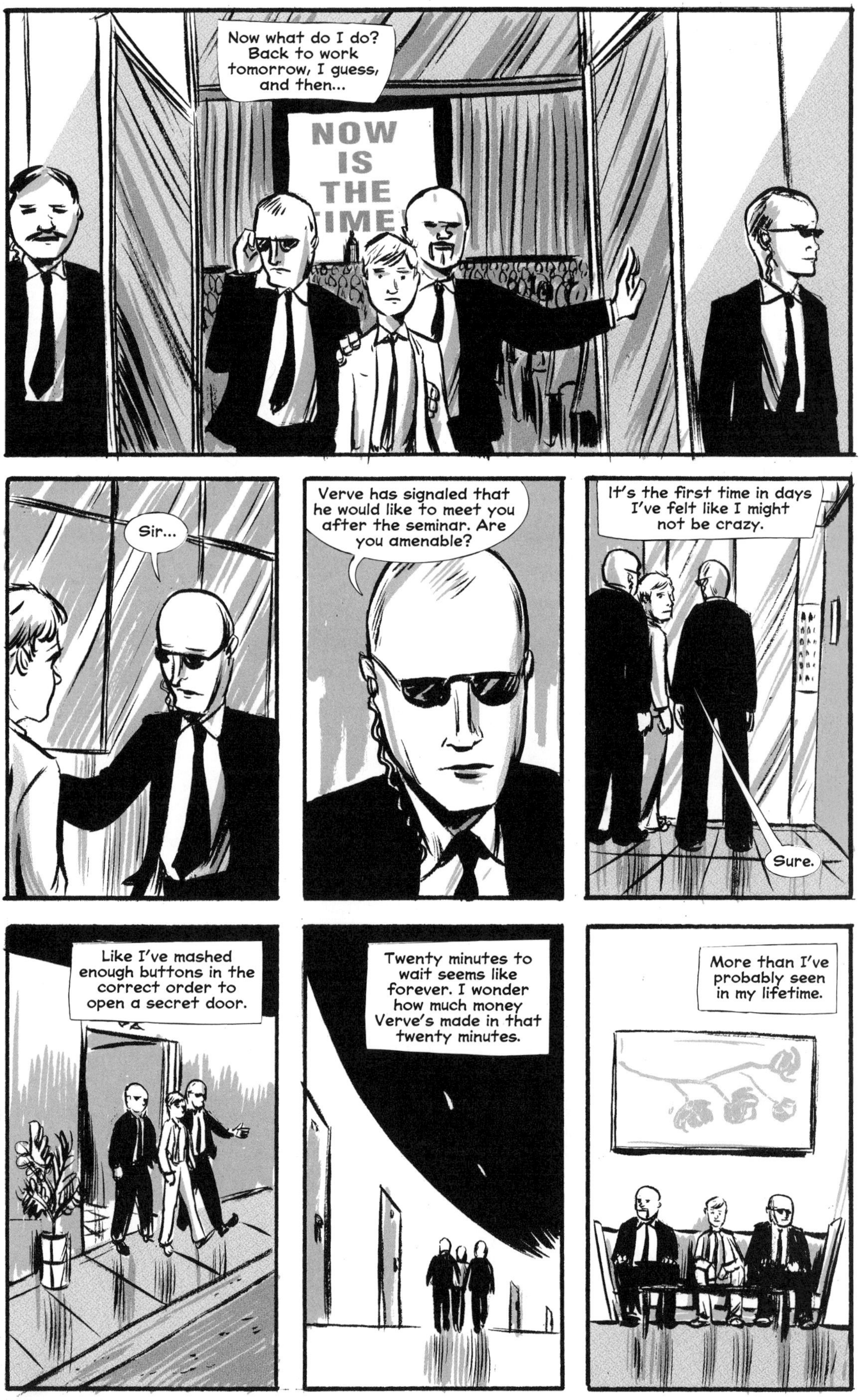
Now what do I do? Back to work tomorrow, I guess, and then...
NOW IS THE TIME
Sir...
Verve has signaled that he would like to meet you after the seminar. Are you amenable?
It's the first time in days I've felt like I might not be crazy.
Sure.
Like I've mashed enough buttons in the correct order to open a secret door.
Twenty minutes to wait seems like forever. I wonder how much money Verve's made in that twenty minutes.
More than I've probably seen in my lifetime.

AIMED SPEAKER REPORTEDLY GAVE THE LEADER OF THE "76ERS" OVER $1.22 MILLION FOR THE RIGHTS TO HIS UNIQUE STORY C

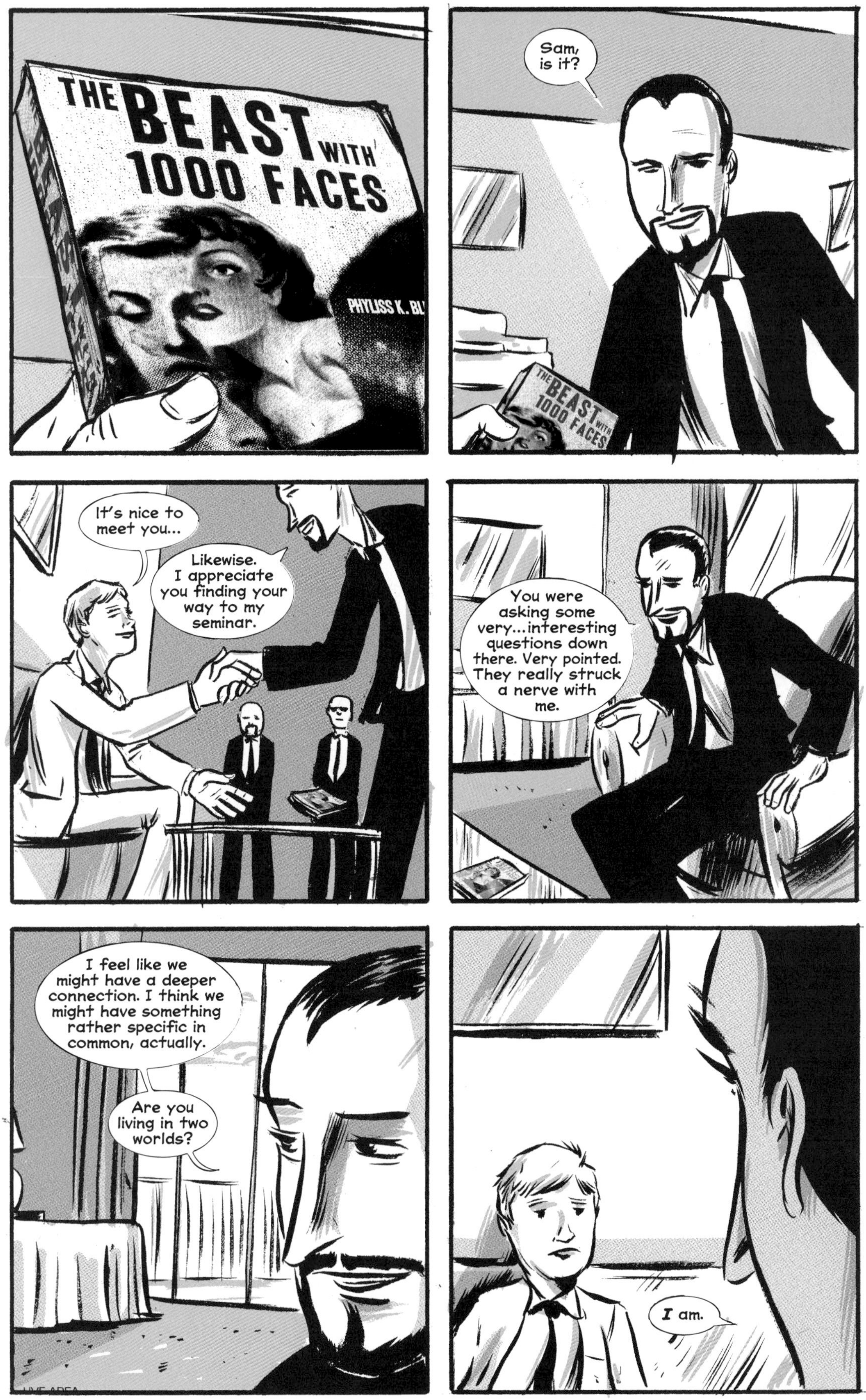
THE BEAST WITH 1000 FACES
PHYLISS K. BL
Sam, is it?
THE BEAST WITH 1000 FACES
It's nice to meet you...
Likewise. I appreciate you finding your way to my seminar.
You were asking some very...interesting questions down there. Very pointed. They really struck a nerve with me.
I feel like we might have a deeper connection. I think we might have something rather specific in common, actually.
Are you living in two worlds?
I am.

LKS TO CREATE A MOVIE ADAPTATION OF HIS LIFE BASED ON HIS SPEECH "SUCCESS, **1**, **2**, **3**" IN WHICH HE OUTLINES THE WAYS

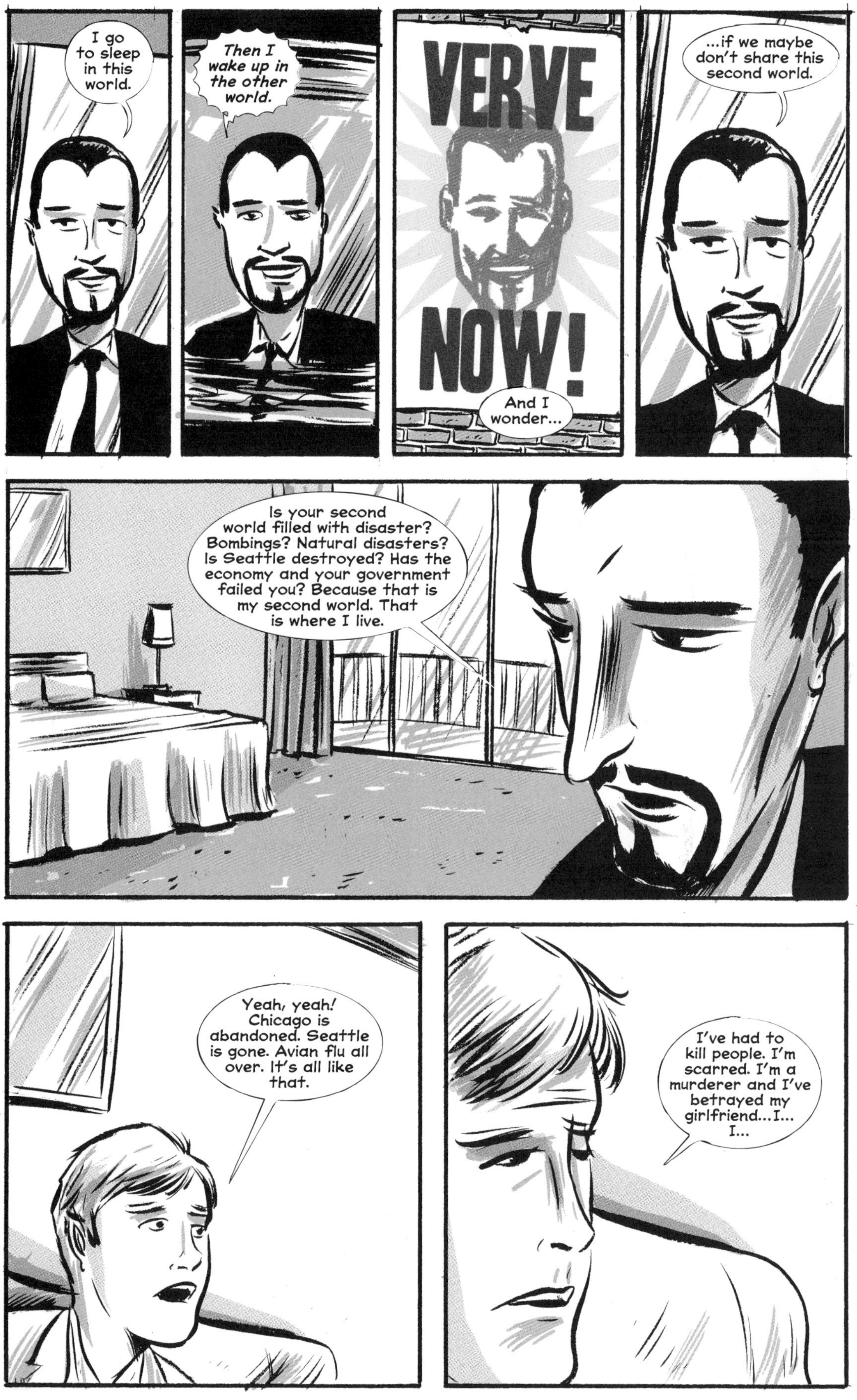
I go to sleep in this world.
Then I wake up in the other world.
VERVE NOW!
And I wonder...
...if we maybe don't share this second world.
Is your second world filled with disaster? Bombings? Natural disasters? Is Seattle destroyed? Has the economy and your government failed you? Because that is my second world. That is where I live.
Yeah, yeah! Chicago is abandoned. Seattle is gone. Avian flu all over. It's all like that.
I've had to kill people. I'm scarred. I'm a murderer and I've betrayed my girlfriend...I... I...

THAT MORE COPIES OF THE NEW ISSUE HAVE SOLD IN **ONE 24** HOUR TIME PERIOD THAN ANY OTHER PERIODICAL IN THE HISTORY

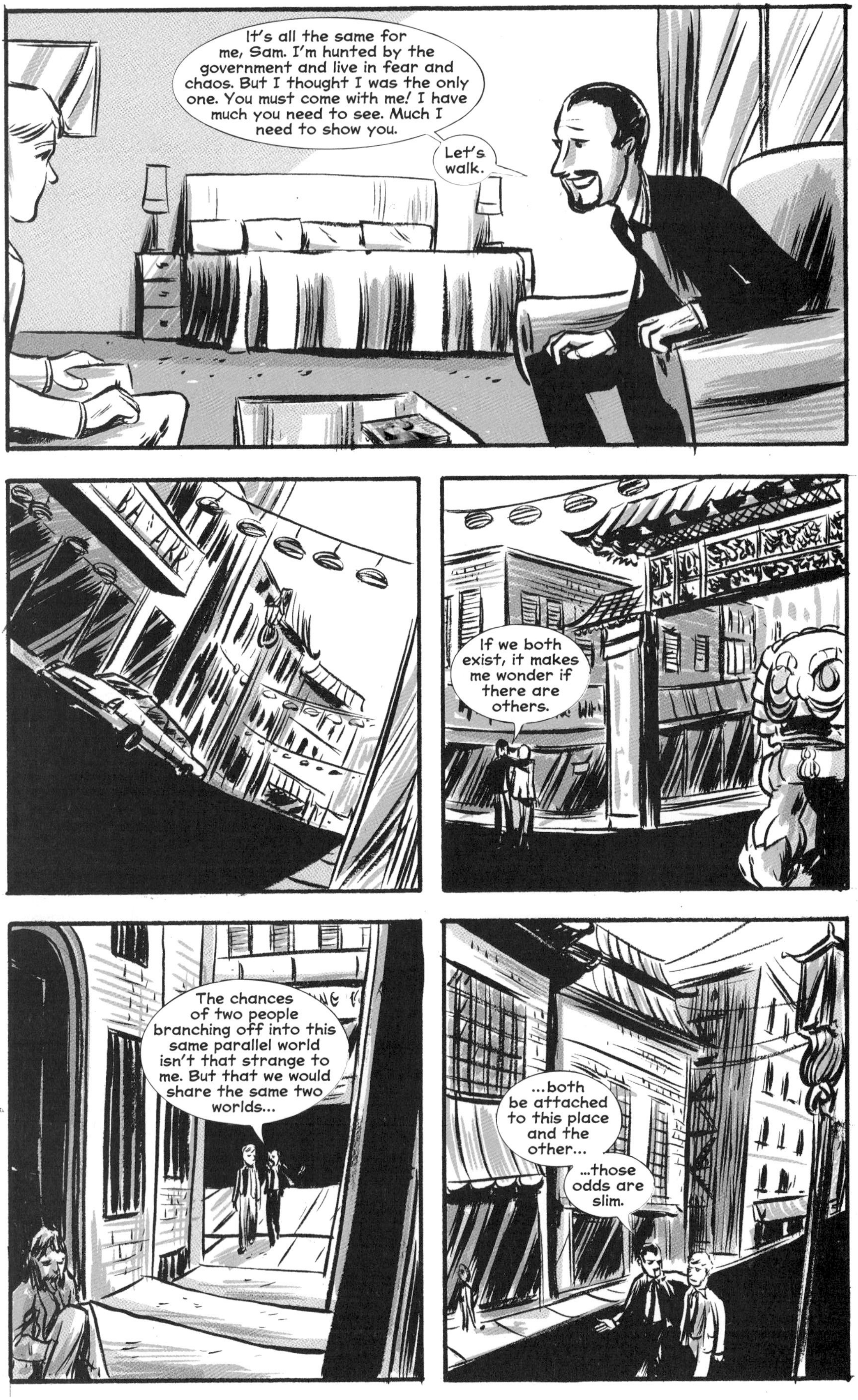
It's all the same for me, Sam. I'm hunted by the government and live in fear and chaos. But I thought I was the only one. You must come with me! I have much you need to see. Much I need to show you.
Let's walk.
If we both exist, it makes me wonder if there are others.
The chances of two people branching off into this same parallel world isn't that strange to me. But that we would share the same two worlds...
...both be attached to this place and the other...
...those odds are slim.

E BETS HAVE BEEN PLACED ON THE HORSE "SUPER SPY'S CHILDREN" IN THE RACE. WITH ODDS AT **1:25** THE PAYOFF WOULD BE

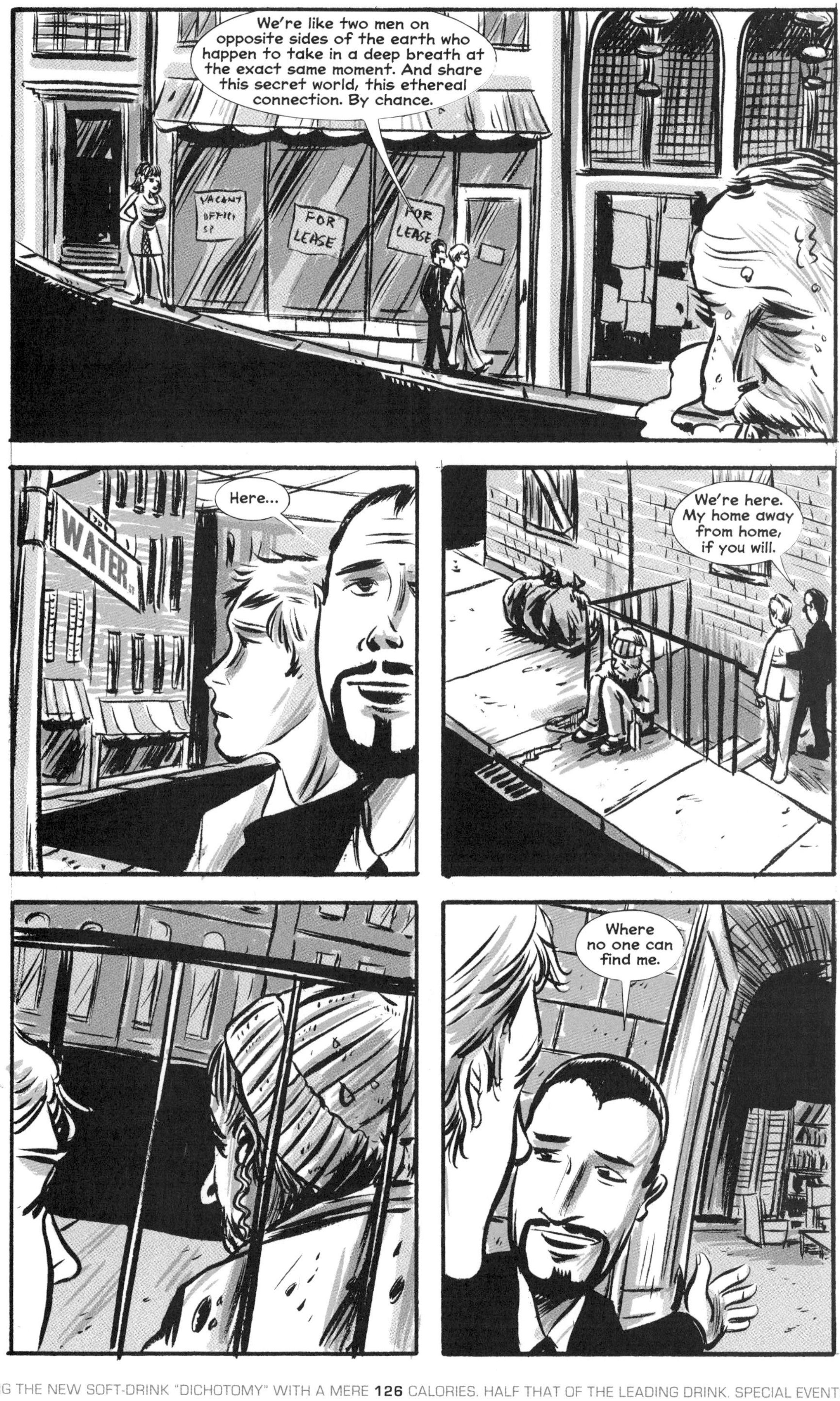
We're like two men on opposite sides of the earth who happen to take in a deep breath at the exact same moment. And share this secret world, this ethereal connection. By chance.
FOR LEASE
FOR LEASE
WATER
Here...
We're here. My home away from home, if you will.
Where no one can find me.

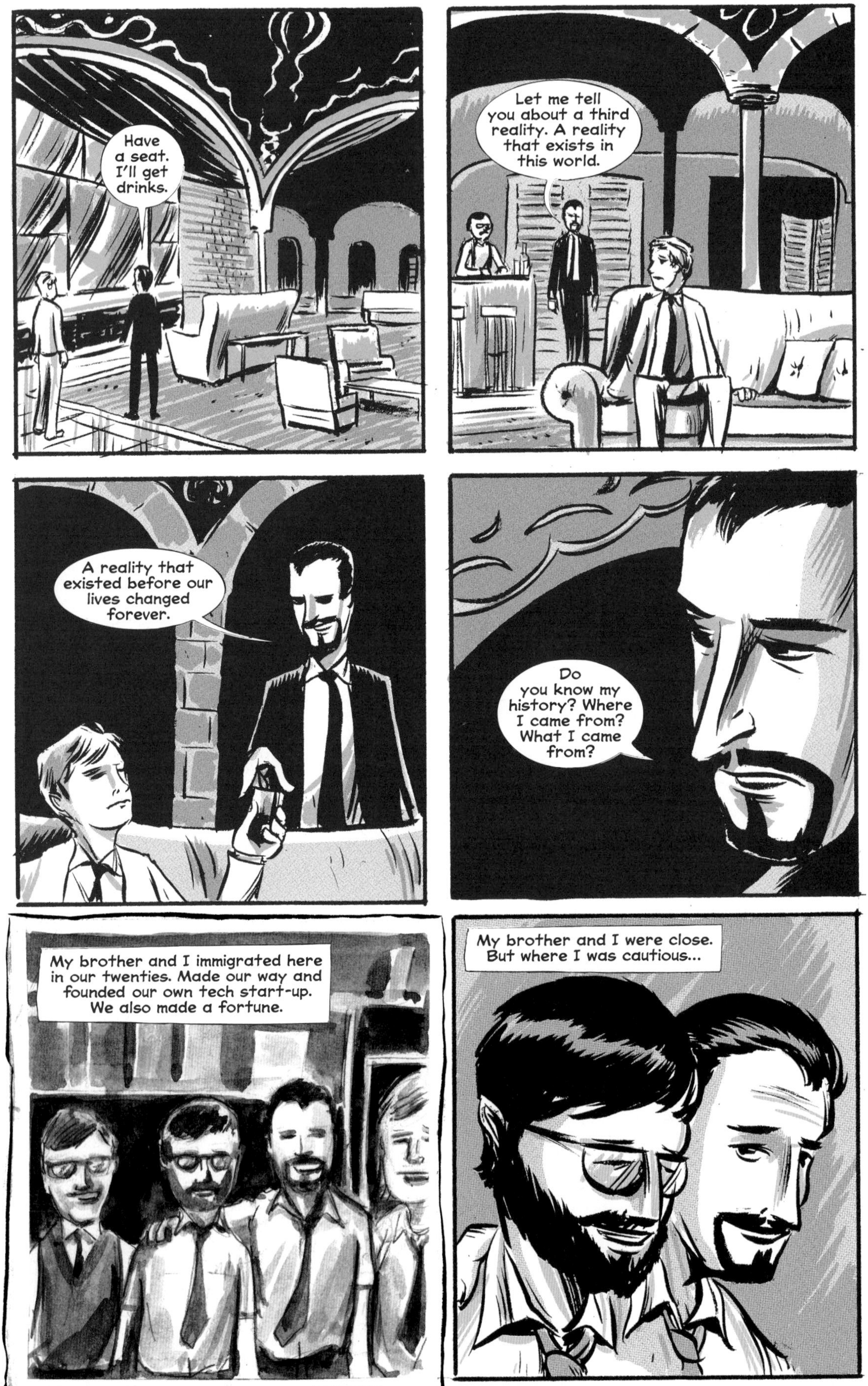
Have a seat. I'll get drinks.
Let me tell you about a third reality. A reality that exists in this world.
A reality that existed before our lives changed forever.
Do you know my history? Where I came from? What I came from?
My brother and I immigrated here in our twenties. Made our way and founded our own tech start-up. We also made a fortune.
My brother and I were close. But where I was cautious...

W EXHIBIT AT THE SMITHSONIAN INSTITUTION, "127 YEARS OF AVIATION HISTORY", INCLUDING SUCH HISTORIC AIRPLANES SUCH

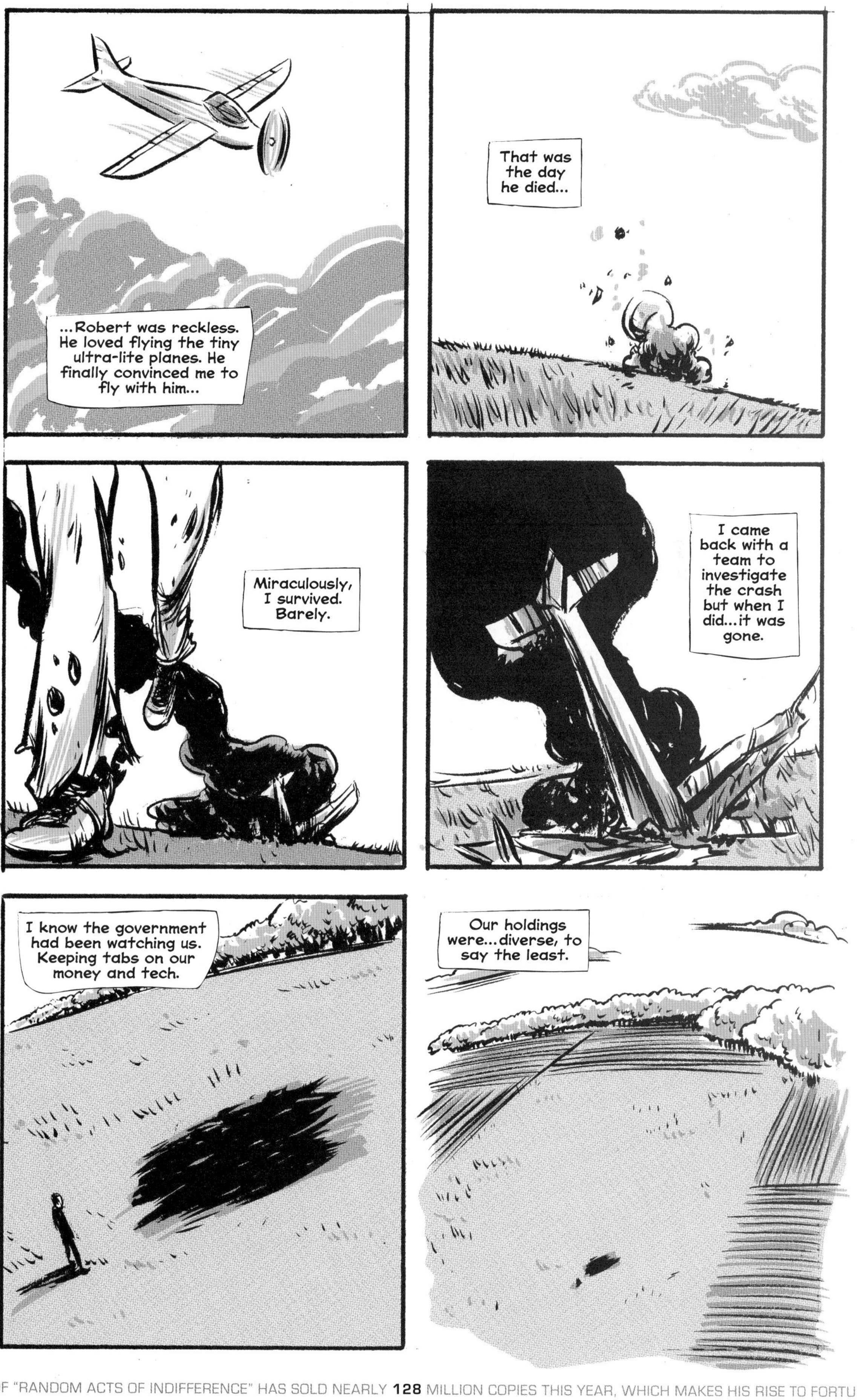
...Robert was reckless. He loved flying the tiny ultra-lite planes. He finally convinced me to fly with him...
That was the day he died...
Miraculously, I survived. Barely.
I came back with a team to investigate the crash but when I did...it was gone.
I know the government had been watching us. Keeping tabs on our money and tech.
Our holdings were...diverse, to say the least.

OF "RANDOM ACTS OF INDIFFERENCE" HAS SOLD NEARLY 128 MILLION COPIES THIS YEAR, WHICH MAKES HIS RISE TO FORTUNE

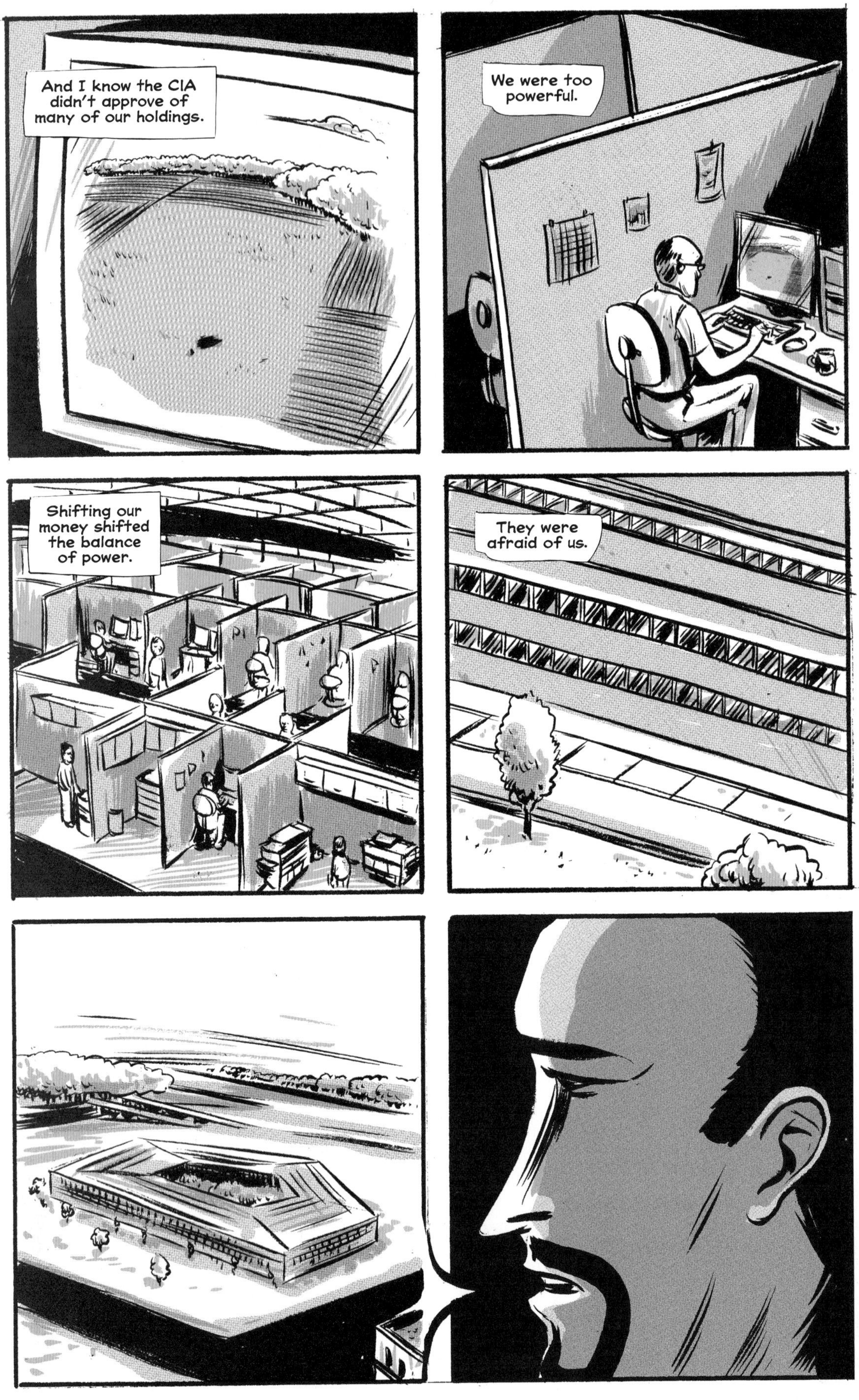
And I know the CIA didn't approve of many of our holdings.
We were too powerful.
Shifting our money shifted the balance of power.
They were afraid of us.

HE RELEASE OF THE BOOK, THE "76ERS" HAVE BECOME A POP CULTURE PHENOMENON. WITH **129** MILLION IN BOOK AND T-SHIRT

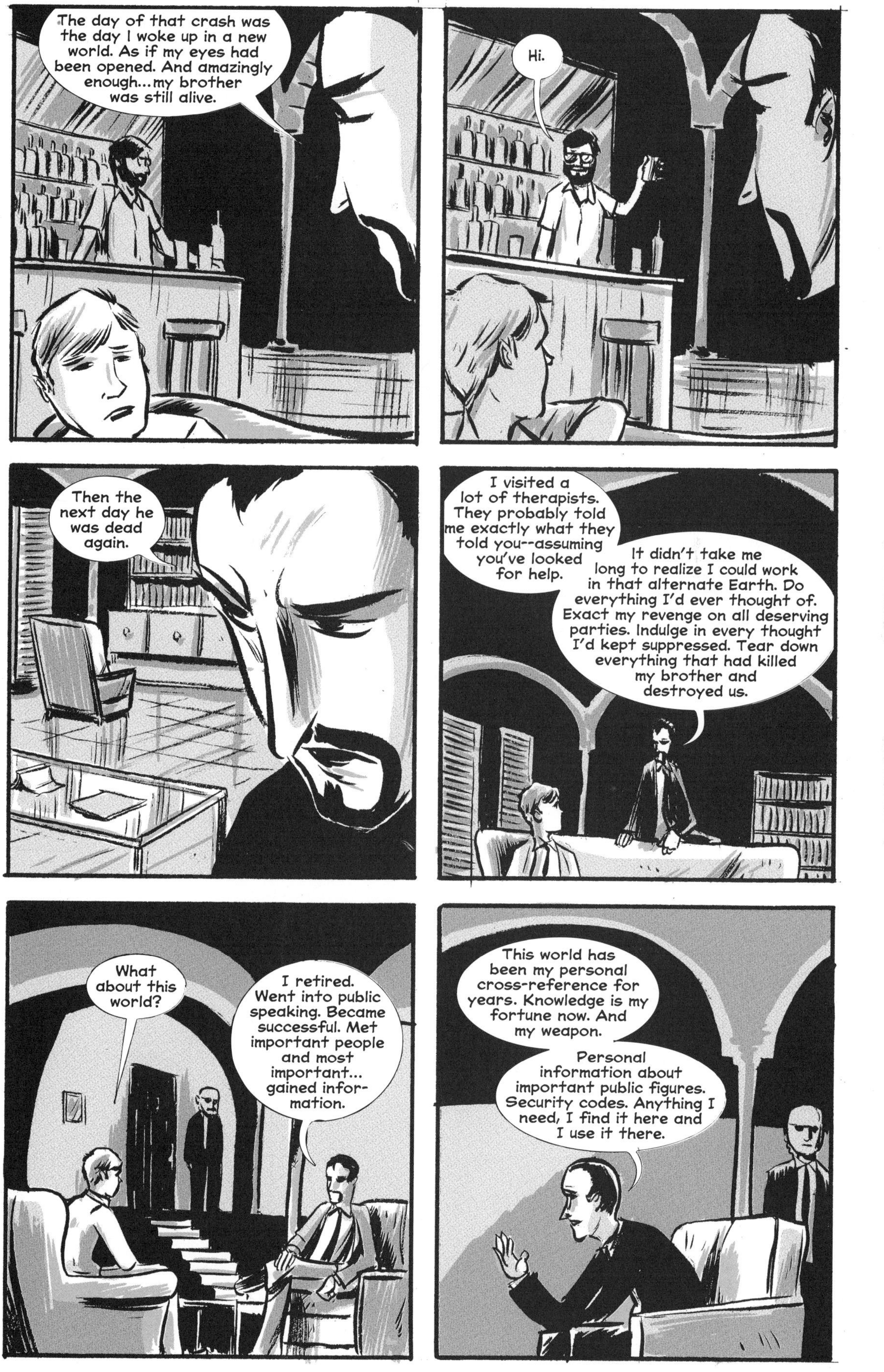
The day of that crash was the day I woke up in a new world. As if my eyes had been opened. And amazingly enough...my brother was still alive.
Hi.
Then the next day he was dead again.
I visited a lot of therapists. They probably told me exactly what they told you--assuming you've looked for help.
It didn't take me long to realize I could work in that alternate Earth. Do everything I'd ever thought of. Exact my revenge on all deserving parties. Indulge in every thought I'd kept suppressed. Tear down everything that had killed my brother and destroyed us.
What about this world?
I retired. Went into public speaking. Became successful. Met important people and most important... gained infor-mation.
This world has been my personal cross-reference for years. Knowledge is my fortune now. And my weapon.
Personal information about important public figures. Security codes. Anything I need, I find it here and I use it there.

NE'S LIST OF RICHEST MEN IN THE WORLD. #3 AT $130 BILLION IS P. K. VERVE, THE WORLD-RENOWNED SPEAKER AND TECHNIC

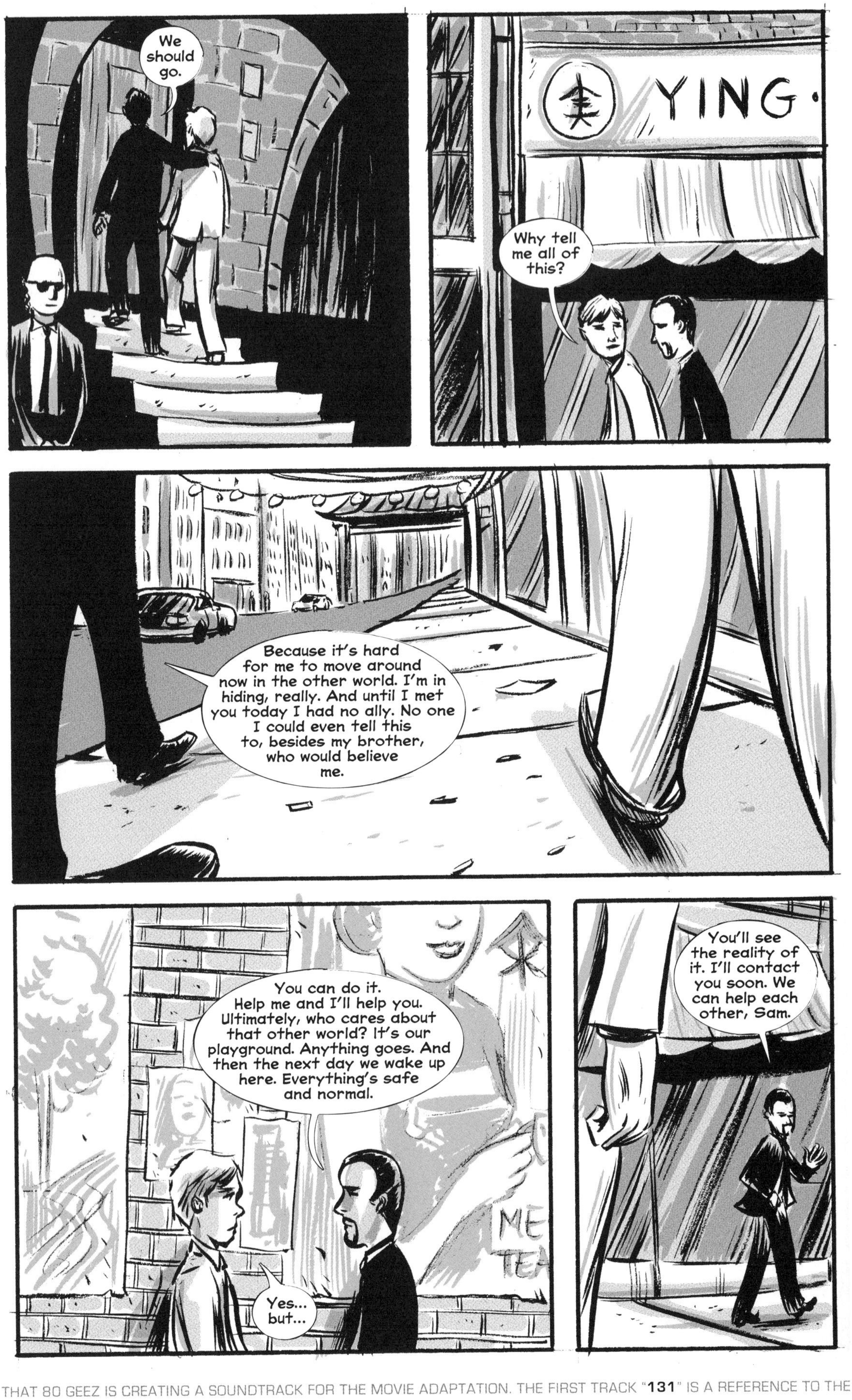
We should go.
YING
Why tell me all of this?
Because it's hard for me to move around now in the other world. I'm in hiding, really. And until I met you today I had no ally. No one I could even tell this to, besides my brother, who would believe me.
You can do it. Help me and I'll help you. Ultimately, who cares about that other world? It's our playground. Anything goes. And then the next day we wake up here. Everything's safe and normal.
Yes... but...
You'll see the reality of it. I'll contact you soon. We can help each other, Sam.

ING THAT 80 GEEZ IS CREATING A SOUNDTRACK FOR THE MOVIE ADAPTATION. THE FIRST TRACK "**131**" IS A REFERENCE TO THE

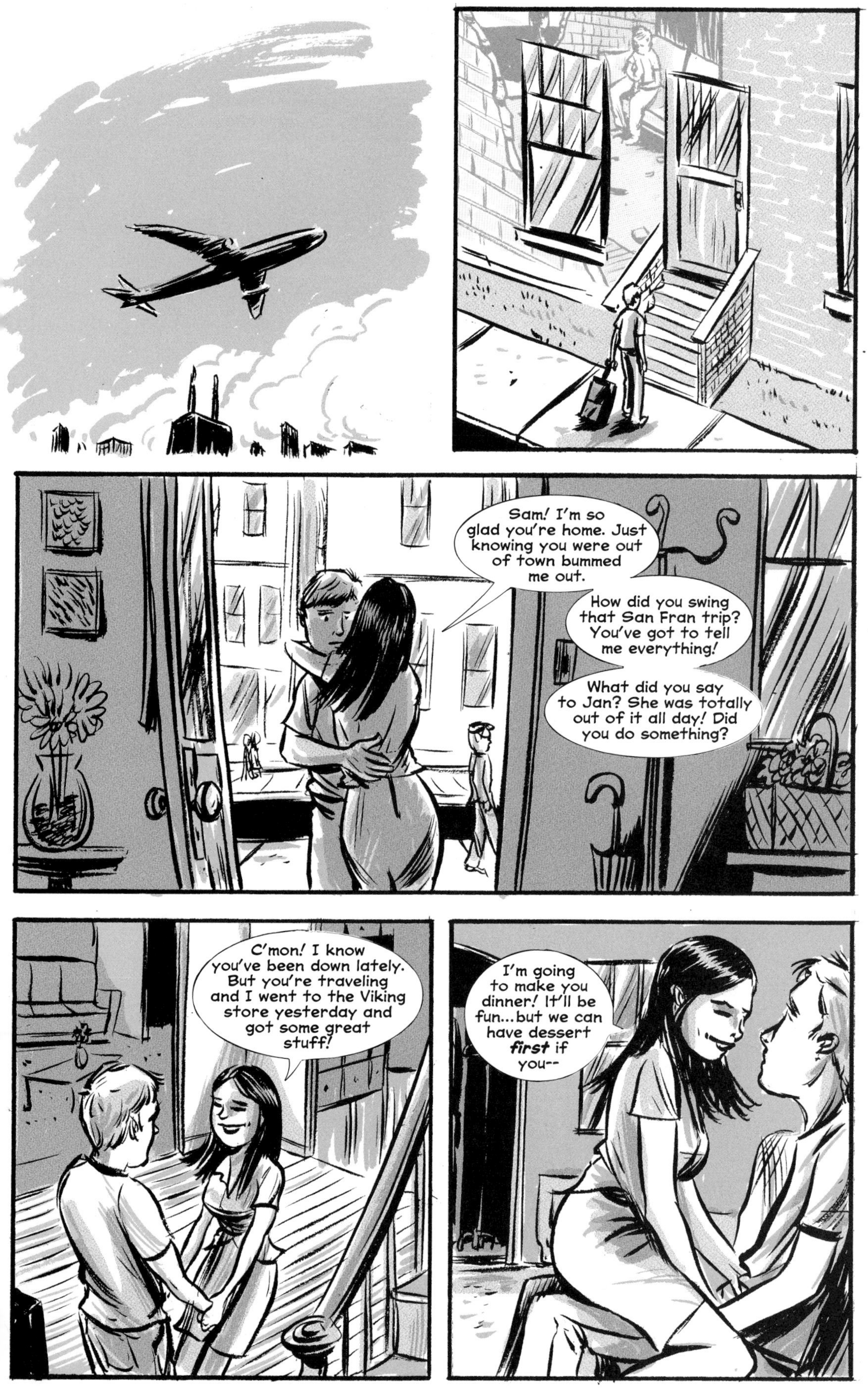
Sam! I'm so glad you're home. Just knowing you were out of town bummed me out.
How did you swing that San Fran trip? You've got to tell me everything!
What did you say to Jan? She was totally out of it all day! Did you do something?
C'mon! I know you've been down lately. But you're traveling and I went to the Viking store yesterday and got some great stuff!
I'm going to make you dinner! It'll be fun...but we can have dessert ***first*** if you--

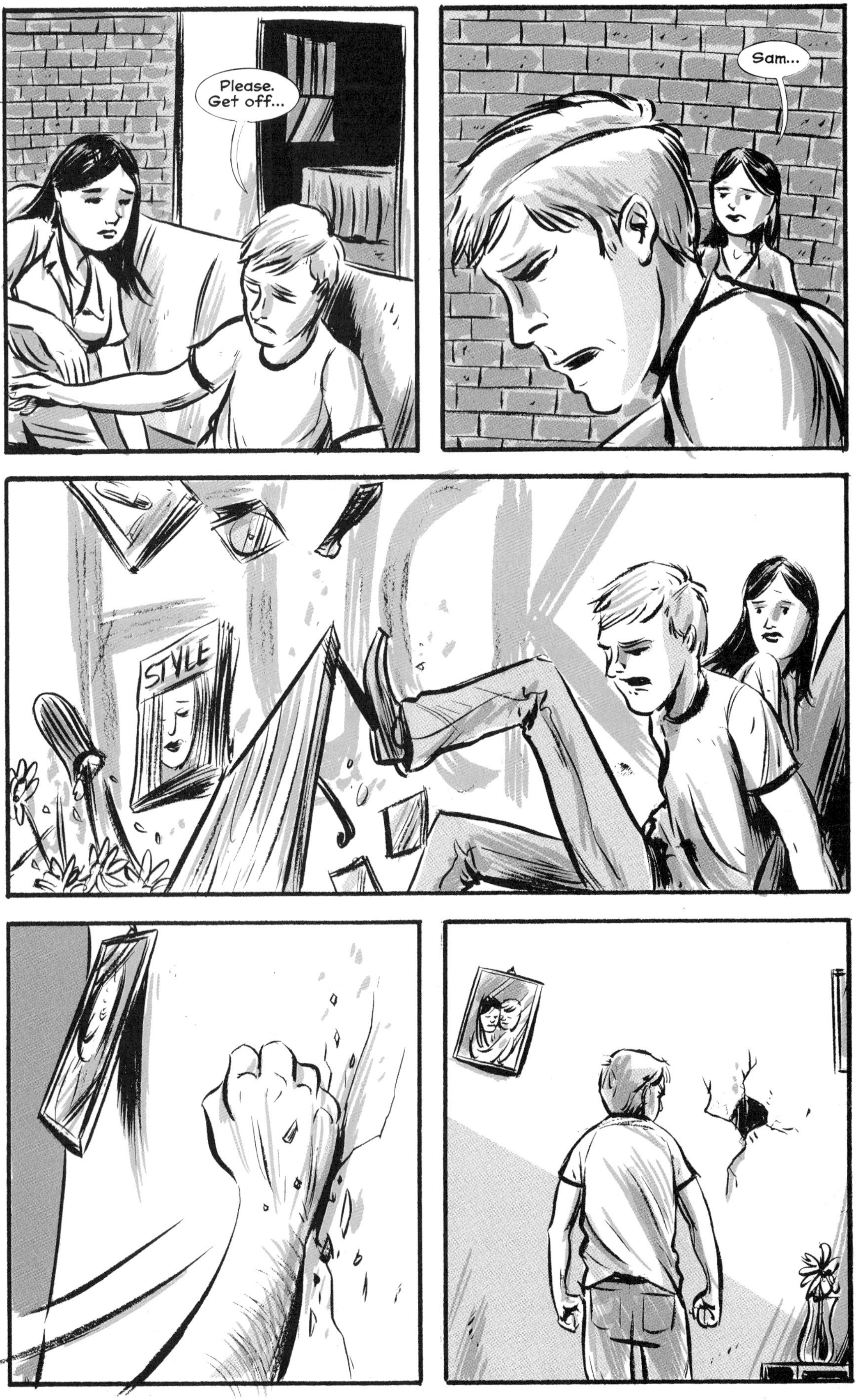
Please.
Get off...
Sam...
STYLE

STATISTICS SHOW **1** OF **33** WOMEN LEAVE THE SITUATION. OTHERS SAY THESE NUMBERS ARE INFLATED AND THAT THE DEFINIT

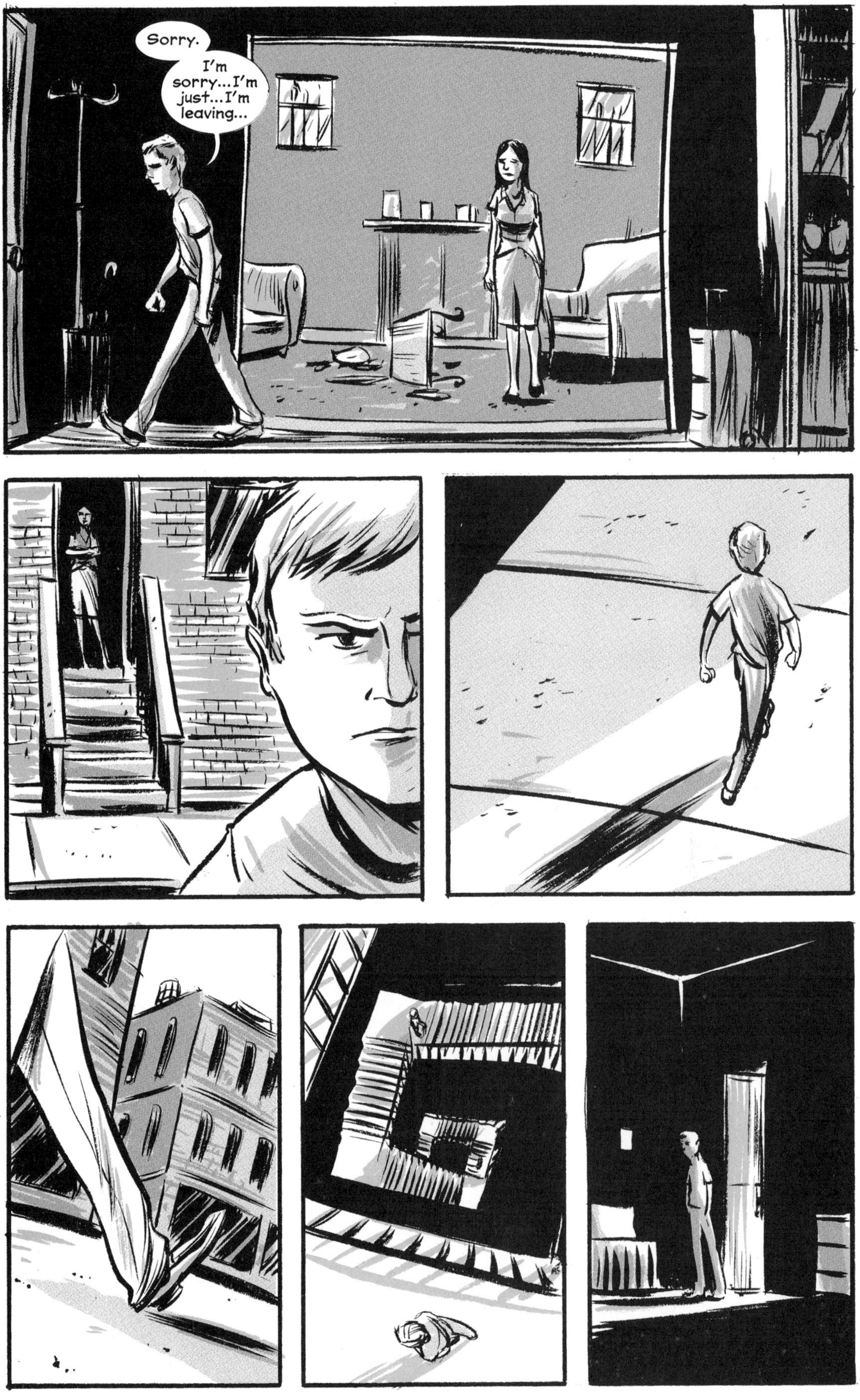
Sorry.
I'm sorry...I'm just...I'm leaving...

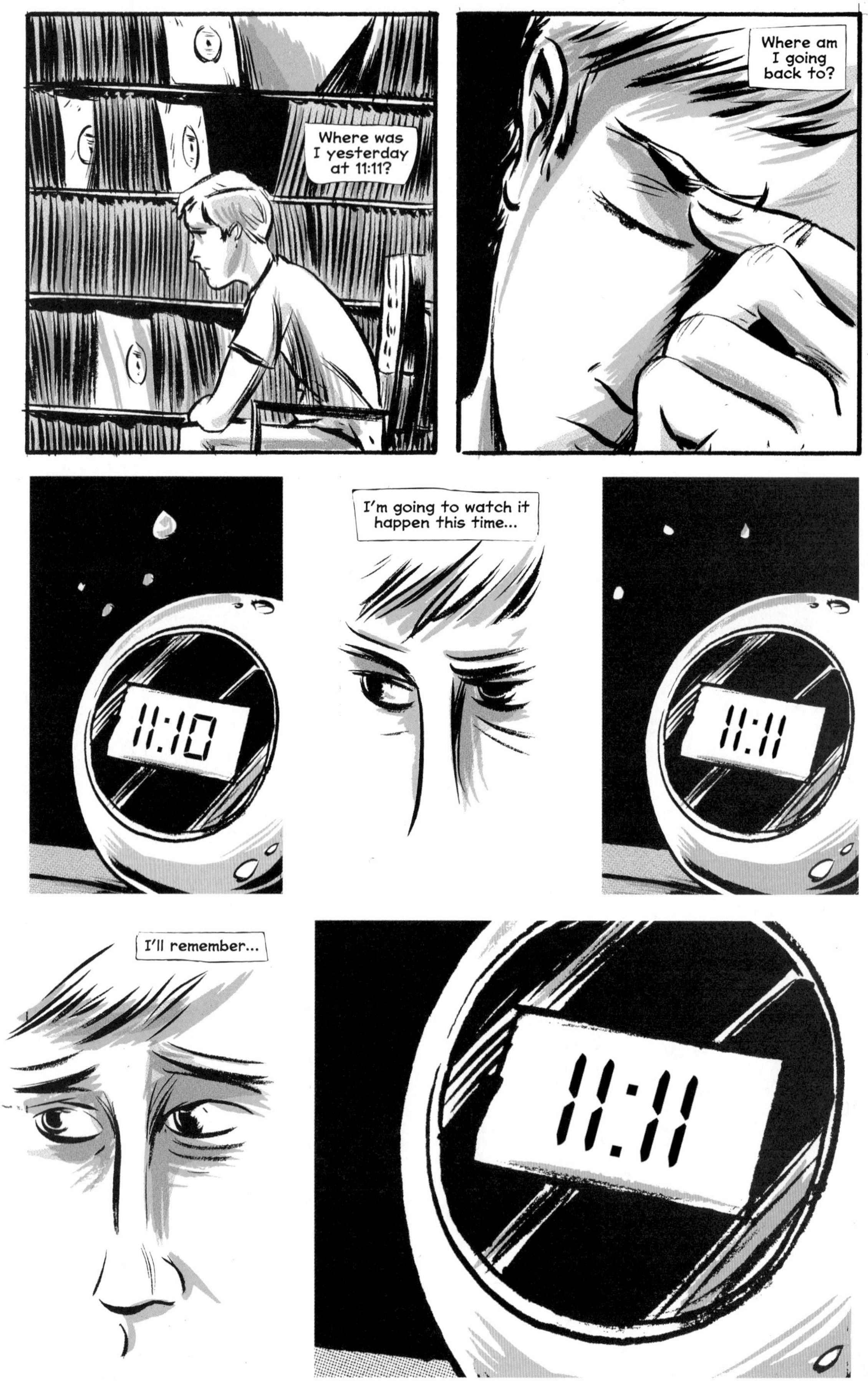
Where was I yesterday at 11:11?
Where am I going back to?
11:10
I'm going to watch it happen this time...
11:11
I'll remember...
11:11

OJECTING THE REMAINING POWER GRIDS WILL GO OFFLINE AT OR BEFORE **1:35** CENTRAL STANDARD TIME. WHAT THIS MEANS

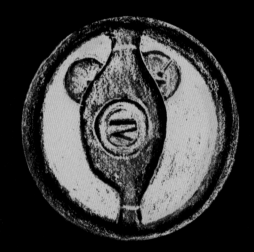

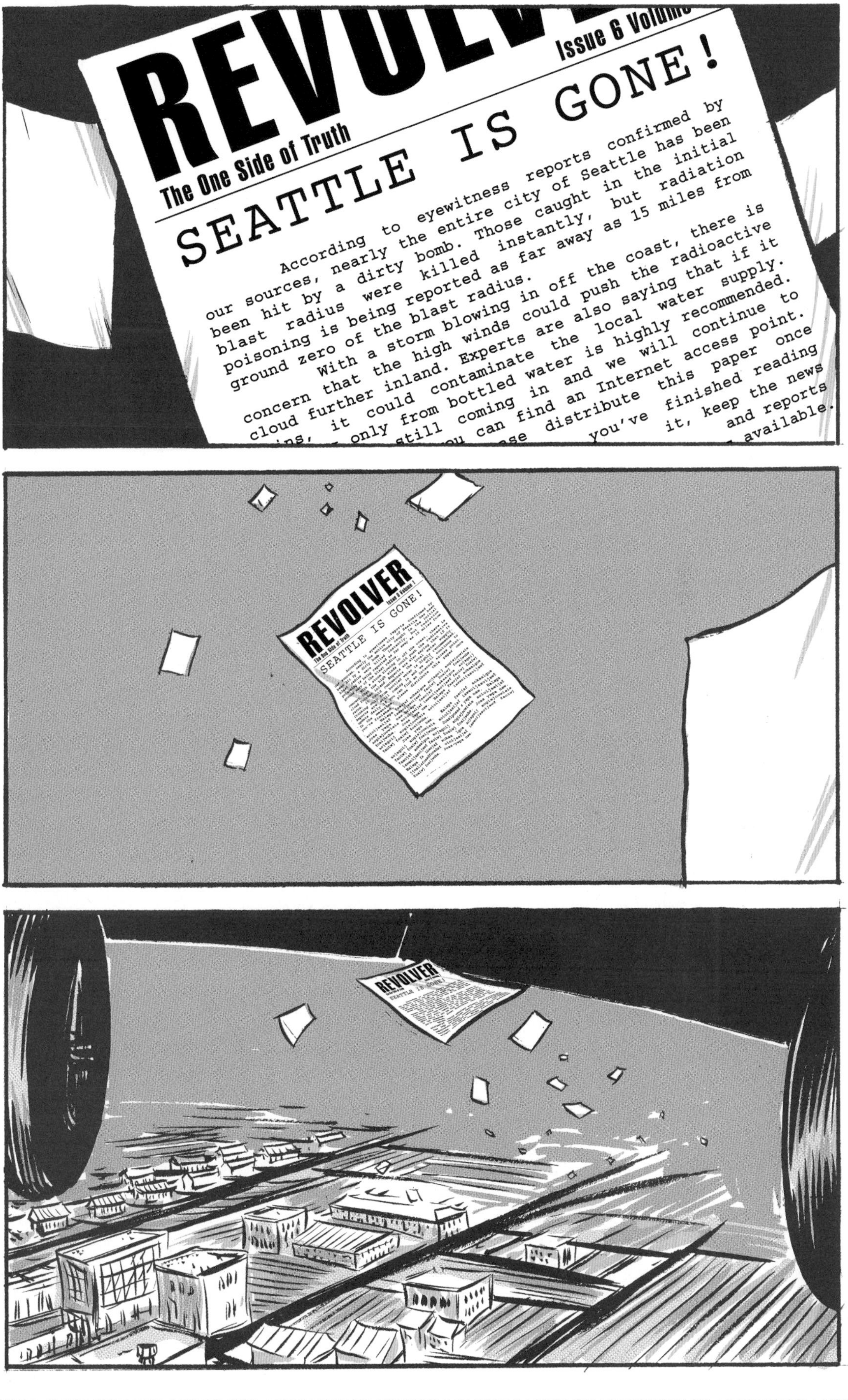
The One Side of Truth
SEATTLE IS GONE!
According to eyewitness reports confirmed by our sources, nearly the entire city of Seattle has been hit by a dirty bomb. Those caught in the initial blast radius were killed instantly, but radiation poisoning is being reported as far away as 15 miles from ground zero of the blast radius.
With a storm blowing in off the coast, there is concern that the high winds could push the radioactive cloud further inland. Experts are also saying that if it
it could contaminate the local water supply.
only from bottled water is highly recommended.
still coming in and we will continue to
can find an Internet access point.
distribute this paper once
you've finished reading
it, keep the news
and reports
available.
REVOLVER
SEATTLE IS GONE!

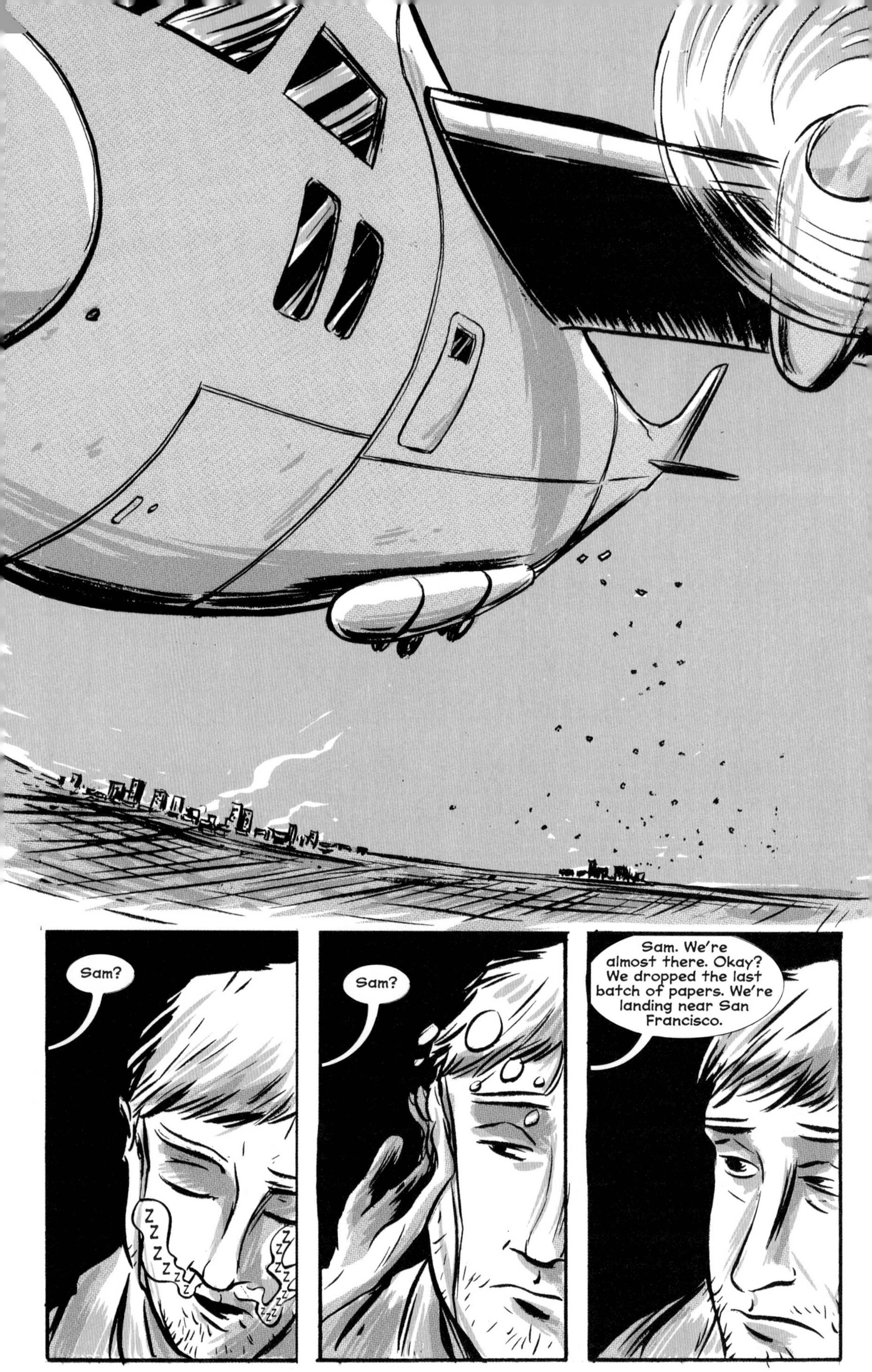
Sam?
Sam?
Sam. We're almost there. Okay? We dropped the last batch of papers. We're landing near San Francisco.

N PARANOIA BUT ALSO ADAPTING TO MODERN DANGERS. OF THE **137** POLLED, MOST SAID THEY WERE ACTUALLY HEALTHIER NO

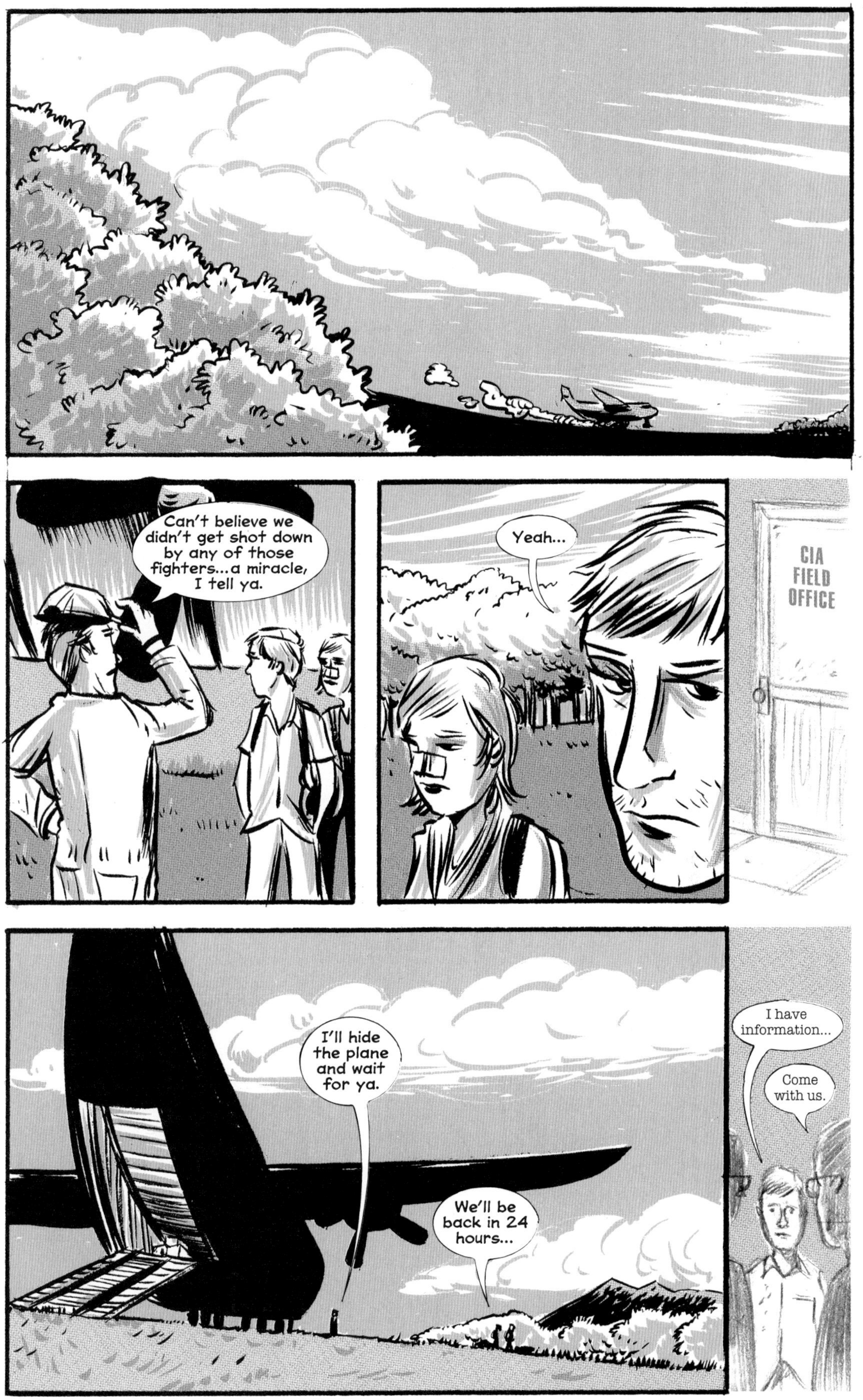
Can't believe we didn't get shot down by any of those fighters...a miracle, I tell ya.
Yeah...
CIA FIELD OFFICE
I'll hide the plane and wait for ya.
We'll be back in 24 hours...
I have information...
Come with us.

TEXAS HAS OFFICIALLY SECEDED FROM THE UNION. AN ESTIMATED **138**,000 PEOPLE MARCHED ALONG THE BORDER AS A CONF

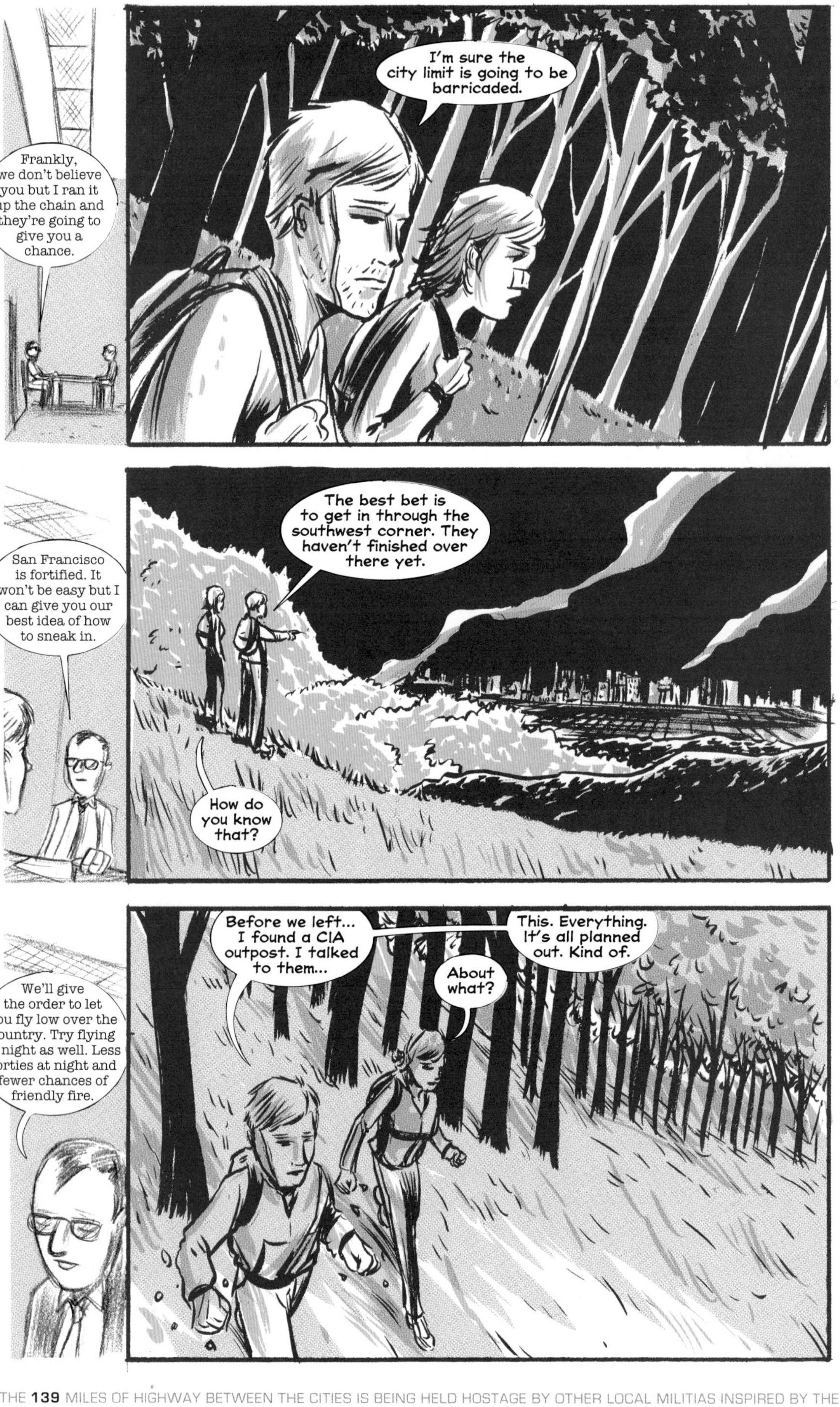
Frankly, we don't believe you but I ran it up the chain and they're going to give you a chance.
I'm sure the city limit is going to be barricaded.
San Francisco is fortified. It won't be easy but I can give you our best idea of how to sneak in.
The best bet is to get in through the southwest corner. They haven't finished over there yet.
How do you know that?
We'll give the order to let you fly low over the country. Try flying at night as well. Less sorties at night and fewer chances of friendly fire.
Before we left... I found a CIA outpost. I talked to them...
About what?
This. Everything. It's all planned out. Kind of.

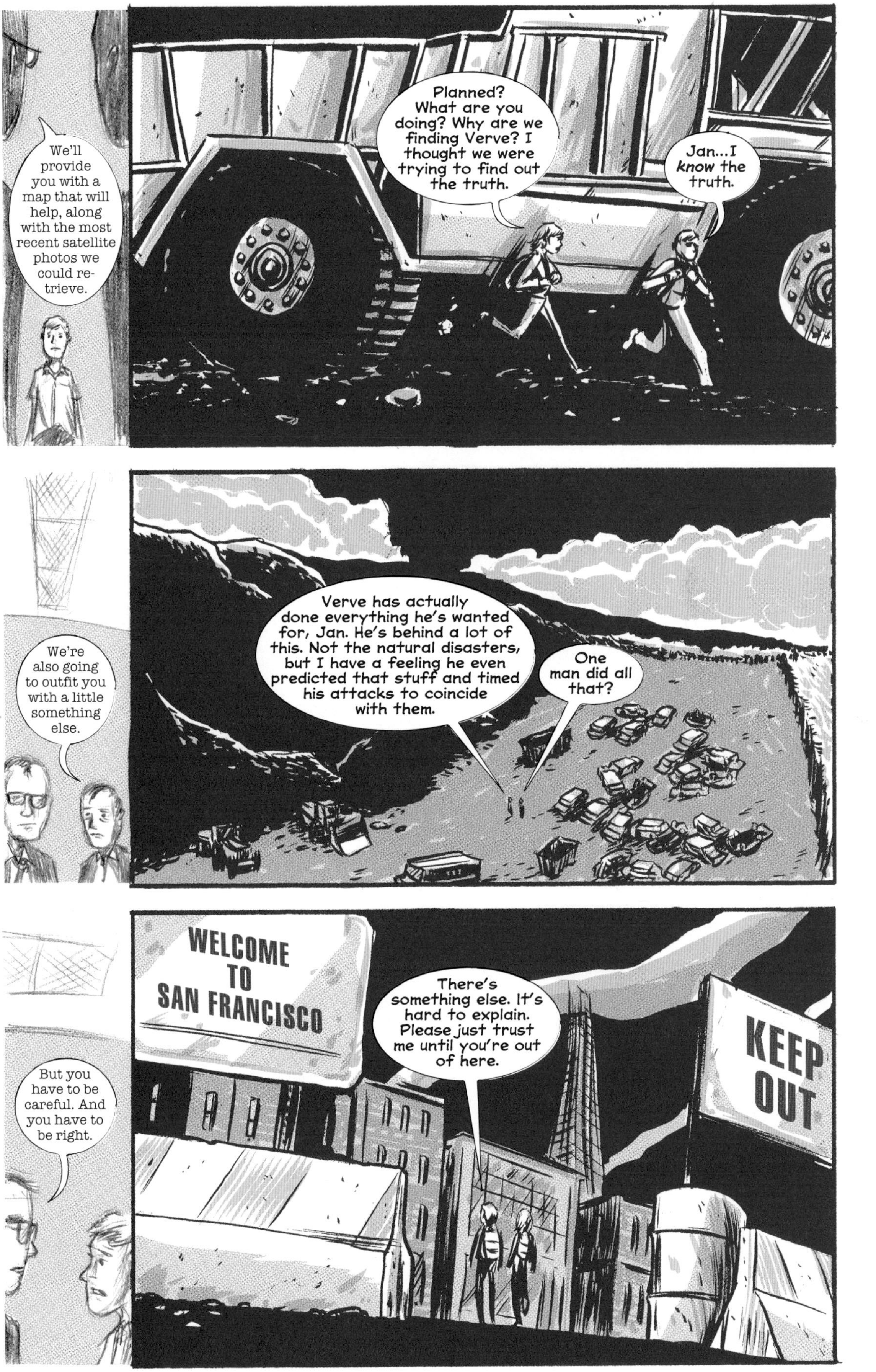
We'll provide you with a map that will help, along with the most recent satellite photos we could re-trieve.
Planned? What are you doing? Why are we finding Verve? I thought we were trying to find out the truth.
Jan...I *know* the truth.
We're also going to outfit you with a little something else.
Verve has actually done everything he's wanted for, Jan. He's behind a lot of this. Not the natural disasters, but I have a feeling he even predicted that stuff and timed his attacks to coincide with them.
One man did all that?
But you have to be careful. And you have to be right.
WELCOME TO SAN FRANCISCO
There's something else. It's hard to explain. Please just trust me until you're out of here.
KEEP OUT

T P. K. VERVE MAY BE INADVERTENTLY RESPONSIBLE FOR OVER **140**,000 DEATHS SINCE THE DISASTERS AND ATTACKS BEGAN.

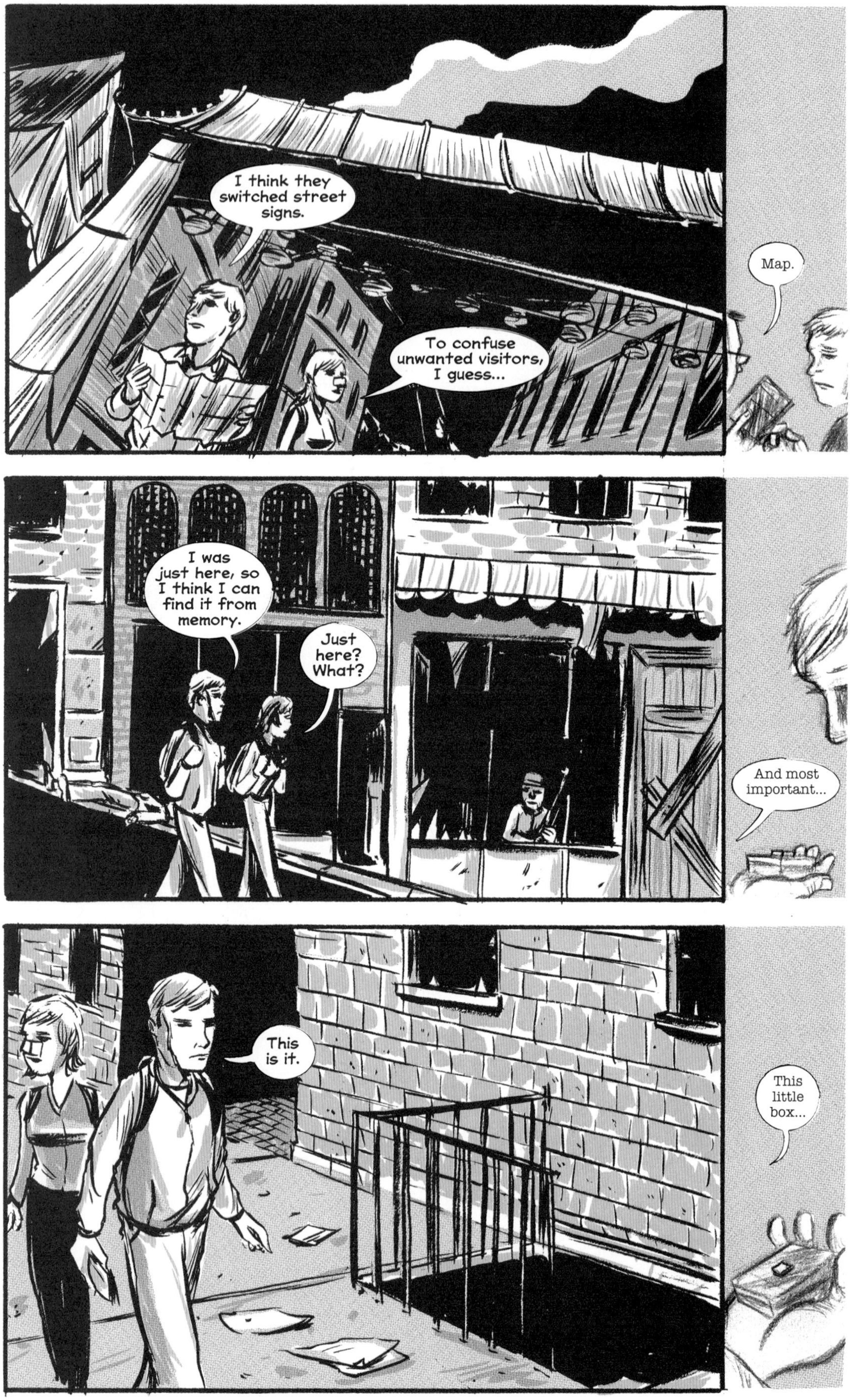
I think they switched street signs.
To confuse unwanted visitors, I guess...
Map.
I was just here, so I think I can find it from memory.
Just here? What?
And most important...
This is it.
This little box...

OUS SIGHTINGS OF THE "76ERS" HEADING NORTH TOWARDS NATIONAL GUARD CAMPS. APPROXIMATELY **141**,000 TROOPS ARE

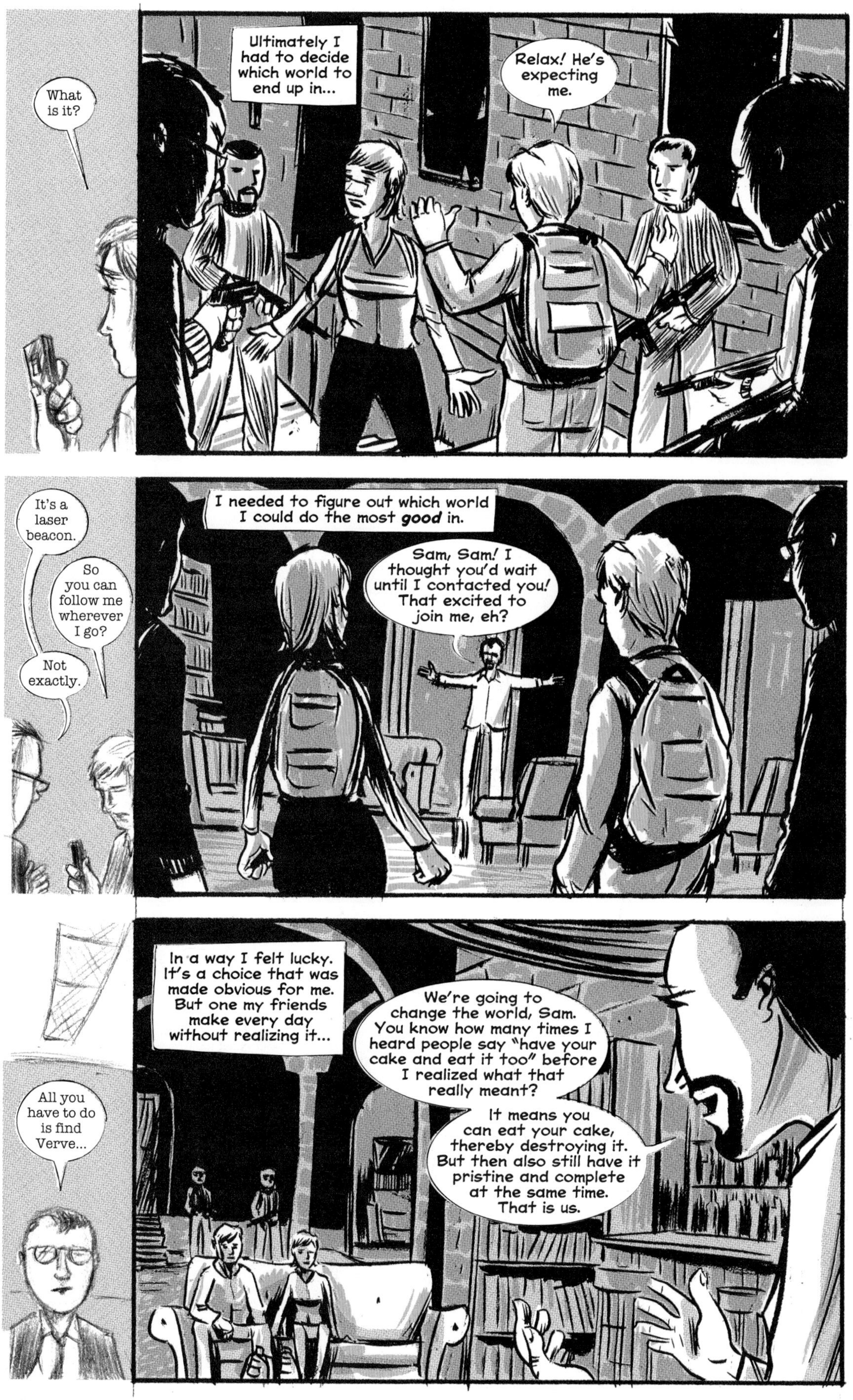
What is it?
Ultimately I had to decide which world to end up in...
Relax! He's expecting me.
It's a laser beacon.
So you can follow me wherever I go?
Not exactly.
I needed to figure out which world I could do the most **good** in.
Sam, Sam! I thought you'd wait until I contacted you! That excited to join me, eh?
All you have to do is find Verve...
In a way I felt lucky. It's a choice that was made obvious for me. But one my friends make every day without realizing it...
We're going to change the world, Sam. You know how many times I heard people say "have your cake and eat it too" before I realized what that really meant?
It means you can eat your cake, thereby destroying it. But then also still have it pristine and complete at the same time. That is us.

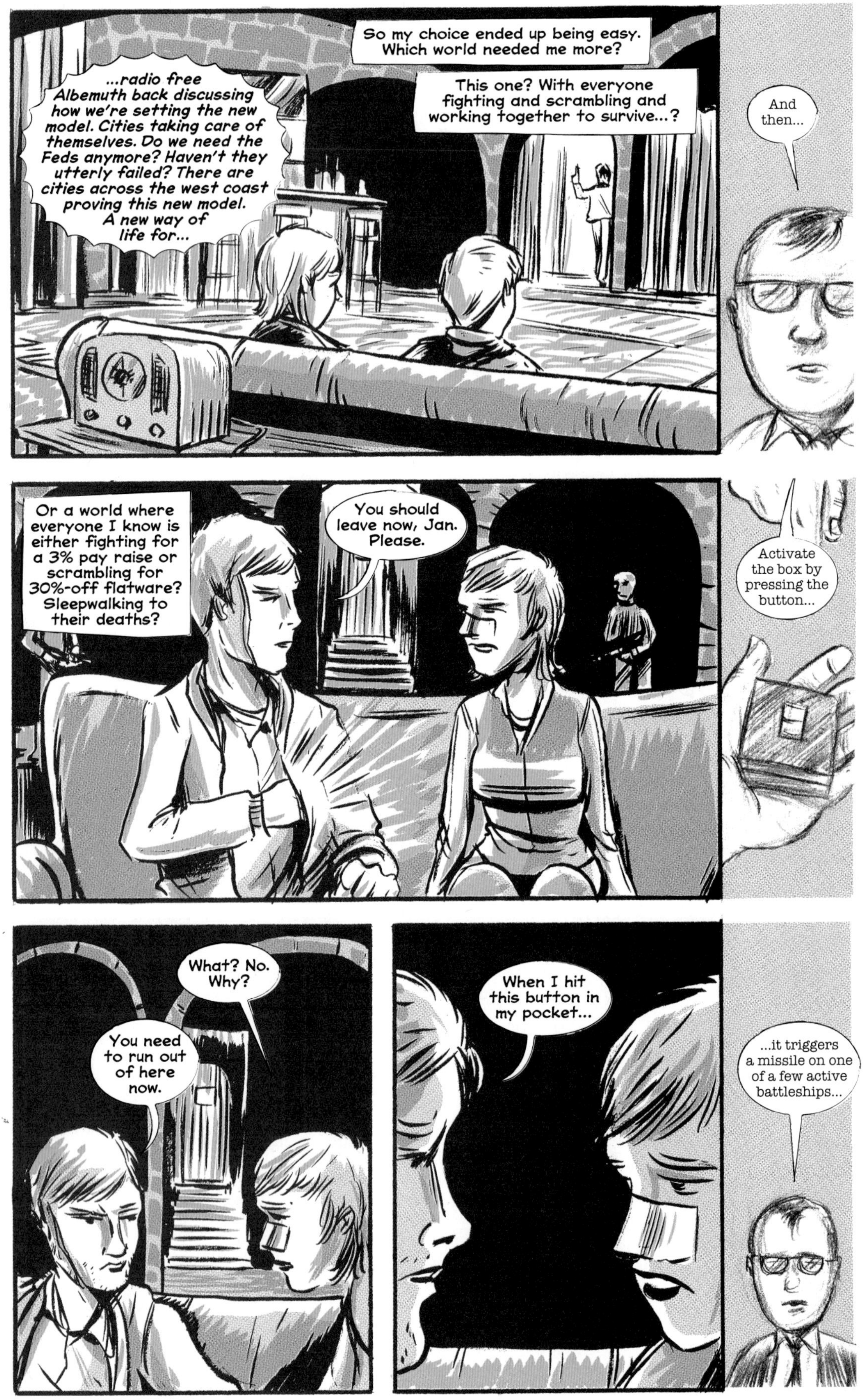
So my choice ended up being easy. Which world needed me more?
...radio free Albemuth back discussing how we're setting the new model. Cities taking care of themselves. Do we need the Feds anymore? Haven't they utterly failed? There are cities across the west coast proving this new model. A new way of life for...
This one? With everyone fighting and scrambling and working together to survive...?
And then...
Or a world where everyone I know is either fighting for a 3% pay raise or scrambling for 30%-off flatware? Sleepwalking to their deaths?
You should leave now, Jan. Please.
Activate the box by pressing the button...
What? No. Why?
You need to run out of here now.
When I hit this button in my pocket...
...it triggers a missile on one of a few active battleships...

IMING A STANDOFF BETWEEN THE "76ERS" AND THE NATIONAL GUARD IS INEVITABLE. **143** CASUALTIES HAVE BEEN REPORTED

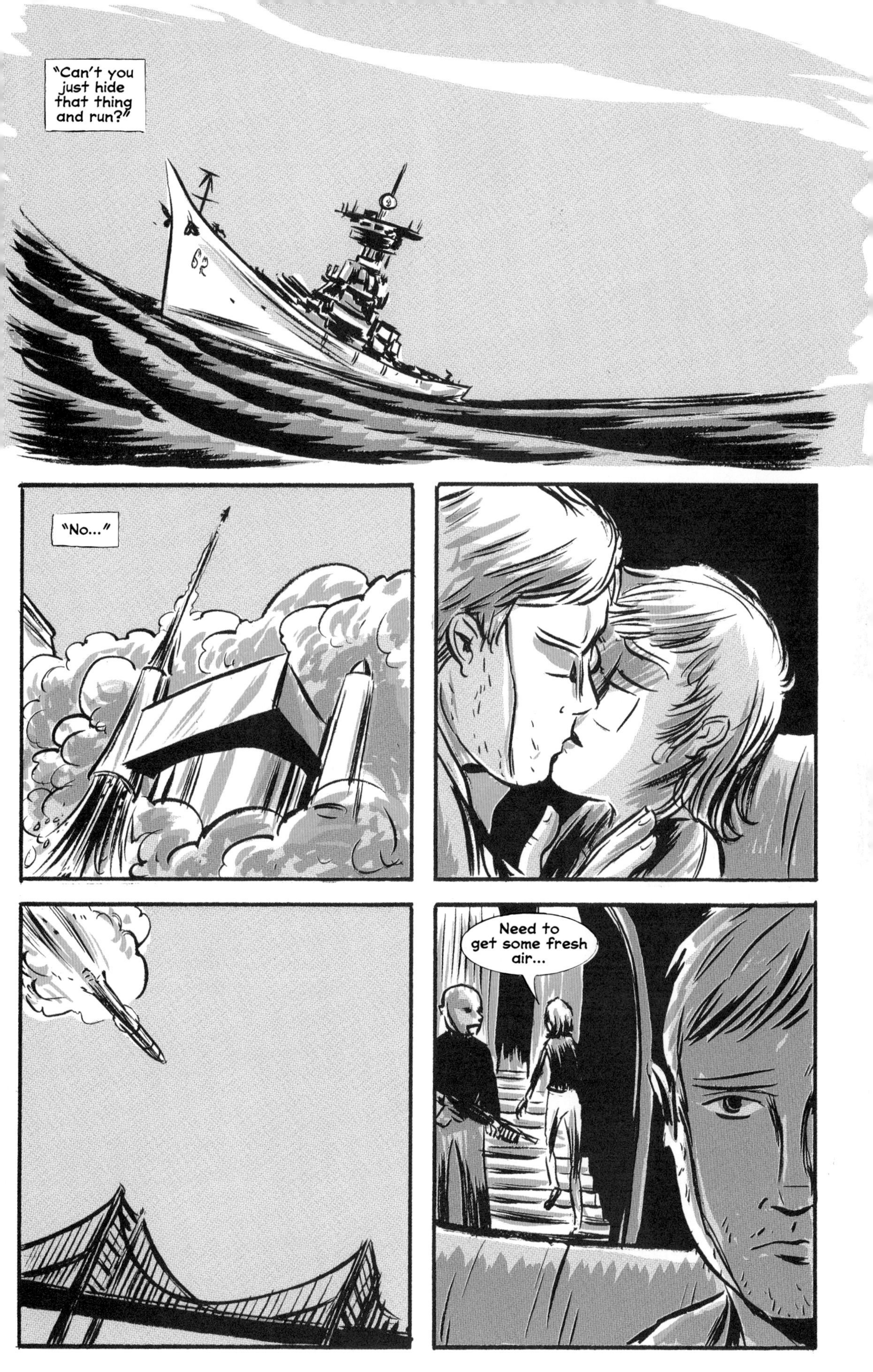
"Can't you just hide that thing and run?"
"No..."
Need to get some fresh air...

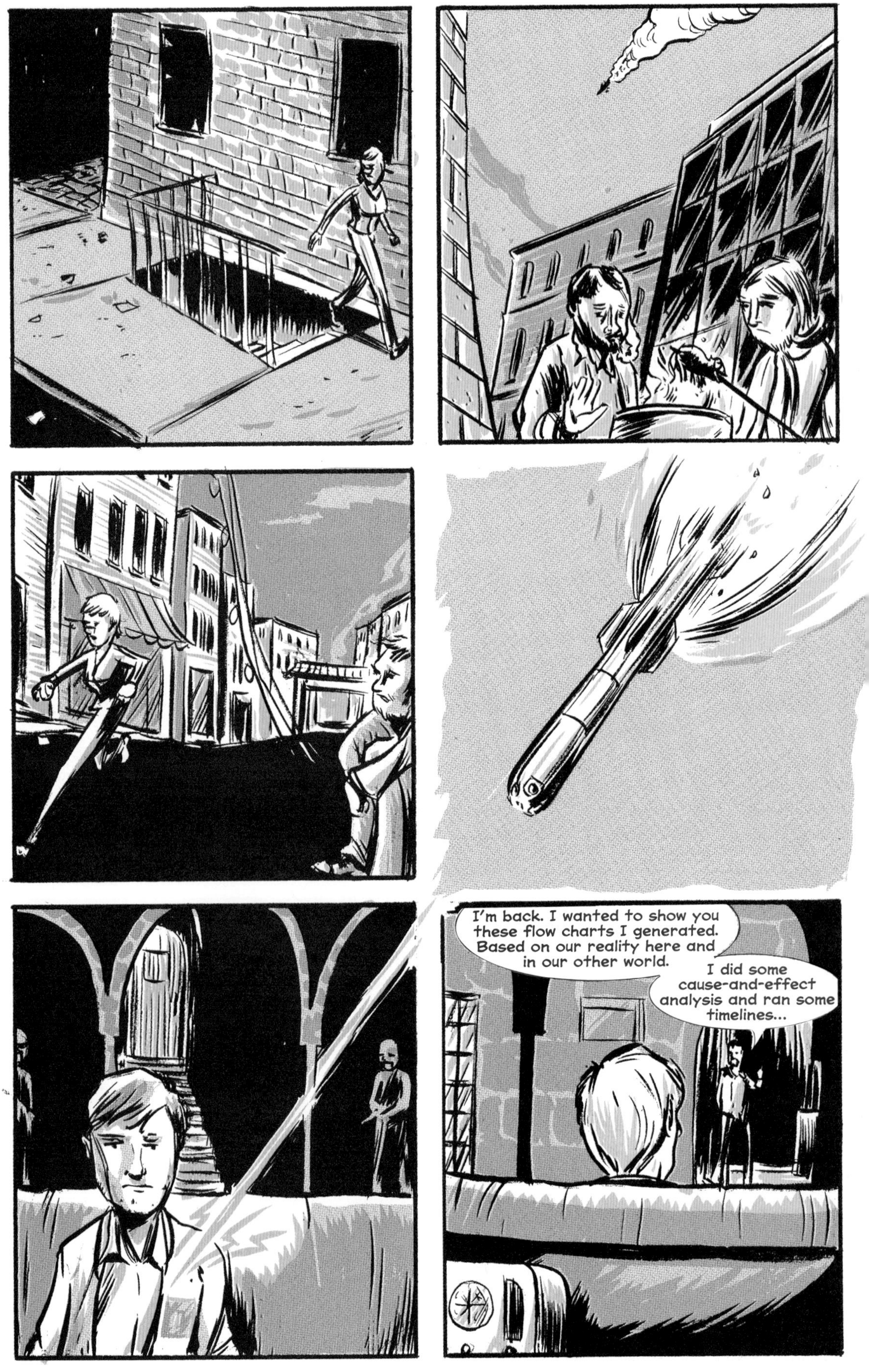
I'm back. I wanted to show you these flow charts I generated. Based on our reality here and in our other world.
I did some cause-and-effect analysis and ran some timelines...

NING AND OFFICIAL WORD FROM THE PRESIDENT. 14,500 U.N. TROOPS HAVE BEEN CALLED IN TO ASSIST THE "76ERS" AGAINST

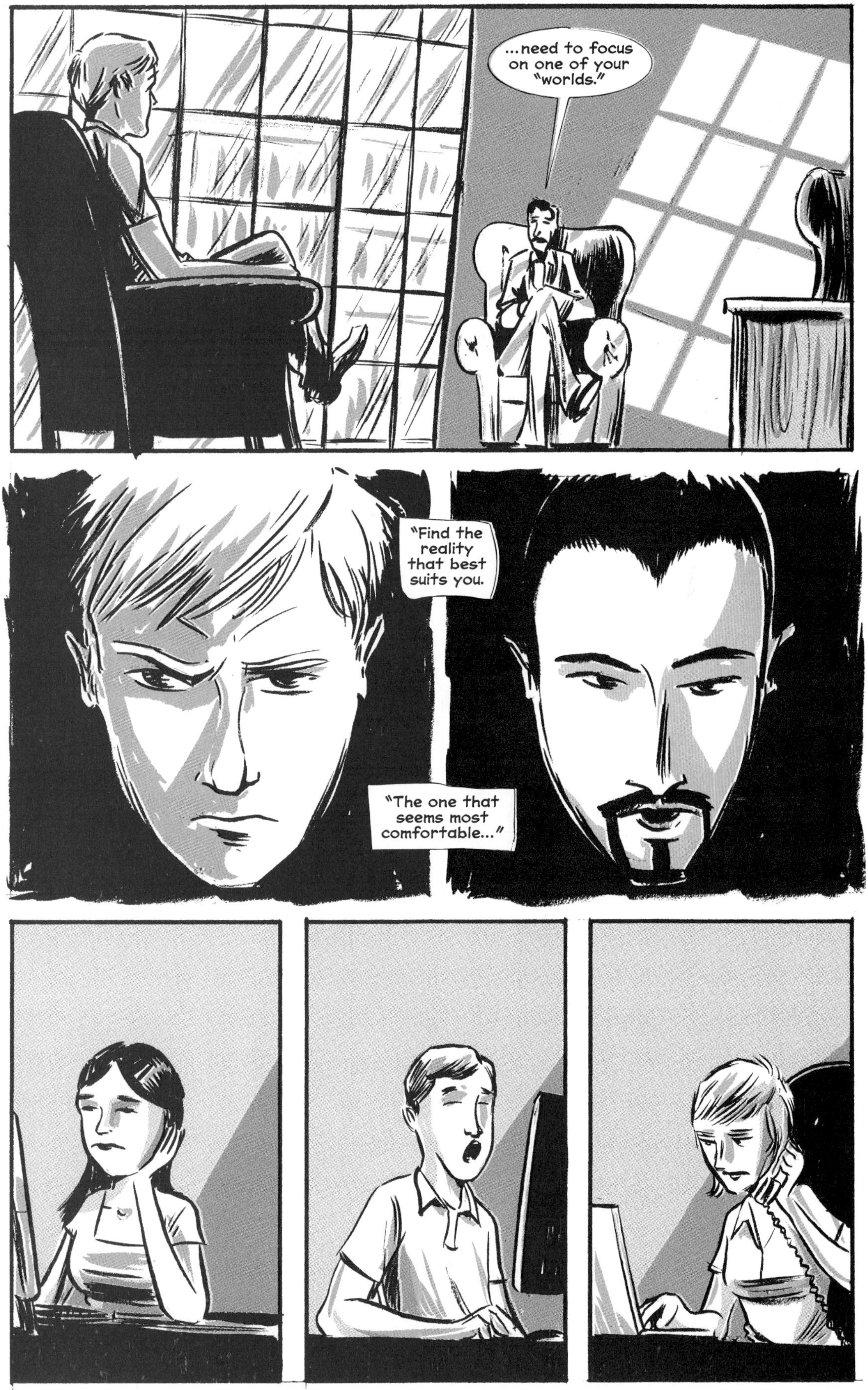
...need to focus on one of your "worlds."
"Find the reality that best suits you.
"The one that seems most comfortable..."

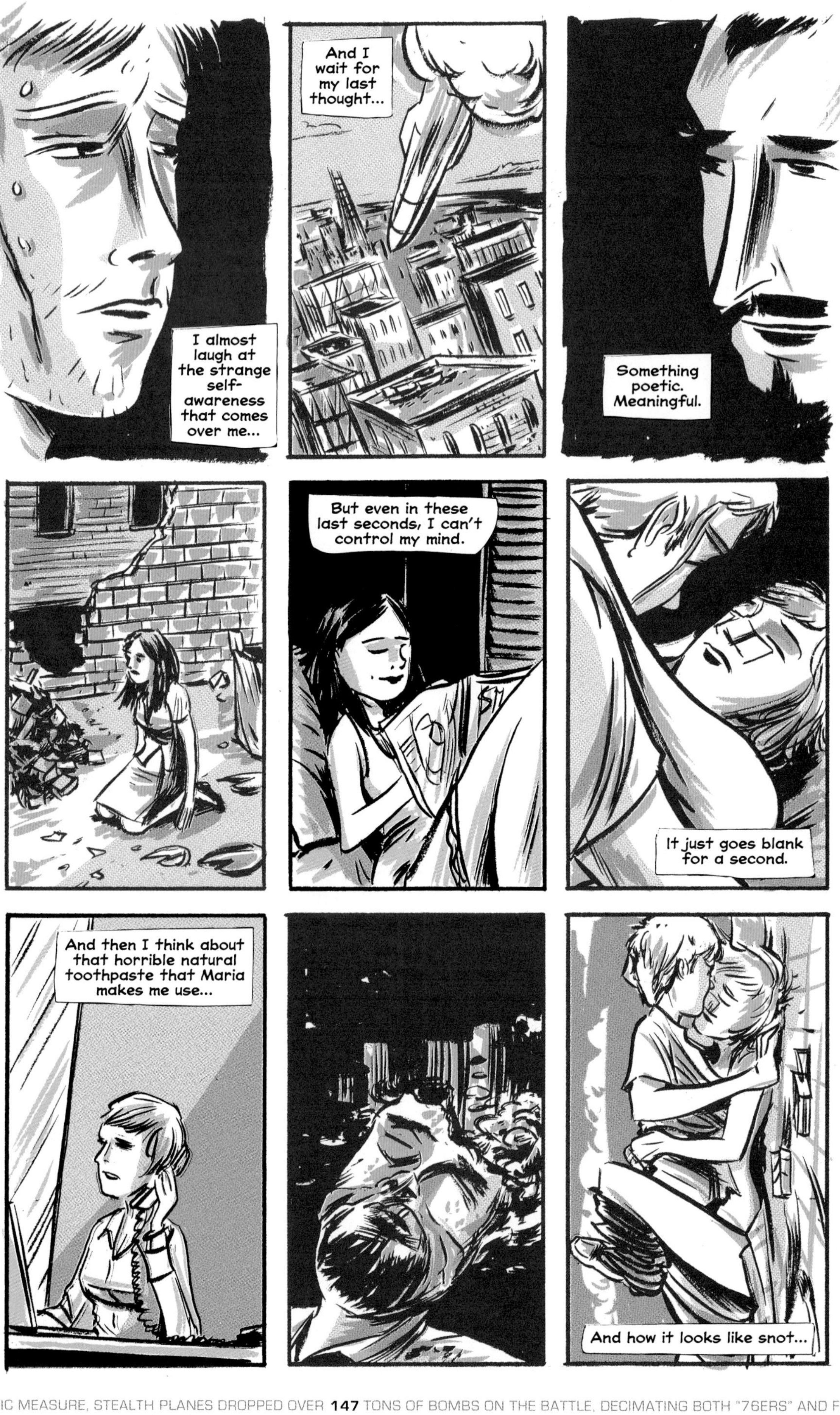
I almost laugh at the strange self-awareness that comes over me...
And I wait for my last thought...
Something poetic. Meaningful.
But even in these last seconds, I can't control my mind.
It just goes blank for a second.
And then I think about that horrible natural toothpaste that Maria makes me use...
And how it looks like snot...

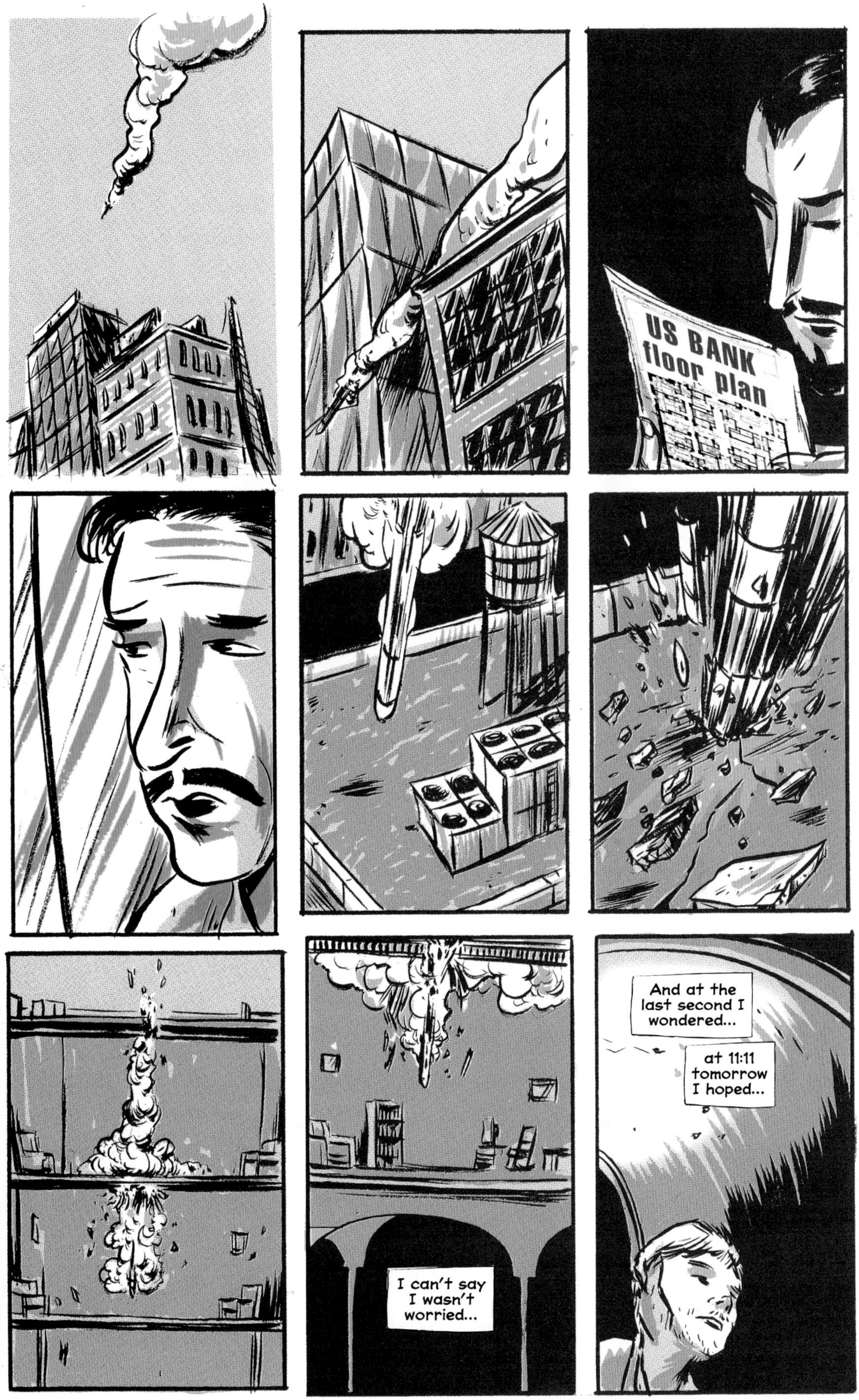
US BANK
floor plan
I can't say
I wasn't
worried...
And at the
last second I
wondered...
at 11:11
tomorrow
I hoped...

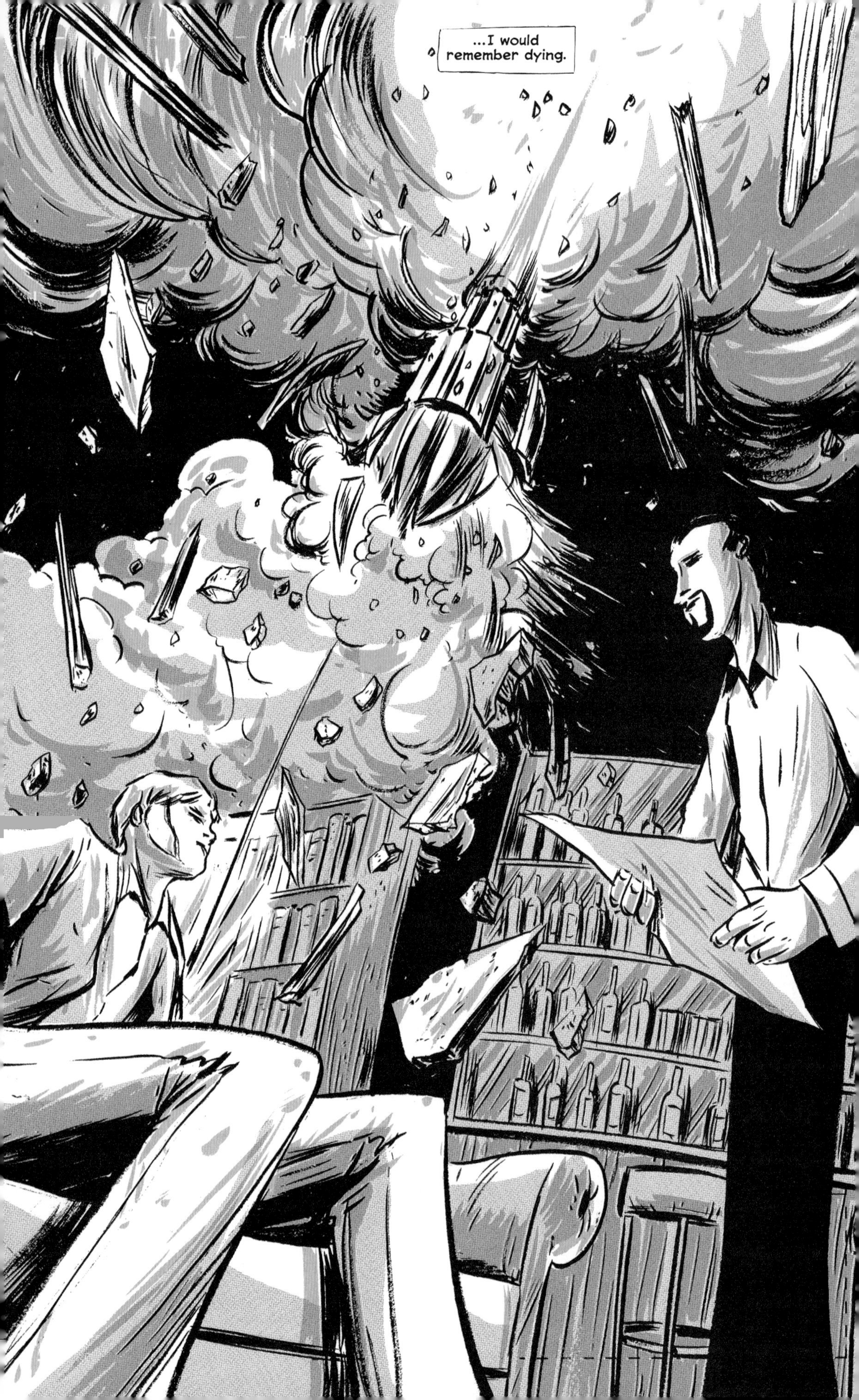
...I would remember dying.

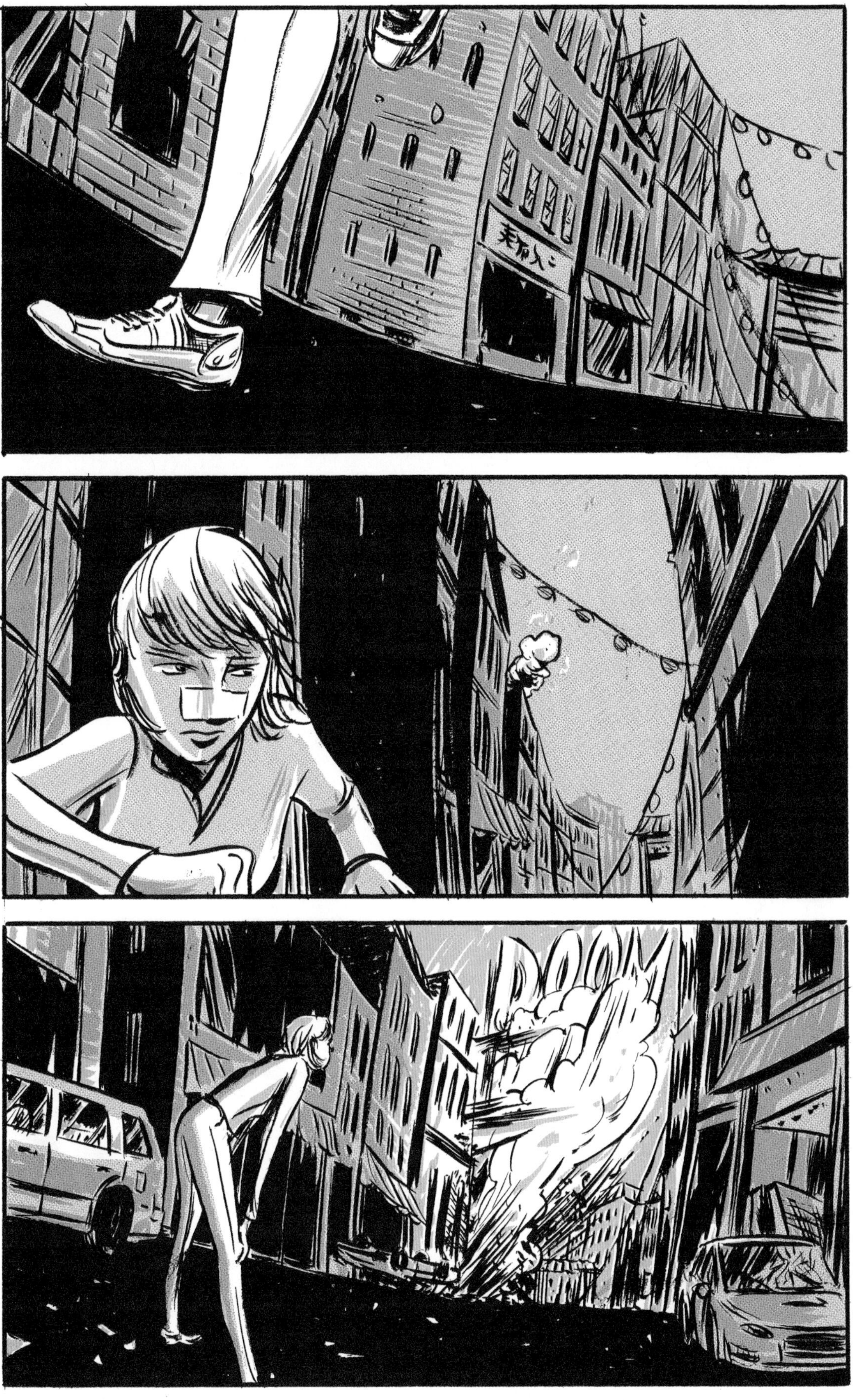
BOOM

RE URGING RESIDENTS TO AVOID THE CITY CENTER. **I-50** IS CLOSED TO PEDESTRIAN TRAFFIC AS WHAT REMAINS OF THE BATTER

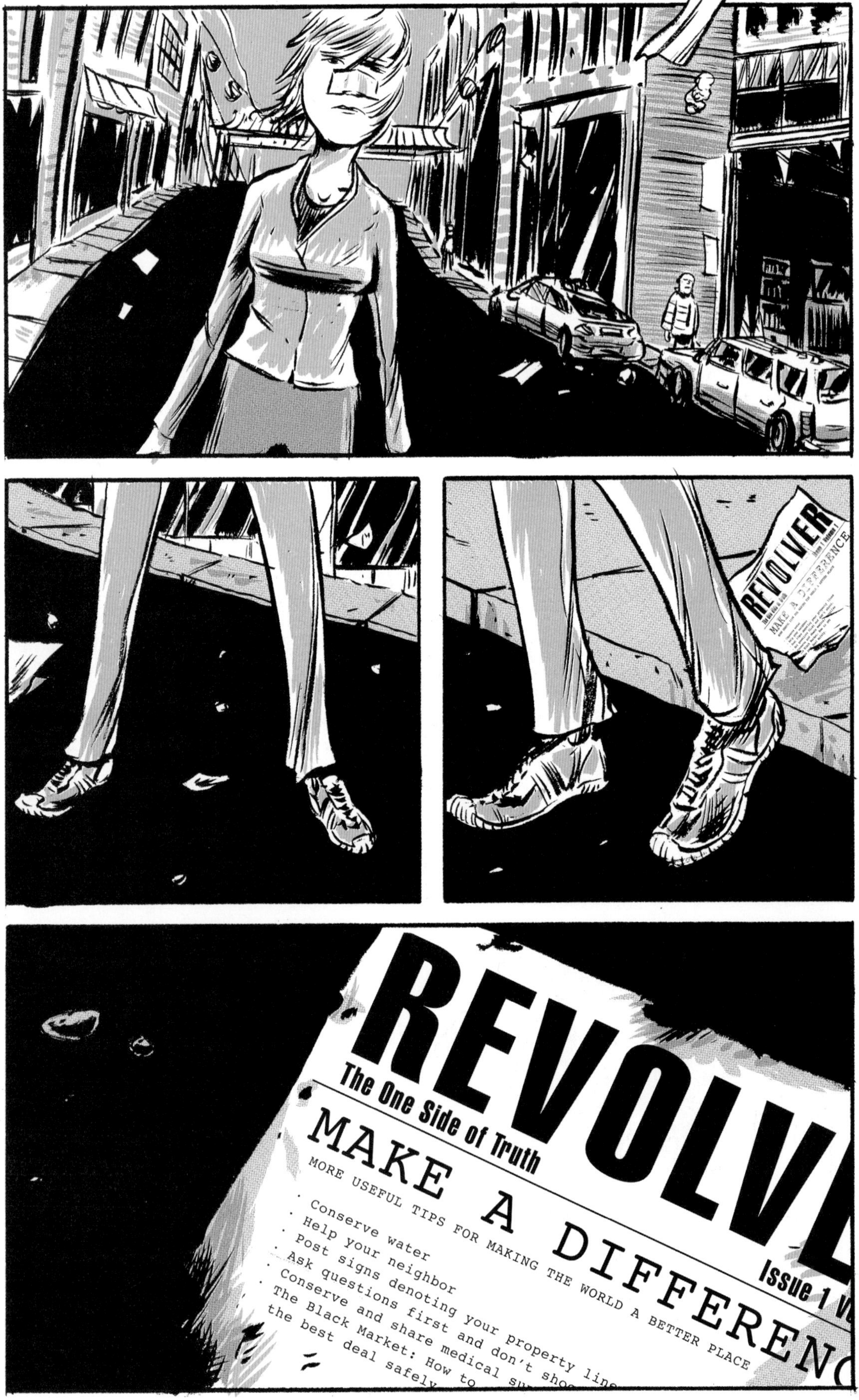
REVOLVER
MAKE A DIFFERENCE
REVOLV
The One Side of Truth
Issue 1 V
MAKE A DIFFERENC
MORE USEFUL TIPS FOR MAKING THE WORLD A BETTER PLACE
. Conserve water
. Help your neighbor
. Post signs denoting your property lin
. Ask questions first and don't sho
. Conserve and share medical s
. The Black Market: How to
the best deal safely

G THAT THE RELIEF EFFORT SPEARHEADED BY THE HOME-GROWN NEWSPAPER HAS PROVIDED OVER **1,51**0 CHICAGO REFUGEES

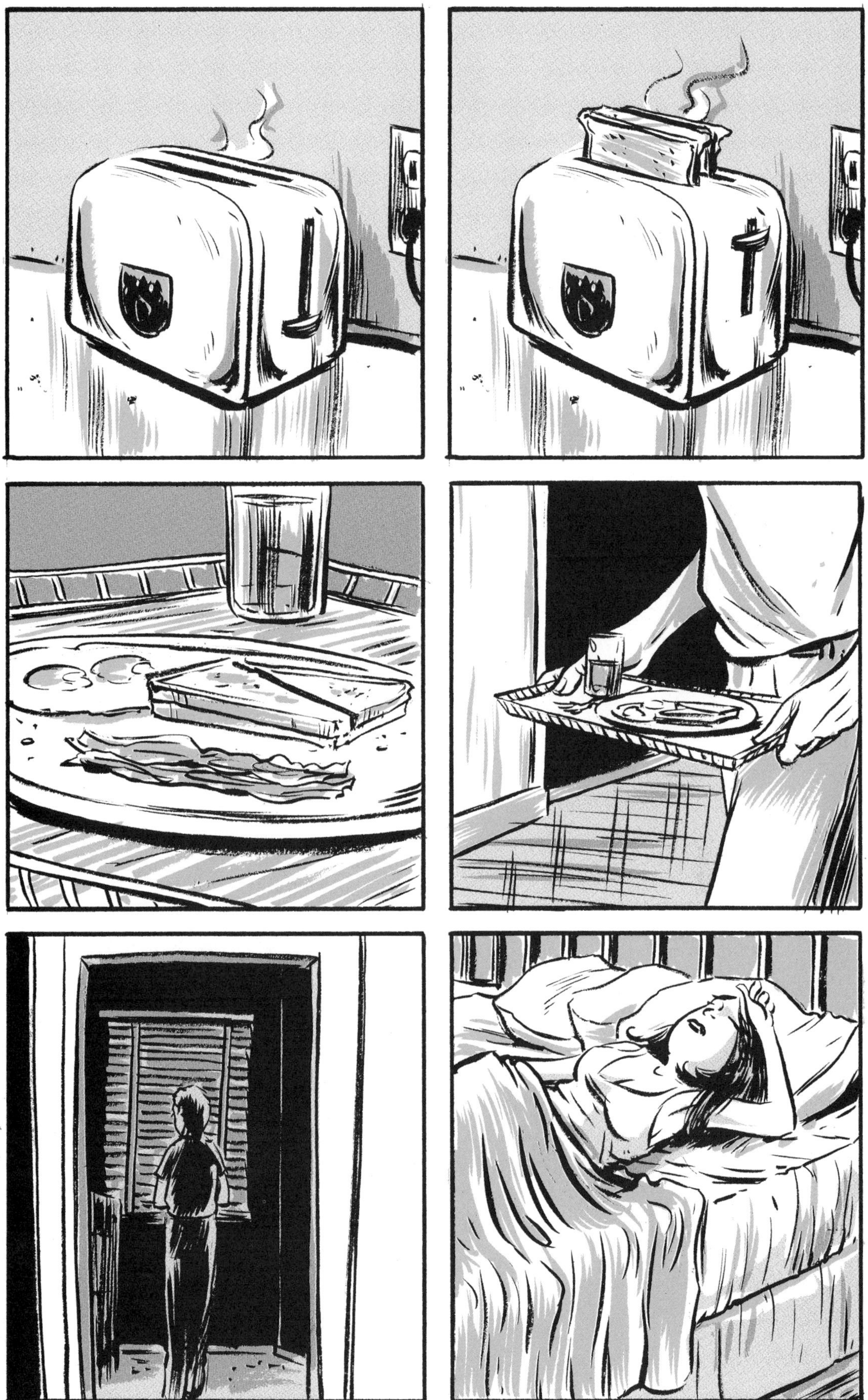

ADAPTATION OF "BEAST WITH 1,000 FACES" BROKE ALL RECORDS WITH AN OPENING OF $**152** MILLION, MAKING THE OWNER, P

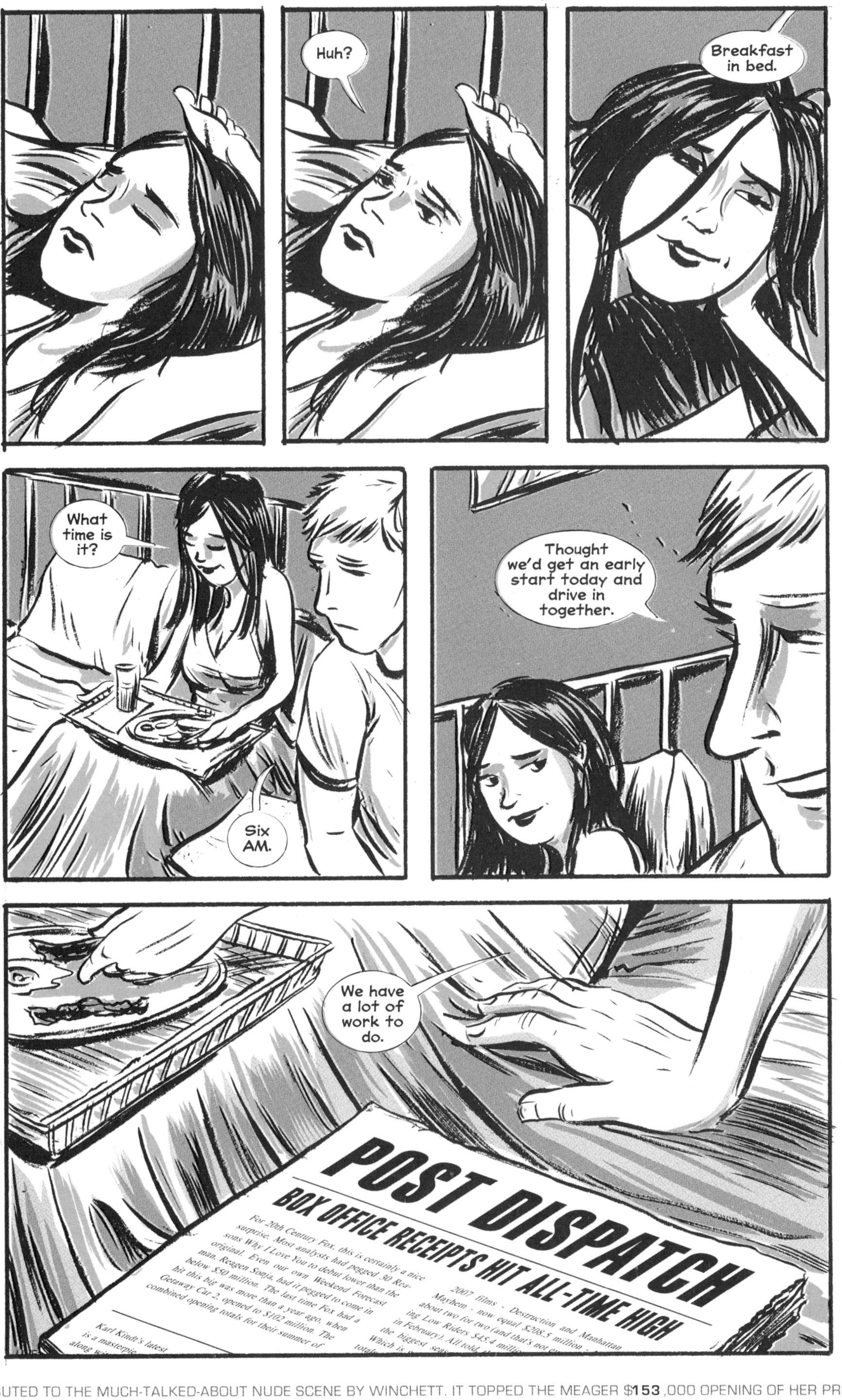

Huh?
Breakfast in bed.
What time is it?
Six AM.
Thought we'd get an early start today and drive in together.
We have a lot of work to do.
POST DISPATCH
BOX OFFICE RECEIPTS HIT ALL-TIME HIGH
For 20th Century Fox, this is certainly a nice surprise. Most analysts had pegged 30 Reasons Why I Love You to debut lower than the original. Even our own Weekend Forecast man, Reagen Sonja, had it pegged to come in below $50 million. The last time Fox had a hit this big was more than a year ago, when Getaway Car 2, opened to $102 million. The combined opening totals for their summer of
2007 films - Destruction and Manhattan Mayhem - now equal $208.5 million
Karl Kindt's latest

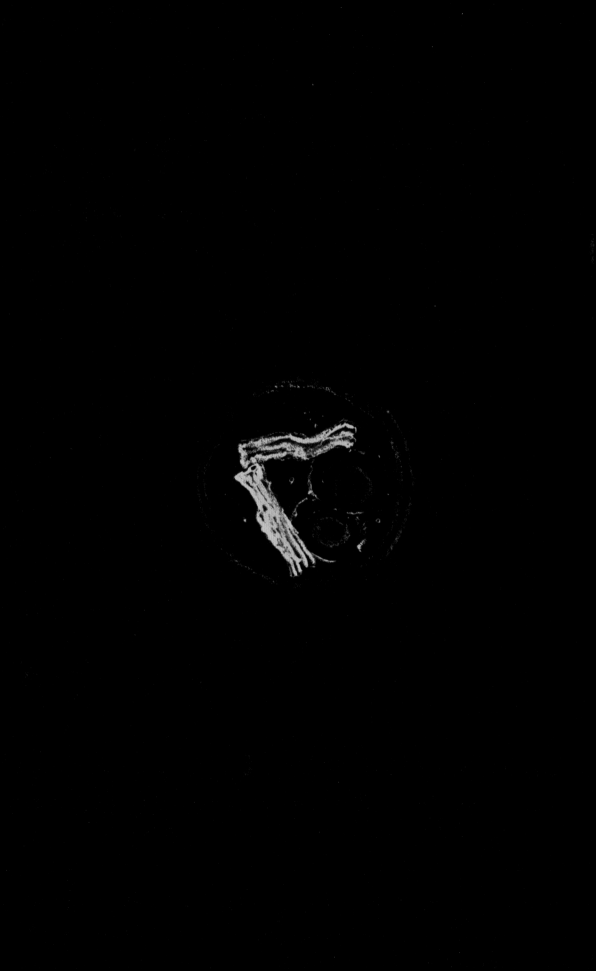

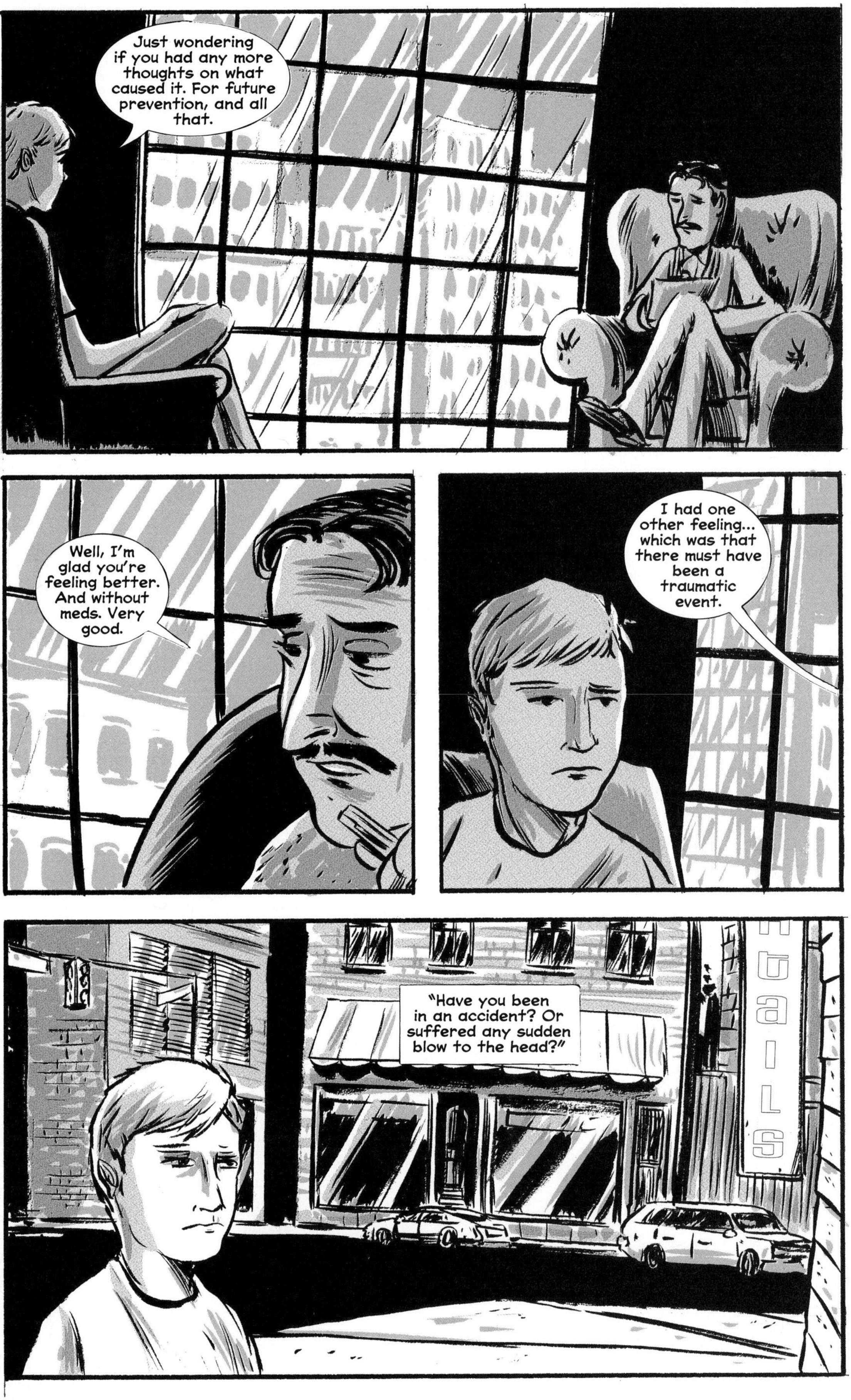
Just wondering if you had any more thoughts on what caused it. For future prevention, and all that.
Well, I'm glad you're feeling better. And without meds. Very good.
I had one other feeling... which was that there must have been a traumatic event.
"Have you been in an accident? Or suffered any sudden blow to the head?"

THE TOP OF THE CHARTS, BESTING 80 GEEZ'S AND CLIMBING FROM #**154** TO #1 IN EIGHT SHORT WEEKS. THE HIT "BUSTANUT"

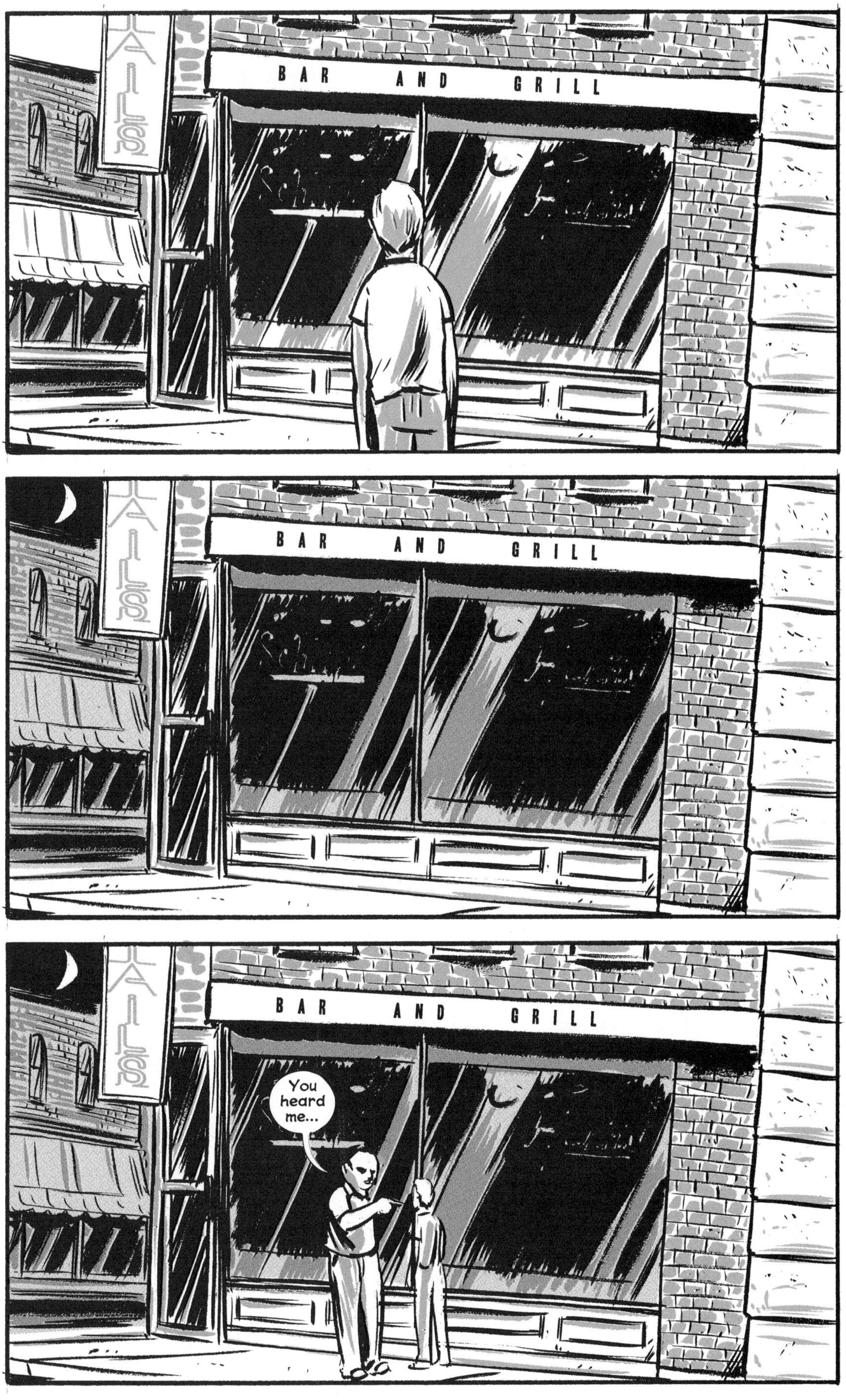
BAR AND GRILL
BAR AND GRILL
BAR AND GRILL
You heard me...

CE FOUND THE BODY OF "76ERS" LEADER DEAD IN HIS CAR NEAR **I-55**, APPARENTLY FROM A SELF-INFLICTED GUNSHOT WOUND

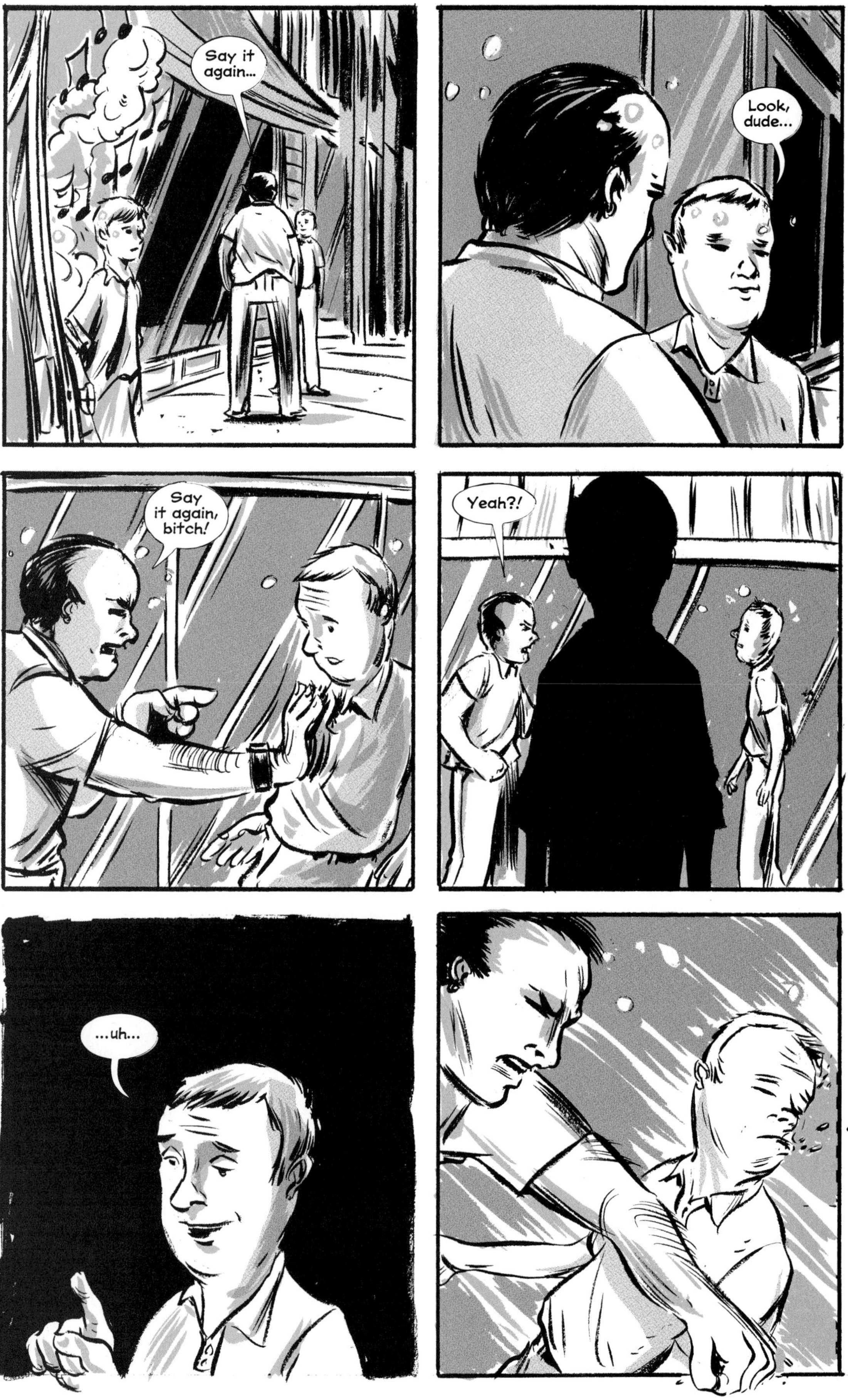
Say it again...
Look, dude...
Say it again, bitch!
Yeah?!
...uh...

STIMONY THAT 156 BYSTANDERS REFUSED TO INTERVENE AS SHE WAS BRUTALLY BEATEN AND THEN DRAGGED THROUGH THE

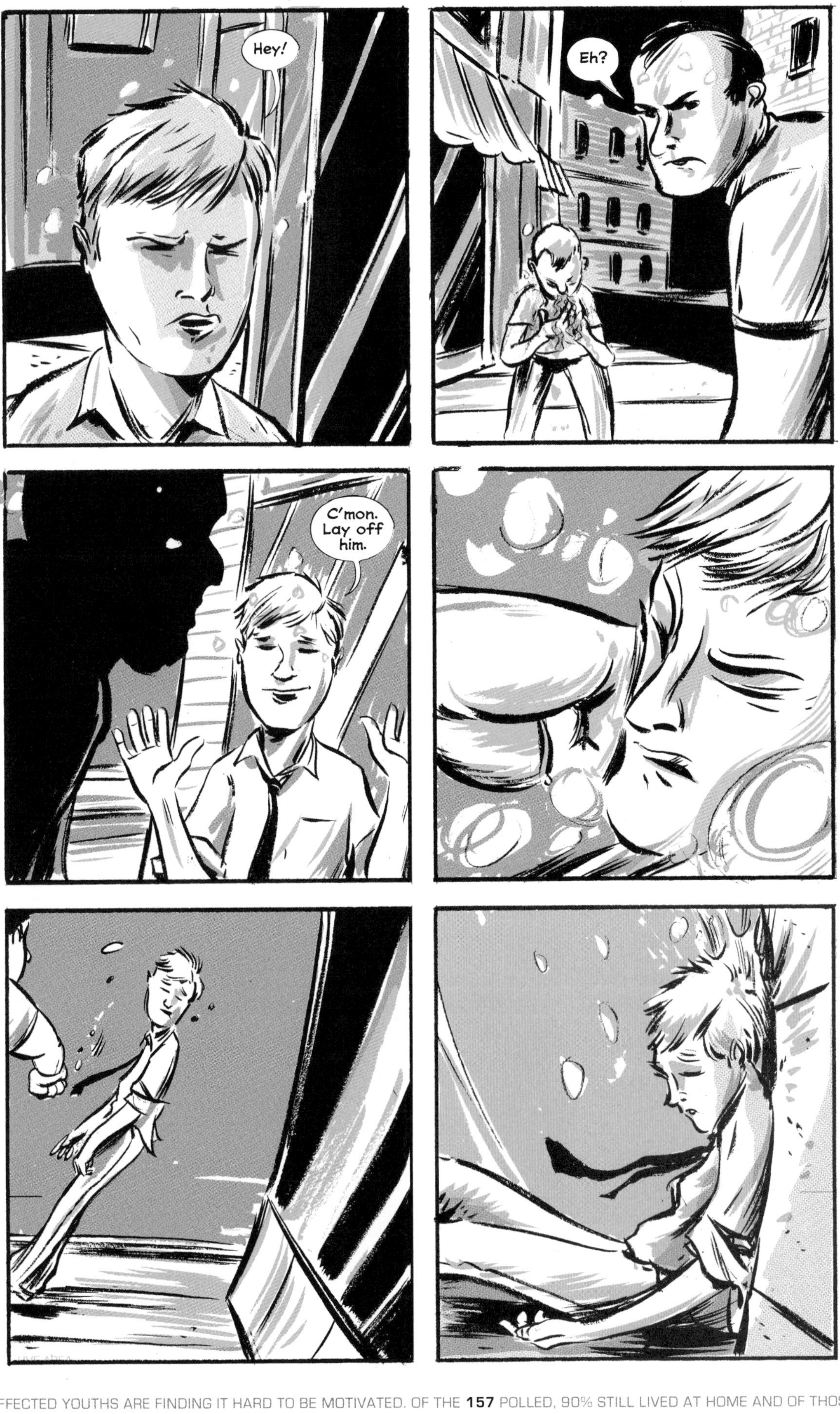
Hey!
Eh?
C'mon. Lay off him.

DISAFFECTED YOUTHS ARE FINDING IT HARD TO BE MOTIVATED. OF THE **157** POLLED, 90% STILL LIVED AT HOME AND OF THOSE

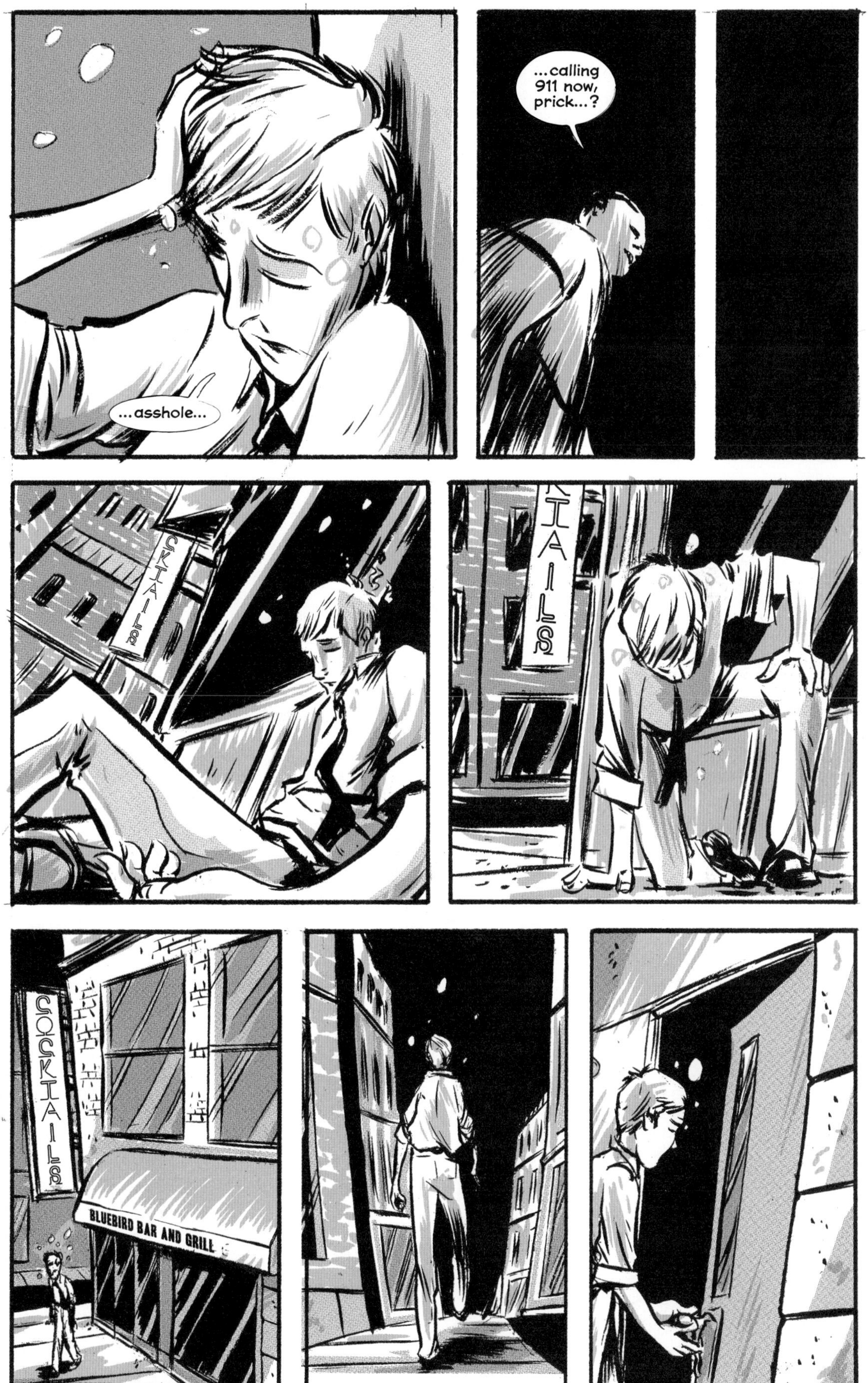
...asshole...
...calling 911 now, prick...?
COCKTAILS
BLUEBIRD BAR AND GRILL

'HE ATTITUDE OF STUDENTS. IT IS THE FIRST PROTEST SINCE THE **JANUARY '58** RIOT THAT SPARKED THE CIVIL RIGHTS MARCH I

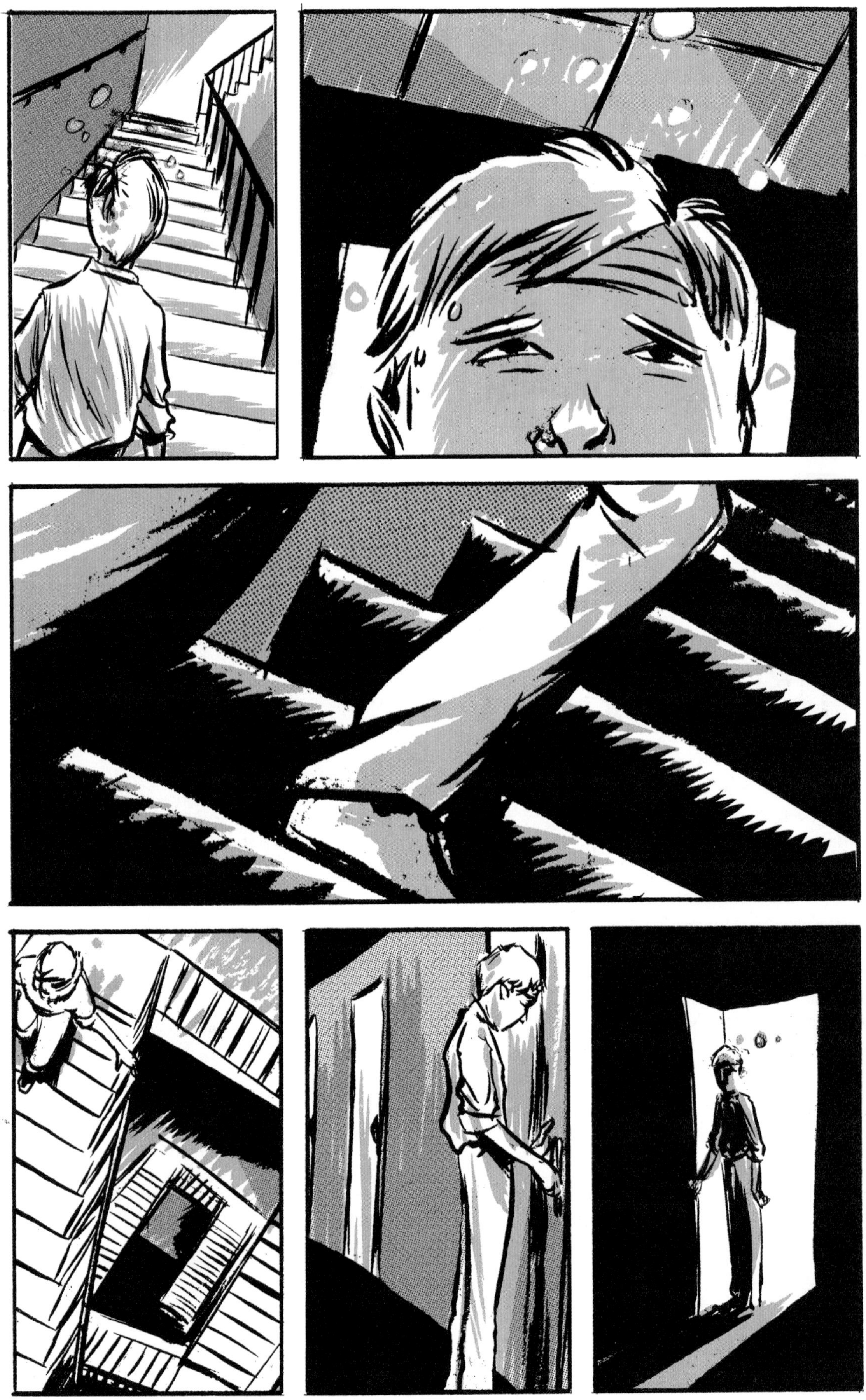

ND MORE CITE DEPRESSION AND BOREDOM. **159**,000 JOB LOSSES HAVE BEEN ATTRIBUTED TO LACK OF MOTIVATION ON THE PA

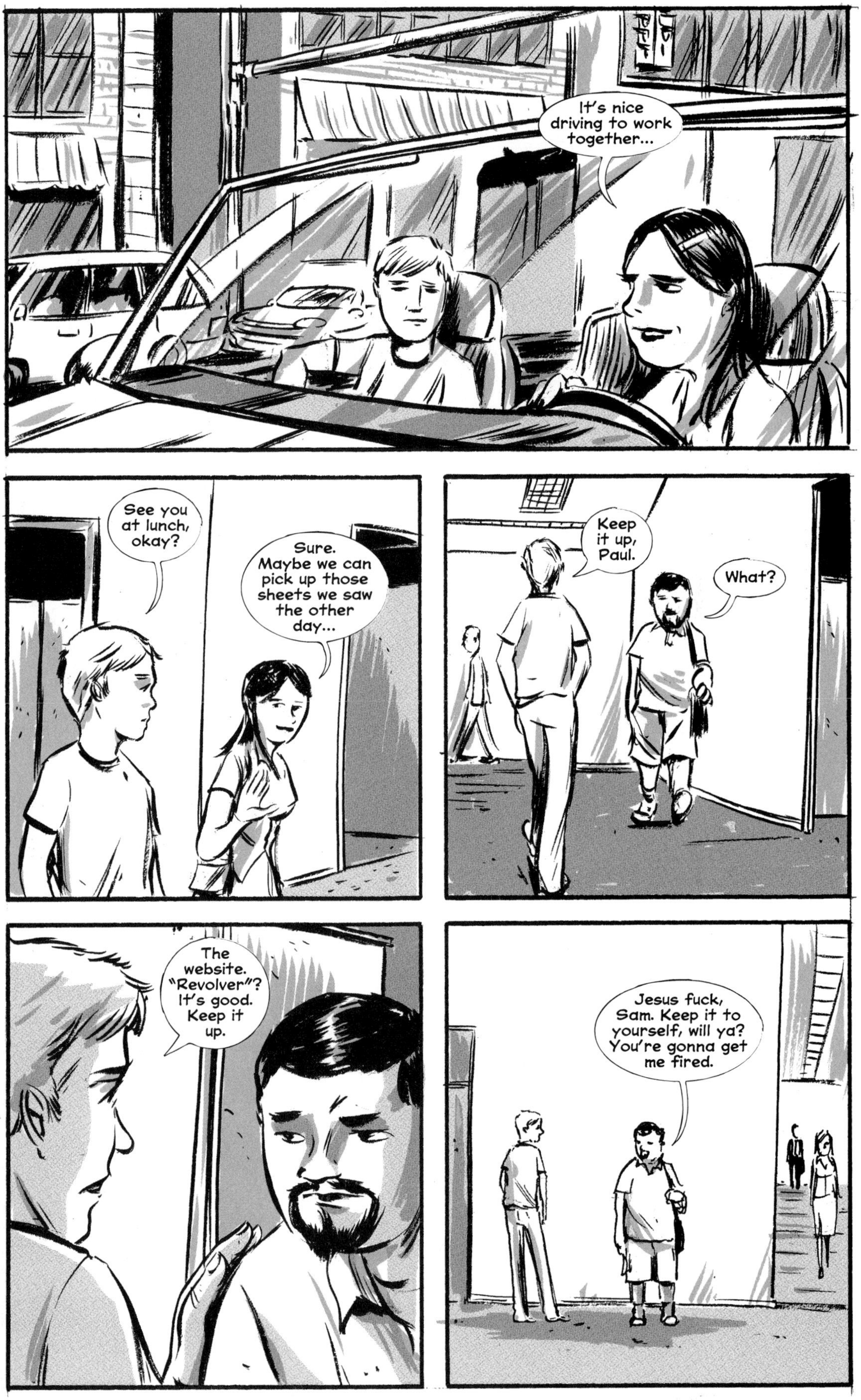
It's nice driving to work together...
See you at lunch, okay?
Sure. Maybe we can pick up those sheets we saw the other day...
Keep it up, Paul.
What?
The website. "Revolver"? It's good. Keep it up.
Jesus fuck, Sam. Keep it to yourself, will ya? You're gonna get me fired.

RIPS THE CAPITAL. IT IS ESTIMATED THAT NEARLY $160 MILLION IN EARMARKED FUNDS HAS GONE MISSING. FINGERS ARE POIN

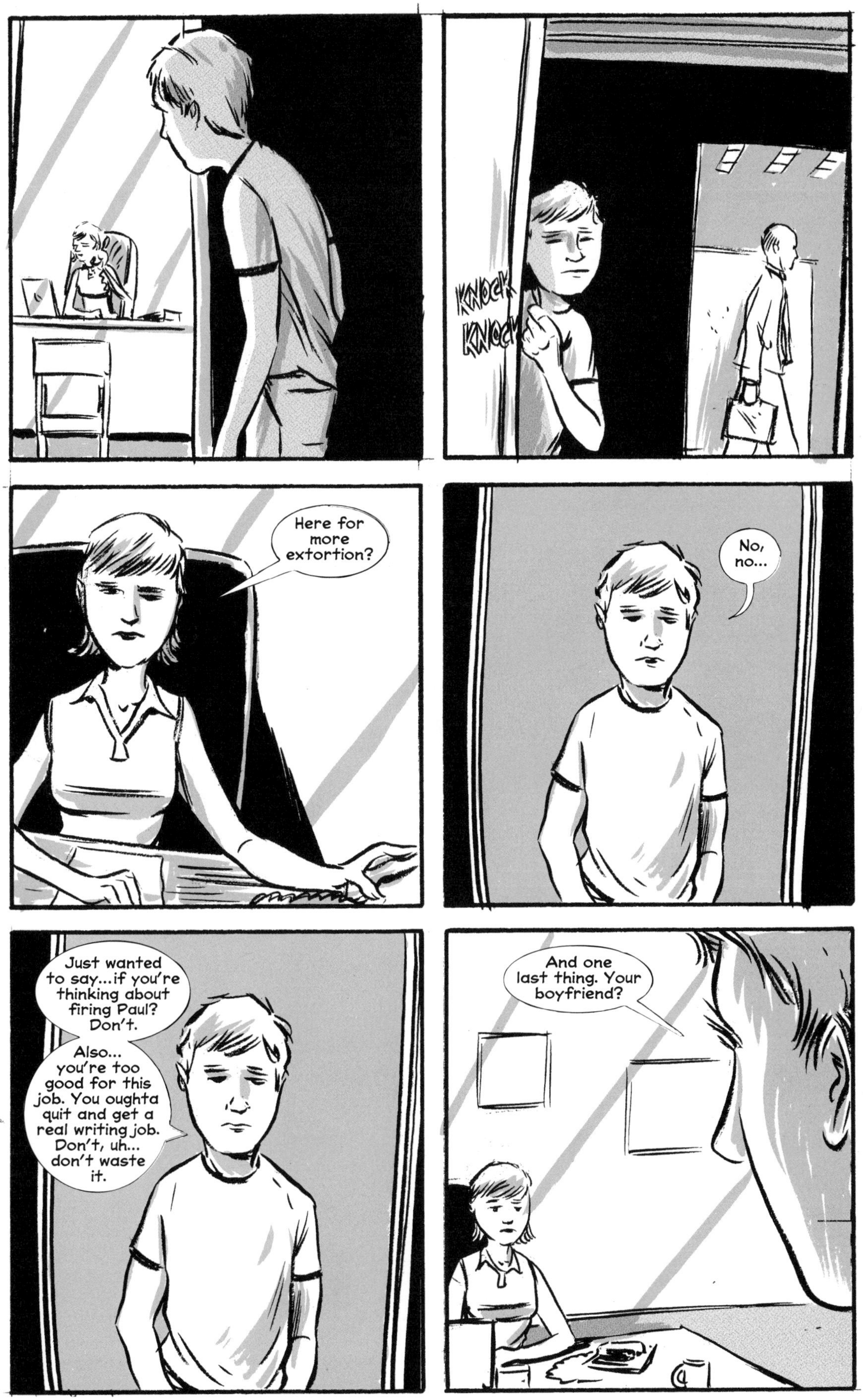
KNOCK
KNOCK
Here for more extortion?
No, no...
Just wanted to say...if you're thinking about firing Paul? Don't.
Also... you're too good for this job. You oughta quit and get a real writing job. Don't, uh... don't waste it.
And one last thing. Your boyfriend?

ORRIED AS A RESULT OF THE INFLUX OF FANS. THE STADIUM HOLDS APPROXIMATELY **161**,000 BUT THE HOTEL RECORDS REPOR

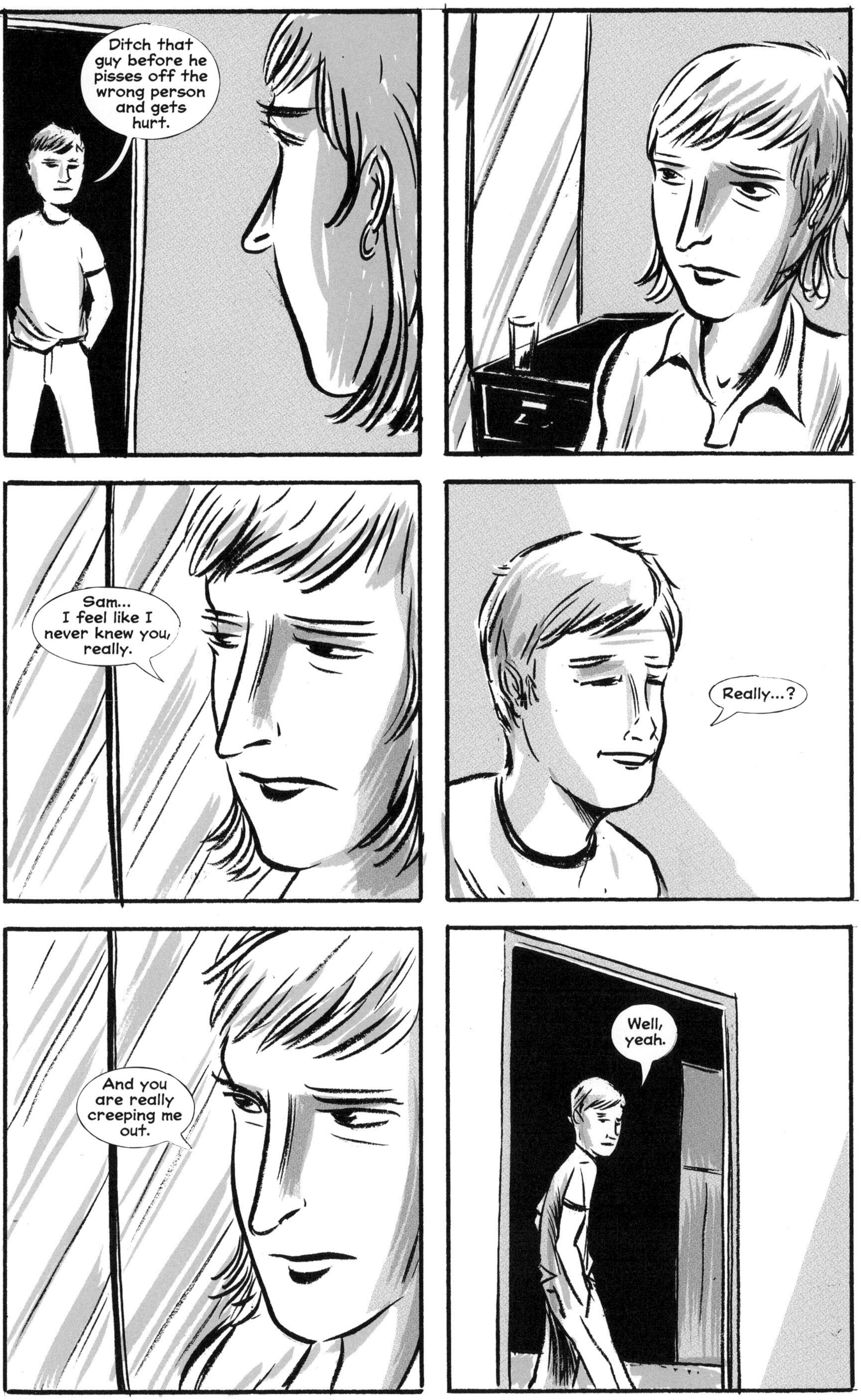
Ditch that guy before he pisses off the wrong person and gets hurt.
Sam... I feel like I never knew you, really.
Really...?
And you are really creeping me out.
Well, yeah.

E CANCELLATION OF THE STAR'S APPEARANCE, NEARLY **16,2**00 TEENAGE FANS AND PARENTS BEGAN A RIOT IN THE STREETS. TH

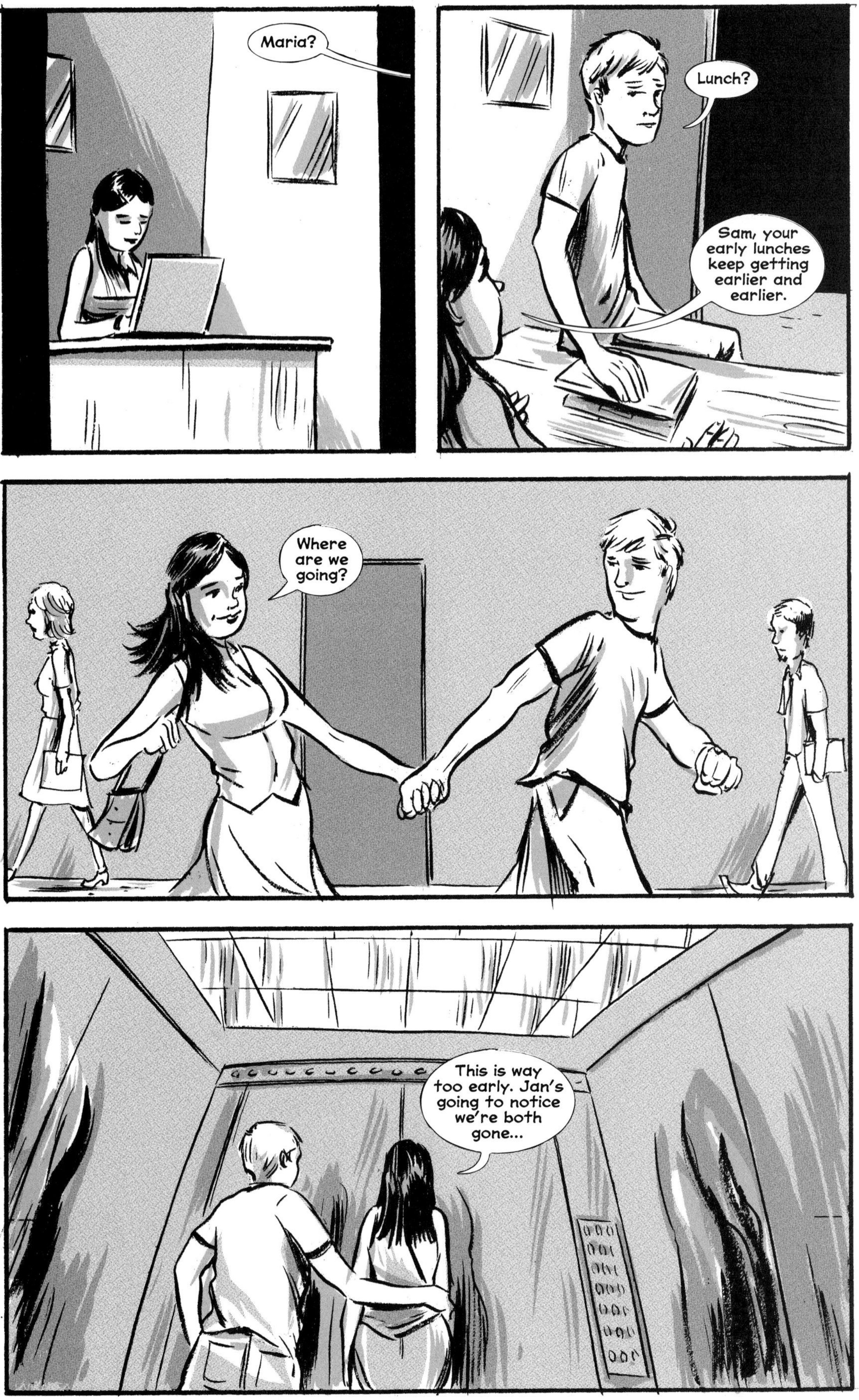
Maria?
Lunch?
Sam, your early lunches keep getting earlier and earlier.
Where are we going?
This is way too early. Jan's going to notice we're both gone...

MOR FOR THE NEW PHONE HAS REACHED A FEVER PITCH WITH ONLINE SALES TOPPING $**163** EACH FOR THE $25 DOLLAR DEVICE

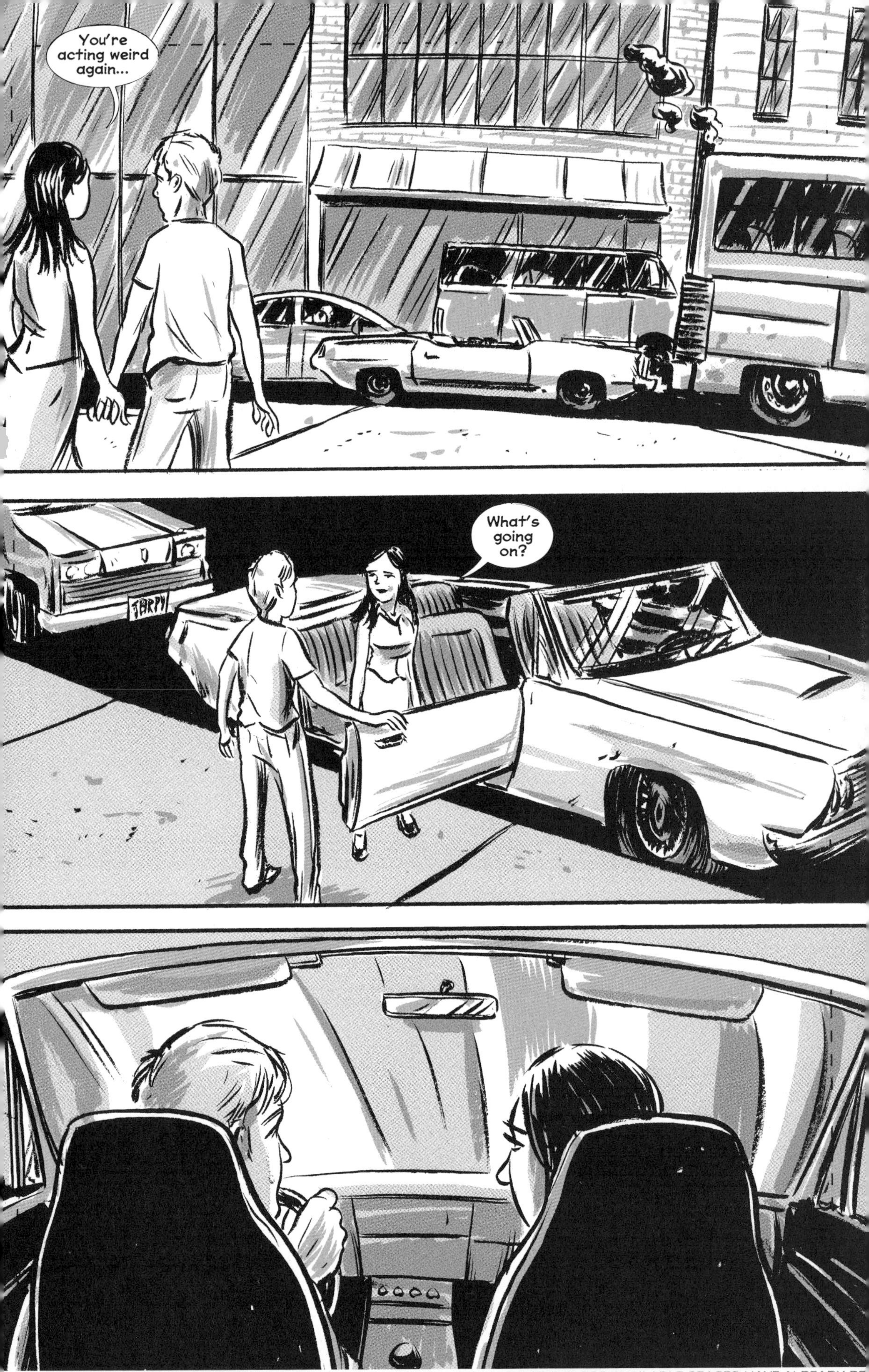
You're acting weird again...
What's going on?

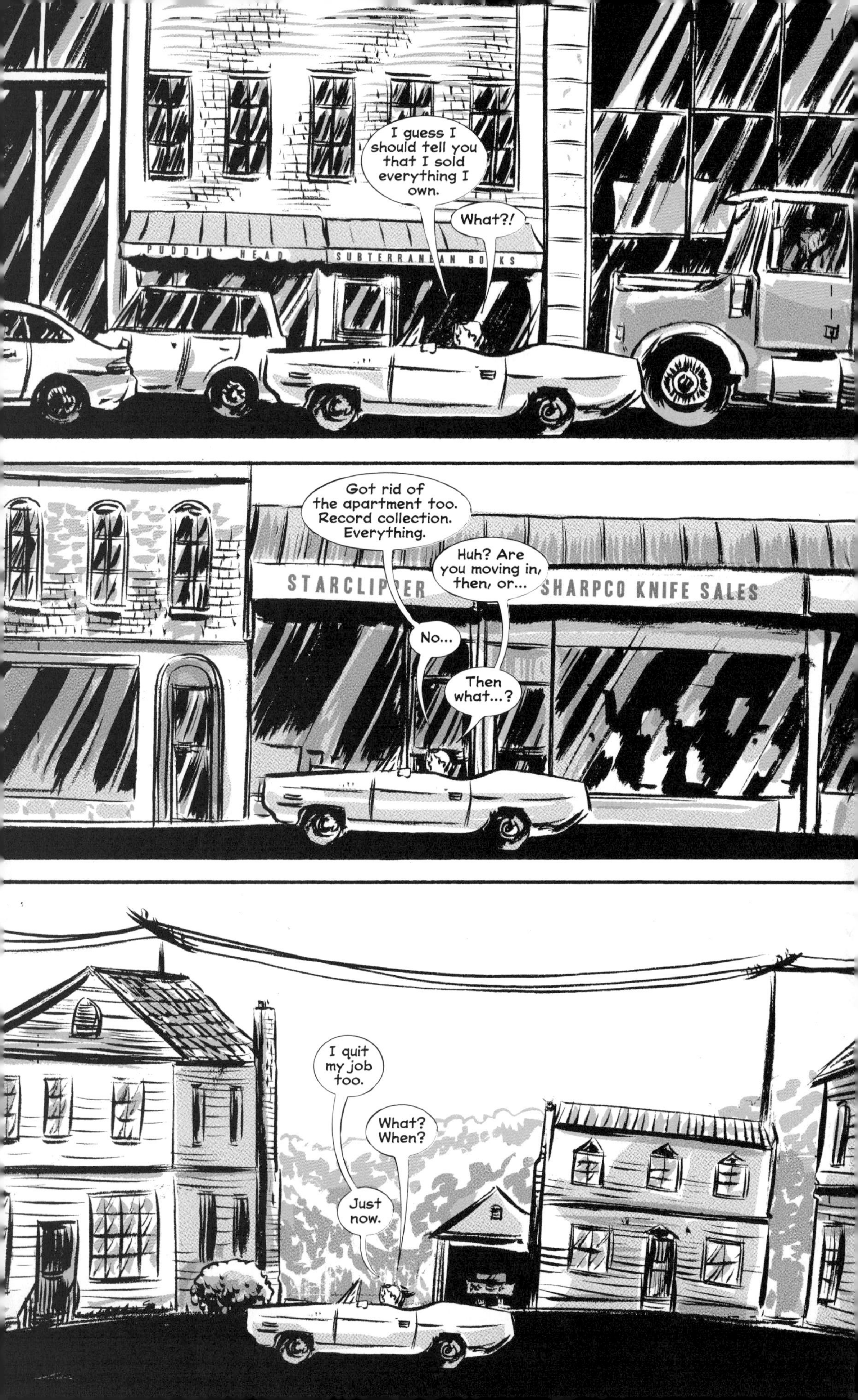
I guess I should tell you that I sold everything I own.
What?!
PUDDIN' HEAD
SUBTERRANEAN BOOKS
Got rid of the apartment too. Record collection. Everything.
Huh? Are you moving in, then, or...
STARCLIPPER
SHARPCO KNIFE SALES
No...
Then what...?
I quit my job too.
What? When?
Just now.

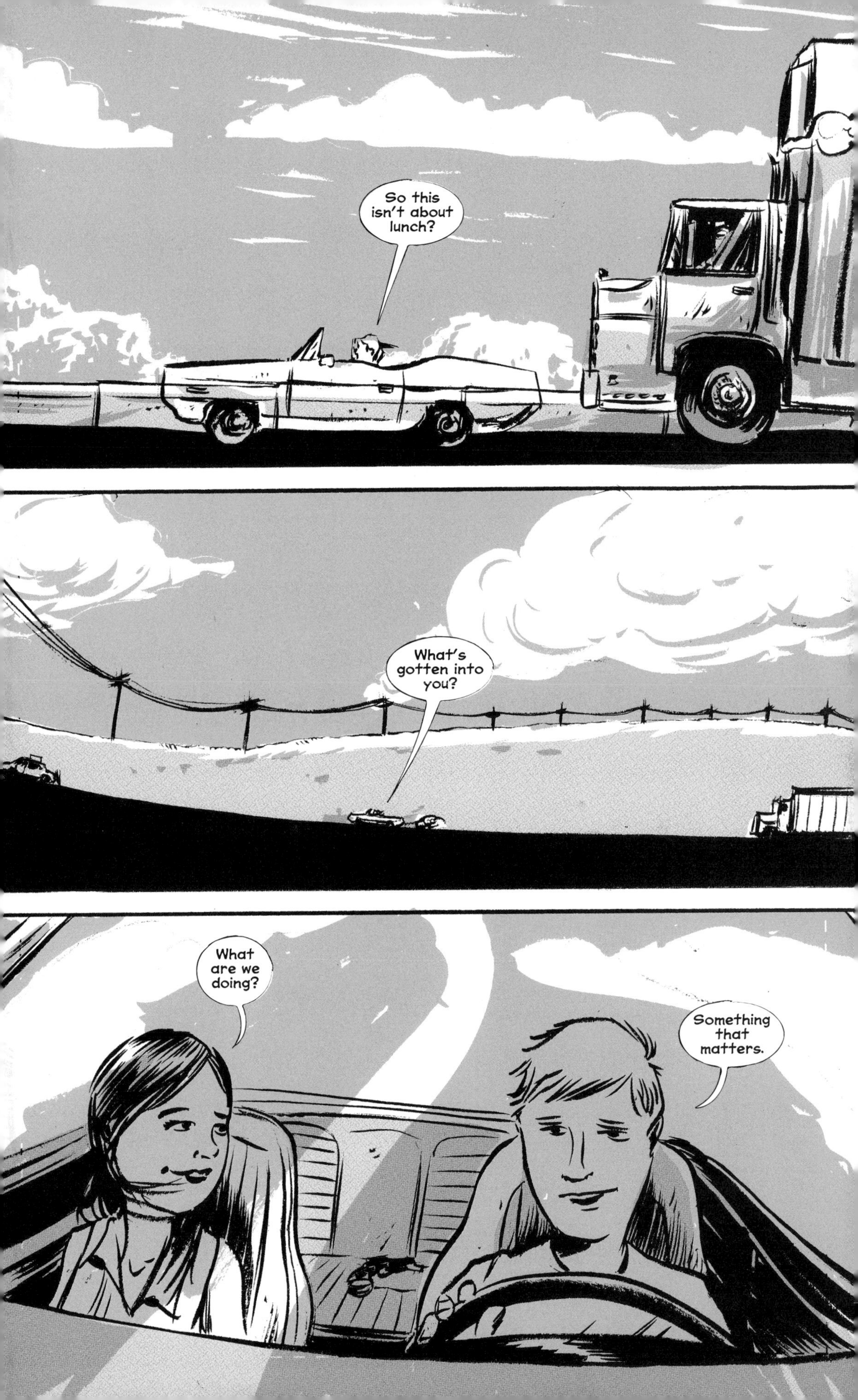
So this isn't about lunch?
What's gotten into you?
What are we doing?
Something that matters.

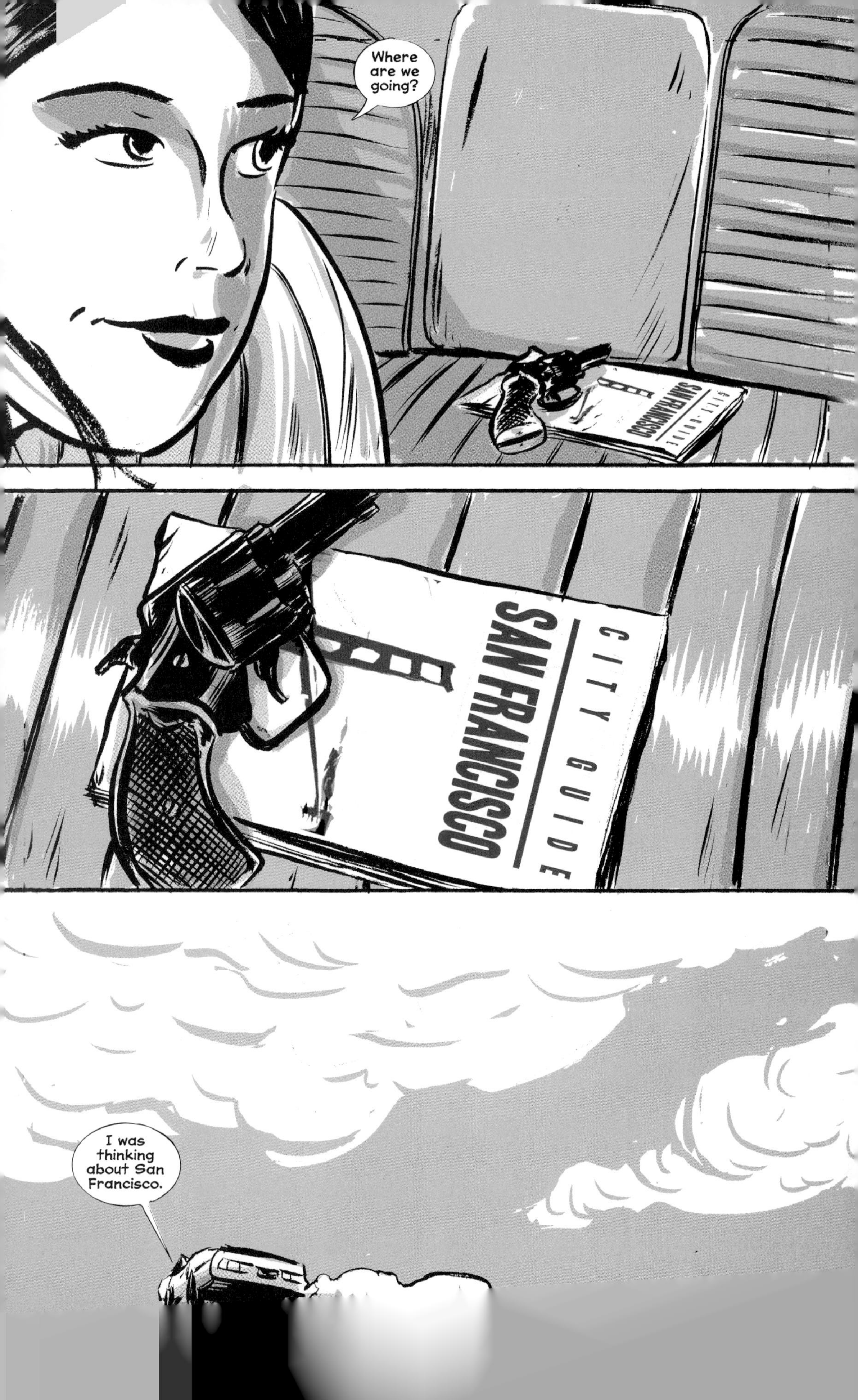
Where are we going?
CITY GUIDE
SAN FRANCISCO
CITY GUIDE
SAN FRANCISCO
I was thinking about San Francisco.

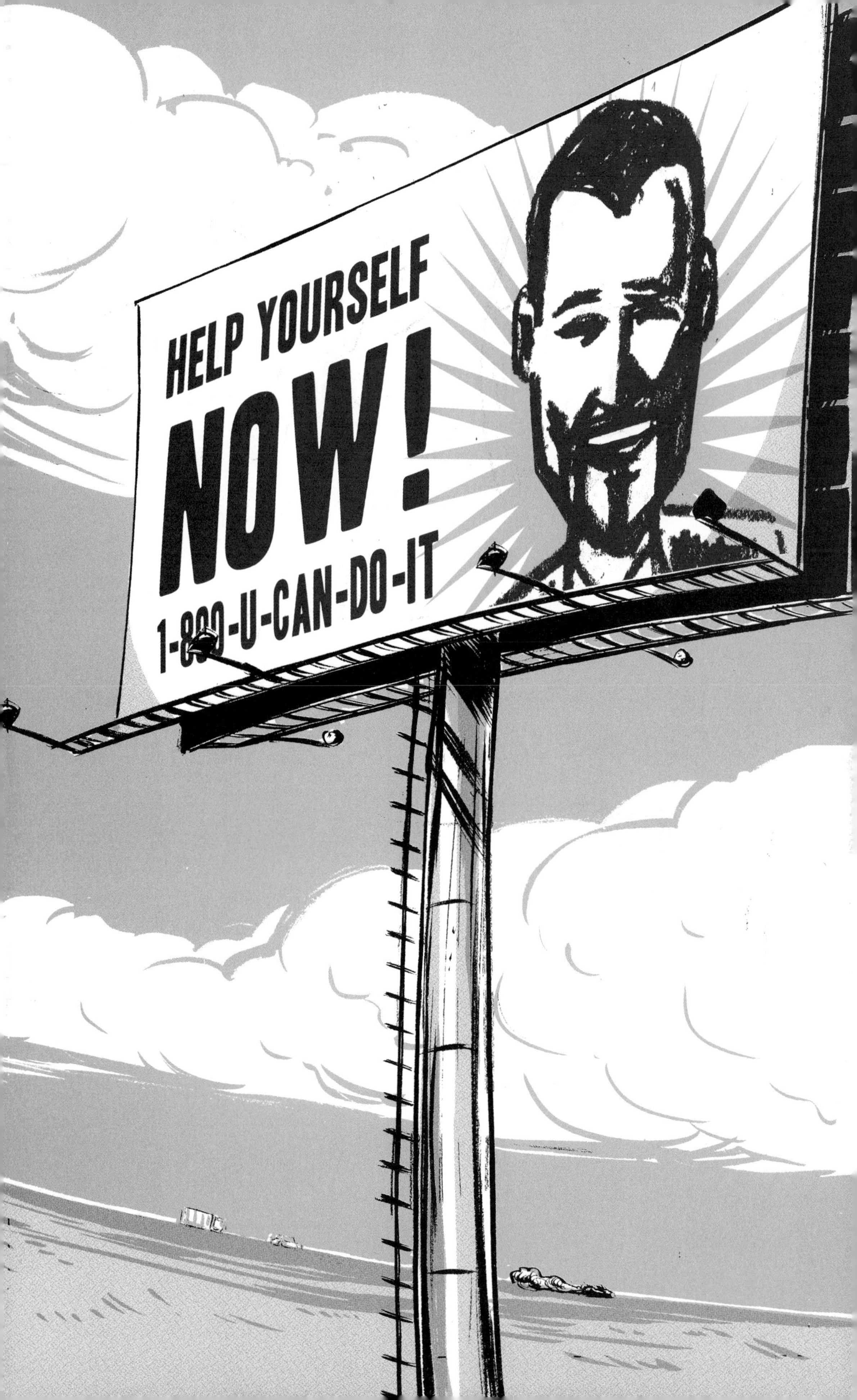
HELP YOURSELF
NOW!
1-800-U-CAN-DO-IT

WHISPERING ABOUT **MATT KINDT**, an award-winning graphic novelist, has been reading, writing, and drawing comics for as long as he's been able to hold a pen. His recent work *Super Spy* was named the 2007 Indie Book of the Year by Wizard Magazine, made Booklist's Top 10 Graphic Novels of 2008, and was nominated for three Harvey Awards and an Eisner Award. Matt won a 2008 Harvey Award for his work on Alan Moore's *Lost Girls*, and his first graphic novel, *Pistolwhip*, was on Time Magazine's Top 10 Graphic Novels of 2001. His website is www.mattkindt.com.